UNBREAKABLE

UNBREAKABLE

A Revolutionary Memoir of Love, Loss and a Return to Wholeness

Debra Hoolahan

Unbreakable: A Revolutionary Memoir of Love, Loss and a Return to Wholeness

For permissions, public relations, and media requests only, please contact debrahoolahan22@gmail.com.

This book is a memoir depicting actual events in the author's life. All persons within are real individuals for whom the author has deep gratitude. To protect the privacy of others, many names, places, occupations, and identifying characteristics have been changed. The story, however, remains her own.

"FARM" and "Regenaware" are fictitious names created by the author and are not related to nor affiliated with any organizations, companies, goods, or services of the same or similar name.

The author of this book does not dispense medical or other advice nor prescribes the use of any practice, technique, or modality as a form of treatment for physical, emotional, or medical conditions without the advice of a qualified healthcare practitioner, either directly or indirectly. The intent of the author is to share her story. If you use any of the information in this book for yourself, the author/publisher assumes no responsibility or liability for your actions.

Kind acknowledgment is made for permission to reprint the following:

Excerpts from "Everything is Here to Help You: Finding the Gift in Life's Greatest Challenges" by Matt Kahn. Published by Hay House, Inc. Reprinted with permission.

Excerpts from "A Course In Miracles" published by the Foundation for Inner Peace. Reprinted with permission.

Excerpts from "The Wounded Woman: Healing the Father-Daughter Relationship" by Linda Schierse Leonard. Published by Shambhala Publications, Inc. Reprinted with permission.

Excerpt from "Revolution 2021: The Importance of Love & Consciousness in Action," a transmission from The Council channeled by Sara Landon. Saralandon.com. Reprinted with permission.

Paperback ISBN: 979-8-9874052-2-2
e-book ISBN: 979-8-9874052-7-7

Published by: Debra Hoolahan, U.S.A.
www.debrahoolahan.com

10 9 8 7 6 5 4 3 2 1
1st edition, July 2023

Printed in the United States of America

For me, and
for my Dad. I love you.

To thine own self be true
And it must follow, as the
Night the day, thou canst not
Then be false to any man.

— William Shakespeare

CONTENTS

(Contents continued)

INTRODUCTION

For many months I wondered why I couldn't finalize this introduction. I thought perhaps I was too far removed from the initial manuscript I'd completed more than two years ago, the exhilaration of achievement now somewhat tarnished by the passing of time. Each attempt fell short, other pressing life issues had begun to arise, and the "right" words just wouldn't come. My mind often rendered a verdict: "Who am I to be incomplete and set this book before you?" What could I possibly offer that would make a difference that matters—that *endures?*

When I recount the circumstances in this book, I no longer identify in the same way as the woman who took the journey. Through the decades, I encountered many upheavals through the often laborious process of self-discovery, stripped to the bone by emotions and past patterns looming under the greater desire to free myself from them in the quest for self-love. In a deep trance, I unconsciously ran from one disappointment to another, attempting to find myself through a person, place, or purpose that would wake me up to who I am and why I came to this earth. The elusive answer to happiness always promised to be anything but *me.*

Ultimately, I found the *one thing* that made me come alive, which truly felt like an extension of my very being: writing this book. I now know why. It is because the expression is *my own;* a result of a commitment I made with myself to finish what I started, a decision to explore something created *by* me, *through* me, and *for* me, a beacon for my freedom from self-imposed illusions and restraints—a completion rendered through grace and sheer determination. I am deeply grateful to the Source that helped me clear the hurdles to bring it to life.

The story of my time in France is truly magical. It is a story of love—a magnificent fairy tale sprung to life from deep desire and a sense of destiny manifesting powerfully through the law of attraction when I finally decided to LET GO. Utterly unaware of those principles back then, I simply wanted to be in love with the man of my dreams. I got so much more than I'd bargained for. I struggled with the idea of bringing my story to life, procuring many excuses to keep it tucked away from the world. Being "seen" was frightening, and I tended to hide, but life and love would never change if I fostered those inclinations.

A Course In Miracles offered me a new perspective, standing many of my firmly held beliefs on their head, especially the deep sense of unworthiness and chronic guilt that had plagued me for much of my life. I describe my profound experience and understanding of the *Course* in great detail within these pages. My interpretations are my own; I am not a scholar, but a student of the *Course*. If you are intrigued by its teachings, seek deeper understanding, or wish to find a study group, you may reach out to acim.org and the Foundation for Inner Peace.

Writing my book has brought healing and validated my heart. It helped me realize I am capable of loving deeply, giving truly, feeling the beauty and the pain, the polarity of expansion and contraction stretching me to the limits of my tolerance.

The story about Jonathan was the most challenging part to write, ripping open my skin to reveal my unhealed inner workings, things I didn't want to face. I hadn't intended it to be part of the book and had only written it to "get it off my chest." Yet, it was the arrival of a new ending waiting for years to be lived, tumbling me into the darkest of nights which forced me to wake up, catalyzing an irrevocable transformation ultimately brought to bear by well-appointed characters who offered me incomprehensible release when I could finally see the forest for the trees. It forced me to reclaim my power from illusory projections that promised my happiness.

I asked for guidance and inspiration in hopes that I could convey the depth of how I felt as I placed my heart vulnerably on the page. I have learned so much about my story and myself from looking back at my journals, from which I gathered extraordinary detail to write the story itself.

Cupped in the hands of the Divine as it shone through the illusion, I have had epiphanies about my patterns that I had not previously seen. It is okay to write this story and to have loved and lost. It is okay that things were messy. There is no wrongness in the journey. I can release resistance and trust myself. If I let my guard down, I will not be swallowed alive. That old story resurrecting itself as a firmly entrenched belief—a program running without my conscious consent—had bowled me over many times, knocking me to my knees. But now I know it doesn't have to be that way, it *isn't* that way for everyone, and I can envision a new way to live. I can choose to surrender, allowing my heart to come through. I can choose to honor my life by being *alive* in it. To feel the edges of myself, the uninterpretable softness of the moment, the glowing borders of my heart as it radiates under my breastbone, wanting itself, wanting just to *be* itself.

No longer willing to change *who* I am, I choose to release the illusions about who I *think* I am, unhooking myself from old paradigms by creating new beliefs that feel good and support me. I don't need to be perfect at this, but the investment will result in a bountiful return. I can simply tell my story, my journey from there to here.

I am not the same woman I was before writing this book. My journey catalyzed a metamorphosis, and I am transformed by the writing itself, having shed the skin of the previous version of me. This skin is in my likeness, but I no longer inhabit it and have no desire to return to it. With that said, I am who I am today because of my deep desire to heal. Everything matters. I had no choice but to hurl myself headlong into the very issues that bound me. There are still places that hurt, but the person I am now is a testament to who I was then, and is ultimately a perpetual state of becoming. More than ever, I ask myself: "Who am I?" And I will keep asking, knowing that I am here to remember the Light in myself and to allow the unfolding of its expression in my life.

What I offer you then is what my book has offered me: This is not the end but a new beginning. I hope you receive whatever you intend to find within these pages; that my story enriches you and brings inspiration, perhaps by directing understanding from a new angle, recollecting something previously unseen, or seeing it in a different light. We arrive at each moment afresh as a new version of ourselves if we release our grip on the past and our expectations for the future. We are inherently worthy. We do not need to live in anyone else's shadow or chase someone else's dream. It is high time we all live powerfully and intentionally, letting our creative wellspring direct our actions to manifest the life we choose to live. We do not need anyone's permission to do so. Through loving consideration and remembering that we are Love itself, I believe all journeys are beautiful, necessary, meaningful, and blessed.

Part One

Fairy Tales Do Come True

CHAPTER 1

Pinch Me, I'm Dreaming

"Oh my God, he's coming!" I squeaked excitedly to Sadie, standing next to me, as I nervously fumbled with the combination on my junior high school locker.

Eddie Schecter was the most adorable boy I had ever seen. Tallish and slender, his shoulder-length light brown hair breezed gently away from his face as he glided down the hall.

"He's so gorgeous!" Sadie swooned, her freckled cheeks flushed with adolescent fervor as Eddie floated by, a vision in tight blue jeans and a black concert T-shirt, chatting with his friends, smiling a broad, white-toothed smile.

"Don't be so obvious," I giggled, equally smitten, as we both ogled the iconic boy of our dreams.

Eddie played electric guitar and had his own band. They played all kinds of popular rock music and a few originals. He was a legend throughout our junior high school. His band would occasionally perform in the enormous gymnasium to a throng of one thousand-plus ecstatic teenagers, waving our arms in the air as drum, guitar, and bass throbbed noisily in our ears.

He had been my first crush, and I was hooked. I'd spent my eighth and ninth-grade years stalking him around the school halls and with Sadie in the neighborhood where they'd both lived. She and I would walk past his house very slowly, hoping to catch a glimpse of him.

Eddie and I were worlds apart in every way except music. I was in the honors program. He appeared to be living the life of a young, happy rebel, passionate about his music and undoubtedly dreaming about a fantastic future, one I would never know. I, however, had skipped over these minor details and was living a fairy tale as his beloved, ever-present girlfriend. In zealous adoration, I had embroidered his band's logo on a T-shirt and had also carved it into a small, wooden, hand-painted plaque. Eventually, I plucked up enough courage to give them to him and tracked him to his locker.

"Wow, you carved this yourself?" he inquired with raised eyebrows, appreciatively running his index finger over the colorful, upraised letters of the plaque.

"Yes. I hope you like it!" I gushed awkwardly, fiddling with a button on my vest.

"I do. Thank you." He smiled shyly, avoiding direct eye contact. He was gracious, but there had been no genuine interest—or much conversation—on his part.

As I sat gazing dreamily out the plane window, I wondered why Eddie had come to mind. Perhaps it was the closest picture to a fairy tale I had conjured all those years ago. Was my time in France destined to be a fairy tale? One that I would experience in real-time instead of solely in my mind? Was love in the cards for me?

The pilot's voice announcing our imminent arrival at Côte d'Azur Airport rained down softly from the speakers overhead, coaxing my mind back to the present. As our plane began its descent through a cloudless blue sky, the breathtaking vista of Nice snapped into focus. I gasped, a rush of adrenaline settling like a simmering sunburst in my chest. Famously sculpted by the Baie des Anges, the burgeoning coastline beckoned its welcome, dotted by myriad terracotta rooftops and elegant white hotels clustered tightly at the shore. The notable seaside boulevard, known as the Promenade des Anglais, girdled the scene stretched out below me, swaddling the panorama that threatened to topple into the brilliant blue of the Mediterranean Sea.

I thought back to the great fortune that had befallen me less than six months prior at the Hotel du Pont in Wilmington, Delaware, and the mantra that may have innocently manifested the great adventure I was presently embarked upon. "Tonight could be my night. Tonight could be my night. *Tonight could be my night!*" I'd chanted under my breath as I yanked the long bronze handle on the heavy glass door of the hotel. It was a refrain I had uttered for months every time I entered the old-world elegance and plush grandeur of the idyllic 1900s masterpiece.

I recollected the opulent lobby adorned in what I imagined was the typical décor of any fine hotel in Europe: striated marble floors and countertops, creamy beige with ribbons of earthy brown tones running in loose patterns throughout; thick mahogany side tables and moldings framing and edging the room, carrying the eye carefully around its perimeter; button-tufted sofas and velvet club chairs, placed invitingly in cozy arrangements around elegant coffee tables, beckoning their invitation; vases and statues in bisques and alabaster with veins of gold delicately erupting into little glittering pools, proudly sitting on tabletops and corbels. The soaring, gilded wood ceiling boasted a warm honey-walnut medallion design, with a central flower motif from which dangled sparkling glass and gold chandeliers. Four majestic pillars extended from floor to ceiling, their squared trunks rising up to the bridled, wooden balconies hovering over the lobby desk far below. Full-length, arched windows lined the walls of the stately lobby, allowing the light to stream in unimpeded. I was overcome by nostalgia every time I walked in.

I knew I wanted to go to France—specifically the French Riviera. Maybe it was because I spoke some high-school French or because France conjured up images of romance. Heaven knows I desperately wanted to be in love with the man of my dreams. Only now, there was a logical *possibility* to manifesting this potential dream-come-true that I hadn't previously considered: getting hired. One of my friends knew of a massage therapist who had met a wealthy couple when she was freelancing in a high-end hotel. They were so impressed with her talents that they hired her to travel the world with them.

If she can do it, so can I! I had thought to myself. And so, the mantra went. I never really considered what a long shot that was. Every night, sitting at my desk, I would pick up the little globe stationed next to my computer. Tracing my finger from the tiny dot called Delaware to the

French Riviera, I would look upward, informing the Universe that this was *precisely* where I wanted to go.

I was also working freelance for another therapist whose massage center was thriving. I didn't really have a plan, other than a half-hearted discussion I was having with my friend Derek Crow, who I had met in the massage program I had recently attended in Delaware. We discussed opening our own place, but I wasn't as intent on that as I was on the idea of getting hired by some wealthy patron of the hotel and traveling the world.

At some point during my France fantasy, life jolted me to my senses. I abandoned the idea of going to France and dove wholeheartedly into the prospect of creating a successful massage practice while still providing freelance work at the Hotel du Pont. Derek was unsure he wanted to pursue this route, but within a couple of weeks, I'd begun evaluating properties and found just what I needed in a historic old house near the estates of Greenville. Focused on the aesthetics of a potential new business, I had forgotten all about traveling the world. That could wait for now. Besides, how could I resist that magnificent sofa I had seen in a nearby shop, regally bedecked in vibrant jewel-toned patterns, that would be perfect for the reception area of my new business?

I was days away from signing a lease when I received a call from Karen, the concierge at the Hotel du Pont. "One of our exclusive guests will be staying with us for the week. He has requested a massage, and I wanted to reach out to you first. His name is Ariel Sorensen. Please give me a call when you get this message." As she spoke his name, an image of a Chinese man's face flashed quickly through my mind, stopping my thoughts. *Strange*, I thought. *His name isn't Asian.* Stranger still that an image popped into my head unannounced.

* * *

I LUGGED MY THIRTY-POUND MASSAGE TABLE down the hall to the room where Ariel Sorensen was staying and plopped it down to knock on his door. As the door opened, I felt an energetic swoosh as the air undulated silently in and out around me.

"Hi, I'm Debra," I said cheerfully as I picked up my massage table to bring it in.

"Hello Debra, come in." He motioned with an outstretched arm, holding the door for me to enter.

I placed the table down in the sitting area of the room. "Ari Sorensen. Pleased to meet you, Debra," he said, extending his hand. I had the feeling he was important. He exuded an air of quiet confidence and a sharp, busy mind that ran on a tight schedule. His brown hair was styled slightly longish, and he was light-skinned. I guessed he was probably European.

He went to the bathroom to change into his robe as I prepared my massage table for him. I looked about the elegant room, swathed in creams and golds with rich mahogany furniture, a granite-topped bar, and a small sitting area with wood-trimmed chairs.

"Make yourself comfortable, face-up on the table," I said to him as he exited the bathroom. "I'm going to wash my hands. I'll be back in a moment," I called over my shoulder, entering the bathroom and closing the door.

When I returned, he was lying naked, face-up on the table. I gasped. "You need to be *under* the covers!"

"Oh, I'm so sorry! This is how I normally lie for a massage," he apologized, nearly leaping off the table as he scrambled to pull back the sheets.

I knew his behavior wasn't lascivious. I viewed the misunderstanding as entirely innocent. I gave him a moment to settle in under the flannel covers. I squeezed some almond oil into the palm of my right hand and rubbed my palms together to distribute the oil.

My routine generally lasted an hour. I encouraged Ari to relax, and we made some idle chit-chat. He offered that he was here on business for a week. He liked the United States but didn't visit very often.

I liked him. He was polite, soft-spoken, and inquisitive. He was very appreciative of the massage and told me that he had been massaged the world over. It was one of the few things that truly relaxed him.

When he had turned to face down, I exposed his left leg and applied enough oil to cover the entire limb. I was surprised at how smooth and relatively firm he was. I could tell his skin was minimally exposed to the sun, radiating a youthful peachy glow. As I made my way down from the top of his thigh to his calf, he lifted his head. "This is the best massage I've ever had! How do you know the muscles so well?"

I told him it was because of the specificity and depth of my chiropractic training. "I have x-ray vision, so to speak." We both chuckled.

After I had completed his massage and he was contentedly wrapped in his robe, he asked me if I was available to come back every night that he was in town. "I would be happy to," I replied brightly, feeling excited about seeing him again and having the opportunity to enjoy his company.

He handed me a generous tip on top of my regular fee and said, "buy some flowers for yourself, Debra." I beamed. What a lovely way to offer a tip, I thought. This man had character and class. I was looking forward to the week. Every evening, to my delight, he would give me the same tip and the same sentiment.

When the massage was complete the following evening, he asked me to join him and his pilot for dinner. "I would love to join you!" I beamed. *He had a pilot?!* My mind set sail on the winds of wonder. Just who was this man who had his own private pilot?

We exchanged pleasantries over dinner as he and his pilot sat opposite me in the elegant booth. I learned that he was in Delaware because of a lawsuit he thought was a frivolous waste of his time. He was meeting with his lawyers here to settle it, he offered drily, obviously irritated by the inconvenience, but taking it all in stride.

* * *

THE FOLLOWING EVENING'S MASSAGE started like the others. Ari's voice lilted upwards as I massaged him. "I live in the south of France, on the French Riviera. Have you ever been there, Debra?" My heart skipped a beat as I felt the back of my neck bristle with excitement.

"I've never been to Europe," I gushed and quickly added, "but I'd love to go." My mind started racing like a greyhound chasing a rabbit.

"France is the most beautiful country in the world, Debra." I noticed he used my name a lot when he spoke to me. "I've been to many beautiful countries, but France is exceptional. My main residence is there," he offered proudly.

He shared that he owned multiple homes throughout Europe and might be purchasing a penthouse in New York City. Never mind those other homes; *he lived on the French Riviera*! Had the Universe been listening to me after all? Was this the opportunity I had been longing for? My brain was off and running, and my hands moved on autopilot as I kneaded the back of his neck, incredulously considering the possibility of Grace.

"It's such an annoyance to have a massage therapist come to the house. I don't like to give my private address, and it's a hassle with the security people on my property..." he trailed off, shifting on the table.

The blood rushed straight up my spine and into my face like a geyser. Before I knew what was happening, I felt the muscles of my mouth moving, words tumbling out. "I could come to France and be your personal massage therapist and chiropractor...!" I stopped breathing; my words hung like static electricity in the air. *Shit!* Why had I said that? What was I thinking? Whatever reason would a man of his stature have to hire me? I felt my chest and throat starting to tighten up.

He peered up at me, eyebrows raised, incredulous himself. "But don't you have commitments, Debra? Family? What about your job?"

"I am single with no kids, pets, or obligations," I rattled out like a rapid-fire machine gun, teeth chattering, still kneading his neck. "My work is freelance, and my apartment lease is up in two months."

Ari's eyes locked on mine as he paused for what felt like an eternity. "Ok, Debra, let's try it for three months. We'll talk about it after my massage." He smiled and closed his eyes, settling back down on the table.

* * *

I STUMBLED UP THE STAIRS to my townhouse, eager to share my fantastic news with friends and family. "Oh my God, Tina, *you're not going to believe this*!" I squawked into the phone, delirious as I flapped around my apartment, my voice two octaves higher, the details of what had happened with Ari at the hotel gushing out of me like a waterfall roaring over a towering cliff.

"It's a dream come true!" she exclaimed, mirroring my joy.

I had met Valentina Parisi on a connecting flight to Long Island several years earlier, on the way home from Virginia. She had been seated beside me, reading a personal growth book that I had read, and we struck up a conversation. A familiar sensation had washed over me as we spoke. It was the sensation of "recognition" that I always got when I knew someone was destined to be a close friend.

Later, we said our goodbyes in the airport parking lot, and I watched her long, curly dark hair bouncing behind her as she walked away, the wheels of her little suitcase click-clacking noisily on the pavement. I'd met many people on planes. Maybe it had just been a chance encounter.

"Tina!" I blurted out before I could stop myself. She spun around as I hurried over to her. My God, she lived half an hour away from me! I couldn't just let her go. "Let's exchange phone numbers; maybe we could get together." She happily consented. Our friendship had gradually grown into a deep camaraderie, a trusted, sacred space for us to share matters of the heart. Tina was a soul sister to whom I confided everything.

"It's even *better* than a dream come true!" I squealed, now pacing wildly about my living room, unable to sit down, as if the excitement would blast me straight up out of my chair like a rocket. At that time, the magnitude of the "law of attraction" was innocently absent from my perception, but the Universe had *indeed* been listening. From my perspective, life was not yet happening *through* me, and on an organic level, that cosmic understanding was still many years away.

My sister had been to Europe for a school semester as part of her bachelor's degree in Art History. She was thrilled for me. "You're going to *love* France!" she exclaimed excitedly. "The food, the wine, the cheese, and oh my God, the *bread!* She nearly swooned, savoring her words in delighted recollection.

I called Derek and his partner Anthony and everyone else I could think of who mattered the most in my life. Anthony believed my going to France was ordained. He could feel it as if it were already happening and was psychically packing my bags.

My mom was exhilarated. And surprisingly, my practical, both-feet-firmly-on-the-ground father did not protest. He even bought me a little pocket translator, which he lovingly bestowed upon me in a humble father-daughter moment. I was in heaven. Well, I was *going* to heaven itself! France, oh *France! I can't wait for your loving embrace.*

My reverie was interrupted as one of the flight attendants made her way down the aisle, glancing from lap to lap to ensure passengers' seatbelts were securely fastened for landing. In minutes, I would be stepping out of the plane and onto French soil.

As our plane lowered itself toward the runway, I felt uncontainable excitement as it skittered dangerously close to the harbor. The mile-long tarmac unfurled and seemed to catch us as we landed, victoriously plunking down into its welcoming embrace.

Small and unassuming, Nice Côte d'Azur Airport was not the sprawling estimation I'd had of this legendary destination. As I waited in the customs line to have my new passport receive its first stamp, I wondered how I would find Theo, the man who was supposed to pick me up and take me to my apartment. The customs officer glanced at me with disinterest as he wordlessly plunged his date stamper onto my American passport. I smirked to myself, wondering if the cliché about how the French viewed Americans was true. It made no matter to me; I was in France!

***

THEO HAD NOT BEEN HARD TO FIND. He held a plain piece of paper with my name printed on it in block letters. Since I'd had no description of him, I had no idea who or what to expect, and this tall, handsome, ginger-haired man was decidedly not who I'd pictured.

I could tell he had spotted me. Surely I was wearing the countenance of someone who was searching for another someone. I relished first encounters, awaiting that delicious little moment of recognition when I connected with someone I'd never met and the little burst of warmth that melted over me like hot fudge on an ice cream sundae.

He beamed a toothy grin as our eyes met. "Hi, are you Debra?" he inquired.

"I am!" I exclaimed with glee.

"Theo Visser. Nice to meet you," he said as he heartily stuck out his hand to greet me. "Welcome to France!" He spoke impressive, rapid-fire English. "First, we'll pick up your rental car, and then I'll take you to your place. You will be staying in the same apartment complex as me, in the village of Biot." I wondered if it overlooked the Mediterranean Sea like I had been promised.

"I'm going to take you there first. We'll drop off your things, and then we'll go shopping at the Géant to get some food and whatever else you need to be comfortable," he said cheerily. A personal chauffeur in France who would also take me shopping? Oh yes, that *definitely* worked for me.

* * *

MY RENTAL WAS A COMPACT SILVER-BLUE Peugeot hatchback. Most of the cars on the road were small, four-cylinder, stick-shift types that ran on diesel fuel. Gasoline was expensive here, nearly four times that in the states!

As we pulled onto the main road, I gazed all around, looking out and up at the hotels parading before me as we drove along the Promenade des Anglais. I marveled at the sights as we casually chatted. My senses were overwhelmed, and I felt as if I were in a dream. Beautiful old architecture, hotels, restaurants, and palm trees accentuated the indescribably blue coast to my left. *Just like a postcard,* I mused, grinning broadly.

"How did you meet Mr. S.?" Theo adoringly referred to Ari that way. I decided to do the same.

"I met him at the Hotel du Pont in Wilmington, Delaware, when he scheduled a massage there."

"So you're a massage therapist?" he queried.

"I'm a chiropractor, primarily. I do medical massage work on the side." I continued to peruse the view beyond and around me, taking it all in. France was gorgeous. I was going to make the most of this opportunity. In all honesty, I had no intention of leaving.

"And he hired you to come here to France?" he asked, raising his eyebrows in disbelief.

I gave him the short answer. "Yes. He said it was the best massage he'd ever had, that I knew all the muscles."

"Wow," he said, chuckling, "you must be really good!"

"Thank you. I hope Mr. S. continues to think so too. I'm looking forward to seeing him again." I was ready to embark on this journey, wherever it took me.

I quickly learned that Theo spoke several languages, adored Ariel Sorensen, his kids, American movies, and pop music. He was a loyal protector-type man who knew what he liked and didn't like. He was high-strung, didn't sleep well, and took medication to quell his paranoia and hypervigilance about life in general. He had recently suffered a tumultuous breakup with his French wife, Vivienne, whom he unapologetically referred to as "that bitch." Ari presently employed Theo to pick up visitors and business associates from the airport, secure rental cars and apartments as needed, and perform other odd jobs to supplement his erratic income as a part-time, though presently unemployed, security guard.

As we turned off the highway and wound our way along narrow, twisting roads into the residential area, my senses were greeted by large properties and farms, spread out and somewhat scrubby in their appearance. They weren't like the farms I was accustomed to. Neat, sprawling, well-delineated, well-hydrated squares of uniform perfection defined my idea of a "farm." Here they didn't get as much rain, and the soil was dry and somewhat pebbly, with sparse patches of grass, characteristic of the low-lying Alps.

We turned onto a little side street and headed to the apartment complex where I would be living. Theo pointed out my unit as we drove toward the entrance. He opened the wrought iron gate with his remote control, and it lurched into compliance as we pulled through to the unpaved, gravelly parking lot.

Most of the compound's units were designed in duplex style, but edging the periphery were a pair of two-story rectangular buildings accommodating about a dozen units each. Theo lived in one of them. The structures were all surfaced with stucco and trimmed in dark wood. The rooftops were red-orange clay tile, ubiquitous in the Mediterranean. The duplexes had pointed roofs and were split right down the middle to form two dwellings. The window openings were trimmed in wood and covered by a single functional shutter door. The entryways were straddled by a pair of French doors that opened out onto a simple cement patio.

We unloaded my suitcases from the back of the car and walked around to my duplex via a narrow sidewalk lined with oleander bushes, their fragrant pink, white, and crimson flowers clustered amongst long, slender, dark green leaves. As we arrived at my unit, my insides prickled with delight. "A *real* French door!" I beamed.

"What did you expect?" Theo teased.

The recessed property was bordered by a four-foot cement retainer wall rimmed with arborvitae for privacy and a simple wooden fence that encircled the entire residence. In front of my street-facing unit was a large patio with oleander bushes on one side, a little grassy area on the other, and plenty of space for gardening.

"Wow, it's small!" I exclaimed as I stepped inside the compact apartment.

"Real estate in France is expensive, Debra," Theo said, chuckling.

"Why are there no screens on the windows?" I asked, surveying the room.

"We don't need them. There are no bugs," he said, matter-of-fact.

"But what about at night? Aren't there any mosquitoes?"

"Not in this dry climate," Theo said, shaking his head.

"Fantastic!" I remarked, looking forward to seeing for myself if this were true. Mosquitoes were plentiful in the humid summers of Long Island, where I had grown up and spent most of my adult life. Delaware, also on the east coast, and my most recent residence, was virtually the same in this regard.

The apartment was quaint and simply furnished with a total of four rooms: A large central room bordered on the back right wall by a galley kitchen; a small bathroom with a full-sized tub to the right of the kitchen; the main bedroom to the immediate front right of the great room—which was just big enough for a queen bed and small nightstand; and a small upstairs guest bedroom atop the primary bedroom. "I love it!" I exclaimed. It would be mine for the next three months, which I already hoped would turn into forever. France was strumming my heartstrings with her beauty, and my mind exploded with possibilities.

"I bought new linens for the bed and towels for the kitchen and bathroom," Theo said proudly. "There are some provisions in the fridge for lunch, but I'll be back a little later to take you to the grocery store."

"Thank you so much, Theo!" I gushed as he headed out the door. "See you later!"

I was ready to burst. My tiny apartment was sunny and bright, facing south, so I would have sunshine all day. Exhausted from my overnight flight, I hauled my suitcases into the bedroom and started to unpack.

Afterward, I laid down on the bed for a bit and let my body feel the newness of my surroundings. *I was jaw-droppingly, unquestionably, astoundingly, in FRANCE!* I giggled and kicked my legs excitedly on the thin, firm mattress below me. What had I done to deserve all this?! Whatever it was, I couldn't wait for it all to unfold. It was a fairy tale come true, and I intended to enjoy every spectacular moment!

CHAPTER 2

Stranger in Paradise

I hadn't been doing much sightseeing since I'd arrived in France as I was still timid about driving in an unfamiliar place, especially given the language barrier. My French was adequate but not advanced. Theo wasn't as available as I would have liked him to be, and touring around didn't appeal to him. I needed a companion. Someone interested in exploring with me and showing me the beautiful little towns, coast, and countryside I pined to discover. I was in one of the most beautiful destinations in the world with a universe of magnificent places to explore, and I wanted someone special with whom I could share it.

My mind raced with questions. Was this a dream? Just how *did* this trip come about? Had I simply "allowed" it? Did I conjure a new belief system, put out different vibes, or was it just meant to be? Had I merely received a signal for something that had already been on its way? Was there a formula? Could I do the same with the love of my life? Was he here in France??

Until now, I'd believed that meeting soul mates had nothing to do with emitting any special something; it was simply a matter of recognizing them when they came. Maybe I was meant to take this life's journey alone. I wasn't looking for someone to *make* me happy; I could genuinely access that. I longed for the man with whom I could open my heart completely, a man with whom I could unabashedly be myself. I wanted a man who could receive me, understand just who-in-the-hell I was, and a love that made me feel completely alive, vibrant, expectant, quivering in its presence. I wanted the fairy tale. To prove that big dreams could come true. To prove that what was in my heart's deepest, most glorious crevices could be made manifest, exploding into life like a great nova of unbounded creation and joy. Maybe this was the proof of God's love that I was looking for, and through having my deepest desire materialize, I could finally believe that God loved me, heard me, and wanted me to be happy.

Theo had a good friend named Erik Henderson, who lived in Switzerland. Shortly after I settled in, he introduced me to Erik's girlfriend, Nadine Baer, who resided in the neighboring town of Vallauris.

Nadine had high cheekbones and kindly blue eyes. She was on the quiet side but very welcoming and instantly trustable. She knew of Ari and had a deep respect and admiration for him. She offered me coffee, which I delightedly accepted; a delicious espresso served in a demitasse with a dab of frothed cream, which the French called "noisette." I spooned in two tiny brown sugar cubes to sweeten it, watching the crystals melt into the foamy dark brew. I would happily discover that many restaurants served noisette with a little biscuit placed on the saucer. Such deliberate delicacy was relatively unknown to my American palate, and it delighted me.

"Debra, how do you like it here so far? Do you see Mr. Sorensen a lot?" Nadine inquired.

"Actually, not so much. He's a busy man. I've only seen him once since I've been here."

She nodded her head. "We should go for lunch and sightseeing. There are a lot of nice walks we can take by the sea. Besides, I have to lose weight," she said, patting her stomach with both hands. She wasn't particularly overweight but had been slender most of her life. It was all relative, I supposed, and it wouldn't hurt me to lose a few pounds either.

Divorced from a Frenchman, Nadine had lived in France for many years. She worked part-time as a gardener, leaving plenty of opportunities to explore the beautiful countryside. "Maybe tomorrow we can have lunch by the sea in my village," she offered. I was overjoyed at the idea. It would be the beginning of a vital friendship and many magical, memorable moments. We were a mutual breath of fresh air in each other's lives.

* * *

THE FOLLOWING WEEK, I met Ari at the Schweizerhof Hotel in Switzerland, near Lake Zurich. As his guest, I was treated like royalty. I found the Swiss people much friendlier than the French and always eager to speak nearly perfect English. Ari was engulfed with meetings that ran into the evening, but I kept myself busy sightseeing in the lively, international city.

Swiss architecture was starkly different from Mediterranean French, with both medieval and modern design comingling on the immaculate wide streets of the downtown district. The facades of the charming Old Town were boldly splashed with reds, blues, and greens, and the flat front, pointy-roofed homesteads huddled uniformly around the winding, cobbled alleyways. Snow still covered most of the mountains, but snowdrops, purple crocuses, and yellow narcissus were blooming in the surrounding parks, punctuating the chilly cityscape.

Sitting in the hotel lobby, I struck up a conversation with a Norwegian man named Benji Pedersen. He was a developer of theme parks in Asia and the Middle East and spent much of his time in Dubai. He was in Zurich regularly and a frequent guest at the hotel. He toured me all around the city and took me to lunch at a brasserie in Federal Station.

"I don't know anything about Dubai," I said innocently.

"You should visit," Benji said definitively. "There's not that much to it. It's kind of an oasis in the middle of the desert, but it has some rather opulent architecture. You can probably get a good feel for it in under a week," he said, biting into his sandwich.

Benji was a gracious guide, but I hadn't particularly warmed up to him. He was very knowledgeable about Zurich, so I was grateful to have the company. Perhaps he was thankful too. Benji knew I was here with Ari, and whether or not that mattered, he hadn't made any overtures.

"I'm not drawn to that part of the world," I said, shrugging my shoulders. "I prefer Europe and am hoping to see as much of it as I can while I'm here," I remarked, ogling the oversized train schedule marquis, and marveling at the elaborate, stupendously organized tram system that Zurich was famous for. Federal station reminded me of Grand Central Station back in New York City, with its high ceiling and expansive lobby, travelers hurrying in many directions to catch their trains.

After lunch, we strolled the upscale ritz of Bahnhofstrasse, one of the world's most expensive and exclusive shopping avenues. I gaped at the well-appointed windows of Cartier, Gucci, Louis Vuitton, and Tiffany interspersed amongst numerous and equally famous watch shops like Türler, Bulgari, and Piaget.

I was well entertained but anxious to meet with Ari. He had been so involved with his business meetings that I feared I wouldn't get to give him a massage, but at last, he was free.

We dined at the hundred-year-old Ristorante Casa Ferlin. I rolled my eyes with delight, wallowing in their Venetian-style, handmade ravioli; pillowy dumplings made of fresh, light wheat swaddling lumps of exquisite, buttery ricotta cheese covered with a sinfully creamy, alfredo parmesan sauce.

"How are you enjoying Zurich so far, Debra?" Ari inquired.

"Very much," I replied, thankful to be joining him. "I met a businessman by the name of Benji, and he's been showing me around a bit. We walked to Bahnhofstrasse," I said, flashing a proud smile.

"Did you spend all your money?" he teased me as he slid a piece of tomato-chunked cannelloni into his mouth.

"No, we just window-shopped. I wouldn't know where to begin!"

We laughed as we lingered over dinner and fine wine, and Ari told me about his humble beginnings. As a child, he'd had dreams of someday becoming a wealthy businessman.

"I was born in Suriname, where my mother is from. My father died in a fishing boat accident when I was a young boy in Paramaribo and was lost at sea. After he died, my family emigrated to Amsterdam, where a few of my father's relatives lived," he recollected quietly.

"I'm sorry about your father, Ari," I said respectfully. I couldn't imagine how hard this loss must have been for a young child to understand.

"Thank you, Debra. It was a long time ago," he said softly.

His family had left Suriname when he was a teen, and they'd had to scramble to make ends meet. Ari worked many odd jobs and managed to put himself through college. He started in real estate, then commercial real estate, and made many astute business investments. By the time he was in his early thirties, Ari had built an impressive enterprise. Because of his impeccable timing, uncanny business sense, and a mind that reached for the stars, he had become a wealthy patriarch of a great, self-constructed empire.

I was astonished at how far he had risen. I guessed there were other stories like his, but what impressed me the most was that he was down-to-earth, honest, and reachable. Later that evening, I gave him a massage. He would be leaving the following morning, but I still had a day left to see the sights.

The city of Zurich had much to offer, but I craved a more rustic setting. I booked a train to Uetliberg, a mountain peak offering a panoramic view of the city and Lake Zurich. The deep windows of the tram car provided an unobstructed view of the snowy pine and fir-covered countryside as the train ascended to an altitude of three thousand feet. It was a cloudy day, and I couldn't see the city several miles away, so I circled back, opting for a visit to the Landesmuseum.

Later at the hotel, I enjoyed a Sri Lankan buffet dinner—compliments of Benji. "Have you had your fill of Zurich?" Benji asked, heaping a mound of white rice onto his plate.

"For now," I said. "I'm sure I'll be back. Ari comes here pretty frequently."

"Be sure to look me up when you return," he said, sliding his business card across the table. My time with him had been fun, but I knew I wouldn't take him up on it.

* * *

BACK HOME ON THE RIVIERA, I was excited to be going for a coastal walk with Nadine. It was a chilly Spring morning, but I adored our seaside "promenades." I hadn't yet been further east than Nice and was looking forward to seeing the sights and supremely happy at having made a friend who enjoyed exploring as much as I did. Nadine always took tons of pictures and appreciated the flowers and birds, as did I. We cherished France's simple, proliferous beauty.

The daytime drive toward Monte-Carlo, the famous casino quarter in the principality of Monaco, was breathtaking. Winding eastward along the A8, as it ducked in and out of seaside tunnels and tremendous, high scenic bridges, I was agape at the mastery of its construction as we navigated through the bountiful sights that unapologetically dazzled my senses. I was in awe of the brilliant blue of the Mediterranean Sea, appreciating it from the soaring heights that enveloped me as bridges and tunnels threatened to collapse like a great landslide, plunging us into the vast watery depths below.

"Oh my God, this view is stunning!" I gasped as I looked out the passenger window of Nadine's little car.

Nadine agreed. "I have been here many times, but I never get tired of the sea from up high, even though I am afraid of heights!"

We stopped at an overlook before we entered the bustling village of Villefranche to take pictures of the resplendent, 300-foot-deep harbor, shimmering in cool hues of cobalt blue and aquamarine, its sprawling coastline peppered with quaint hotels and restaurants. Residences with bright facades of yellow and rust tones overlooked the sunny beachfront.

Entering the village, we made our way down to the Promenade des Marinières, the main road along the coast. I admired the mellifluous bougainvillea, with their heart-shaped leaves and masses of papery flowers in pink, purple, and magenta, clamping their thorny branches onto the stucco walls of the buildings in swaths of vivid color.

We lunched at a quaint café. I enjoyed sitting outside, taking in the sights and sounds of the streets, and gazing at the sea from the restaurant terrace high above. Outdoor street dining was a hallmark of the Riviera itself, French culture in general, and one of my fondest recollections. You could dine al fresco in many towns and villages year-round. Even in the late fall, winter, and early spring months, warmed by the rays of the noon-day sun, you could dine comfortably, sporting nothing more than a light jacket.

After lunch we headed to the billionaire's playground of Saint-Jean-Cap-Ferrat, a magnificent peninsula jutting into the sea between Villefranche and Monaco. "I can't!" Nadine protested, eyeing the steep, unpaved seaside trail.

"It's not that narrow, Nadine. Here, I'll walk on the outside," I offered, extending my hand to her.

It was an almost humorous scenario that happened on many walks, but we never turned back. Neither of us cared to miss out on catching a glimpse of the luxurious villas hiding behind mounds of flowering hedges and dignified, wrought iron gates.

Our walk led us to the restored seventeenth-century Chapelle de Saint-Hospice, and the understated Église Saint-Jean-Baptiste overlooking the sea, where a towering, thirty-foot-high bronze statue of the Madonna and child, cast early in the twentieth century, watchfully guarded the sacred site. On our return, we stopped at a Paloma beach bistro for a late afternoon espresso, where we sat gazing at the turquoise water and pebbly shore, enjoying the nippy spring air before we headed home.

* * *

ARI HAD INVITED ME TO A LUNCHEON with his family several days earlier. I was unsure of his motivation, but perhaps he simply wanted to introduce me. How could I say no?

This was not a meal I was looking forward to. I had only met Celeste—Ari's second wife—once before, and I bristled at the thought of spending *hours* with her. Their children would be there as well, and although I hadn't met any of them, I didn't have high hopes. I had bought two dozen long-stemmed pink roses for Celeste, hoping they would stave off the iciness of her personality long enough to get me through the meal.

I pulled up in my little Peugeot and pressed the call button on the wall beside the tall, pointy wrought-iron gate at the entrance to the Sorensen residence. The gate opened slowly inward, and I drove nervously to the carport just fifty feet inside. The property was well-manicured, with flowers tastefully displayed in ringed gardens, wrapped colorfully in raised beds around the well-placed mimosa and linden trees that decorated the courtyard. Their pretty pinks, reds, and whites reminded me of cotton candy, and the short, green grass was in sharp contrast to the grassless and rubbly landscape outside the perimeter of the enclosed property.

Carrying the long narrow box of roses, I unhurriedly made my way up the flat-stoned winding sidewalk that reminded me of the yellow brick road in Oz. *Interesting analogy*, I mused, a smile erupting on my face. I would not be disappointed.

The house was simple in design, constructed of ultra-smooth white cement, rectangular frameless windows, and a sleek modern facade. Like many modern homes in France, it was built so that the bedrooms were on the lower floor, semi-submerged, facing the back of the house. Typically oriented north or east, the goal was to diminish the heat of the intense summer sun of the Côte d'Azur while preserving exposure to the natural light. Europeans, I found, were much more conscious of energy usage. The French were no exception.

I rang the bell and was greeted by Izabella, the older of the two girls. Slim and very pretty, wearing chic, tight jeans and a pastel-colored T-shirt, she extended a slender hand, forcing a polite smile. "You must be Debra," she oozed, unimpressed. "So nice to meet you. Please come in."

I followed her into the main sitting room, which was sunny and bright. The décor was very modern. The floors throughout the house were highly polished, large, white marble tile. Three white leather couches with brightly colored yellow and blue floral pillows were arranged around a large glass-topped table in a U-shape. Gold-veined, mirrored tiles covered the main wall in the otherwise white room and were separated by full-length marble columns lying flush against the wall. Several small, delectable plates of hors d'oeuvres were placed invitingly on the table. I took a seat on one of the couches as Izabella disappeared to summon her mother and father. I was relieved to see Ari. I arose, and he shook my hand. I reached for the box of roses and offered them to Celeste.

"Oh, how sweet of you! They are quite beautiful," she smiled, placing an appreciative hand dramatically over her chest. I was relieved. Perhaps, all would go smoothly. "I've prepared fish for dinner, Debra. I hope you like salmon?"

"Yes, it's one of my favorites," I replied eagerly.

"It's quite healthy, you know." She tilted her head to the side and quickly examined me. "It appears you have lost some weight. Likely the French diet," she concluded with a crooked smile.

"I'm sure it is," I replied, taken a little off guard by her comment. "I have been doing a lot of sightseeing and walking the coast."

We headed through the modest all-white kitchen and took our seats at a table in a small yellow room surrounded by long windows. I sat down next to Ari. Celeste sat at the head of the table beside a large platter containing a grilled salmon, its head still attached. Their children and a few friends who had been invited to join the festivities sat opposite Ari and me.

Celeste was petite and quite attractive, with cat-like amber eyes and short dark hair cut in a modern angular style that accentuated her firm jawline. Clad in a form-fitting pearl pink dress with long sleeves and sporting high-heeled gold stiletto pumps, she was gorgeous.

She stood to cut and serve the two-foot-long fillet, and Ari distributed the fish-laden plates around the table. Celeste sat down gingerly, pleased with herself, and glanced around the room. "Bon appetite," she chirped.

"Bon appetite," we chorused in reply.

"Are you enjoying your stay here, Debra?" she inquired politely.

"Very much, thank you," I said, contemplating my plate of delectable fare. I slid a succulent lemony forkful of the fish into my mouth. "This meal is delicious!"

"I'm glad you're enjoying it. What does your family think about you living in France?" she inquired.

"They're happy for me. I've always wanted to travel," I said enthusiastically.

"Yes, but I'm sure they miss you. Do your family members live close to one another?" she asked.

"My parents are in New York. My sister and her family live in Delaware," I replied. "But they visit each other often enough, I suppose."

"How very nice." Celeste paused, glancing around the table and then directly at me. "Only *my* husband would invite his massage therapist to a *family* gathering," she quipped, her mouth a full smile, baring her teeth. I shouldn't have been surprised, but her words stung, nevertheless. Mildly flustered, Ari ignored her comment, refilling my half-empty champagne glass. Satisfied she had made her point, Celeste picked up her fork and resumed eating. It appeared no one else had noticed.

Lively chit-chat encircled the table. Feeling self-conscious after Celeste's biting remark, I was hesitant to join in the dialogue. Natasha, the youngest, was the most spirited and engaging of the three siblings. She resembled a younger version of her mother but with long blond hair. Zachary, Celeste's son from a prior marriage, was quiet and wholly uninterested in my presence. His dark, close-set eyes made me uncomfortable, and I actively avoided his gaze. To make matters worse, Natasha and Izabella smoked at the table while everyone was still dining, and I'd developed a headache.

Ari opened a window to relieve us of the offensive cloud. Izabella shot him an icy glance. "Close the window! I'm cold!" she scolded.

"We have guests, Izza," Ari countered firmly.

It pained me to see how his family addressed him, and I was anxious to leave. After dessert and waiting for what I thought was a tasteful amount of time, I announced my departure. "Thank you so much for the lovely luncheon, Celeste. You are an excellent cook. I appreciate all the trouble you must have gone through to make such a beautiful presentation," I said as graciously as I could muster.

"You're welcome, Debra. I'm glad you enjoyed your meal," Celeste said, shaking my hand.

I said goodbye to the others, and Ari walked me to my car. "I hope you had a nice time, Debra," he said, making no mention of Celeste's inappropriate comment. Maybe he hadn't noticed after all.

"Thank you, Ari. It was very generous of you to invite me to share a meal with you and your family," I said.

I was somewhat deflated and hoped I had seen the last of Celeste. Why had she made it a point to announce that it had been Ari's idea and not hers to have me join them for lunch? Had I done anything to deserve a comment like that? *No*, I shook my head; *it probably had nothing to do with me.* I shrugged it off, relieved as I backed out of the driveway and headed toward the gate. Thank God that was over with.

* * *

NADINE HAD A FRIEND named Yvette Toussaint, who lived in Bar-sur-Loup. I had met her once before and liked her immediately. Warm and friendly, she sometimes accompanied us for a long walk or a trip to the beach. On this occasion, we decided to take a walk from Yvette's house to an old, defunct railway viaduct a couple of miles from her home.

Her community was tightly nestled in and about the low-lying Alps, miles north of the coastline. The narrow streets wove in and out of neighborhoods and wooded areas, meandering up and down the brush-covered, rugged terrain where olive trees, mimosa, pine, linden, and oak grew abundantly. I coveted these walks where occasional panoramic views of higher mountainous areas and unobstructed valleys could appear suddenly and unexpectedly as you rounded a humble bend in the road.

Houses of different shapes and sizes dotted the unstructured landscape in varying shades of pastel. Wooden shutters in light blues and greens, pink, yellow, or violet framed the simple window openings and could be closed and locked.

Landscapes exploded in brilliant color. Large, poisonous oleander shrubs festooned their beautiful crimson, pink or white blooms proliferatively in gardens and woods alike. Lemon trees earthed in lively colored pots burst with bright yellow fruits, window boxes billowed with hardy, thick-stemmed, fiery red geraniums, and bougainvillea plastered the stucco walls like a vibrant, colorful blanket, coveting my adoration.

Yvette, Nadine, and I turned down a narrow street toward where the old railway viaduct was located. We climbed upward along a rocky footpath, obscured by low-hanging tree branches. Suddenly, and quite remarkably, there it was. I stood agape at the extraordinary architecture before me, thrilled by the craggy, treelined valley far, far below. The single-laned, paved crossing stretched like a giant ribbon across the open valley, and exhilaration whooshed inside me.

"I'm scared!" Nadine squealed excitedly, taking a step backward.

"You're always scared," I shook my head teasingly.

I took her by the arm as we carefully made our way to the middle of the great span, proceeding slowly and deliberately as if we were walking a tightrope, the sheering height threatening to suck us over the edge. "I can't. It's too high!" she protested.

I tightened my grip on her arm. "You know you can't resist," I lovingly taunted, pressing us both forward.

As we neared the center, I wanted to look over the side, so I slowly let go of her arm and proceeded gingerly to the edge. "Take care, Debra!" she cautioned, standing with her feet wide apart, bracing herself.

The bridge was bordered by a waist-high railing enforced by a rusty chain-link fence, so there was no danger of falling off. *Magnificent!* I was breathless as I beamed at the privilege of experiencing the grand panorama before me. I didn't ever want to leave this place. I had to figure out a way to stay in France.

* * *

ARI PHONED LATER TO TELL ME he had been busy the entire weekend. "I'm sorry I let you down, Debra," he apologized. "We had unexpected guests, and I couldn't get away."

"It's okay, please don't apologize. I know how quickly things can change for you," I offered understandingly.

"Would you like to accompany me to the race in Paris this weekend?" he asked, brightening.

Would I?! "Oh my God, really?! Yes! Yes! I would love that!" I practically whinnied into his ear as adrenaline surged through every cell of my body.

"Theo will take you to the airport, and I will meet you there." I could tell he was excited too. There was an easy rapport between us, and it would be fun to have his undivided attention for the duration of the flight.

Ari and I had previously but briefly discussed the possibility of my working for the race team that he owned. His son Brock was a race car driver, and the entire team could benefit from my chiropractic and massage services. There were six races in all—one per month—and if Brock was satisfied after the practice race at Le Mans in Paris, I could potentially continue to work the other races.

I jumped up and down in my living room, shrieking with delight. I was euphoric. How did I get so lucky?! All I had asked for was to live on the French Riviera with an income source that allowed me to stay as long as possible, leaving a yawning funnel of potential that could be filled with all sorts of magic and miracles. Heaven and Earth were in symphonic collusion as providence unfurled its imperial carpet at my feet. I could hardly wait to meet Brock. I had only once been to a racetrack and had no idea what to expect. I was ready for anything.

CHAPTER 3

Love at First Sight

My legs shook with excitement as I mounted the steps to Ari's private jet for the first time. Still adrift in a tailwind of utter disbelief, I floated on the steady breeze of stupefaction that had clonked me over the head just months ago at the Hotel du Pont. I settled down into the plush white leather seat, Ari across the aisle facing me.

He beamed at me. "Are you excited about the race, Debra?"

"You can't even imagine," I brimmed, smiling from ear to ear. The Sorensen experience had descended upon me like a regal thunderclap, obliterating my daily grind like a 360-degree wind bomb.

"It is just the practice race; the actual race is in June," he said proudly.

"I'm looking forward to meeting the team and working on Brock and the other drivers," I chirped.

"Some of my CEOs and business associates will be there, so I may not get to spend time with you," he said lightly, preparing me in advance. "But there will be a lot of excitement and plenty of time for you to meet the team and enjoy the atmosphere." He organized the stack of newspapers lying on the seat beside him: The New York Times, the Wall Street Journal, the USA Today, and the Nice-Matin. "Would you like some coffee, Debra?" he asked in a singsong voice.

He wanted to serve *me* coffee. "I would love some," I said giddily. I watched appreciatively as he carefully prepared a noisette for me in the tiny galley, swaying lightly with the gentle rocking of the plane. "*Pinch me, I'm dreaming,*" I uttered under my breath, gazing around the ten-seat aircraft.

***

ONCE ON THE GROUND, we were greeted by a bulky man with white hair and kindly, twinkling blue eyes like Saint Nick himself. I liked Liam instantly. He was one of the truck drivers for the race team. "Hallo, Debra. Pleased to meet you," he said in a thick accent, extending a meaty palm to shake my hand. Liam spoke little English, so we often resorted to body language and hand gestures throughout the weekend, which created much laughter and bonding between us.

The "Circuit de 24 Heures Du Mans" was enormous. There were dozens of teams, mainly from Europe, that would be competing. We hopped into a shuttle, like a golf cart, Liam stuffing his large frame behind the wheel, to drive us to the garage where the race team was. There were rows of gigantic trailers with colorful emblems spanning the length of the rear pit road behind the track that transported the race cars: Ferrari, Lamborghini, Audi, Porsche, Maserati, Mercedes-Benz, Bentley, BMW, and more. My senses soared. Ari got out of the cart and hurried over to Brock, leaning against one of the team's trailers. I followed suit.

His confident eyes locked on mine, and I felt a laser beam go straight to my heart as he smiled playfully at me. I was momentarily immobilized, riveted as I experienced an internal flush of warm, sizzling chemistry I hadn't felt in years. I had just met Brock, the dashing son of Ariel Sorensen. World champion race car driver.

This is your future husband, my brain whispered. I was surprised, but it hadn't been the first time my brain had told me that. "Pleased to meet you, Debra," Brock said politely, his gaze playing with mine, flashing the sexiest eyes I had ever seen. Ari hadn't seemed to notice.

As we entered the pit, my senses were bombarded by a sea of men in uniform, busily working on or around the two race cars parked side by side in the wide garage. Power tools clattered and whirred, echoing their unapologetic cacophony. The rev of car engines throughout the track created a drone that required everyone to raise their voices to hear one another.

The crew snapped to attention when Ari entered the room. He, of course, was oblivious to this. His eyes darted around the garage to see if any of his guests or business entourage had arrived.

Ari introduced me to his brother Willem whose skin was somewhat greyish from smoking. He was one of the mechanics. We made polite conversation as Ari's eyes ping-ponged back and forth surveying the surroundings, and he ducked away from time to time with his finger jammed into one ear to take a phone call.

After a while, Ari and I retreated to a quiet trailer behind the garage that served as Brock's "office" so Ari could make some phone calls in private. "How do you like things so far, Debra?" he asked proudly.

"I'm thrilled," I said to him. "I can't wait to get to work!"

I walked around the outer premises. Liam directed me to the service trailer, where I would set up my table to work on Brock and the drivers. A double-wide guest trailer decorated with brocaded sofas, mahogany tables, stylish club chairs and Persian rugs opened out onto a green-carpeted patio area filled with folding tables and chairs. There was another large tent for the main dining room and a smaller tent housing the kitchen. I smiled broadly. The elaborate setting was surreal, like a tiny city: everything and everyone in its place.

Later, when things had quieted down, Brock came into the trailer. He asked me to work on his right shoulder, a source of considerable pain. He had sustained a permanent injury from a racing accident years earlier, and there was no long-term antidote. Palliative care seemed to take the edge off.

He removed his shirt, revealing significant scarring around his shoulder from a couple of rotator cuff surgeries. "Wow, it looks like you went through some pretty extensive repair," I said quietly, inspecting the scars on his shoulder.

"Yes, it was a mess," he said, shaking his head slightly. "My hand slipped and got stuck in the steering wheel as I tried to avoid hitting the barrier wall, and when I crashed into it, my shoulder was nearly yanked out of the socket. I tore a lot of the tendons and ligaments. I've had two surgeries and lost some of the mobility of my shoulder," he said, raising his arm and moving it into different positions to indicate his limitations. I offered an understanding smile. "I'm sorry you had to go through all that, Brock."

"I have good days and bad days," he shrugged. "It's the price of competing at this level," he said, flashing the same smile as when I'd first met him. "I've heard good things about your therapy from my father. I hope you can help me too," he said, his eyes still holding my gaze.

"Well, I hope I don't disappoint you!" I said, flushing as we both laughed in agreement.

With my heart somewhat aflutter, I carefully administered a deep tissue massage working as therapeutically as possible without causing undue discomfort. The next day he was incredulous, as he had no pain. I was elated.

Everything and everyone revolved around Brock, and the crew genuinely admired him. I would linger in the rear of the pit for hours, taking it all in. He appeared to have a lot on his mind as he and Ari co-owned the team. Watching him in conversation, I gathered these exchanges were likely as much about "racing" as they were about "the business of racing."

Throughout the weekend, I worked on the other race car drivers, the crew, the lorry drivers, and Brock. I was focused and felt confident in my work. It seemed my life had taken a refreshing turn. On more than one occasion, Brock and I would lock eyes in the pit or while walking around outside, and my heart would skip a beat. I knew it would be a challenge for me to remain objective, given my growing attraction for him, but I prayed to be able to put these feelings aside when I performed my chiropractic and massage work. I was there to help.

On the last day of the race, Ari pulled me aside. "Debra, I'm sorry to tell you this, but you won't be able to fly back with me to France after the race. I have to accommodate my business partners, and Brock has to go to Italy to see about a part for one of the cars," he said to me apologetically.

I felt my innards sag. "It's okay. I understand."

"You can drive back with some of the crew who will drop you off in Amsterdam to explore the city for a few days, or I can buy you a ticket back to France." I chose Amsterdam. I hadn't yet been there and figured there was no time like the present to take advantage of the opportunity to explore a new city.

One of the crew members had already taken my luggage back to Ari's jet, so I would have to retrieve it. When I arrived, Brock was there.

"Sorry I stole your seat," he smirked playfully.

"You can make it up to me," I flirted back. "I'm going to Amsterdam for the rest of the week. I haven't been there yet."

"Queen's Day is in a few days. It's a major celebration in the Netherlands." I had never heard of it. "Everyone wears orange and drinks a lot of beer," he chuckled.

"Sounds like St. Patrick's Day back in the States," I quipped. It would be an adventure.

"See you in Monza," he smiled with a wink. And just like that, I found myself employed. I was exhilarated to be part of the team. He called me an hour later. Apparently, I was still on his mind. I had missed his call, but I listened to the message he left several times over to hear his soft, sultry voice.

As I lay in bed that evening, I thought about Brock and the impact he'd had on me when we first met. Was it just a flight of fancy? Could there be a future with him? The situation conjured images of Hunter, a man who'd had the same immediate impact on me nearly a decade ago. It was a relationship with an ending that left me confused, wondering what I'd done wrong and if I'd ever love again.

***

HUNTER MACDONOUGH LANDED in my life with a fiercely beautiful smile and sparkling blue eyes that made my knees go weak. He flashed that smile like a calling card, and in the weeks when I'd first met him, he made me flush like a schoolgirl, stopping my heart in its tracks. He lived in Arlington, Virginia. I'd met him at a hotel conference for a network marketing company for which we both were distributors. I sensed I would meet someone and wasn't sure it was fate or wishful thinking.

I recalled the loud dance music that thrust my body backward as I stepped into the packed ballroom of the hotel. The beat of the bass thrummed through me, vibrating my chest. My eyes were intent on the dance floor, penetrating, searching, looking for the man of my dreams. After a few minutes, I felt my heart sink as I heard the words inside my head. *He's not here, Debra.* Dejected, I spun around to leave and felt a tap on my shoulder.

"Will you dance with me?" asked the tall, attractive stranger, barely audible over the pulsing music.

"No thanks," I said, turning to go, already deflated by the words that had just rendered a verdict in my head.

He scampered off to the dance floor, and I walked toward the door. Suddenly, he was back again.

"Did you say 'no' to me?" he asked, blinking incredulously.

Hadn't he heard me? "I don't feel like dancing," I offered, trying to leave. He wouldn't entertain that answer, and I reluctantly succumbed.

He was a decent dancer. We enjoyed a couple of songs, but I wanted to go. He offered to buy me a drink. I resisted the urge to decline.

Hunter leaned back, stretching his long body in the comfy club chair, legs straight out, crossed at the ankles, as we sat chatting in the bar lounge. He was smart, quick, cultured, and sexy. As the conversation unfolded, I felt a prickling around my heart, a flicker longing to become a flame.

Later, he walked me to my room. "May I kiss you?" he asked politely, possibly ready for another "no" answer. A few moments later, I was plastered to the wall next to my door, his tongue soft as it rolled around mine, his hands cupped around my face, my head, my neck, our bodies pinned together in the hallway.

I smiled as I remembered our six-month relationship. Embroiled in an ugly divorce, Hunter hadn't been ready for me then. It didn't take long before he started pulling away. My response was to try harder. Maybe if I gave more, did more, he would change his mind and stick around.

One day, while visiting him for a few days, I rearranged all of the furniture in his house while he was at work. He was surprised but didn't seem perturbed. And he seemed grateful when I drove down from New York on another occasion with a carload of perennials I had uprooted from my parents' house to plant in his garden. I'd spent the entire day digging and planting. His yard looked beautiful when I finished. He was appreciative, but it only seemed to push him further away.

"Wow," he'd marveled, glancing in disbelief around the perimeter of his house, "you did all this yourself?"

Was I doing too much? Not enough? I hadn't wanted our relationship to end. I'd surged toward him, not knowing what else to do. What had I done wrong? Early on, he told me he was in love with me and that I could be the one for him. He apologized. "It's not you; it's me," he had said.

Wasn't that what they always said? Was he being honest? Maybe he was paying attention to an inner knowing I hadn't discovered in myself, a whispering voice that I rarely obliged, brushing it away impatiently, like a fly buzzing around my face.

I'd gone kicking and screaming, calling him often. He was always polite, but the answer was always, "I'm not ready." One day he just stopped taking my calls. I suffered. I sobbed. I prayed. It took three years for me to be over him, but eventually, I was. I had tearfully pulled myself together to wait for the next Mr. Right to show up, sublimating the experience of love that I'd wanted with Hunter like a sleeping giant. Could Brock be the man for whom I was waiting? Had Hunter merely pointed the way to greater love?

* * *

IT WAS MONDAY MORNING, and I would be driving back to Amsterdam with Willem and a couple of the other crew members. Willem took care of all the details. Keith, the team's public relations manager, drove me from the country club where I had stayed with Ari, Brock, and the drivers, back to the track to meet Willem in Brock's luxurious, black LP640 Lamborghini Murciélago Roadster with red leather interior.

Brock always brought a couple of his cars to the track; it was part of the "show." Keith leapt at the opportunity to drive such a fine machine, and I basked as the mighty engine responded to Keith's foot heavy on the pedal, the force sucking me back into my seat as we whisked through the winding countryside roads on the fringes of Paris.

Ari's wealth was incalculable to me. He had accumulated one of the finest vintage race car collections in Europe. Understandably, I was impressed. And so was Brock. He examined exotic sports cars with the same lusting perusal as he gave to most women. Unfortunately, I considered his first glance as romantic interest. Objectification had never dawned on my smitten naiveté.

* * *

IT WAS GREAT FUN DRIVING back with the crew. They had many questions for me. "How did I meet Ari? What did I do for him? Did I like living in France? Was I going to come back and do my work with the team?"

"My brother sure has the life," Willem smiled. He was different from Ari; he was an earthy type, mechanically inclined, quiet, somewhat reserved, comfortable working alone or in a group. Like Ari, Willem had a great sense of humor and the capacity to care for people who mattered to him. Yet, he seemed content with a simpler life.

* * *

I CHECKED INTO THE HOTEL AMSTELZICHT near Rembrandtplein, where Ari was a frequent patron. After I checked in, I decided to walk to the center of town to explore the remarkable city of Amsterdam.

As I strolled the city's main streets, I was floored by the physical characteristics of the people. "My flock!" I exclaimed, eyeing the tall, ample-bodied, blond-haired females, comfortable and confident in their skin, arm in arm, happily chatting and laughing, enjoying each other's company. Even their noses were slightly sloped, like mine. And the men! It was lovely to be around tall, attractive, smiling men; their long strides and relaxed camaraderie with their friends made me feel right at home. It was an absolute surprise and delight. I didn't have any Dutch heritage as far as I knew, but in my heart, I did. They may have felt the same and were surprised when I started speaking English!

I considered it impeccable orchestration on behalf of the Universe that I would get to experience Queen's Day, one of the Netherlands' biggest festivals, rippling throughout the country on the last day of April every year. Hailing from the lineage of King William III and dating back to 1885, Queen's Day was a carnival-scale countrywide birthday celebration of the Queen, most notably Queen Juliana and later her daughter, Queen Beatrix.

The cityscape was an explosion of orange, the royal color of the "House of Orange-Nassau." Amsterdam's canals swarmed with boats draped in orange streamers and orange balloons. The bars were packed with noisy crowds, celebrating loudly with beer mugs in hand. The Dutch were lively and expressive, emitting a vibe that reminded me of Americans. And my insight had been correct; it was just like St. Patrick's Day in New York City!

Ironically, I even met a man from Orange County, New York, reveling in the festivities, drinking an orange beer. The next day he accompanied me to the Rijksmuseum, where we got to experience the masterpieces of great artists like Rembrandt, Frans Hals, Johannes Vermeer, and later the Van

Gogh Museum, exhibiting the brilliant works of the artist and his contemporaries.

The timing couldn't have been more perfect. I was happy to explore the iconic city of the beautiful country to which Ari had immigrated with his mother, brother, and sister many years ago. I had a perspective that expanded my heart and my mind. I looked forward to the time when I might be spending a lot more of my time here, maybe even with Brock.

***

A MONTH LATER, I drove to the racetrack in Monza, less than five hours from my apartment in Biot. Driving in Italy was even more confusing than in France. All those roundabouts! I was exasperated. And the fact that I spoke no Italian didn't help. At least I knew enough French to get me around France.

When I finally arrived in Monza, I made the mistake of relying on the locals to get me to the Autodromo Nazionale di Monza. Most of them spoke little to no English, and I went around in circles. I was exasperated and flustered. I had wanted to get to the track early to meet everyone and set up my workspace.

Suddenly, it occurred to me that I'd mistakenly thought the street signs for the "motocourse" I had been seeing was the racetrack. No! The motocourse was the highway. *No wonder,* I thought.

Once that dawned on me, a local who spoke English appeared out of the blue, escorting me to the nearby track. Completely unaware, I'd passed it several times. I let the poignancy of that sink in. Something could be right under our nose, and if it weren't what we expected, we might not even see that it was there.

Brock was harried and distracted when I arrived. He was mildly amused at my escapade. "Well, at least you got here," he grinned. "Italy can be very confusing, even if you know where you are going."

It was my first paid race. Seeing Brock again swept me off my feet. His prowess and power captivated and thrilled me. I was enthusiastic about working on the team and contributing to their success, and it didn't take long before I was under his spell.

Keith, on the other hand, was an entirely different story. I had first met him at the Le Mans Practice race, and I had been instantly uneasy around him. His cavalier approach to life grated against my sensibilities, and the very sound of his rapid-fire voice triggered my hypervigilance; I did not trust him at all.

He followed Brock in long strides, leaning close to him like a puppy, prattling in his ear, and was annoyingly ever-present. His attention darted nervously about, vigilantly scanning the environment for anything out of place, and he frequently raked his hair with his fingers. He had an adept, busy mind, which adapted quickly to sudden changes, and he excelled at his job.

Often on the phone, Keith had a harsh, drawling voice, and I felt he talked *at* people rather than *with* them. His passion had something to prove rather than being an expression of an engaged heart. He appeared regularly in many of the photos taken at the events, smiling triumphantly with his arm around Brock, which smacked of self-promotion. It was the cost of doing business, even to my inexperienced evaluation, and what I lacked in business savvy, I believed I made up for in personality assessment.

I felt a seething undercurrent of jealousy from Keith. Sometimes he would burst through the trailer door as I was working on Brock's shoulder, coming to an abrupt halt, surprised at my presence. I was a new addition that upset the status quo, and my attention primarily focused on Brock. It was apparent that Keith was unwilling to share his precious moments while I was in the room. Brock was unaffected by this and spoke freely about business while I was present. Keith made infrequent eye contact with me, directing all his attention to Brock, and refused my offer to work on him.

To make matters worse, many crew members were suspicious of me, and I could feel their questioning, non-accepting glances: Why was I hanging around with Brock? At Le Mans, I had been a guest of Ari's, so there was no threat, no question; like so many others who came and went, my relationship in the scheme of things had been unknown to them. Only Ari and Brock knew that I was the newest team member. My attempts at friendly conversation met with polite but unengaged responses. I couldn't figure out why they were distant and unreceptive to me.

Later, Willem confirmed my suspicions. I addressed it with Brock. "The crew don't seem to know why I'm here," I said to him. He admitted that he hadn't formally told them about me. "No wonder!" I exclaimed. "You have to tell them, Brock." He wasn't accustomed to someone in my position telling him what to do, as this was new for him too. Furthermore, the crew were unaware of many details about how things operated; it wasn't their concern. "I'm here to work on them too, Brock," I said. He looked at me inquisitively. I spelled it out for him. "They are very physical in their job as mechanics. If they get hurt or something is hampering their performance, I can help them."

"I will make an announcement at dinner," he said, now understanding. I was satisfied.

Most of the races took place over four to five days. Day one was set up, and the second and third were for practice: working out the bugs in the cars, the drivers familiarizing themselves with the track. The last days were for racing.

There were a lot of hungry men to feed. The cooking was done on-site by a vending company that provided the food, the cooks, and the servers. Everything was buffet-style and always delicious. I sat, munching expectantly, happy that Brock had agreed to inform the crew about my presence. I hadn't anticipated the reaction I would get when he called me to the front of the large tent.

"I know many of you probably don't know why Debra has joined us," Brock said, smiling and relaxed as he glanced around the room, knowing his announcement would be a pleasant surprise for the crew and a morale booster at that; I was here to help the whole team. "I'd like to introduce Dr. Hoolahan as our new team doctor and massage therapist."

They all clapped! Suddenly, I became the woman they all wanted to talk to, and their acceptance spread over me like a cozy blanket. Could I help them with their lower back? Their neck? Shoulders, knees, ankles, wrists, and fingers…?? Yes, yes, and yes. I beamed with delight. I was going to be busy.

Some men came to me, and some did not. Most accepted me, and as I stood in the rear of the pit, appreciating their quick and facile talents, I sensed their growing respect. I felt a stirring inside me—and them—which brought great satisfaction.

* * *

IT WAS DAY FOUR, RACE DAY. I mused at Brock's capacity to be in the moment at will. All those years of mindful presence at the wheel could be summoned instantly, even off the track. My mistake was believing this was an indication of an evolved consciousness. I would suffer that misperception for months, which, unfortunately, distorted all true objectivity on my part thenceforth. My schoolgirl heart was off and running. But if that were a nail in the coffin, Giuseppina would be the hammer.

Keith had been behaving strangely all morning. He would blast out some idle chit-chat and then gaze off in the distance, snickering. It was as if he knew something I didn't, which gave me the creeps. The less I saw of this guy, the better. A couple of hours later, I found out the little secret his twisted mind was cherishing.

Giuseppina arrived in a flurry of pomp and circumstance. My heart sank. I didn't entertain the idea that Brock might have a girlfriend. As far as I knew, he was in the middle of a divorce. I really shouldn't have been surprised. Confident on the outside, a constant stream of female companionship might have been a mechanism to stave off insecurity.

Italian, petite, slender, with long shiny hair, Giuseppina was scolding, withholding, and bewitching, but Brock was hooked. Ari confided in me, lamenting their union, suspecting Giuseppina was there for the money. So apparently, did everyone else except for Brock. But, likening the son to the father, history was destined to repeat itself, and mine wasn't the only poor, codependent heart spinning in the swill.

Giuseppina's personality and gestures were almost a carbon copy of Celeste's. Both were shrewd in a barely concealed, self-serving manner—however gracious their transparent smile appeared to be. Shopping came naturally, and they were a substantive channel for the workaholic ways of the Sorensen men, albeit Ari was the only one making any money *per se*; their open palms were never far from his obliging wallet.

I was crushed. I wanted Giuseppina to disappear, but I mustered up the courage to connect with her and accept her. I offered her a full-body massage. I reminded myself that Brock's romantic life was none of my business. It was hard to be around her. She fidgeted on the table, and we chatted superficially. It was energetically exhausting for me. I felt like a revving engine that couldn't shift out of first gear, and I was relieved when the massage was over.

Feeling vulnerable, I wanted to run and hide but couldn't find a spot alone. Finally, I went into Brock's trailer, wanting desperately to speak with Valentina. She knew how I felt about Brock. Miraculously, she must have picked up on my vibe, and the phone rang!

"My God, Tina! You must be psychic!" I chuckled.

"Why?" she asked, chuckling along with me.

"You're not going to believe what's happening. These people are driving me crazy." I felt myself unwinding as I recounted the latest drama and how difficult it was for me to find my balance.

She soothed my jangled nerves, stabilizing me. "Regardless of what is happening, Brock needs you there. Nothing is wrong," she reminded me, "this is just how his life is. The drama is not about you," she reassured me.

"You're right." I felt myself recentering. Like it or not, this was the way things were. I didn't know what the future held. I had to be more allowing and let things flow.

***

THE FOLLOWING DAY BROCK TOLD ME that Giuseppina had cancer. "*WHAT? She's so young!*" My mind screamed to analyze the information as a dagger pierced my heart. Something was not quite right. My "bullshit meter" had just swung wildly to the right. I looked deeply into his eyes, searching for something that would tell me otherwise.

"She has lymphoma. Can you help her?" He was earnest.

Why was I so dubious? Cancer was not in my scope of practice. Had he meant via energy work, which I would be glad to offer, or intense nutritional support? I wasn't going to foray into questionable territory, but I could speak with her intelligently and support her choices. He was happy to hear that.

Later that day, after the race, she confided in me. She had the same look in her eyes that Brock had, but I didn't see fear there. Searching for something that would offer me the truth, I questioned her about her medications, history, treatments, and conversations with the doctors. I couldn't knit together the information she furnished in a way that made medical sense. She hadn't offered me much except the pharmaceutical company's name on the side of the pill bottle that she didn't happen to have with her. I stopped pressing her, lest she pick up on my suspicions.

I felt guilty about questioning the validity of the situation. Suspicion would never be my response to circumstances so potentially dire. I understood the fear and disorientation people suffered when rendered diagnoses like cancer. It just didn't seem like that was the case here. What was I picking up on?

Later that evening, Brock put his arm around me while we walked outside. "I'm so glad Giuseppina told you about her cancer," he said, relieved of the secret he had been carrying.

"Does your father know?" I asked.

"Yes." I wondered what Ari thought about it all. Why was Brock glad I knew? What did he think I could do for her? After our conversation, I felt he'd dropped the ball as if it belonged in my court instead of his. But I wasn't going to pick it up. I didn't want to get involved, primarily because I was concerned about the validity of the situation.

After I had returned from the race, Ari invited me to his house to give him a massage. "Was the girl there, Debra?" he asked, tight-lipped.

"You mean Giuseppina?" I asked, surprised he was referring to her this way.

"She needs a lot of attention," he said bluntly. He shared his concern and disappointment over Brock and the romantic situation. "Brock falls in love too easily. Besides, the girl is so young."

"How did he meet her?" I asked innocently.

"He met her at a nightclub when he was racing in Italy. I fear Brock is lost, Debra," Ari said without further explanation.

I could hear the discomfort in his voice as he spoke, but I didn't press him for more details. "I will take care of Brock and the team," I offered. I had my own ideas about Brock. I wanted him and Ari to be happy, and I could envision Ari as my father-in-law.

CHAPTER 4

Blurred Boundaries

Happily, Rochelle was coming to France. My two little worlds were about to collide. She would be a witness to the fairy tale I was living.

By the time she arrived, I was already head-over-heels in love with Brock, and I was looking forward to sharing all that schoolgirl stuff with her. Rochelle Laroux was the only childhood friend that had accompanied me into adulthood. I had first met her in my tenth-grade French class, the only class we'd had in common. She sat behind me, and we shared many giggles. I'd lost touch with her until twelfth grade when our desire for boys and bad choices came crashing together.

On a typical school day, standing in the lunch line at the cafeteria, I barely recognized the dark-haired beauty waving at me, approaching me with a big smile.

"Hi Debra, remember me?" she chirped, happy to see me. I searched my mind and came up short. "Rochelle," she offered, smiling, "from French class. I used to sit behind you."

"Oh…hi...Rochelle!" I stammered. Two years had changed a lot. She was slim and radiant. Her long hair bounced stylishly around her shoulders, framing her strawberry-shaped face. Smooth porcelain skin accentuated her almond-shaped eyes, rimmed by thick, dark lashes.

One Saturday night, she had arrived at my parents' house with her friend Peony, who drove a blue mustang. I was excited to have a place to go as I wasn't yet driving. They wanted to go bowling. I had never been bowling and was not interested but obligingly acquiesced.

Hanging out with Rochelle was the beginning of several years of looking for love in all the wrong places: bars, endless concerts, and wayward men. She and I became close, spending many weekends together, growing up, sharing dreams, drinking too much, searching for ourselves through others, and getting our hearts broken. She'd met Vincent on one of our many nights out long before college. They had gotten married and had two children, now teenagers themselves. And here, nearly a lifetime later, we were about to share another escapade. I smiled. Rochelle was my good-time adventure friend.

* * *

THEO TOOK ME TO THE AIRPORT to retrieve her. I was excited that they were going to meet. Rochelle had never been to Europe, and she was ecstatic to be joining me for a week. "You made it!" I exclaimed, my arms wide open for an embrace as she exited the baggage claim area into the main lobby where we'd been awaiting her arrival.

"Hi, Rochelle! Welcome to France! Debra told me all about you," Theo gushed, wrapping his arms around her in a bear hug. They liked each other immediately, as I knew they would. Both were outgoing, welcoming, and loved being around people.

"Oh my God, I can't believe I'm in France!" Rochelle beamed, her white teeth sticking out from under full rosy lips. Although she had gained some weight over the years, she still looked great, and I was happy to have her here with me.

She sat in the back seat, her head turning from left to right, taking in all the scenery as we engaged in lively conversation. "Look at all the beautiful flowers everywhere! And palm trees right along the coast! You and Theo are so lucky to live here. It's gorgeous. I love the old architecture and especially the tile roofs!" she gushed in delighted appreciation as we made our way along the Promenade des Anglais through the city of Nice.

"Wait until you see all the quaint little villages!" I added cheerfully. There were so many places I was looking forward to taking her.

Theo was happy to have a new person to talk to, and he was very fond of Americans. "I've lived here for almost fifteen years," he offered. "I love everything about France, except for the French people." We laughed uproariously. Theo had a direct, biting sense of humor, likely basing his assessment of the French on his ex-wife Vivienne.

Fortunately, Rochelle didn't press him for details. "It's so much fun to speak French!" she giggled. Her French was never that developed, but she would have plenty of opportunities to say "Bonjour!" and "Merci!" over the next week.

* * *

MY APARTMENT HAD A TINY second bedroom upstairs with a twin bed, a simple nightstand, and a small chest of drawers. Rochelle was thrilled to have her own little space. A single window covered by an appliqué lace curtain overlooked the street below.

"What was that strange croaking noise I heard last night?" she asked as we sat drinking our coffee on the terrace the next morning.

"Oh, that," I laughed. "I think it's a big bullfrog." We giggled.

"How do you say frog in French?" she asked.

"Grenouille."

"Gren-oo-ee!" she trilled, clapping her hands together. "Well, that grenouille had better let me get some sleep tonight!" We tittered gleefully. Accustomed to the outside sounds, the grenouille no longer awakened me from my solid night's sleep.

I reveled in the French countryside's sights, smells, and sounds, as they were different from home. I didn't, however, appreciate the tradition of burning refuse that the French farmers employed. Every day, as I gazed up into the foothills or drove around the neighboring towns, I could see little wisps of smoke rising from the farms. Mostly, it was brush that had been cleared, heaped into an ever-present pile. Farmers were permitted to burn organic waste year-round except for the hot, dry months of July and August. Depending on how the wind was blowing, the smell and the soot could be overpowering, and the unmistakable stench of illicit burning plastic occasionally overcame me. It pained me that all those petrochemicals were polluting the atmosphere.

* * *

BY NOW, I'D ACCLIMATED TO DRIVING and took Rochelle to some of my most cherished places. My favorite was Tourrettes-sur-Loup, which looked exactly like the paintings of artists depicting typical French Riviera charm.

Little cobblestoned streets wound upward like spokes on a wheel from the central part of the town square lined with tightly packed, stuccoed, two-story apartment dwellings. Clay tile roofs dotted their timeless charm throughout the village. There were potted plants everywhere; ascending staircases, crammed onto balcony ledges, and cascading in brilliant hues from simple, wooden window boxes.

I stood behind her, one hand on her back, pushing gently to assist her as we leaned forward to navigate the inclining landscape. "Is everything uphill?" Rochelle puffed as we ascended the street to a panoramic overlook.

"You get used to it," I said as we both laughed, unaccustomed to hilly terrain. We weren't really complaining.

As we reached the overlook, we breathlessly observed the sweeping vista below. I never grew tired of the simple, unmanicured, colorful countryside that generated an ancient longing from lifetimes past.

Afterward, we drove upward toward Gourdon, an old medieval village perched high above the scenic Gorges du Loup. As we gazed out over the low rock wall of the village square to the coast, we could see Antibes, the Marina at Villeneuve-Loubet, and Cagnes-sur-Mer, as our gaze swept down over a vast mountainous cavern to the sea.

We enjoyed a tasty noisette at the famous Nid D'Aigle, as had Nadine and I a month earlier. Perched on the very edge of the sheer south cliff of the communal village, we gaped at the plummeting 2,500-foot drop that took our breath away and sighed as hang gliders sailed overhead toward the magnificent canyon.

Winding our way down to Bar-sur-Loup, we pulled over to take photos, captivated by another plunging cavern that loomed panoramically before us, its schists of yellow rock covered with dark green vegetation as majestic as the Grand Canyon itself. As we continued our descent, we stopped to visit the Gorges du Loup, enthralled by deep crystal-green pools, into which water plunged noisily over mossy-covered cliffs and jutting rocks.

Ari had invited Rochelle and me to attend a dinner in Monte-Carlo. Brock would be racing in the Grand Prix Historique over the weekend preceding the Formula One World Championship race, and many of the race team entourage and crew would be there to work or attend. The timing of Rochelle's visit was exceptionally fortuitous, as I had no idea this was going to occur.

"What time are we going to the Hotel de Paris restaurant tomorrow night?" she asked excitedly, thrilled by the idea of dining at Monte-Carlo's famous landmark and meeting Brock, Ari, and some of the race team entourage.

"Probably around eight o'clock," I said. I was looking forward to seeing Brock. I knew Giuseppina wouldn't be there, and I was relieved that she would be out of the way. It never occurred to me that he would move forward with her. In my mind, it was just a passing thing. I was on a mission to win his affection and his heart.

"I can hardly wait to meet everyone!" Rochelle gushed.

"You won't be disappointed. There is always excitement on planet Sorensen." *Sometimes a little too much*, I grinned to myself.

***

DINNER STARTED INNOCENTLY ENOUGH. There were more than two dozen people in attendance. Keith was there, and I wanted to ensure I wasn't sitting anywhere near him. Ari sat at the head of the table with some of his business associates and people I didn't recognize. Brock preferred to be in the middle of the action and centrally located himself at the long table. I sat next to him with Rochelle on my other side. Keith was across the table, as was Theo. Bottles of red wine stationed along the table were draining rapidly, and I could feel my head starting to buzz.

"What time does the race begin on Saturday?" I asked Brock.

"I'm not sure. I haven't yet heard where my starting position will be," he said, shrugging his shoulders.

The Historic Grand Prix of Monaco, or Grand Prix Historique, as the French called it, occurred once every two years, about two weeks before the Formula One World Championship race. It featured old, historic race cars and collector cars. I wanted to see Brock race. I knew there would be a sea of people in attendance and that Ari would likely be conducting business.

When I questioned Ari, he was reluctant to invite me. "Let's see how it goes, Debra. I will let you know." Brock seemed to be equally distancing.

The drinks continued to pour, and the conversation grew more lively. Rochelle was joking across the table with Keith, who enjoyed her spunk. At some point during dinner, I had placed my hand on Brock's thigh. I don't remember why or what his reaction had been. We'd all imbibed a lot of alcohol, and I didn't recall much of the conversation. But I vividly remember the gut punch I subsequently received from Brock in the parking lot that made my heart sink.

Everyone was exchanging goodbyes, and I again asked Brock about attending the race. He brushed me off as he headed across the parking lot. I followed him. Had I somehow offended him over dinner? "I just want to see you race!" I exclaimed. "I'm not trying to make you uncomfortable…," I trailed off.

"You're lucky to be on the team, Debra," he said coolly, still walking.

"Yeah, well, you're lucky to have me!" I countered, stunned.

He whirled around and grabbed me by the shoulders, looking me squarely in the eyes. "Debra, I love you! It's not about you! I don't even know where I'm starting on Saturday!" His eyes pleaded for understanding.

My heart dropped. I desperately wanted to attend the Historique. "I'm sorry, Brock. I don't mean to push you," I said dejectedly, knowing I had come from feelings that weren't reciprocal for him.

"Then don't," he said, hands still on my shoulders as he held my gaze. I appreciated these honest moments with him and didn't want to invite disharmony. I wanted him in my life. Likely, things were happening behind the scenes that were none of my concern. Motor racing was big business. Nevertheless, I longed to spend more time with him. I was falling in love.

Theo had abstained from drinking, being the designated driver for Rochelle and me. Not much of a drinker, his poisons were coffee and cigarettes. He'd had a wonderful time, as had Rochelle. She had gotten to speak with Ari, and he enjoyed her gregarious nature and mirthful laughter. Theo rarely spent any time with Ari, so anything was a plus. Having taken things personally, I felt left out and disposed of as it concerned the Historique race. Was I part of the team or not? I rarely got angry, but I'd had to swallow so many emotions that had become bottled up inside me over the past few weeks. I erupted uncharacteristically and flew into an accusatory tirade, cursing Ari and Brock as we drove home.

"So I'm not good enough to attend their highfalutin little party in Monte-Carlo?!" I clucked at Theo.

"This has nothing to do with you, Debra!" Theo retaliated. "They probably have business to conduct. You can't expect to be invited to everything just because you work at the other races. Mr. S. doesn't owe you anything!"

"I'll bet if I was one of his fat cats, I'd be able to get a seat at the damned show!" I countered, raising my voice even more.

"What's your problem, Debra?!" Theo was flabbergasted and defended them both mightily. I felt guilty but justified about flying off the handle; they had blown me off. They could have given me an explanation. Rochelle hadn't said a word, but I could see by her expression that she was surprised at my unexpected outburst. High drama wasn't my style.

Theo dropped us off at the curb outside my apartment. He was going to Switzerland by himself for a few days to visit his friend Erik so I wouldn't see him until he got back. He'd promised to drive Rochelle back to the airport. "You'd better," she teased. "I don't want to leave without seeing you again."

"I promise," he said, flashing a big smile for her.

I'd calmed down after I'd let the steam blow off. "Thanks for driving us, Theo. Sorry I made a big deal over things. I appreciate you taking us there." I truly did. He was a light in my life. I was glad Rochelle was here to distract my mind from the dizzying rumination that would ensue from this incident. Would Brock tell Ari what had happened between us? What would Ari's reaction be if he knew I had behaved that way?

* * *

TWO DAYS LATER, Rochelle and I sat outside a cozy Trattoria, soaking up the sights and sounds of the quaint side street restaurant situated on a small canal just minutes from the bustling Piazza San Marco. Content to be away from the larger crowds, we ate our pasta as we sipped a deep, red Chianti from round-bottomed glasses. "This is the best spaghetti I've ever had!" I remarked, somewhat surprised that semolina flour, ground beef, and tomatoes could come together in such splendor. Hungrily spinning the wriggling heap of pasta with my fork, long threads of it dangling and slapping saucily against my chin, I slurped the delicious strands into my mouth.

"Maybe, it's because we're in freaking *Venice,"* Rochelle giggled, dabbing the edges of her full lips as we gazed out onto the canal, no more than twenty feet in front of us, bobbing our heads in raucous agreement.

We had driven to Venice the evening before. I was astounded at how near Nice was to this premier destination. Living so close to the Italian border had its perks. We promised each other that we would return to this very spot to seal our journey, but there were oh-so-many yummy places to eat, and we never did make it back.

We strolled arm-in-arm along the enchanting brick street bordering the narrow canal, gently undulating with small boats drifting past in either direction. Ducking into a small jewelry store, I spied a beautiful turquoise ring in a small glass case, sitting on a tiny, black velvet pillow. It was a lovely oblong piece that spanned nearly half the length of my middle finger. The stone was flat and unpolished, with raw, slender, brown veins running through its matte blue-green surface. Sitting crowned in a latticed, sterling mesh, tiny flecks of black marcasite glittered unobtrusively along the edge where the silver met the stone. "Que bella," I said, glancing up at the pretty, dark-haired clerk behind the counter. "Quanto costa?" I asked, intending to buy.

"Oh, you speak Italiano," she said in English, raising her eyebrows, a charming smile spreading across her face.

"It must be the red wine," I countered playfully. The three of us chuckled as the girl wrapped the pretty piece in tissue paper, placing it into a simple paper bag and tying it with a slender raffia ribbon.

Later that evening, Rochelle and I went to a local disco for the opportunity of dancing with the ever-romantic Italian men. We would not be disappointed. We had already imbibed too much red wine when Roberto and his friend Miguel singled us out at the long bar. Fortunately for us, they spoke enough English to have some conversation, but the real magic happened on the dance floor.

Wow, I thought, as Roberto deftly pulled my body to him, his hand pressed firmly against my lower back, his swaying hips tempting mine into a surrendered reply. He was tall and solid, with a triangular torso that sat well-honed over equally proportionate long legs. European men had an innate passion for recreational soccer playing. *American men do not have legs like this,* I sighed silently.

We danced and drank, and danced and drank some more, letting the moments fold unselfconsciously around us. Later that evening, Roberto kissed me. His kisses weren't as exciting as the dancing, but, laughing and weaving along the cobbled street, the four of us made it back to the hotel where Rochelle and I were lodging. We promptly said good night to our gorgeous companions, and she and I whooped with drunken reverie as we sat on our beds recounting our great fortune.

The next day we hopped aboard a speedy northbound ferry that took us across the choppy waters of the Grand Canal to the island of Murano, where we would experience a glass-blowing demonstration at one of the factories. Rochelle and I got to try our hand at the craft. Guided by an adept artisan, I held the long, heavy, iron poker as he put his arms around me, securing the cumbersome rod. Slowly, I twirled the glowing blob on the end of the poker, trying to shape the amorphous mass into something recognizable. "This is really hard!" I exclaimed, appreciating the deft skill it took to wind the unruly orange glob into compliance.

* * *

IT WAS THE LAST DAY OF HER VACATION, and Rochelle wanted to visit Cannes, as it was film festival time in France. Theo was happy to oblige. It was one of the first places I had seen when I'd arrived. I wasn't as impressed as I was with Nice, although there were similarities. Cannes felt very Beverly Hills to me, with all its expensive shops, and in my opinion, didn't have the character or old-world charm of the older cities.

Rochelle, however, was in her glory, content to sit and people watch, hoping to spy someone famous. We ate a delicious pasta lunch under the awning of Caffé Roma as we watched hordes of tourists traversing the palm-lined, seaside walkway of Boulevard de la Croisette and headed back after we'd had our fill. Satisfied, Rochelle was already anticipating her return in late autumn.

* * *

THEO CONFRONTED ME ABOUT OUR DINNER at the Hotel de Paris while driving back from the airport. "I don't like that you were talking shit about Mr. S., Debra!" he fumed, music clacking on the car stereo as he blew a deep drag of smoke out his open window.

"I'm sorry, Theo. I didn't mean to upset you so much. I was pissed off about Brock. There's a lot of drama because of Giuseppina, and it all just got to me."

Theo hadn't slept for two nights after my raging about Ari and Brock. I wasn't a yeller, and my outburst had entirely upended him. I felt guilty. I didn't want to hurt Theo. His allegiance to the Sorensens, especially Ari, was fierce. Ari was like a father figure to him; I had forgotten that the sun rose and set around him, and I had never heard Theo utter an unkind word about this man. He was enamored and beholden, and although he could see Brock's foibles, he defended Ari strongly; nothing was ever his fault.

"I know you were frustrated, Debra. But please, don't do that again." His tone was resolute and uncharacteristically succinct.

I loved the Sorensen men too, but I'd felt hurt, left out. The truth was, I was just a hired hand, like Theo, who had no resistance to that fact. No amount of wishing or hoping, or clinging to signs that weren't there, would bring me any closer to the inner circle or Brock. Many wanted to be there, to feel significant—purposeful because "important" people were in their world. Many of us hadn't discovered our intrinsic worth and were still looking to outside events for proof.

* * *

THE FOLLOWING DAY I SPOKE WITH ARI. He did not bring up my antics at the dinner in Monte-Carlo, and I sensed from his tone of voice that Brock hadn't mentioned it. He was concerned about Brock and "the girl." He told me Giuseppina went to a hospital in Italy after the Monaco Historique, availing herself of his private jet. He commented on her "playing a comedy." It was clear he didn't trust her. I didn't either, but it wasn't my business. I would be leaving for Le Mans in a couple of weeks, where I was sure the drama would continue to play out.

Questions continued to tumble out of my mind and onto the page. Why was I attracted to Brock? Was he capable of a normal relationship? Consumed by a wealthy world, did he even know who he was? Ari had said

Brock was lost. And what about me? Why was I attracted to another unavailable narcissist? Was *I* unavailable? Was it the chase that compelled me?

I struggled with the pomp and circumstance, the high drama, chaos, and phoniness that I was privy to in the Sorensen world. My breakup with Hunter had been so painful, and I certainly didn't want a repeat. After him, my spirit and desire to love were exhausted. I had been closed for so long, and Brock had been the first opening in years. Why was it all happening like this? I wanted real love, consecrated with an available man. Was there something inherently wrong with me? Was what I wanted unattainable? Why was love such a struggle?

CHAPTER 5

Was it Something I Said?

A *Course In Miracles*. The words on the binding grabbed my attention. *I could use a miracle*, I mused, sliding the heavy, dark blue tome from the shelf. *Wow, this thing is like the Bible*, I thought as I gazed at its simple gold-lettered cover. I opened the book to the middle, its tissuey pages covered in old-fashioned, classical font and numbered paragraphs mildly alarming my new-aged sensibilities.

As I started to read it, a strange sensation overcame me, as if I was being drawn into a tunnel to some long-ago forgotten time and place. The words appeared to come from an authority that was not human. My eyes were pulled from left to right, magnetized by the very sentences themselves as I struggled to understand where the message was coming from and its effect on me. I read on. Capitalized words like "Holy Spirit," "Father," and "Son" started to appear, and I bristled, disappointed. I snapped the book shut, placing it back on the shelf.

Too bad, I thought, feeling my hopes somewhat dashed. But a primeval spark deep inside me had been fanned. I felt both annoyed and nervous, afraid to discover something that I did not want to know. "I'm not ready yet," I said aloud. I shook it off and continued perusing the shelves, looking for a book or two more aligned with my developing perspective.

* * *

I SAT OUTSIDE ON MY LITTLE PATIO IN BIOT, warmed by a freshly brewed cup of coffee and the mid-morning Riviera sunshine. Here I was seven years later, reading a book by Joel Goldsmith called *Beyond Words and Thoughts* given to me by a close friend and colleague in New York before I'd left for France.

Goldsmith examined and explained the meaning of Jesus' words as he understood them. I did not follow any Christian faiths, and it wasn't clear why my friend had given me this book. Still, he was excited about Goldsmith's clarity in presenting the deeper meaning of Jesus' teachings beyond traditional interpretations.

Somewhat tongue in cheek, I had started reading it a few months after I'd arrived here. I struggled through the Christian English of Jesus' words, relying on Goldsmith to navigate my understanding. I don't know what made me keep at it. I resisted my way through one hundred pages, and something shifted when I got to page one hundred one.

Suddenly, the scripture-like words uttered by Jesus became crystal clear. I giggled in accord, my head bobbing up and down with new understanding. I no longer "saw" the words but felt them emanating from my heart as if I had spoken them myself. *It's so clear*, I thought, incredulous that it had taken me this long to understand. I was peaceful. I felt loved by the Universe. It wasn't Jesus who said we were sinners. There was no separation; that was an illusion. The great I AM of myself filled me until I was only that.

I closed my eyes and turned my face up to receive the warmth of the brilliant springtime sun. I was ready to let go of self-limiting thinking that no longer served me. Would this book be the bridge I needed to enter the deep dive of *A Course In Miracles* that I hadn't been ready for almost a decade ago?

* * *

"LE 24 HEURES DU MANS" was the biggest race of the season. Tensions were high. There were big stakes, big problems, and big disappointments. Car 42 broke down and didn't finish. Everyone was wired. Brock stayed out of the pit and only came over to me once. Was this all because of what had happened at the restaurant in Monte-Carlo?

Keith's energy felt dangerous as if he were hurling energetic daggers at me. Giuseppina must have caught wind of my exploits because her name had suddenly appeared on the back of Brock's motor scooter, and I was certain that Keith had moved in for the kill.

Ari arrived a few hours before the race began. My heart lifted every time I saw him. I felt myself inhale and exhale slowly. He always had a warm, genuine smile for me, although he was generally distracted by all the goings-on. Racing was big business—many phone calls, many little meetings, agents, sponsors, publicists, vendors, Brock—all manner of men pulling him aside.

Everyone knew when he was coming. It was a fast-spreading rumor, a hush rippling through the pit. It was always the same when Ari entered the noisy room. Everyone seemed to grow taller. The team climate would instantly change from unselfconscious but focused puttering to an at-attention reverence and respect for the man paying for all of it. The man who created the empire, the man who humbly told me he "wanted to be a businessman" when he was a kid.

I delighted in his presence, usually. He could be calm one minute, hands raking wildly through his hair, eyes darting the next, energy spluttering from him like a sparkler on the fourth of July. One phone call could change everything: a short tire order; an engine part needed replacement; so and so, or such and such wouldn't be arriving until tomorrow or the next day; one of the drivers was sick or injured. More money, *always more money*, was needed for this or that.

This time things were different. There were many more guests in the pit than usual, most of whom I didn't recognize. Ari's eyes were shallow and vacant, and he was way out of sorts. He frequently walked away from me in the pit.

"Leave Brock alone, Debra," he said without explanation. I was shocked. Why? Wasn't I here to work on him? This race was important. I was deflated and worried. Would he be shipping me back to the States after the race?? I could feel my heart twisting into a knot inside my chest. His phone rang. He raised it to his ear and hurried out the pit door.

Brock approached me shortly afterward. Staring out into the pit, he said warily, "I don't even know half of the people with team shirts on."

"Really?" I countered coolly, surprised he had approached me given our last encounter at the restaurant in Monte-Carlo.

Ari walked briskly over to us and promptly put his arm around Brock's shoulders, steering him away from me. What had I done now?

The environment was emotionally fragile and unnerved me, making me question myself. I was insecure. Everything got measured and analyzed in terms of what I did or didn't do. In my mind, I was the epicenter of everyone's good or bad behavior, and I was reeling as I tried to figure everything out, to no avail.

I retreated to Brock's trailer. *I am too normal for these people*, I thought. I don't belong here. Grayson, the team manager, entered and gave me a walkie-talkie radio. We made some small talk. He was down to earth, and I liked him. His gesture made me feel a little less unwelcome.

Theo called to check up on me and wish the team luck. *Ari is lucky to have him*, I thought, relieved to hear Theo's voice.

I'd had a dream a couple of nights prior. I frequently dreamed about Ari and Brock, sometimes separately, sometimes together. It usually involved working with them on some level. In this dream, Brock was closing the trunk of his car, and I was standing next to him, about to walk away. He blurted out, "Debra, you make me *feel*." I woke up right after that. Many months earlier, Louisa, a psychic friend, said, "Ari wants you to bring his family together." *Really? How??* I thought to myself, shaking my head.

Brock had finally come to see me for a brief massage session. The tension between us was uncomfortable. I performed a deep tendon massage on his shoulder and did some energy work on him. I could feel the heat being sucked through my hands as I placed one on his chest and one on his back.

"Wow, are you depleted!" I remarked. "I guess the only place you get any peace is in the car." We laughed in agreement, but he remained tight-lipped.

The rest of the crew was very receptive to me, and even some of the men who previously hadn't received my work showed up. Sem, the head mechanic, confided in me that he'd known Brock a long time and that he'd changed. Brock didn't hang out in the pit with the team anymore, and his attention was elsewhere.

Ari's brother Willem and a couple of the other drivers echoed the sentiment. Some thought Giuseppina was the reason. According to Brock, only he and I, and his father, knew about her cancer. I felt sad for the team. They devoted their heart and soul to their work, and I felt solidarity between them. It was a shame that Brock couldn't appreciate their dedication, their need for his leadership. He probably had never even considered it.

Once I got home, my mind continued to mull over everything. I wanted Brock to know that the team needed him. I decided to send him a text. "I stayed in the pit to give the crew and drivers support, but it wasn't mine they needed; it was yours. You were missed, Brock. See you in Nürburgring."

He shot back at me, "I do not have to give an explanation to you. I was there Sunday until 3:45 p.m. and spoke to all the guys."

I was a bit unsettled but realized he'd taken it as criticism, which hadn't been my intention. *One of the foibles of texting*, I thought. I sent him another text. "I am giving you honest feedback. I have ears and eyes. I care about you and this team. For some reason, I think you no longer believe that. It doesn't change the truth." I didn't hear back from him after that.

Of course, my conscience grabbed me around the throat, and I suffered for the next week until I saw Ari. I had taken everyone's behavior personally. Why couldn't I see it was not about me like Brock and Theo had said that night in Monaco? I didn't come from their world. I didn't realize the stakes, the risks, the betrayals, the entanglements, the estrangements, the deception, or the lies that were borne and perpetrated by playing at this level of wealth. I didn't want to know.

* * *

"DEBRA, I WILL PURCHASE A MASSAGE TABLE that you can use for the team," Ari said the next time I massaged him in his guesthouse as he lay contentedly on his back, obviously moving forward with our agreement. "And I'm going to pay you upfront for the remainder of the races."

"Wow, that's very generous of you. Thank you." I was floored. I'd had fantasies of him shipping me back home for good. Maybe Louisa had been right.

"I'm going to pay for a round trip for you to return to the States. Since you don't have a visa, you can't be here longer than six months," he said plainly. After the massage, he gave me his credit card number so I could purchase the ticket.

We talked about Le Mans, and I shared that I preferred the smaller races. I told him that he and Brock were too stressed and that these events should be fun. We agreed that Brock had been distracted by many things. I told him I had only seen Brock once during the race but that the other team members had kept me busy.

I cared about Ari. I felt the warmth return to our conversation. Even though I only provided him a massage about once a month due to his demanding schedule, I knew he appreciated having me here.

The next day I felt unstable again, vulnerable over my feelings for Brock. I was so tired of revisiting my self-worth because of him. I needed clarity.

I reached out to Concetta, another psychic who had long ago become a friend. Over the years, she provided numerous tarot readings for me, presenting astute and incisive guidance about people and circumstances in my life, especially my love life. Her readings offered me a deeper understanding that did not always occur to my waking consciousness but often elicited nods of confirmation from my subconscious. She had guided me, quite specifically, about prior relationships and their unfoldment; I trusted the information that came through her. She had been accurate.

The race at Le Mans had been unsettling, and it was painful to see Ari and Brock scrambling around, unstable, eyes lost at sea, no sign of the shore. I had wanted to comfort them both but was flailing around in my own emotional sinking ship, with nothing safe to grab onto.

In her readings, Concetta saw me coming together with Brock. She said there was deception with Giuseppina and that "the shit will hit the fan." She told me I was very much in the right place, that Ari was totally behind me, and that the team adored me. I was relieved. She also did not see me leaving in November. Neither did I.

* * *

THE NEXT RACE WAS IN NÜRBURGRING, Germany. I decided to drop all my needs and treat Brock like I treated the rest of the team. I was pleasantly surprised. He was warm and friendly. The more I smiled and touched him, the more receptive he was to me. When I got pushy, he pushed back. I didn't take anyone's behaviors personally, and overall I was exceptionally pleased with the weekend.

Grayson confided in me and confirmed my suspicions about Keith. "Brock spends way too much time with Keith," he said. "He fills Brock's head with shit he doesn't need to worry about." He shook his head. "Brock is too easily distracted and focused on girls." I smirked. Concetta had said that Brock was merely confused.

After the race, Brock drove me back from the track to our hotel. It was a beautiful summer's night ride through the forested German countryside. The air was fresh as we whisked down the narrow roadway in his Lamborghini Roadster. He voiced his concerns about the team management and that it needed improvement, except for the changes in the driver lineup, which pleased him. When we got to the hotel, Giuseppina called. I could hear her yakking at one point, and Brock locked eyes with me. I grinned, wondering if he was comparing us. There really was no comparison.

***

ONCE HOME, I WAS HAPPY to be away from the drama. It was late afternoon, and the sun streamed golden through the windows in the little guest house on Ari's property. I arranged the sheets and blanket on my massage table, folding down the corner nearest him. I turned to give him privacy as he climbed aboard, naked, pulling the coverings up to his chest.

"Debra, have you been dating since you've been in France?" he wondered.

"No, I haven't been looking. Mostly, I go for walks and lunches with my friends," I offered cheerfully, hoping this would satisfy him. He knew nothing about my feelings for Brock.

"But you need someone to share your emotions with," he said thoughtfully.

"True," I acknowledged, pondering his choice of words. A woman's emotions, let alone mine, weren't something I thought he would consider. I adored him, and he was brilliant in his own right, but he didn't strike me as deep on the emotional level. Maybe I just hadn't spent enough time with him to know. I wondered if Brock would be the man with whom I could share my emotions.

And with whom did Ari share *his* emotions? Certainly not Celeste. I had seen her in action all those months ago at the luncheon in their home. I brought up the subject of inner peace.

"I *have* no inner peace, Debra," he said matter-of-fact, looking into my eyes, the tiniest wince of pain visible in his face, cracking open the door to a vulnerable heart.

What? My mind protested. How could that be? He seemed so happy, so full of *life*, so confident. He had everything money could buy and then some. He'd created an empire and had so many incredible people in his life. But my heart knew this wasn't the remedy.

"You may want to look to your childhood for clues," I offered respectfully.

"Yes...," his voice trailed off. "Maybe I should do yoga," he said with a wink, steering clear of the childhood conversation.

"That could be a good place to start," I said lightly, wanting to provide the space for whatever was on his mind. I told him he was a gentle soul, not as chaotic as he might believe.

"What do you think of me, Debra?" he asked humbly.

His question surprised and humbled me too. I didn't know what he needed to hear or what to offer him. "You are a good man. I see you as a grand and beautiful, fatherly soul. I have a lot of gratitude for you in my life."

He grinned. I was happy to share these feelings with him. He had shown me nothing but kindness, respect, and generosity. "You've lived on both sides of the coin, and I believe this has made you appreciate what you have. You treat everyone with respect. You know what it's like to have nothing. I admire your responsibility and commitment." It was the truth.

"Thank you, Debra." His eyes shone with gratitude. It brought me joy to acknowledge what I saw in him.

"I feel a sense of destiny about our relationship. I hope it continues to grow into the future." I could feel my heart expanding as I said it. My preferred conversations were those of the heart. I adored having this man in my life.

"I feel the same way too. We will always have a relationship," he reciprocated. He was calm, peaceful, thankful.

"You wear many hats, but I am most comfortable when you are yourself. Ari the man, lying on my table," I uttered quietly, the cadence of my voice slowing down, sensing the stillness in the room. "It seems no one else gets to see this part of you, the real you."

"This is true, Debra," he sighed as he relaxed, expelling all the air from his body. I knew he trusted me. I trusted him too. The mutual admiration between us came from a place out of time. I held onto the moment, centering my attention in my own heart. I was satiated and at peace.

* * *

LATER, THEO AND I WATCHED a rerun of *When Harry met Sally*. I had always liked the movie, but this time around, I felt sadness.

Theo laughed heartily after the famous scene where Meg Ryan fakes an orgasm while seated at a table in a diner with Billy Crystal. "Look at Billy's face! I wonder what he really thought when they did this scene. She obviously doesn't need a man!"

"Apparently not," I muttered glumly. I was thinking about the other scenes when they started falling for each other, and I realized that all I wanted was to be in love. I didn't want a simulated orgasm; I wanted the real thing. I wanted to feel alive in the arms of the man who was my destiny. I was surprised at how sharply the movie had brought that into focus and wondered why I continued pouring my heart into Brock. If I was honest, he didn't have all the qualities I wanted in a man. I had always felt I'd made good choices easily in other areas of my life, but I wasn't sure when it came to love.

I thought about Eddie Schecter, my high school crush, and the plaque and T-shirt I had made for him. Sadie and I used to creep by his house slowly, hoping to catch a glimpse of him. He was probably terrified of me, pushed away by the intensity of my pursuit. And when Hunter had said just a few short months into our relationship, "it's not you, it's me," was it? *Really?* And why was I interested in Brock, another Peter Pan, who was not interested in returning my advances? I was acutely aware of my pattern of chasing unavailable men, but why didn't that knowledge *change* it? What compelled me to act this way? Wasn't shining the light on it supposed to break the spell?

Maybe I was attracted to men who were just as afraid of love as I was. Perhaps if I continued to chase, I wouldn't have to settle for a mere mortal. I was weary of asking questions and drawing endless conclusions about myself and men. None of my inquiries brought me an epiphany, yet all of them eventually brought me to my knees. What was it that I was after? It was exquisitely distressing for me. I felt stuck in a pattern I didn't know how to resolve. Was something inherently wrong with me regarding romantic relationships? Would I ever get to be in love?

* * *

NADINE AND I HAD BECOME close friends and travel buddies. We went everywhere together. Throughout the summer, we frequented seaside restaurants with beachfront lounging areas. Every establishment had a designated bathing zone bordered on either side by simple ropes, but beach walkers maintained the ability to stroll the shoreline uninterrupted. Well-padded chaise lounges sprawled in uniform colorful rows with little tables in between.

We spent many leisurely hours luxuriating on the azure sea, eating simple lunches like "moules frites" (mussels and French fries), "salade niçoise" with chunks of tuna, egg, and avocado, or "gambas" (large shrimp), served with heads and tentacles intact. It took me some time to get used to their bulging, cooked-black eyes staring dead from the plate but preparing them this way preserved their sweet, buttery flavor. We often ordered a tart, fruity "quart carafe" of French rosé to accompany our tasty meal.

The beautiful beaches of the Riviera rambled unendingly in either direction. Preferring to stay local, Nadine and I often enjoyed the bright, sandy strip of Juan Les Pins near Cap d'Antibes, Ari's hometown, a coveted playground for wealthy expatriates, locals, and tourists alike.

Sometimes we opted for a walk around Port Vauban to ogle the luxury yachts moored at the marina or hiked the picturesque Sentier du Littoral, a striking, narrow seaside trail starting at Plage de la Garoupe that wound up and down the coastal fringes of the peninsula, featuring some of the most breathtaking beach and cliffside views on the Riviera. The trek meandered and stair-stepped over a thick coastal perimeter of chunked-up limestone, stubbled with Aleppo pine trees on the interior side, their long spiny leaves sprouting from bent and funky-shaped branches and trunks, some growing side-slant from the wind.

At its southernmost apex, the trail bowed outward into the astonishing turquoise of the Mediterranean Sea, corralling the protuberant ramparts of the rambling private estate of the Château Croë, en route to Villa Eilenroc, where we would often take a break to wander through the pinks and reds of the proliferative, multicolored rose gardens.

Approximately 75,000 residents populated the large resort town, and the prosperous Antibes sidewalks flourished with pricy boutiques, inexpensive souvenir shops, and restaurants galore. The narrow streets of the Old Town area were charmingly cobbled, lined with antique street lamps and hanging flower baskets brimming with fragrant, vivid hues of pink, purple, yellow, and red.

The street market of Le Marché Provençale was a favorite stop for Nadine and me. Its stalls overflowed with pungent, delectable olives and cheeses; savory herbs and spices; the heady fragrance of fresh flowers, and sprays of lavender bound together like broom bristles; sweet sugary perfumes of strawberries, tangerines, mangoes, and papayas, interposed by the briny funk of fish on ice, heaping platters of gambas, and all manner of delicacies from the mountains and the sea.

The market also offered homespun crafts like aromatic soaps and sachets. It was a place where painters, sculptors, ceramists, and other artisans could exhibit their art on hot afternoons in the shade of the market hall.

* * *

THE RACE IN SILVERSTONE was less than a week away, and I looked forward to being in England. I had recently returned from a relatively uneventful two-week visit to the States. Even though it had been nice to see my friends and family and receive a tarot reading from Concetta, I was happy to be back in France. Something had shifted for me; I was unfulfilled back in the U.S. Nothing and no one had changed. It was as if everything had stood still while I was gone. There was no thrill, no movement, and it no longer felt like home.

Dreamily, I sat looking out my French doors. I wondered "who" I was and where I'd been. Where I *was* was not as important as *how* I was. I missed Ari and longed for Brock. I pined as I experienced the eternity of myself, life, and love. I felt the magnificence and beauty of my old, wise soul. I yearned to be with someone who could appreciate me. Could Brock? I looked around slowly. *This earth is so beautiful*, my heart whispered to me. *Let love be as beautiful.*

* * *

RACING SEASON, AND SUMMER ITSELF, were almost over. My feelings for Brock were changing. I was starting to outgrow the fantasy, and I decided to let the chips fall wherever they may, enjoy the moment, and everything and everyone *else* in it.

I was excited to be in England. London was about two hours away by car. I longed to see it but didn't feel the option was there. I met Keith and Brock at the airport. I asked Keith why my return flight was so late. Brock piped in before Keith could reply, "Why didn't you schedule Debra to fly back in the morning like us?"

Keith mumbled a few excuses. I remained silent. Brock called Farah, one of Ari's assistants, who changed my flight on the spot. I felt appreciated. I knew Keith likely hadn't *intended* things to be inconvenient for me, but neither had he gone out of his way.

Things fell wonderfully into place, need by need. I allowed myself to go with Brock's flow. Our conversation was easy and flirtatious. He was showing me the real version of him. It was fun to let things unfold without any effort.

Arriving at the track, the crew was more receptive than usual, with kisses and hugs to greet me. Some drivers who had typically given me the cold shoulder were friendly and kissed me hello. Had something been said on my behalf? I felt uplifted, acknowledged, and accepted.

Two days were devoted to preparing for the race and ensuring the cars were ready to perform. Activity was the main course. The pit buzzed like a giant beehive amidst a backdrop of revving engines and the zhoot-zhoot of mechanics' power tools.

On race day, the contagion was palpable. Guests arrived one by one, and the arena's vacant seats became dotted with color. Individual sounds blended into a din, as empty spaces filled with people and the cacophony of power tools and car engines.

Brock and I chatted in his mobile office, and he showed me pictures of his children, his mother, and his grandmother—Ari's mother, Citri. I was happy to see what she looked like.

Our conversation turned more serious. "I want to understand what is happening with her diagnosis, but Giuseppina won't let me take her to a doctor near me," Brock said.

"Why is that?" I asked, judgment taking hold of my mind.

"She says she's already been to seven hospitals and doesn't see why she would need another diagnosis," he said, somewhat frustrated.

"Do you doubt Giuseppina has cancer?" I asked, cutting right to the chase.

He shrugged. "I've seen her receive some sort of injections."

The pieces of the puzzle just didn't fit. "You have the right to know, Brock," I said assertively. I could tell by his eyes that he might not have wanted to. He was confused and did not understand why she wouldn't comply, but he made plenty of excuses for her. *Love is blind*, I thought to myself. We see what we want to see. Wasn't I doing that with him?

I walked back to the pit and stood in the rear of the garage. I felt privileged to be an observer. Thoughts of peace spun around me like a gently pulsing cocoon, stilling me within the bustling scene before me. I no longer doubted my contribution to the team.

The race was going well, but the temperature in the cars had spiked to a dangerous 160 degrees Fahrenheit. The drivers were quickly overheating. Brock had recently emerged from one of the cars, red as a beet, eyes bloodshot as if cooked by the extreme heat.

A little while later, I returned to his trailer and found him lying on one of the couches, sweating profusely, his racing suit peeled down to his waist. "Are you okay?" I asked, trying not to sound worried or intrusive.

"I'm just hot," he nodded.

"Are you sure?" I pressed lightly.

"Sometimes I get dizzy when I get out of the car," he offered reluctantly.

"Little wonder," I said, smiling, respectful of his efforts. "You could be boiled alive in there."

I found a big pot in one of the cabinets and filled it with cool water. I gently sponged Brock's skin using a small washcloth to bring down his temperature. He hadn't eaten any protein. I rummaged around the little fridge and found some bread and cheese. As I tended to him, I watched his eyes change from observation to affection. He was starting to feel better, but I knew he was still exhausted.

"Give the protein a little time to kick in, and take a shower once you've cooled down enough," I said as I turned to go. "I have to go treat a driver from another team who is friends with one of the crew."

When I returned, he had a towel around his waist and had just finished his shower. "Every time I see you, I am undressing," he said playfully.

"I'm not touching that one," I said, flushing.

He winked. "Are you going to work on my shoulder, or are you on holiday?"

Giuseppina arrived as I worked on Brock's shoulder. I gave him a few mineral supplements to bring his electrolytes back up to par.

"I don't want you to give Brock drugs," she pouted.

He and I looked at each other, rolling our eyes and laughing. "They're supplements, Giuseppina. I don't prescribe medication." She gawked at me like a five-year-old.

* * *

THE NEXT DAY, BROCK, KEITH, and I checked into the airport. My line moved quickly, and I went to a coffee bar to get an espresso.

My phone rang. "Are you going to leave without saying goodbye?" Brock teased me.

He and Keith made their way over to me, and we exchanged farewells. This time it was Brock's energy that was pulling *me*. I knew he was sorry to see me go. Nothing was said, but I felt it when he hugged me. *Funny how things change when you stop pushing*, I thought to myself with a smile.

I took an inside seat and gazed out the window at the tarmac. It was the best time I'd had yet at the races. I had finally found my footing with the team and with Brock. I could love him and let him be himself. I could be myself. I pondered my last visit with Ari. There was a shift happening between us too. Our conversation had a closeness and ease that I could envision blossoming into a valuable friendship. He trusted that I cared about him. I trusted that he wouldn't change his mind and ship me back to the U.S. He wanted me around as much as I wanted to be here.

* * *

BACK HOME, IT DIDN'T TAKE LONG for the high of Silverstone to wear off. Race season was over. I was riddled with anxiety and doubt, reeling and off balance from my feelings about Brock. I wondered when I would see him again. Would he reach out to me? Would I have to wait until next season?

All grown up and still falling for unavailable men, I seemed a prisoner to the Jekyll and Hyde memories of my father, his alcohol, and the emotional unavailability that had admonished my self-worth. Did I have to chase men to resolve the deep pain of unlovability and not being enough? Was I trying to prove to my father that I was worthy of a good man? Whose affection was I trying to win?

The analytical tirade was exhausting. I thought I was done with all the self-therapy. I had put myself through years and years of deep self-reflection, journaling, and leaping straight into the searing flames of my youth that threatened to scorch me to the bone. Yet, I had survived, emerging like a Phoenix, renewed, forgiving, and forgiven.

I had deep love and respect for my father and his arduous journey. I appreciated the difficult lessons that I had learned. I was strong and believed my sights were future-focused, but my very way of being and relating to men romantically seemed *entirely driven* by my past. I felt I had hit a plateau. What was it going to take to resolve this pattern? Was I capable of manifesting true intimacy in my life? *What* wasn't I seeing?

CHAPTER 6

A Course In Miracles

It was late September. The sun was golden, and it was still hot in the middle of the day. I sat on my sofa, gazing out the wide-open French doors into the brightly lit outdoor space, my begonias full and bushy from months of growth, rimming the edges of my patio in pretty splashes of pink, red and white.

My palms unexpectedly started to sweat. Suddenly, I was thinking about *A Course In Miracles*. I paused and nervously told myself I would look online to see if I could find anything about it. No commitment, just curiosity. I consoled myself as if what I was going to find would conflict with my philosophy in a way that would make me doubt myself, and I strongly resisted that idea. *I have enough doubt*, I rationalized. *Why am I even doing this?* But as much as I wanted to dig in my heels, I could not ignore the compelling sensation guiding me to explore.

Grimacing, I scrolled through the *ACIM* website. I took a deep breath and continued searching. There were *six* meetings in all of France. Did I understand enough French to try to find someone I could have a conversation with? Maybe there would be something in or near Nice. I scrolled down the list of available locations and found a meeting in Tourrettes-sur-Loup, about a half-hour away. What were the chances of *that*?

I excitedly dialed the phone. No answer. I sat in stunned disbelief as the voice on the answering machine chirped sweetly into my incredulous ear:

"Hi, you've reached Gwyn. I can't come to the phone right now, but I will happily return your call if you leave me a message. Au revoir!" *She was American!*

I was thrilled at the thought of a potential new friend. I was content and happy on my sojourns with Nadine, but my spiritual side longed for a kindred soul here in France.

The next day she phoned. Gwyn Pettiman was a breath of fresh air. Her singsong, mellow voice serenaded my ear as she told me her story. She had been living in France for about ten years. While living in the U.K. years earlier, she had started *A Course In Miracles* study group by placing an ad in the local paper to garner interest. The group ran for nearly fifteen years. While there, she married, divorced, and subsequently moved to France.

We decided to meet at a little café in Cap d'Antibes. I remember the rush of energy I felt when we first embraced. Her round green eyes and pretty, white smile radiated warmth like a miniature sun. She was a giving, effervescent soul and called me "cutie" a lot.

Gwyn and I had plenty to share. We took turns exchanging bits and pieces of our lives with each other. I learned she was a musician who played the flute, and she had a boyfriend named Niccolo, who was also a musician. She had recently retired from L'Orchestre Philharmonique de Nice and enjoyed a relatively unencumbered lifestyle. Like me, she'd had no children. We were both grateful for the freedom this offered us.

She marveled at my story as I told her the details of how I was fortunate enough to be living in France. She didn't know Ari. Wealthy people were quite common on the French Riviera and lived relatively undisturbed among the sizeable coastal population.

I wanted to know about *A Course In Miracles* and how it came into her life. I had read Marianne Williamson's book, *A Return to Love,* which introduced me to some of the *Course's* concepts and Marianne's journey with it as both a student and teacher.

"Well," Gwyn began pensively, "*A Course In Miracles* is a path to Truth. It teaches you to recognize the ego construct as separate from the divinity within us. It guides us to remember who we truly are, as sons and daughters of God, and that our pure essence is not the ego, but Source itself." It sounded like what I had recently read in Joel Goldsmith's book *Beyond Thoughts and Words,* and I was very intrigued.

"I was thinking of buying a copy online, but I'm not sure it will be my cup of tea," I said hesitantly.

"I have an old paperback version I can lend you to help you decide," she offered, raising a forkful of fresh salad to her lips.

"That would be wonderful!" I beamed, appreciating her generosity. She wasn't hosting meetings anymore but hadn't removed the listing on the acim.org website as more of an oversight. Lucky for me. It was another one of those serendipities gracefully put into place by a benevolent Universe.

* * *

I FELT LIKE I WAS TURNING UP STONES with nothing underneath them. Gwyn had given me a copy of her *ACIM* text. It was cumbersome to read, and I felt my resistance rise up strongly against its Christian-type language, although it spoke of my inherent "holiness" and "sinlessness" as a child of God.

From what I could comprehend, the *Course* was a spiritual-psychological path to help the student understand that the world we "see" is only a reflection or a projection of our perception. It explained that our *interpretation* of what we were "seeing" caused our suffering.

To that end, its curriculum endeavored to reorient the student through the use of lessons and text designed to catalyze an experiential understanding of this truth. The *Course* was not a religion—as it encompasses "universal" spiritual themes; its goal was to help the seeker recognize self-constructed illusions and unlearn or correct these errors to reveal the truth.

After almost two weeks, the *Course's* "language" was still a hurdle for me. I had just completed lesson thirteen, "A Meaningless World Engenders Fear." Little glimmers of light were beginning to dawn on me. I started to understand that the ego was in competition with God and that we had to hold tight to our little concept of what the world "is" because we had no other reference point but our own. It stressed that recognizing the meaninglessness of *our* perception as a defense against the truth of God's Love would initially be intensely distressing.

It was. What the hell was *ACIM* saying? Weren't my thoughts coming from my higher consciousness?

I felt hot anger gurgling up into my throat as my mind refused the ideas surfacing. So you're going to tell me that my father's alcoholism didn't harm me?! That only *my thinking* caused my suffering? That I chase all these stupid guys because I am seeing something that isn't there, objectifying them through the eyes of my illusion?! Hadn't I ever given love? Received it? Was I the reason for my misery?

No way! I was pretty perceptive, I thought, now flinching as my mind contemplated the word. My analysis was accurate, wasn't it? What else did I have? What wasn't I getting? I felt the bottom drop out, alone and cold with my thoughts, utterly meaningless, bankrupt. I was nothing, nobody. I had been asking for the Light every day for so long, and was this what was being offered? I felt so deceived. By God. By myself. Was my happiness real?

The *Course* said I do not know what happiness is, that the only happiness I'd ever felt had been based on illusion. But what about the times when I thought I'd felt inner peace? Was that an illusion too? Was I looking for someone to save me? Was that the propelling force of my entire existence?

I didn't trust myself, didn't trust anything, anyone. I was cynical. Is this what God wanted? This groveling version of me? It felt like another trick. My brief dabbling with the Bible years ago made me feel the same way. I hadn't ever been this uncomfortable reading a spiritual book before, nor needed much clarification or interpretation. I felt fingers pointing at my unworthiness. Was I a fraud? I didn't know how to make sense of the words pelting my eyes from its pages. Why couldn't Jesus just speak English?

A few days later, I called Gwyn. I let everything gush out; my fears, the extreme resistance I had, and the inability to grasp what the book was saying. "I don't think this is the book for me," I cried, feeling like a failure because I couldn't make a go of it.

"Oh, it's the book for you, all right," Gwyn said brightly. I was aghast. How could she be giddy in the face of my plight?

"You don't understand. I feel *bad,* Gwyn. Isn't this book supposed to make me feel better? Like I'm on the right path?" I clucked petulantly.

"The beauty of the *Course* is that it doesn't support false perceptions. You're struggling because you've lost your reference point, which is your *ego*. And that is good news because now real understanding can arrive. Just go easy with yourself and allow new learning without trying to force it. I'm so happy for you!" she beamed.

She was. I could feel it. I felt blessed by her arrival in my life and so much gratitude for her level of understanding. She had studied the *Course* for many years. She had come out of the blue, like everything and everyone else. Sometimes the significance of it all overwhelmed me, and I took it for granted. I wanted desperately to trust life, to allow it to show the real me to myself. Over the years, I had built a wall around myself. Like yanking a molar, the *Course* had just removed a solidly placed brick.

* * *

ROCHELLE WAS BACK IN TOWN, eager to drive to Florence, Italy. I hadn't yet been there and was excited about going to the capital of Italy's Tuscany region to visit the many masterpieces of Renaissance art and architecture and to shop at the well-known outdoor markets.

We entered the city and drove to our hotel in the heart of town, dominated by the bulbous, red-tiled rooftop of the Duomo Cathedral. I had thought Florence would be much larger. A decidedly compact city, it was tightly populated by national monuments, classically decorated hotels, countless shops, and street-corner trattorias flanking the Arno River, straddled by the well-worn arch of the Ponte Vecchio.

The smell of leather goods, chocolates, espresso, and exquisite pastries wafted out of open doors. The aroma of baking bread tantalized us unforgivingly, weaving its magic in and around the streets and alleyways. We breathed deep, gluing the memories to our olfactory cells, the heels of our boots adding to the din of the footsteps of other travelers.

Rochelle and I decided to take a scenic taxi ride early one evening. It wasn't yet dark, but the streetlights were lit, showcasing numerous statues. It felt like Christmas, with many sights to see. The Florentine people, like most Italians, were quite proud of their heritage; our taxi driver was no exception.

He spoke little English, mashing words together in sentences that were difficult but amusing to decipher. We'd asked him to take us to a fine restaurant with a city view. We weren't sure he'd understood, but he nodded enthusiastically and proceeded out of the city limits. Rochelle and I lounged in the back seat, snickering at the god-sized statues stationed like petrified trees in hotel fronts, parks, piazzas, and front yards. As our car wound its way higher into the darkening landscape, we glimpsed the hilly farms of the classic, Tuscan countryside, erupting with emerald cypress totems and leafy, fan-shaped olive trees waving unkempt, silvery-green fronds.

Uncountable statues of Michael assailed our senses. We were agog at the cornucopia of stony penises dotting the simple landscape, unselfconsciously basking in phallic splendor under the brightly-lit moon and ornate streetlamps. "Never mind everything else," they seemed to say. "Behold us!"

Watching us in his rearview mirror, the proud taxi driver joined in our mirth. "Bueno! Yes?"

"Si, si!" we nodded, lost for an explanation.

"How do you say statue in Italian?" I asked Rochelle, lowering my voice.

"I don't know…edificio?" she offered. Her son was taking Italian classes in school back home, and I hoped it had rubbed off on her.

"No, an edifice is a building," I reasoned. "Hmm… what's another word for 'statue'?"

"How about a monument…monumento maybe?"

I turned to the driver, still watching us in his rearview. "Bellissimo monumento!" I exclaimed, wondering if I had gotten close enough. He nodded and laughed as his eyes connected with mine, but I wanted to tell him why we had laughed at the statues.

"How do you say 'all' or 'every'?"

"Tutti," Rochelle said.

I tapped the driver's shoulder, motioning for him to look at me. I parted my thighs. "Tutti monumento—" and I abruptly pointed to my crotch. He erupted with laughter, bobbing his head up and down as the three of us connected in uproarious glee, tears streaming down our faces.

We arrived at La Leggenda dei Frati, but to our great disappointment, the restaurant was closed. It was now dark, and we couldn't adequately appreciate the view. It didn't matter; we'd had an enjoyable, hilarious ride.

I don't even recall where we wound up dining. I will, however, never forget the power of body language.

* * *

THE REST OF NOVEMBER and most of December had disappeared into the approaching winter. It was just after midnight, Christmas morning. I felt the need to process what had happened with Ari a week earlier when I had given him a massage at his house, so I took out my ever-present journal to write.

I had believed he was making a sexual overture. He tried to touch me a lot while he was on the table, which was a first. Nude under the sheet, he usually remained face up when I finished the massage. I would then retire to the bathroom to wash my hands of the oil, allowing him to get dressed. Instead, he rolled immediately onto his side, and I got nervous.

"Don't get up off the table yet!" I blurted out and scurried to the bathroom. My heart beat rapidly as I washed my hands under the warm water. What was I going to do if Ari made an advance? I stalled as long as I could, and to my relief, he was fully dressed when I emerged. He noticed. I felt the wall I had worked so hard to break through refortify itself.

I'd had a tarot reading over the phone with Concetta regarding the incident. Her insights surprised me. "He's afraid of losing you," she said plainly, "and he's upset about his feelings for you." Did Ari know I had feelings for Brock? I would have "a shift of perception," she continued, my heart tugged in "two different directions." I hadn't seen Brock for four months, and my feelings for him were somewhat diminished, but my feelings for Ari were not romantic. There would be a "real change" within me, Concetta said; the "understanding" would come and "then a burst of joy." Her reading ended with the "future card" and "wish card" side by side. "You will have an epiphany, Debra. You will get what you want," she had said. What did I want?

I tried to recall the details of Ari's prior massage. Had I been giving him mixed messages? That evening when I'd gone to bed, I had to admit I'd felt a surge of sexual attraction for him, which made me exclaim in surprise, "I *am* attracted to him!" Had he simply been picking up on that?

The feeling had been fleeting. I adored seeing him and spending time with him. I relished the friendship and the trust that was developing between us, but I wanted Brock. Didn't I? I certainly didn't want to ruin my relationship with Ari.

Later that evening, I pulled a single tarot card regarding Ari and received the "Sun" card, representing divine marriage and the truest love possible. I still wanted it to be Brock. Sadly, I felt I couldn't connect with Brock anymore; I wasn't able to feel his presence, his essence; he was fading. It had been too long.

I hadn't seen Ari since his massage, and I scrutinized everything that had happened between us to see if I had done something wrong. That, I believed, was because of my father's drinking and the hypervigilance it created in me as a child struggling to figure out if my behavior could have precipitated his verbal onslaught. Sadly, I hadn't known then that it wasn't about me. None of it had ever been about me.

***

IN JANUARY, I ATTENDED the race team's New Year's reception. Brock didn't even make an appearance. He was sick with the flu. I wasn't surprised that he didn't "show up."

According to his frustrated teammates, Brock's behavior at the last couple of races had been appalling. I observed that he had been decidedly scarce. He was all wrapped up with things, one of them being Giuseppina, and had been absent for much of the time except when it was his turn to drive.

They'd had a baby since the end of the race season. I was not surprised. Maybe Giuseppina had secured what she wanted. I never heard another word about her cancer.

Ari's first wife, Marcie, was at the party and invited me to stay with her the next time I was in town. I was amazed at how Ari accumulated people in his ever-burgeoning life. Ari's brother Willem and his wife Faye were there too. Faye seemed to accept me wholeheartedly. They were all down-to-earth, engaging people, from my experience with them.

So far, I had met everyone in Ari's family except for his sister Sarena, and his mother, Citri, whom everyone called "Honey." She'd felt her name was too "ethnic" and had adopted a new one. I hoped I would meet her too, as I had only seen her picture.

As I walked into the team showroom on the first floor of the building, I gasped. A sea of dazzling Italian race cars in black, red, and yellow sprawled before me, tightly packed together on a black granite floor that sparkled like diamonds. Little wonder Brock was "lost," I thought. Born into this, from Ari's demanding climb to the top, he'd had no reference point for an ordinary life.

CHAPTER 7

Mr. Right Steps Forward

The end of January was cold, and the mountains in Gréolières were packed with snow. Nadine and I decided on a day trip to go cross-country skiing, and Gréolières was only an hour away.

It was my first time, and I was nervous, but the tracks were well-worn, and I didn't fall once. We spent a couple of hours going uphill and down, and it was exhilarating to feel the sun warming the cold crisp mountain air. Afterward, we enjoyed a steamy cup of hot cocoa and a "croque monsieur," a melted ham and cheese sandwich, at a simple picnic table outside the little lodge, our frosty breath sending little white puffs into the air.

The snow's surface was somewhat icy on our second run because of the high-noon hot sun, but I managed to keep myself on the tracks as I whooshed down the largest of the hills. As I gazed out over the bright white landscape rimmed with soaring evergreen trees, I thought perhaps I could do other work for Ari. He had a home office and needed someone to compose letters and organize things. I was open to possibilities, and knew he wanted me to work as the team doctor next season. I also wanted to stop calling him "Mr. S.," as that felt awkward to me now. I wanted to stay in his life, but just what that looked like, I didn't know.

I felt my friendship with Ari had moved up a notch. We were more physically expressive with each other. Even though the massages were infrequent, I was very relaxed and "filled up" when I was with him. Our conversations were deeper, more spiritual. When I touched him,

I was happy. I could massage him for hours and never tire. We hugged before and after his massage. I started to miss him when the weeks mounted between us.

Ari had told me he had no inner peace. Inner peace was essential to me, and I wanted him to have it too. Months later, when I started studying the *Course*, I asked him if I could send him a lesson once a week. He had agreed.

Every Monday, I would search through the table of contents for something that would be uplifting and non-threatening for someone who had "no inner peace" and no experience with the lofty voice of the *Course*. Faithfully, I texted him in the morning as soon as I awoke, carefully and lovingly typing the words onto the tiny screen of my cell phone.

He seemed receptive, although he never replied to any of these texts. Sometimes we would talk about it, and he would thank me. He said he wasn't very spiritual, but he thought the lessons I sent him were inspiring.

I was still in love with Brock even as I texted Ari those beautiful sentences of peace and guidance—which sustained me, too, through the trials and tribulations of life on this beautiful Riviera that was home for the moment. Surely Brock would not be able to "hear" these words, but his father could. "Brock is not his father," Concetta had said to me. Yes, I did confuse them sometimes.

Although Ari didn't consider himself a spiritual man, I observed how he treated others, treated me, and thought otherwise. My respect for him was deep. I felt appreciated, even though I didn't see him very often. Texting him the lessons brought us closer, as the words of the *Course* came from the realm of absolute truth and divine love. He'd gotten a glimpse of what was most important to me: my spiritual development.

One day, as I crossed the threshold of my bedroom, I had an epiphany about Brock that halted me sharply, as if I had walked into a brick wall. "*He doesn't want me*!" I said aloud, stopping in my tracks. Simple, common sense fell on my head like Newton's apple, as if I were discovering gravity for the first time. "Well, *of course,*" any logical person might say. But yes, I could be that dense about love, and my pattern, which had thick leather blinders on, obscuring even the obvious from my sight.

And then: "Oh my God, it isn't Brock, it's *Ari!*" I blinked hard as the words tumbled out of my gaping mouth, still riveted to the same spot as these thoughts magnetized my feet to the earth. Is this the shift Concetta had seen me having?

As my heart quickly pondered the unthinkable, my mind protested its defense. "Oh, no, no, no. I'm not going *there.*" I shook my head emphatically from side to side. "I'm *not* messing with my bread and butter." Besides, I reasoned, incredulous at my impetuousness, what would Ari want with *me*? If Brock was the Prince, Ari was most certainly the King. The great Patriarch of his self-made kingdom, I could hardly envision a role for myself other than the one I was playing. "*And a happy, thankful one at that,*" I sternly reminded myself. "*Get hold of yourself, Debra. Do not go there.*" But, of course, it was too late. I already had. I could be pretty stubborn once my heart made its decision. Like an obedient servant, my mind relegated itself to the back seat, and my heart grabbed hold of the steering wheel with gusto as I nestled myself into the driver's seat. I was off and running.

Was I crazy? I certainly needed to think this one out. I thought about Brock and even Hunter. There were consequences to impulsive choices. Could I project a future with Ari, a happily ever after? Did I genuinely want the kind of life I thought he would offer? Was he emotionally and spiritually deep enough? Capable of being truly intimate in a relationship with me? If he rejected me and sent me home, I would likely never forgive myself for ruining my chances of staying in France. Was I merely following another romantic chemistry destined to fail? I needed sage advice.

"They're telling me you need to move forward with Ari," Concetta said slowly over the phone, weighing the gravity of the situation. She was serious. Although I trusted her guidance, my feelings for Ari conjured up deep and moral resistance within me; Concetta was about to guide me *in, not out* of the most meaningful, reciprocal relationship I had had to date.

She listened carefully and offered what came through her, trusting what she heard. My protests and exceptions were being lovingly guided by an Intelligence that knew more than I did. I could see her sharp eyes on the small, square, sturdy face in my mind as I imagined Concetta glancing up at me over her narrow spectacles like she always did when making a point that needed to settle into my understanding. Could I trust my heart to make the right choice for me? Would loving Ari be the highest good for us both?

* * *

JANUARY MELTED INTO FEBRUARY. The tiny buds on the mimosa trees were bursting into yellow cotton candy. Their sweet, fresh fragrance lightly punctuated the chilly air, filling me with anticipation for the spring, their bright lemony color contrasting boldly against the blue azure of the Mediterranean sky.

The floodgates of my heart were uncontainable, and I thought about Ari all the time. My feelings for Brock had virtually slipped away, but I was still trying to hold onto the illusion of something that wasn't there. Now, of course, there was new guilt, something for my ever-active mind to chew on that I hadn't had to contemplate: falling in love with a married man.

Concetta had said that I would know in a moment of clarity. My fears of rejection loudly reared their head, and although I had a long history of trust regarding Concetta's readings, part of me thought I was out of my mind to contemplate a romance with Ari. When I allowed myself to be present with the feelings bubbling up from the well-stream of my true desires, I realized this was the best love ever felt, like a carefully watered seedling now unfurling into a magnificent flower. There was a fullness, awe, and unconditionality between us. It was okay to be myself around this man. I didn't have to change anything about myself or him.

I reflected on the luncheon last spring at Ari's home and his family's behavior at the dining table. It had all seemed so mechanical. No one was sharing anything that made any difference; it had all been idle chit-chat. I recalled asking Celeste on an earlier occasion if she would like me to give her a massage. "I don't like to be touched," she had said, her voice tight and clipped. I wasn't surprised.

She talked *at* Ari rather than with him, a stark contrast to how everyone else in his world treated him, including his first family. I knew him enough now to see how affected he was around them. He was always on guard. I wondered how he even wound up in this relationship.

"She is dangerous," Concetta offered. "He can't trust her." Celeste would be fierce if he decided to end the relationship, and according to Concetta's readings, he was headed in that direction. "You bring him joy, Debra."

It was Ari's birthday. I wished I could see him but had no idea where he was. I texted him: "Dear Ari, have a very happy birthday. May you find the light of Love within yourself today and always."

I still wanted to provide other work for him beside the massages and the races. Concetta had said that all I needed to do was open my mouth, and it would be done. She was right. The next time I massaged him, I felt the energy and the closeness shift even more. I applied Reiki to his solar plexus as he lay face up, his hand resting on my hip the whole time. "Debra, do you think you could help me in my home office over the next couple of days?" he inquired.

"I would be delighted!" I said excitedly. I hadn't even needed to ask!

* * *

CELESTE WAS OUT OF TOWN for the week. When I walked into Ari's office, I noticed a framed picture of her in a floral tiara. Her stony smirk and wicked amber eyes glowered from behind the glass. I was relieved when Ari took the picture and discreetly put it away inside one of the cabinets. Had he picked up on my vibe?

It was pure heaven spending so many hours with him. Stacks of papers and magazines were piled high on his desk. Initially, he was a bit scattered, and it took a little time to get him to focus, but we eventually found our groove, and by the end of two days, we were eighty percent complete.

Ari had saved all his briefcases over the years and proudly recounted the big business deals corresponding to each of them and which one he had when he'd made his first million dollars. I enjoyed this aspect of our work together, and working with him felt completely natural. I wanted more.

I filed away a mountain of Forbes 100 and 500 magazines. He had a whole bookcase filled with them. "Do you read *all* of these?" I inquired.

"I have to keep up with my competition, Debra," he said demurely, standing on tiptoe as he slid a magazine into the lineup on the top shelf of the bookcase.

It was getting late, and we were hungry. Ari had promised Theo one of his extra computers. We decided to join him for Chinese food in St. Laurent."

* * *

AS WE SAT AT THE SIMPLE SQUARE WOODEN TABLE, I could feel the tension between Ari and me. He would sit close to me for a few minutes and suddenly become hyperactive, abruptly pushing himself away, the wooden chair legs scraping across the tiled floor. I wondered if Theo was picking up on the push and pull of our attraction. He was very intuitive. After a while, we settled in, joking and teasing each other like old friends. I felt right at home with these two men I adored.

Ari told Theo about the time he had overbooked his private jet in Le Mans, and I couldn't fly back with him to Nice, which had provided me the opportunity to visit the Netherlands for the first time. "You should have seen Debra's face; so surprised!" he said as we all laughed.

I remembered feeling hurt and disposed of at the time, but going to Holland had turned out to be a very fulfilling side trip. The people and the architecture of Amsterdam delighted me. Wandering through a sea of tall, statuesque blond men and women, I had found my genetic lookalikes.

Recounting a recent business trip to the States to handle an ongoing lawsuit, Ari had stayed at the same hotel where we met. He was a frequent guest there. Karen, the concierge, said to him as he stood at the front desk with his U.S. lawyers, "Oh, Mr. Sorensen, you took Debra away from us!"

Her comment had caught him off guard. "You can imagine how embarrassed I was," he said with a smirk. Theo and I laughed. Ari gazed steadily into my eyes.

"You got a taste of your own medicine," I teased, laughing heartily, giddy at his attention.

A couple of hours later, we were back at his house so I could give him a massage. He had decided over dinner to buy me a car instead of continuing to rent them for me. It would be more economical that way. He was also going to increase my salary, as he anticipated more work in his home office. He was thrilled with our progress and how quickly I had caught on. I had written a couple of English emails for him, although Ari's written English was quite polished and eloquent. It appeared he had his eyes on the future, like me.

He felt guilty about asking me to work so late. I was exhausted but happy to reciprocate his generosity. "I don't mind at all. I enjoy your company, Ari," I said, addressing him by his first name. I hadn't done that before; I usually called him "Mr. S." like Theo. "Do you mind if I call you by your first name?"

"Of course not, Debra. You could have called me Ari the whole time," he said happily, settling onto the massage table.

I reflected on the day's conversation. "Thank you for being so generous and taking care of me. You are a good man."

"You always say such nice things about me, Debra," Ari sighed contentedly. He told me he couldn't always honor his truth at work and was often deceived, which kept him on guard. Sometimes I observed his eyes piercing mine like a laser when he asked me a question. It was how he sniffed out the liars.

Ari wasn't the only good man I had attracted over the years. I'd met Shane Kelly in a bar in my early twenties. I'd never thought I could meet a man anywhere else. Perhaps it was because I didn't look anywhere else. I was drawn to him immediately, liked how he moved his lean body, and trusted his genuine smile.

Essentially, he was my first boyfriend. He was a hard, reliable worker, an honest man with a good sense of humor. He was down to earth, and my family liked him. We stayed together for eight years and had been engaged for three. We became true friends and had each other's back, but what we didn't have, was the same idea about "happily ever after."

Shane wanted children, a house to raise them in, and a wife to take part in the journey of creating a family. I longed for a different fairy tale. It was undefined then but didn't include children or a house with a white picket fence. This was never an argument because I don't think either of us had considered the disparity of our desires. Besides, we were young, having fun, and had plenty of time.

But you couldn't *have* kids and not have kids. It was an all-or-nothing consideration. We rolled along for years. I know he was in love with me. I had been in love too, but having had no prior significant relationships, I couldn't substantiate the doubt that was starting to creep into my heart. I longed for a life that flung me far and wide. I had a romantic view of things, and although I loved Shane deeply, he wasn't wearing shining armor.

Towards the end of my chiropractic education, I'd had to move close to campus, as the school had relocated hours away. During that time, separated from Shane, it became clearer that I wanted something different than what my mind could extrapolate into a future with him. He had a more pragmatic view of things, like my father, and practicality was a temporary inconvenience that didn't interest me in the least. I wanted a life of movement and adventure.

When I graduated, I was contemplating a practice in Maryland, another disparity that Shane and I hadn't critically considered. In the end, we chose the paths that were closest to our hearts.

"I'm *not* moving to Baltimore, Debra." He was clear.

I had been sleeping on my sister's couch for three months, searching for chiropractic practice opportunities in Maryland. "I don't want to practice in New York, Shane. The potential is better down here." I was firm.

He was frustrated. "You can't have a relationship with someone while sleeping in separate beds," he said.

Perhaps he'd been right. We wept in each other's arms and parted as friends. He was the only love I'd ever known, and I grieved for many months. Had we made the right choice?

Shane eventually got married and later divorced. Perhaps we had needed to grow into adulthood together to crystallize our visions about life. He helped inform the woman I had become; our impressions were indelible. We had offered each other love, stability, and groundedness. Even after our romance ended, we shared many fond memories, including the birth of his two children and a longstanding bond that felt like family. I hadn't moved to Baltimore. Decades later, our important friendship still endures, and ultimately, he became the brother I'd never had.

Ari had fallen asleep on his back and emitted a snort that jolted him awake, bringing us both back to the present moment. I smiled to myself. Relaxed in each other's company, I cherished my time with him. I had recently given him a copy of *The Power of Now,* by Eckhart Tolle. He hadn't yet read it and hoped it wouldn't be evangelistic. I chuckled to myself. *Hardly,* I thought, smiling.

We started to speak about love and trust. He told me he had divorced Marcie after finding out she was having an affair. He said that was long ago, and he had no hard feelings. He was still supporting her financially, much to the chagrin of Celeste. He said Celeste was more "down to earth," that they had a friendship, and he would never leave her. I cringed. Would she ever leave *him*? Concetta had pulled two cards about her that pointed to deception. One of them might have been another man in her life.

"Sometimes I get excited when you give me a massage, Debra," Ari offered innocently, somewhat surprised. I *wasn't* surprised. My massage instructor had told us it was common for men to get aroused.

"I'm attracted to you too." The words slipped out of my mouth and into the air before I could suck them back in. Ari smiled, lying contentedly on his back. The air in the room was kinetic. I continued to apply long strokes to his smooth skin, enjoying the rhythm of my movements, grounding my awareness into the moment, drawing my physical excitement upward into my heart, letting it rest there and expand, dissipating the tension.

Later, as I lay in my bed, I couldn't get his words out of my head. What was the highest good? Why was I here? Yes, I was falling in love with him, but what was our true destiny? I was sure we were brought together for a reason, maybe several reasons. Was this just a crazy fantasy?

"He does love you," Concetta said. "You make him feel connected and safe." I felt the same way around him. "He would love to show you the world and introduce you to everyone. He wants his world to see you. He doesn't want to keep you a secret." She told me he wanted to "take care of his mess," putting it all behind him. "*Let him make the first move,*" she said, emphasizing her words. "And no matter what you choose," she said clearly, "he will always be here for you."

Concetta's guidance was steadfast, but Ari had said he would never leave Celeste. I wondered if true love would change his mind. I continued to swing wildly between guilt, anxiety, and unbounded joy. Naturally, the days I didn't see or hear from him were worse. Sometimes he would plan for me to work with him the next day, and then he would disappear without a trace. No call, no text. It was very frustrating.

I felt like I was in a rocking boat. On these occasions, I would always wonder what I had done wrong. I overanalyzed everything, and my negative emotions intensified my anxiety. In my racing mind, he was Dr. Jekyll, then Mr. Hyde, but that wasn't my *experience* with him. He had a steady personality and never treated me with anything but respect and kindness. My patterns around men confounded my thinking.

All of these aberrant thoughts slipped back into their dark cave at the sound of his voice. He had canceled a dinner meeting, having felt the need to take care of himself. I worked in his office earlier that day, so I was surprised to hear from him again in the evening. I was already emotionally preparing to be away from him for two weeks, as I would be traveling to New York. "I desperately need a massage, Debra," he said over the phone. He sounded tired.

* * *

ARRIVING AT ARI'S HOUSE, I looked at his face and realized he needed to talk. He protested that he wasn't a "talker." I sat on one of two small sofas in the guest cabana and motioned for him to do the same. "You have been sick with a bad cold three times in the past couple of months. Sometimes things are symbolic. Maybe you're 'sick of things.' Does that apply anywhere in your life?" I asked him gently.

The floodgates opened, and everything spilled out. The tabloids were trying to damage his reputation by propagating lies. He was hurt, angry, and fighting back, thus the lawyers. He was fretting a lot, hadn't slept well for several months, and was always nervous.

He proceeded to tell me his personal life was okay, but within minutes he related to me that he had an ongoing battle with Celeste. She was furious that he continued to support his first family financially.

The two families were like oil and vinegar. His second family reflected his severe self-judgment, endlessly criticizing, nagging, and condemning, making him feel guilty about his attention to his first family. It was as if the two families divided him in half.

I could see the strain and sadness in his eyes as he related this to me. Celeste and the girls were also threatened by me because they didn't trust *him*. "I'm sure you feel it," he said, looking into my eyes. "But having you in my life is good for me, Debra." It was my truth too.

Our hour-long chat had unwound him sufficiently, and he opened up more deeply once he was on my massage table. "Our relationship is very special to me, Debra," he said, lying on his back with his eyes closed. "I can't explain all the feelings I have for you," he paused, looking up at me sitting at the head of the table. "I can *feel* you with me even when you aren't here. I've never experienced that before." It was the same for me. I felt his presence next to me when I lay in my bed. His energy was powerful, and my connection to him was as natural as breathing. He told me he experienced a lot of emotion when he spoke my name.

He had started reading *The Power of Now*, which I had given him weeks earlier, and was applying the idea of being present when he shaved or ate an apple. The thought of him connecting to the peace of his inner presence brought me joy.

He told me again how excited he got when I massaged him. It didn't feel lustful. He was being honest, sharing his truth. "I've never crossed a professional boundary," I said to him. I had never even contemplated it. The line was the line. I told him it would be too easy to cross that line with him.

"Debra, will you miss me when you are in New York?" he asked softly. *With every inch of my being*, I thought. I almost couldn't bear being an ocean away from him. We hugged for a long time before I left. I breathed in his clean scent, filling myself deeply with his essence.

I wanted it to happen in the right way, with him single and available. I didn't want to be part of his pattern of infidelity. I didn't want him to be part of my pattern of falling in love with unavailable men. Clearly, I loved Ari. I'd kept hitting brick walls with Brock; he didn't *want* me. Ari moved *toward* me. Our friendship was more profound. Our connection was real, sturdy, and strong. He was confiding in me. Was I kidding myself?

* * *

I PONDERED ALL THIS ON THE LONG PLANE RIDE from Nice to John F. Kennedy International Airport. Soon I would be back in the hustle-bustle that permeated the very being of metropolitan New Yorkers. Many transplanted city dwellers populated Long Island, and the energy radiated out to its North and South forks.

I didn't miss being in the States, but it was fun to be back in New York to see family and friends. I had forgotten how big the plates were in the restaurants. Sitting in a local diner with Tina, I marveled at the oversized hamburgers and mountains of French fries the servers were doling out to overweight patrons, who predominated the scene. I was accustomed to the adequate but smaller, satiating servings in France. It was enough. I preferred quality over quantity, and my waistline had benefited from this simple lifestyle change.

"What are you going to do about Ari?" Tina asked, leaning forward.

"I don't know. I think I should let destiny unfold," I said, sighing.

Tina smiled. "I couldn't agree more."

I was happy to see Concetta while visiting New York. She told me that I "knew" I'd had the shift. It was true. In my mind, Ari and I were already a couple. "He fantasizes about you," she said. "This is out of character for him. He wants to take you into his arms." She saw a significant shift happening for him once our relationship became physical. My God, she was so *sure* about this. I did not plan to fall in love with Ari, but I was ready.

Two weeks flew by, and in no time, I was back on the plane, pointed in the direction of my true love. I was relieved. I was going *home.* My chest warmed with the expansion I always got when joyously connected to my inner being. I was ready to follow my heart. This idea was firmly implanted in my mind, and there was no turning back.

* * *

ARI HAD CALLED EARLIER IN THE WEEK and wanted a massage. Nervously, I offered to do it at my apartment. He agreed.

It was a typical sunny spring day. The light streamed through the beautiful lace panels that covered the French doors, which spanned nearly the wall's length of my compact apartment. The air was still cool, but the sun was warm and the colorful pansies edging my patio glowed in pigments of perfection as the sun dappled their petaled faces. *If a panda bear could be a flower, this is what it would look like,* I thought, a delighted little grin playing at the corners of my mouth as I peered through the curtains. "Flowers raise the earth's vibration," a friend of mine had once said to me. *Indeed,* I thought as I lovingly admired my little garden. Ari would arrive shortly and I had already set up my massage table in the middle of my modest living room.

While in New York, I had purchased an expensive camera that he'd wanted. Computers, and electronic equipment in general, were much less costly in the States. Being a consummate businessman, Ari always appreciated the best price he could get, even though he could easily afford to buy Nikon or Canon itself. I was amused that saving a couple of hundred dollars mattered to him. I shrugged, countering my thoughts. *His financial prowess is why he is so successful with power and money.*

I watched him cross the small patio to my door and waited for him to knock. My heartbeat quickened as I let him in. He stepped to the center of the room, looking around the confines of the small dwelling, taking it all in. The calculation pleased him, and he exclaimed proudly, "it's all you need, Debra!" He was delighted to have provided me with a tiny piece of paradise in this magical country. I couldn't have agreed more. He opened his arms wide and gave me a big embrace. It was so good to feel his arms around me again.

We exchanged pleasantries as we sat on the sofa, opening the boxes of camera components. He thanked me and placed a small envelope on the round dining table to compensate me for the expense. "Shall we begin, Debra?" he motioned toward the massage table. My throat tightened as I felt a flush of nervous excitement flooding my body.

Sitting at the head of the massage table as he lay face up, I put my hands over Ari's heart, letting the energy flow through me to him. I felt it surging through my hands, like a cool breeze entering from the tops and exiting as heat from my palms. He gently but firmly held onto my hands as I did this, and my heart filled to bursting. I loved this man so much. I lowered my forehead onto his and felt the warmth of his smooth skin against my own, lingering, wanting to memorialize the precious fleeting *moment.* I kissed him on the forehead, and he smiled. With eyes still closed, wriggling contentedly, he uttered, "I feel so much energy from you, Debra." I thought he'd said "imagery" instead of "energy," feeling he could read my mind.

Our friendship had deepened considerably over the past few months, and I knew we'd moved to higher ground. We revealed to each other through words and small gestures—like a hug before or after his massage, frequent little touches on the arms, shoulders, or back—the changes we were both experiencing. I had been seeing him more frequently, occasionally working in his home office. He confided personal family matters to me, some of which I knew from working the races and observing the dynamics that unfolded like a great drama before me.

I undraped his left leg and began applying the sweet-smelling almond oil in broad strokes to cover his skin. Overwhelmed with the emotion of falling in love, I could no longer stifle what I was feeling, and I blurted out, “I need to hug you!”

He enfolded me with his arms as I bent over him, and we hovered there. My heart pounded with longing and excitement. I kissed his shoulder, then his neck and his cheek. And then, in an exquisite, delirious instant, I kissed his mouth.

What am I doing?? The words whizzed through my mind like a hummingbird in flight as he flung his arm around my neck, gluing our faces together, kissing me deeply. My heart seared with all that I’d been holding back for months. *He’s married!* My head tried to counter. I could feel my heart racing, thumping in my throat, my mind dizzy with a million thoughts and no thoughts, desperately enjoying his lips on mine. I didn’t want this moment to end. He arose, and I grabbed his hand. We gaped at each other, blinking incredulously. Flushed with passion, my legs wobbling like a spotted fawn, I pulled him into my bedroom.

All of our resistance melted into that moment. Questions, protests, and judgments clamoring their disapproval were briskly swept away by a stronger wind, slamming them into a far corner of my mind. We made love passionately, gently, and wholly. He took my face in his hands, so tenderly, so adoringly, and kissed me again and again. My Knight. My beautiful King. This was Heaven, and I was in it. I had been in love before, but not like this. I felt a wave in him equal to my own, something prophesied long ago, waiting for us to arrive. More than our human vessels could hold, it overflowed in rippling cascades, crashing around us, undulating, rocking, honoring, adoring, worshipping, tearing us willingly open. Seen, heard, and held, we breathed each other in deeply, tasting sweet, salty flesh as our mouths clambered wetly about.

Part Two

The Emperor Has No Clothes

CHAPTER 8

Forbidden Fruit

"What are you doing to me? I'm a married man, Debra," Ari said somberly, looking into my eyes. His words were like a knife to my heart. It hadn't stopped him from climbing all over me. His guilt was intense. He hadn't wanted to jeopardize our friendship, but I knew his feelings were like mine. I didn't feel any remorse. I couldn't. I loved him with all of my heart, laying myself bare. He told me he wouldn't have gone there. "This will complicate my life," he said as he tenderly held my face in his hands. "The massage will never be the same." Apparently, he *was* going there.

"He would have swooned if he could have," Concetta said, chuckling over the phone, delighted about what had happened. "He feels trapped in his marriage, and this is changing everything for him," she continued. "He's going to be conflicted. It will be like a roller coaster, yes and then no. You need to let it ride. He's a man of honor and a man of commitment. Give him time and space. He'll come up with ideas of how to make it all work. He is a caretaker for everybody, and it will take him some time to ensure nobody gets hurt. He is completely elated and scared shitless around you." She giggled. Was this *real?* "You must stop the fear you feel; there's no need for it. Be joyful around him. Love is what he needs to feel. He trusts you and knows you love him. Tell him you will never betray his trust and that no matter what happens, you will always love him even if he doesn't want a relationship," she said confidently.

Could I *do* that? He hadn't asked for my advances, although his gestures had been very affectionate over the past couple of months, pushing the boundaries himself. I knew I would have these moments and was trying to stay in the now. Had I made a mistake? Was I hurting anyone? Was this love or just another illusion? Did I know what love was? What was Ari going through?

My mind continued its endless commentary and stream of questioning as if I were on trial. I could stand on both sides of myself, listen to both sides of my arguments for and against what I was thinking, feeling, envisioning, and expressing, and then throw it all away. I knew the answers I was looking for weren't outside of me. I felt flawed, wrong, and ashamed in my worst moments and filled with joy when I tapped the stillness and realness of the love I felt, both for him and from him. I needed to trust that it would all work out for the highest good and that I had to feel joy and allow my heart to open to Ari completely.

He started sending me short little texts to say goodnight. It was both strange and delicious. I sometimes felt like I was dreaming but was glad I wasn't. One night, we had sent an identical text to each other at the exact moment!

I had waited all my life for Ari, a man who met the power of my own heart. This was the fairy tale I had always dreamed of. My conflicts had nothing to do with my feelings. There was no doubt that the love I felt for Ari was the best it had ever felt; honest, raw, and vulnerable in a breathtaking way. Epic. His world was chaotic, but aside from the races, I was shielded from all that. Could I handle being in his world if our relationship moved up and out into the open?

* * *

SOON NADINE AND I WOULD BE TRAVELING to the Netherlands. Ari had offered one of his guest cars, and we gladly accepted. I wanted to see as much of Holland as possible. It was a small country, so Nadine and I could cover a lot of ground: the Atlantic Ocean, the old historic windmills, and the manifold splendor of Keukenhof Gardens, bespectacled with every color tulip one could imagine. I welcomed a week away from my racing thoughts, excited about staying at the Krasnapolsky Hotel in the heart of Amsterdam.

"Mr. Sorensen is so generous! You are so lucky to be working for him!" Nadine exclaimed with delight as we booked our hotel reservation. Ari had insisted on paying for our airfare and hotel. I was beaming too. I'd never had a man who took such good care of me. Having come from humble beginnings, he knew the value and scale of things and took great pride in sharing his good fortune, especially delighted by the "wow" factor it provided others. The money it cost for our trip was pocket change for him and a week's salary for us. He was a provider and a caretaker, roles I was unaccustomed to in most of the men I'd dated. Of course, Nadine didn't know about our romance. Nor did anyone else in France. He would have happily paid for our trip, nonetheless.

* * *

THE NEXT TIME I SAW ARI, we were both more relaxed. It was delicious to experience him flush against me or beside me. "Your kisses are sensational," he said adoringly.

"I know it may seem sudden, but I'm in love with you, Ari," I said softly. Guided by my heart and buoyed by Concetta's readings, I spoke freely. "I knew our coming together was imminent. I've known it for a while now, and I don't want to hold back my feelings," I offered tenderly, feeling vulnerable in the sincerity of the moment.

"This is so new for me, Debra. My feelings are not there yet. I don't want to deceive you or hurt you," he said, looking into my eyes, his arm draped over me as we lay facing each other.

The air seemed to bristle around us, electric, but serene, like a moment out of time. I sighed, letting myself be present in the stillness. "I know what your life is like, Ari. I don't want to make any demands on you." My words made me feel defenseless, as if inviting him to nip our love affair in the bud, but I knew I could be frank with him.

The following day Ari called me to give him a massage in the guest cabana at his house. He kissed me when I got there, which felt awkward. I gave him a professional massage and a big hug afterward. He was relieved that I was still willing to massage him. He'd thought he was being selfish. "You give me so much love, Debra. I *feel* it. I'm not used to that," he said humbly. I knew he was being honest with me.

"Ari, I don't want you to look at me and feel anything but joy and love, not guilt or sadness. Even if you choose not to be intimate with me, I will still love you." It was the truth. I would only ever be honest with him too.

But deep longing and harsh self-criticism were the other side of the bliss I felt with Ari. I was not his wife. Was I his mistress? That word didn't feel right. It was so tiny, lopsided, and too restricting for the heart of love. What was the great Source that had brought us together?

One morning while still living in Delaware, I had risen from bed, halting abruptly. Ten feet away, I felt an invisible force fixed undeniably in front of me. My mind searched for a reference point, some other occurrence that would offer me an explanation. Locked in the moment, feeling awe and a little alarm, I demanded, "Where are you?" The presence lingered strongly, like a ball of energy. It was different from the pervasive experience of "presence." It was a distinct, alive, *individual*, other beingness. And "he" had been "there," right in front of me. I didn't know who it was, but it was undoubtedly a "who." In my mind, always searching for my soul mate, this was the "who" that had appeared before me.

When I met Ari, I had forgotten all about it. I was now confident it was him. Like a great, cosmic GPS, he'd had to "locate" me before he arrived, a powerful being who had set his course to move boldly toward it.

Why did things happen in life in any particular way? Why could it be so grand one moment and so bland the next? Was it just the necessary polarity of things? Had I just become too accustomed to longing? What about contentment and satisfaction? Would these ever become a reality, like those couples who had both feet planted in the soil of each other?

I desperately wanted to seed my garden in Ari's love, in this cornucopia that I knew we were creating together. I was the judge, the jury, and *always* the analyst. It was easy for me to see the situation's wrongness or rightness. I questioned everything, swinging wildly from one perspective to the other. I was on my knees or up in the clouds. I just wanted to be, and to stay, in love. I wanted to come home to this place in my heart. I was exhausted from the metronome of my emotions battering me against the jagged rock of my tired brain.

Ari could have been in much the same place, experiencing deep guilt or complete abandonment as it pertained to me. How were we supposed to live our love gracefully without the severity that threatened to lurch it from some rightful place on the path of our soul's most profound expression and evolution? Was there a price that had to be extracted, a pound of flesh? Was this true love or just a bitterly selfish fantasy?

I was weary of fleeting glimpses of love and even more weary of unrequited love. I hadn't known I had a *pattern*, let alone how to change it. Ari appeared to be an exception. He didn't run from me. I thought that was a good place to start—a crumb along the path to healing my heart. My sparsely romantic past had been dominated by short-lived relationships that bored me, floored me, or left me still attached, yoked to my illusions and desires. My mind reeled, spent from rumination.

***

HOLLAND WAS PLUSH AND GREEN in the springtime. Ari's driver, Thomas, met Nadine and me at the airport with a Mercedes sedan we would borrow for the week.

She and I made good use of the car and drove around the countryside. We visited the beautiful centuries-old, still-functioning windmills of the marshy shores of Zaanse Schans, their elegant blades silently cutting the swamp-scented air, and the Atlantic Ocean of Zaanfort, with its ultra-wide, flat beach and shoreline, hypnotized by the low waves ambling in lazily from way out in the distance. We visited the lush port village of Enkhuizen, home to the Zuiderzee Museum and one of the principal harbor towns of international trade in seventeenth-century Holland. We strolled through the old town region, its swamps, canals, and long, luxuriant grasses reminiscent of the eastern North Fork of Long Island. Time seemed to stand still as we chatted with the townspeople and workers dressed in period style.

Nadine and I strolled along the bustling cobblestone streets of Amsterdam, dodging bell-ringing cyclists and heeding the whistle of the trams that seemed to sneak up behind us as we took photos. We goggled at the jaw-dropping stripes of vivid color as we drove by the swaths of tulip farms splattering the countryside in brilliant lanes of color, like gargantuan flags sprawled out over the expansive fields. We visited the famed Keukenhof Gardens in Lisse, overflowing with endless rows of dazzling tulips along ambling storybook paths.

I spotted a ladybug, my sign of love, and thought about Ari. The love I felt for him threatened to crack me open. I had never felt such joy in loving before and so much trust in the Universe. *This feeling* is what was real; there was nothing else. I was safe, enveloped by the light of Love, cradled, humbled, and filled with immense gratitude.

* * *

FRANCE DIDN'T LOOK AS BEAUTIFUL as I drove to chorus practice a week later. My mind was still in Holland. The countryside and architecture reminded me of the home I'd known growing up in New York. The Atlantic Ocean, with its familiar, brownish-blue color—quite dull compared to the striking azure of the Mediterranean Sea—was nevertheless embedded in my cellular memory.

My heart longed for Ari, and my restless mind was conjuring resistance. I wanted this relationship. Part of me didn't believe I deserved stability, safety, or lasting things. I wanted to learn about love by loving, not losing.

The sounds of approaching summer rose ceremoniously from bushes and trees as birds and frogs vied for morning airspace. The ensuing heat of the afternoon sun riled the cicadas into a whirring frenzy as it beat down drily on the burgeoning landscape. Intermittent yearnings aside, I adored the South of France and didn't plan on leaving.

I'd had a dream the night before about Ari, in which he had given me a card filled with little cartoons and loving words that he had scribbled around the printed words on the card, some of which he had crossed out. He was pledging his heart to me. I recalled the word "leifje," which means "sweetheart" in Dutch, and the card said something about knowing when you're with the right person. I felt apprehension and consoled myself in the dream: "He loves you and *wants* you. Now that you have his heart, he's not running. He's turning to face you." I thought about it and smiled. *Yes, this is what I want.*

It was a small, significant moment for me. I'd never pursued a man who'd acquiesced. A flush of excitement washed over me. The Dutch words he had used in the card made it very personal, precise, and private. It was also significant because he had written it down, making it real. Even though it was a dream, I knew it was true. I didn't have to chase. How did that make me feel? Did I want him? Did I want *anyone*? Was I more in love with the thought of love than an actual person? Could I commit, or would I always have one foot out the door?

Tina said these thoughts were normal and Concetta told me it would be up and down, even for me. I had to be patient, remain calm, and stop mind racing.

Ari was driving with Brock in a rally through Italy. He had texted me briefly here and there about the race status but hadn't phoned me. They had lost the rally because the car broke down. He was understandably disappointed. He wanted to come by and see me when he returned. I was exhilarated but uneasy as several weeks had elapsed since our last meeting. Each encounter was like starting over again.

* * *

THEO AND THOMAS STOPPED BY that evening and invited me to dinner. It was a welcome reprieve from fretting over Ari. We went out for Thai food, and I got an earful about Celeste. My perceptions of her and the girls were right on target. I'd needed only one afternoon with them to gather that.

Thomas recounted an impromptu barbecue at Ari's house to which Ari had invited a couple of prominent neighbors. "Celeste went into a tirade, yelling and slamming the bedroom door because she said she needed at least a week's notice for a party." He chuckled and shook his head as he recalled the scene. According to Thomas, the theatrics overwhelmed Ari, who later escaped to the sitting room to watch the Grand Prix and clear his head.

"That bitch!" Theo spat, his lips pulled tightly across his face. "She only thinks about herself." I looked at him and nodded my agreement.

Thomas shifted his large frame on the small wooden chair and leaned forward. "I often hear Celeste or their daughters berating Mr. Sorensen over the phone from the driver's seat. I don't know why he puts up with it," he puzzled. I recalled how nervous Ari would get as we descended into the nearby airport on his jet, shifting in his seat and raking his hand through his hair, gaping out the tiny window as if someone were spying on us way up in the air.

According to Thomas, Ari's second family differed significantly from the first one. Was Brock destined to follow in his father's footsteps with Giuseppina? Thomas was privy to that relationship as well. "The apple doesn't fall far from the tree," he said with a grin. He reached for the bill as we stood up to leave.

"I'll go pull the car around," Theo offered.

As we departed the restaurant, Thomas turned to me. "I thought Mr. Sorensen would leave Celeste after the kids were grown."

"Why didn't he?" I asked, eager to know this myself.

"I don't know," he shrugged, shaking his head.

Later that evening, I sent Ari a loving text but received no reply. I had the feeling that the atmosphere was challenging at home. Before drifting off to sleep, I said a quiet prayer for his protection and peace of mind. My meeting with Theo and Thomas had been no accident. The Universe always provided me with the information I needed to know.

The next day I awoke at 4:00 a.m. I thought of Ari, as I often did at this time in the morning, but felt his presence more strongly than usual as if he were lying beside me. Suddenly, I felt significant pain in my left arm and substernal region, immediately followed by intense worry and emotional heaviness that nearly made me cry. I knew the sensations were not about me. Spontaneously, I clasped my hands and started to pray.

CHAPTER 9

Naked

It was June, and the temperature was delightful. Nadine, Yvette, and I headed to the exclusive coastal town of St. Tropez to relax and bask in the sun for a few glorious days. The legendary destination was renowned for its white sandy beaches, sparkling blue waters, and picturesque landscapes, with hundreds of luxury yachts cramming the spectacular harbor of the small village in the summertime. Overflowing with exclusive shops and fine restaurants, St. Tropez was a frequented hot spot for the rich and famous.

We spent our afternoons lounging at a well-known nude beach in Pamplonne. Swaths of bare well-tanned tourists on colorful blankets surrounded us. At first, I resisted being stark naked but figured I would be less conspicuous if I took everything off. I started with my bikini top, as many women in France sunbathed topless. After a few minutes, I found the nerve to untie the sides of my bottom. Sitting on my blanket, shaded by an umbrella, I yanked it out from under my rump and held my breath, anticipating gasps. None came.

Nadine laughed. "Everybody else is naked too, Debra!"

"This feels so strange!" I chuckled softly so our neighboring sunbathers wouldn't overhear. Not that they would have cared. We giggled at the freedom we felt not having to adjust our swimsuits with every turn on the blanket, and within moments dared to stand up from under our umbrella, strutting out into the bright, golden sunlight to the water's edge.

It felt wonderful to have the warm breeze gently caressing places on my body unfamiliar with the outside air. I was exhilarated, beaming, totally exposed, with nothing to hide. It was odd how being undressed made me feel less self-conscious. People frolicked with their families, their naked children running and splashing in the shallow water. Heterosexual men chatted at the shoreline, unmindful of their shared apparatus in different colors, shapes, and sizes, dangling in broad daylight.

Nadine and I walked into the gently lapping surf and waded to our waist. We dipped down to our neck and paddled out further. Buoyed by the intense saltiness of the sea, we could almost stand still without treading, legs dangling, arms outstretched like a "T" in the ultra-blue water. It was delicious to feel the coolness of the water against my skin without my swimsuit, my breasts bobbing freely. I wished I never had to wear one again. I was happy in my little microcosm of nakedness.

Ari had called during my stay and wanted to see me before a weeklong trip to his father-in-law's house in Copenhagen with Celeste. Our rendezvous was not going to happen this time. It was so hard to turn him down. I wanted to run to him, but I knew I still had to live my life and keep my plans. I realized how quickly life could change and was mature enough to entertain the thought that he may not be the last great love of my life. Nevertheless, loving him made me feel so alive, and the *feelings* were a gift.

Some days were bittersweet. There was poignancy and pain in loving him. If only I could look upon everything the way I looked at flowers; their beauty was so intense, perfect, and satisfying; their loveliness never brought sadness, only gratitude. There was no expectation, only appreciation of their beauty, and I could give tender and complete thanks. Could I do this with Ari? Even in seemingly undesirable circumstances? Could I relinquish control of the future and simply let it unfold?

"We have to take the opportunity when it arises," he often told me. He was the center of my universe, and my mind was unendingly on him. I didn't want the intense love I felt for him to be *wrong* because then I wouldn't know what was *right.*

Concetta's readings were unwavering. He would be guided out of his marriage, and I was part of his guidance, a shining star. "You are the star, Debra," Ari had once said. What had he meant? Concetta said he'd never had a relationship like this in his life. He told me that too. "He isn't walking away," she said. "Your childhood issues have nothing to do with this relationship, Debra. He's not going to leave you. He will commit to you. Stop obsessing. The relationship is fine!" she said emphatically. "His only question is, why did you take so long to come into his life?" I had the same question. "If you die tomorrow, it will have been useless to be afraid today. The rules in this world are not God's rules Debra," Concetta insisted. "Listen to your heart."

* * *

ARI TOOK ME ON ONE OF HIS business trips to Basel and Holland. We sat on opposite sides of his ten-seat jet, facing each other. I spied the usual lineup of newspapers: The Wall Street Journal, the New York Times, the USA Today, and the Nice-Matin. Tiny bottles of Evian water were swaddled in cocktail napkins and placed in our cupholders by the pilots. Pinned to the white leather seats from the G-force, we skittered down the runway and rose quickly into the cloudless blue sky.

"Would you like an espresso, Debra?" Ari asked me cheerfully once we were at cruising level.

"Of course," I said, smiling broadly as he got up to serve me. His voice lilted when he spoke my name, and my heart warmed as I beheld him carefully preparing the demi-tasse, placing a tiny biscuit and a lemon rind on the saucer. He was a caretaker. Concetta had picked that up in my readings. I felt sheer gratitude for this moment, and I loved him dearly.

"Do you want a family, Debra?" he casually asked as we sipped our frothy noisette.

His inquiry took me off guard. "I never wanted children," I replied, feeling uncomfortable. It was true. *Never.* Why was he asking me this?

"But you do like children, don't you?" he asked, a bit surprised, raising his eyebrows as he brought the tiny cup to his lips.

"Not for myself," I answered cautiously. To my relief, he didn't press further.

It would be our first night in a hotel room together. Our visits had been at my apartment every other time—which could be counted on one hand. I basked in the oversized king bed dominating the large room. He'd come in late after a long dinner meeting. He unfastened his tie, and we were all over each other in seconds. He held me tightly on top of him and whispered playfully, "you can't sleep with anyone but me."

"What makes you think I would want to?" Didn't he know I was crazy about him? I was a one-man woman. There was no one else for me but him.

"I'm just saying," he sighed. "I want you to be happy."

"I love you, Ari. There *is* no one else," I said, looking deep into his eyes.

"Our relationship is poison, Debra," he murmured drily, rendering me momentarily speechless. Although I had grown accustomed to his guilty objections, they still blindsided my open heart. Concetta had told me several times that he would go up and down about us.

"Ari, we don't know what the future holds; please just love me and let me love you," I squeaked out, my words bordering on a plea. I had no idea what the future held, but I trusted that whatever the outcome, it would be for the highest good, and ultimately, our deep connection would endure. I needed to learn to let it roll off me like water off a duck's back. Our time together was so limited and precious. I wanted to fill the vessel with love.

"I love you too, Debra," he said softly, finally letting his heart speak for itself.

I was amazed at his libido after a fourteen-hour workday, given that he was significantly older than me. He was determined to please me, and receiving his sexual and sensual adoration was heavenly. Afterward, we promptly fell asleep.

I kissed him awake in the morning, and he rolled over, tangling his legs with mine as he held me. His passion rose quickly, but he wanted to save it for the evening.

"How was your visit with Willem and Faye yesterday?" he inquired. His brother Willem was suffering from neuritis in his leg. I thought it might be related to his spine, so I volunteered to take a look at him.

"It was nice. We had lunch, and afterward, I did some massage on Willem's back and leg. He said he felt a bit better after my treatment." I hoped he would get more relief as time went on.

"Do you think it's something serious?" he asked, concerned.

"I don't know," I said plainly. I never made any assumptions about people's health.

I ordered breakfast while Ari was in the shower. He'd left for work before it arrived. I tingled all over when I signed the check upon which was written "Mrs. Sorensen." I had not ordered it as such. Was it a sign?

After eating and showering, I went to a local lingerie shop to buy something sensual, thrilled to indulge in a bit of laciness I could share with Ari. I had a drawer full of sexy bras and panties that no one but me ever got to see.

We had dinner with Thomas that evening. The three of us joked lightly, but Thomas was not as lively as when he and I had eaten dinner with Theo. A big, sturdy man with a bulbous nose and thick salt-and-pepper eyebrows, he was always polite and unreadable, a relatively unexcitable type of man. I wondered what he thought about Ari and me, sitting side by side, so comfortable in each other's presence, the electricity of attraction dancing playfully between us. How many other women had come before me? Would Thomas be happy for Ari if he knew about the love, joy, and deep respect we shared?

Later, I gave Ari a long massage. It was our last night together at the hotel. Exhausted from another typically long day, he was asleep within minutes. It was an easier sleep for both of us, as most of the nervousness of our first overnight together had abated.

The following morning, he became excited, releasing his passion deep inside me. Making love with him swept me away. His touch was deliciously scintillating and intuitive to the erotic crescendo blossoming within me. Satisfied by his release and bathing in the afterglow, I also felt a twinge of panic as my mind attempted a feeble calculation. What day of the month was my cycle due?

* * *

NOW THAT ARI AND I HAD CONSECRATED our relationship, a new set of emotions were ushered in, taking up residence in my ever-analytical mind. In Concetta's readings, her guidance always pointed to continuing my relationship with him. "Open your heart to Ari, Debra. Stop worrying and judging the situation. Be in love." It was a constant emotional juggling act for me. When I was with Ari, I could abandon all criticism of myself, the relationship, and him. When we were apart, it varied. I spent a lot of time questioning and holding myself accountable for his behavior and my own.

Fortunately, I had the chorus. We met every Sunday morning in the mountains of Fayence, about an hour from my apartment. Gwyn always did the driving, and I treasured my time with her. Singing filled me up, recharging my soul batteries and bringing me peace. We sang at holidays and weddings. The beautiful churches we sang in and the resonance of our voices inspired me beyond words.

Deeply engrossed in *A Course In Miracles,* I spent many hours reading the text and the daily lessons. I understood the messages and felt profound shifts when I was able to apply the teachings.

On Saturday, our chorus was scheduled to perform at an outdoor wedding in Seillans. I decided I would employ the instructions of the *Course* to let myself be guided by a force greater than me.

I had spoken to Concetta the night before. Her guides told me I was a powerful "manifestor" and that I should be mindful of what I said. I decided to put some ideas out to the Universe regarding our performance. I would relinquish my expectations just for a day.

Everything I asked for came to be! I was in awe. Our performance was videotaped, and we sang like angels. Several of the guests acknowledged the quality of my voice, and a few choristers, including Gwyn, said it was the best the chorus had ever sounded. I was so uplifted.

Why couldn't I do this every day? Why did I have to grunt, grovel, plead, and control my way into happiness? I hadn't asked for huge miracles, just a bunch of little ones. They had all come to pass. Could I allow the big miracles? The *Course* said there was no difference between the "magnitude" of the two. Could I allow myself to envision a future with Ari that was out in the open? Could the Universe untangle the matrix he had created or was I just another anchor he had slung over the side of his barnacled ship?

* * *

IT WAS A CHILLY MORNING. I cracked the front door open so that I would hear Gwyn's car when she pulled up. I hadn't told her about the new developments with Ari. No one in France knew, as I was very protective about our romantic engagement. Tina and Concetta in New York were the only friends who knew my secret.

"Hi, cutie!" Gwyn said, leaning over to kiss my cheek as I settled into the passenger seat of her car.

"I finally finished the text of the *Course*," I said proudly as we wound our way west on the A8 to Sunday practice. It had taken me nearly nine months to finish the unwieldy tome, chipping away for hours on end, determined to reach a goal that would merely signify another beginning.

"Oh, that's magnificent!" she exclaimed. "You've certainly committed yourself to this practice." Gwyn was a bright light in my life. Music was a bright light in hers. Aside from her flute playing, she was a long-time chorus member. She had nudged me to audition. I was a little apprehensive and unsure about my sight-reading skills, but it had all fallen into place once I started to sing. I had secretly hoped Gwyn would extend the invitation; it was another example of conscious manifestation.

I drove to Ari's later that day. I pulled through the high wrought-iron gates of the estate as they slowly folded open and parked in the carport. Ari walked toward me, and we headed to the guest house. Once inside, he kissed me. It was uncomfortable, like the first time I had kissed him there, and felt stolen, as if someone would burst in on us. We both shouldered enormous guilt about our relationship, but there was no turning back. I don't know who suffered more, him or me.

"You give me so much love, I can't hold it," he said, looking out and in at the same time, searching for words to express what he was feeling. "I've never been in love, Debra," he said humbly. I found that remarkable. And sad.

What I felt for him was natural, unrestrained. It flowed out of me like a gutter in the pouring rain, uncontainable, spilling everywhere. His guilt angled itself sharply into his moments of joy with me. I reassured him. "You're a good man, Ari."

"I am selfish, Debra," he promptly refused. I disagreed. I was glad he had a conscience, not that I wanted us to suffer. We both desired the highest good. But what was that? What was morality? What did being true to yourself mean? We approached it from a somewhat different perspective, but neither he nor I wanted to hurt anyone. I was already in love but needed to be patient with him. He was wading in more slowly. "I'm still not there yet, Debra." Yet. There was plenty of time.

I couldn't stop thinking about my conversation with him on the plane. Why did men always assume a woman wanted children? Was I headed down a path I had always avoided? Was it my destiny to have a child? Ari and I had never discussed protection. Would he be angry with me or place blame if I were undesirably pregnant?

I went to the pharmacy as soon as they opened Monday morning. The "morning after" pill was legal and readily available in France. The instructions said to take it within 72 hours. Anxiously, I stared at the little white tablet in the palm of my hand. "Please let this be one hundred percent effective," I mumbled.

* * *

ARI CALLED ME THE FOLLOWING EVENING. I was surprised to hear from him. He had a houseful of people but had stepped out to buy the paper. He was afraid to call me from his house. I echoed the sentiment. Should I tell him I'd taken the pill? Our phone conversations usually lasted only a few minutes, and I didn't want us to be interrupted. Besides, I didn't know what his reaction would be.

He was going to Paris for the rest of the week to meet with his sister Sarena. I never knew when I would hear from him. Some days I was undisturbed by the reality of his unavailability, and some days I was angered by the two-minute phone calls and incomplete sentences that came via his texts. On the days when he said he would come over, I felt my energy rising to delicious heights, only to be smashed by disappointment as the day wore on with no sign of him or receiving a text which indicated he had to cancel suddenly. I would hold all the tension inside me like a clenched fist. It was impossible to release it instantly, and when I finally did, I was mentally, emotionally, and sometimes physically exhausted. It was excruciating at times. There were moments when I just wanted to walk away.

* * *

OVER THE NEXT FEW DAYS, I worked on a nutritional protocol to help Willem with mounting health concerns. I was happy to do so. He had been one of the saving graces for me at the races. His down-to-earth personality and sense of humor made me feel instantly at ease. I hoped nutritional support would help, but I was glad he was under the care of a medical doctor. Was he still smoking cigarettes, I wondered? If so, that was never a good thing.

Ari reached out to me unexpectedly. I hadn't heard from him since he went to Paris. We chatted cheerfully, and he said he would stop by. My heart leapt. Two hours later, he canceled. I felt all the cells of my body squeeze shut like trillions of microscopic heart attacks.

I flopped onto my bed and picked up *A Course In Miracles*, opening it randomly. "What would love do now?" the text read. "*I don't know!*" I whined. Was I helplessly bound to suffer the assault of my ego? Did I know what healthy love was? I knew the *Course* wasn't talking about human love. It was referring to the Love of God.

"The highest good for you becomes the highest good for another," it continued. Did I know how to put myself first? I recalled a mature psychic woman named Millie, who had told me many years earlier, "what is right for you will become right for everyone else." I will never forget her words or the long white hair hanging down in front of her shoulders. Had she read *A Course In Miracles* too? The words were so similar. *Truth is truth*, I thought. I didn't know what putting myself first meant. I knew I had to do right by myself and that ultimately things would work out all around, but I wouldn't learn that lesson intimately until many years later.

Ari came over the following evening. I played a Dean Martin disc as we danced, and he sang to me. My heart soared, pushing against the limits of my physical container. This was love despite our attempts to clip its glorious wings with guilt and circumstance.

"Debra, I hate to think of you here all alone," Ari said later as we lay in bed lingering in the aftermath.

"You don't need to worry about me, Ari. I have friends here. I'm not always lonely," I said, pulling him close. I paused, letting the words tumble out. "Are you in love with Celeste?"

"Of course not, Debra. But it is a long-term relationship," he said plainly, without explanation. "I have my joy with you," he said brightly. Sometimes he *did* say the sweetest things. When he spoke from his heart, his words were tender and loving. He always told the truth and didn't hide what he felt from me in either direction. "Debra, do you feel all the love coming through me to you?" he asked softly, using his hands to emphasize what he was saying. I did. I rejoiced in it, holding it deep inside, letting his words caress me, feeling the aliveness and honesty of his touch.

I considered what he said about long-term relationships. I reminded him that he had made significant changes in his life before and shouldn't base staying in a relationship on a sense of obligation. I told him to trust God and follow his heart, that he had a long life left to live and should think about how and with whom he wanted to spend it. He had no objections. I knew he was not only listening but *hearing* my words.

As he climbed the apartment fence to leave several hours later, I called out, "read your *Course in Miracles*!"

"Debra, you are my miracle!" he called back. And there it was. You could have knocked me over with a feather.

* * *

A COUPLE OF WEEKS PASSED, and Ari felt far away. I had lunch in Nice with Nadine, and we took a short walk along the Promenade des Anglais. Although I had heard from Ari two nights prior, I often felt both connected and disconnected from him. I sensed that no particular person's love mattered because it was all God's Love, coming through anyone and everyone, and could be manifested just like that. There was nothing to fear. I could create whatever and whomever I wanted at any time. Whatever was destined with Ari would be, and *that* would be our perfect happiness because that *is* God's Love. I felt so free in these bright moments, and in them—just as in the dark ones—I couldn't imagine the opposite. It was a strange and persistent dichotomy, and the clarity was a welcome relief from the onslaught of guilt and analysis that plagued me almost daily.

When Ari arrived the following day, I expressed concern about our hotel stay weeks prior. "Debra, I had a vasectomy years ago," he reassured me as he put his arms around me. "I'm sorry, I thought I'd told you."

"Well, I can't imagine I would have forgotten that, but I guess it doesn't matter now." I didn't mention the pill I had taken.

He kissed me gently and climbed onto the massage table in the middle of my living room. Afterward, we made love on my bed. "I love you, Debra. I hate to think of you missing me and waiting for me."

"Ari, I am filled up when you're with me, but I'm also full when you're not here. Our joy comes from within, not from someone else—although we can share that fullness," I said wistfully, reflecting on how I'd felt in Nice with Nadine yesterday.

"That is what the book says, doesn't it, Debra?" he asked demurely.

"Yes, but it's something that has to be *experienced*," I added, feeling deeply satisfied in the moment, content to be held.

"Do you still love me?" he whispered, gazing expectantly at me.

I was surprised he questioned this as I repeatedly bequeathed my love to him. Maybe he just needed reassurance. "Sometimes I love you so much I could cry! I could never have sex with you if I didn't love you, Ari." These tender moments where I could share my deepest feelings were heavenly, affirming my soul's desire to let myself be present with them.

"I feel the same way, Debra. I'm not too old for you?" he continued shyly. Was he thinking about a future, opening to the vulnerable and frightening unknown of intimacy?

"Of course not. I like your age and your experience. It's part of why I love you. Honestly, I don't see our age difference anymore," I said, tightening my arms around him as we lay wrapped together.

I could tell he was relieved and delighted. I adored his innocence, the eternal child in him. I felt safe, joyful, and blessed by his presence. Sometimes I was incredulous at how this ultra-powerful man could have any doubts, especially about my love, which I pledged incessantly to him. I treasured his kisses, his smell, and the way he held me. Our friendship was built on mutual respect and trust. Undoubtedly, this was a solid foundation for a great relationship.

Ari swung his legs over the side of the bed and sat facing the window wall. "I wish I was a free man, Debra. I hate to leave you," he uttered sadly, dropping his chin to his chest. Maybe one day, he wouldn't have to.

* * *

"YOU'RE A CATALYST, DEBRA. You shift others," Concetta had recently told me. "Give yourself to him as you are. He will make up his mind. There is nothing you have to do. Just let him love you."

I had recently finished reading *The Alchemist*, by Paulo Coelho, per Ari's recommendation. I smiled, thinking about him reading a story that was decidedly about the Hero's journey, faith in the unknown, and the magic of creating life in the moment, ultimately returning "home" to the divine within.

Intrigued by Coelho's passionate writing, I read *The Pilgrimage*, a novel recounting his journey through Spain on the Camino de Santiago, a centuries-old pilgrimage to the Santiago de Compostela in northwest Spain where the remains of St. James the Great had been discovered in the ninth century. Reading the book gave me a different sense of peace. I experienced a stillness, a knowingness where nothing I was doing or not doing, no one I was loving or not loving, truly mattered. The purpose of my journey "here" was to detach myself from the details because all journeys are ultimately the same. They all lead to the same place: to Love, to God, to Truth, to the soul of the Self; to Oneness.

It was late afternoon, and the sun shined hot and golden. I decided to take a walk in the little "cimetière" at the end of my block. Suddenly, something hard smacked into my neck and bounced off, falling to the sidewalk. Dazed, the tiny creature cocked its head and looked up at me. As we held each other's gaze, I felt a swell of warmth in my heart that brought emotions straight up into my throat. At that moment, I loved him as much as I could love anything or anyone.

I pondered how all attachment to form must necessarily be relinquished and that the distinctions of love were not real. The more we could experience that, the more true joy would be able to flood our hearts. This example of the simplicity of life, staring at me with its tiny praying mantis eyes, held life's greatest joys and needed no words.

Allowing myself to maintain this feeling, I walked back to my apartment to call Nadine. I'd had a vision earlier that she would be the one I would walk the pilgrimage with. She was going to the Netherlands for a week, and I wanted her to pick up a Dutch copy of *The Pilgrimage* that I could give to Ari.

"It's funny that you're asking me this!" she laughed. "I just put a copy of the French version inside my suitcase to take with me to Holland!"

"What a coincidence! If it weren't for Ari, I wouldn't have known about Paulo Coelho. I've got to take this pilgrimage. The experience must be life-changing!" I sighed jubilantly.

"Me too," Nadine echoed. "When I worked at a hostel six or seven years ago, two of the guests told me they had taken the pilgrimage. Ever since then, I have wanted to go!"

"Maybe you and I will go together!" I brimmed with the thought of it. Another knowing was dawning. I was certain I could create this beautiful story any way I wanted; that life's creative power was waiting for me to let go of controlling everything so that it could woosh in and deliver circumstances beyond my wildest dreams.

CHAPTER 10

A Tree for Honey

"It appears Willem has cancer." Ari's late-night text snapped me into reality. The following morning he called to give me the unhappy details. It prompted him to consider his own mortality, as these things inevitably did. "The prognosis is not good, Debra. The cancer has spread to other places in Willem's body."

Deeply saddened, I called Willem to offer my support. He was in complete shock. Toward the end of our call, he became emotional. My heart went out to him. I hung up the phone and sobbed. I didn't know him well, but I could put myself in that place. Anyone could, I supposed. Metastasis was a deadly word. I was flying to Holland tomorrow to visit him. I was numb.

Concetta said that my energy-healing work would bring Willem comfort. She also said that he and Faye "knew" about Ari and me and were delighted. Ari hadn't told anyone, but hiding things from your family was hard, as I knew all too well. They could read you. Concetta told me Ari loved his brother very much. "They have a strange, atypical bond," she said, listening closely to her guidance. "They use humor to navigate their relationship, but on a deep level, they are committed."

Thomas picked me up from Schipol airport, and we drove to Honey's house near Amsterdam, where she had lived for more than fifty years. Some of the décor was in its original condition. Linoleum covered the kitchen floor. A simple metal spigot stuck out from the melon-green tiled backsplash behind the white ceramic sink. The wood floors were worn, but the living area had been updated and finished in a modern style, which seemed a little out of place compared to the old kitchen. A simple Catholic shrine rested on an end table near an upholstered chair. It was a small, cozy place. I smiled, imagining Ari and Willem here as young teens, their whole life ahead of them.

A superstitious woman, Honey asked me to draw a picture of a tree so she could read my character. I had brought my amethyst crystal with me, as I always did on my travels. It was a beautiful hue of deep lavender and shaped like a spire. I used it to meditate and quiet my mind. She waved a little pendulum over it and told me I had made a good choice. I'd thought so too.

She looked carefully at the picture and then at me. "You will meet a man in later years and share your life with him." She paused. "Have you met him yet?" *Had I ever!* I glanced discreetly at Thomas. "No," I lied, aching to tell her the truth. She then waved her pendulum over my outstretched hand to check my health. She told me I was consuming too much fat. *Hmph, who could resist French cheese*? I thought.

* * *

SEEING WILLEM IN THE HOSPITAL was uncomfortable, and I was glad there had been other visitors. I performed energy healing on him. He said he believed in this type of work. I was not surprised, having just come from his mother's house. I thought of giving him a couple of crystals and some inspiring spiritual books to uplift him.

They asked me if I'd seen Ari recently, and we talked about family. According to Willem and Faye, Celeste had enticed Ari away from Marcie by getting pregnant. I thought of Brock and Giuseppina.

Why couldn't we see our patterns? They were as plain as the nose on our faces, and undoubtedly other people could see them and even point them out to us, kindly or not. They were so *charged*, as addictive as candy to a child. They could control us and bring us to our knees, yet, like childbirth, we would forget about the pain and do it all over again. Were we destined to blind repetition? Was it just me that understood this all too clearly? Was I in a pattern with Ari? I'd never experienced anyone like him. He wasn't like Eddie, Hunter, Brock, or others I had chased. Concetta had said my childhood issues had nothing to do with this relationship. Was it true? Was there an ugly monster waiting to come up and grab me? Could I handle his family drama? I wanted the truth, whatever was in my highest good. I loved Ari and didn't want either of us to be hurt. I wanted an honest, trustworthy man who would be monogamous with me. As I had this thought, I received Ari's text: "Thanks for your caring love. Hugs."

The next day I cried for hours. I wasn't sure why. Maybe it was just everything. I felt helpless around Ari's family, an outsider, and I worried about what everyone thought of me. All the secretiveness was difficult. I craved transparency. Would I ever have that?

Regardless, I was happy to be in Amsterdam. The Dutch people were more akin to me than the French and quite receptive to Americans. Many spoke perfect English. They were lively, curious, and direct.

Letting my thoughts drift, I walked around Vondelpark for three hours, holding my amethyst crystal. I bought crystals for Willem, hoping they would positively affect his spirit and immunity. The doctors didn't believe he had much longer. I felt a bit desperate, and I wanted a miracle for him. Life wasn't fair. What was my role here?

That night in my hotel room, as I lay in bed, I thought about how difficult it would be for Ari to lose his brother. Tears formed in the corners of my eyes. At that moment he called me. I felt the tension release from my chest. It was the first time I had spoken to him since I'd been here, and I was relieved to hear his voice. He was understandably sad. He told me he would spend the following week here with his mother and Sarena so that they could see Willem together. He appreciated that I was offering my support. I felt like a fish out of water but was happy to be here for him.

Willem appreciated the gifts I had gotten him. Many friends were visiting, and I saw some of the race team crew. They were a tight-knit, supportive group. I was happy Willem had comrades to laugh with and lighten his burden. Marcie and Honey were there. Sarena had just left.

I hovered my hands over Willem's body, letting the healing energy flow. I glanced over at Faye. How was she taking it? I didn't want to intrude, only to help and bring comfort to Willem, who wanted me to return. Ari's mother took pictures. I felt accepted. Willem seemed heartened when I left, a bit less fearful. I prayed for him when I returned to my hotel room.

The following morning after breakfast, I headed for Vondelpark again and walked through the rose garden. Something silvery caught my eye, and I spied a tiny locket shaped like a heart! I stooped to pick up the dirty trinket, feeling joyful and light. I resisted sending Ari a text as I breathed in the fresh rosy air. Just then, he called. He was at the Vatican waiting in a long line at St. Peter's Basilica so he could light a candle for Willem. The Vatican! I thought excitedly about my trip to Rome with Nadine next spring.

Ari had heard all about my visit to the hospital. He was enormously grateful and saluted with "big hugs and lots of love." After the park, I walked back to Rembrandtplein and ordered a pizza. As I sat down to enjoy my lunch, Ari phoned again. He was eating spaghetti. The Vatican was swamped with tourists "like Disneyland," so he'd opted for a church nearby. He was frustrated. I giggled. I could imagine him fidgeting in the queue, impatiently raking his fingers through his hair. Time was essential to Ari, and he didn't like to waste it.

"I'm anxious to get to Willem, Debra. I need to be strong for him," he said with quiet resolve.

"Just be yourself, Ari. Willem needs to feel your love and how important he is to you," I said, remembering Concetta's words. "Just feel your feelings when you are with him."

"How did Willem's eyes look when you saw him?" he asked with intent curiosity.

"He appeared less fearful than the first time I saw him. He seemed determined, and his sense of humor was back. I think it's important that you share the laughter and the tears. Make sure you touch him," I said gently.

The next day, I stopped at a local church to light a candle for Willem before returning to France. I had phoned him earlier that morning. He was emotional. He wanted me to come back and see him when he began his chemo and radiation treatments. I could hear the fear in his voice. I felt a deep sadness as I hung up the phone. I would be there for him in whatever way was appropriate for all concerned. I was tired and looked forward to being back in my apartment. It had been a very emotional week.

* * *

IT WAS A TYPICALLY HOT, dry day on the sunny Riviera. I was glad to be home. Everything was surreal. I felt like a character straddling different worlds. Which one was real? I felt uneasy about all the texts I sent to Ari while visiting Willem. Did he erase them? What would happen if Celeste saw them? I wondered what her side of the story was. Life was likely not easy for her spiritually or emotionally, and I sensed she didn't trust anyone or anything. Maybe she had good reason not to. I also sensed that she didn't think about any of this. It was just me overanalyzing and trying to figure out what everyone was thinking and feeling, wondering if things would end up in a way that would eventually benefit us all.

From what I could see, many were judging Celeste's behavior. All of Ari's first family and entourage had something negative to say about her, unable to understand why he was still with her. I was sleeping with her husband. Wasn't that the most significant judgment of all? He and I both had enormous guilt over it, but our relationship continued. Was I attacking him? Myself? Celeste? Was our relationship true love, or just my way of becoming more present in his life? Were my intentions pure? Could he and I make it in a partnership, or would he eventually leave me too?

Questions streamed through my mind like water running downhill as I searched for a foreseeable future to latch onto. It would have been so much easier if Ari were already divorced or, at the very least, separated. Was this the only way to extricate himself from Celeste, a perfect reason to leave? Was true love the only thing that would pry him away? I wanted and loved him. Was he the man I could say yes to in all ways? I put my journal away and walked into the living area.

Glancing out my French doors, I saw two white butterflies twirling around each other, flitting about my garden. Was that a good sign? I walked out onto the terrace and spied two ladybugs, one atop the other. I laughed out loud. The Universe certainly had a good sense of humor. Couldn't I lighten up just a little?

Ari called from Zurich the next day. His voice was uneasy. "I think Celeste knows about us," he said without explanation. I grimaced. I didn't want to have this conversation over the phone. I didn't want to run through all the guilt again. It was almost a mantra for him. It was frustrating and draining for me to continually reassure him that everything would work out as it was supposed to. Energetically, I felt his alignment was with me. What did he want to do about it? Did he want to be a free man, or were we merely trying this on for size? Was he hiding behind his guilt so that he didn't have to face his real feelings? Did I need to walk away?

"I'm going to have a full-body MRI to see if I have any cancer." His words jolted me, but I understood. My heart softened. Concetta had said he would be up and down. And now, with the added stress of Willem's condition, it would be unfair to press him toward a resolution. He would be experiencing a massive loss in his life and likely had guilt about Willem. I needed to be a loving vessel for him and brush my desires aside for a while. We had time.

* * *

THE AFTERNOON WAS HOT but comfortable in the shade. I sat outside on my terrace, writing in my journal. I thought about one day writing the story of my life. Many years prior, a psychic named Beatrix had told me I would write a book. She had also said, croaking out the words in her deep, crone voice, "if you don't do your healing work, you don't get the man, Debra." The torment of that had followed me around for years. I often looked at my healing work as a chore. It was not my passion. But it had led me to Ari. Beatrix had also said that the second half of my life would be very public and external, that I might be famous, and that the man in my life would be wealthy. My God, had she predicted Ari all those years ago?

Ari called me late the following evening. He, his sister, and their mother had visited Willem in the hospital, and it was a very emotional day. Willem was delighted to see Ari, and I was happy they were together. "I did energy work and put my hands all over him, Debra!" His voice was light, and I could feel the love and connection he shared with his brother. Willem would receive radiation the next day, and Ari would have the chance to be alone with him. Yes, I could love this man for the rest of my life, I thought tenderly.

* * *

IT WAS A TUESDAY MORNING. I awoke feeling alone and far away from my own life. I sent Ari a weekly *Course in Miracles* lesson via text. I typically sent them on Monday but had forgotten to do so. I always chose loving, supportive messages, not those that bludgeoned you with the errancy of the egoic mind. "Let miracles replace all grievances," I typed. To my surprise, Ari texted back, "big hugs." I started to cry. I realized how deeply my heart wanted to love him, and I had been holding back because of fear and the anticipation of rejection. I let myself sit tenderly with that thought.

Theo stopped by, and I discovered that Katrina was in Holland with Ari, visiting Willem. My heart dropped. I had met Katrina when I first came to France and had given Ari a massage at her home on a couple of occasions. They had been in a relationship for a long time and seemed to be good friends. I liked her from the start. Physically, she resembled Celeste, but that was where the similarity ended. She was quiet and kind, a person you could trust immediately.

Ari had bought her the house she was living in years ago. They didn't appear to be romantically involved but had a comfortable camaraderie. Of course, it hadn't mattered to me at the time. I didn't give it much thought until he and I became intimate more than a year later. My mind jumped into an all-too-familiar gear. Had Ari been lying to me the whole time? Was he having sex with Katrina or even Celeste? Was all the guilt-tripping just a facade to make him feel less remorse about us? Was our relationship really "poison," as he had said?

Concetta told me Katrina was just an old friend and I had nothing to worry about; Ari's heart was with me. Could I believe this? I decided to ask him about his relationship with Katrina when I saw him again. I wouldn't judge it, but I could determine where I went from there, choosing what felt right to my heart.

One of us might reject the other. I knew things would never be the same if either happened, but I had been through rejection before and survived. Was Ari going to be another sad lesson on unavailability? Did I have to be schlepped all the way to France to fall on my face, or was Ari my true love? Why did I swing so wildly between the two thoughts, applying the past to the present simply because it was all I had experienced? Could I open my heart and mind to a new possibility for myself? Would I get to write the story the way I chose? I loved Ari and would always love him no matter what happened.

Ari phoned at 5:15 p.m. He was going to Germany to have his MRI and would return to France the next day for a week. He wanted me to do energy healing on him. Willem was feeling better, and his spirits were up. Ari had been seeing him daily and was hopeful about Willem's progress. It brought me joy that they were connecting on a deeper level. Ari mentioned my text from *A Course In Miracles.*

"I'm sorry I sent it a day late," I said lightheartedly.

"Debra, I have no complaints about you. You should be the one complaining about me," he said, half-jokingly. I wasn't complaining either. I prayed for the courage to ask him about Katrina.

Willem and I spoke later that evening and the next day. The doctors had postponed his surgery because they felt he wasn't strong enough, even though he was mobile, had an appetite, and felt better. I had no close experience with cancer patients. I could only hope for the best, like everyone else.

* * *

ARI CALLED ME TO BRAG ABOUT how healthy he was. The MRI was negative. I was happy he had gotten peace of mind and couldn't wait to see him. I tried to resist projecting the entire relationship into the future. When I kept my thoughts in the present, all my doubts about Ari vanished, and there was trust.

Fortunately, I also had constant guidance and support from Tina, who phoned me regularly from New York. "Remember, Debra, no matter what traits a person has or doesn't have, the basic problem is that we expect them to meet all of our needs. We expect them to take the place of God. They can't uphold our expectations of them, which is why we suffer," she offered introspectively, making perfect sense. Our conversations were critical for me, keeping me on an even keel as I navigated a relationship not only with Ari but with myself.

Ari told me his brother was holding up, but their mother was pessimistic about Willem's plight. "Your mother has Willem dead and buried already," I offered honestly. I had spent enough time with Honey to know where she was coming from. "From what I've seen, she's a very selfish woman. It's always about *her*. Her needs are seldom met, and she is never to blame."

"She's always been like that, Debra," Ari said, resigned to the idea.

"That's where your guilt complex comes from," I said gently.

He paused. "She used to say I was a naughty boy." I could hear the sad reflection in his voice.

"You didn't do anything wrong, Ari. You are a loving child of God," I said softly, wanting to reassure him and let him know that I thought nothing of the kind.

"I am melting as you speak to me, Debra," he said with relief.

"Ari, I miss you so much. It's heaven for me to be in your arms." The words gushed out from the center of my being.

"It is the same for me, Debra. I want to see you today," he said brightly.

It had been four weeks since the last time we were together. I longed to feel Ari next to me. I knew he wouldn't be able to come that evening, but all was okay; there was always tomorrow.

Feeling a burst of creativity, I bought some multicolored, slender ribbons to create bookmarks in my *Course in Miracles* book. I stuck them into the book's binding, where the cover bulged away from the spine, gluing them securely into place. I grinned. The binding was no longer tight, as I had hurled the heavy tome on more than one occasion against the wall on the road to discovering, as Gwyn lovingly pointed out, my "reference point."

Satisfied with my work, I selected six of my favorite passages and draped a ribbon along the inner crease to refer to them often. This book was going to be my companion for life.

Willem's surgery was the next day. I prayed for a miracle. Ari called me from his plane in the morning to connect briefly and again in the evening from Holland. I smiled as I thought of him jetting from country to country, his little plane like a taxicab in the sky. I was missing him desperately, and by the tone of his voice, I imagined it was the same for him. The spaces between our infrequent meetings were challenging, and I longed for the comfort of regular contact. Nevertheless, incremental shifts were occurring, and I felt we'd moved to a deeper level. I was confident that he loved me.

"I'm a prisoner in my own life, Debra," Ari offered dejectedly.

"That's because you're always trying to please everyone," I reflected.

"I'm stupid to do that," he said, his voice riddled with self-deprecation.

"Please don't refer to the man I love that way," I teased, hoping to lift his spirits. I couldn't wait to see him, hoping I wouldn't have to wait much longer.

***

THE SUMMER WAS IN FULL SWING, with tourists from all over Europe vacationing in the South of France. Nadine and I went to Plage La Gougouline in Cagnes-sur-Mer, to soak up some sun and have lunch. Willem called to tell me his surgery had gone well, and the physical therapist had him up and moving. I told him I wanted to see him soon.

Nadine felt moved as he and I spoke. "Tell him *beterscap*," she said compassionately. Willem was delighted.

Ari called me the next day. It was Izabella's birthday, and many guests were at his house. "They all make me feel guilty, Debra. It's *worse* than being a prisoner," he joked. "I miss your kisses. Don't practice on anyone else," he teased. We both chuckled, but I was feeling a bit shut down. It had been more than five weeks since I had seen him. I loved him dearly, but he was a ghost at times. I knew there was a big mountain to move. Would we move it, or not? I wanted action, availability.

Tina said it was still early in the relationship and that Ari needed time to process his feelings of being trapped in his life. Concetta said he would make the right decision. I would have to be patient. The next evening when we spoke, he told me he wanted to take me to Zurich with him so we could spend the night. Yes, there had been too much time in between. "I'm glad I have your picture to remind me of what you look like!" I teased.

We never made it to Zurich, but he was on the massage table in the middle of my living room a few days later. I climbed on top of him. We laughed playfully. It was delicious to feel the warmth of his body against mine. "Debra, I hope the table is sturdy enough to hold us!" He laughed, taking my face in his hands. "I want to take you to the Italian Riviera." I knew there were many places he wanted to take me, and I wondered if it would ever come to pass. Slathered with guilt, he saw himself as a traitor to Celeste. They hadn't had sex in almost five years but still had a "friendship." *Five years?* That was not my idea of marriage.

I looked him in the eyes, holding my breath, letting the question spring from my chest. "Are you having sex with Katrina?"

"No. We were in the beginning, but now we're just friends. I have known her for fifteen years," he said, steadily holding my gaze. Concetta was right about Katrina! I was thrilled. "I'll answer any questions you want, Debra," he said, his eyes still fixed on mine.

"Does she know about us?" I wanted her to know. I trusted her and hoped she could be objective with Ari and tell him to follow his heart, which I knew was with me.

"No one knows about us, Debra. She did ask me about it, but I didn't tell her." I felt his sincerity and willingness to be open with me. I wanted to ask him why he thought Celeste knew about our relationship, but I couldn't.

Making love with him that day was the best yet. Maybe it was surrendering to what was and what would never be. Perhaps life's uncertainty and the honesty of our conversation made us both realize that we should enjoy the precious moments we had.

Holding me gently, he said, "I come for your kisses, Debra, not the sex. But you *are* the best lover I've ever had." That was where I could pour all of my love out to him. He could feel it. It was the same for him.

"I have so much time invested with Celeste…." His voice trailed off. I felt his mind flipping back over the years, but he offered no further insight.

"Trust that God brought us together for a reason. Just feel your love for me," I whispered as we held each other tightly.

We showered together before he left. Afterward, I called Concetta and placed her on hold when Ari unexpectedly phoned me from his car. She said she could feel so much joy between us as she waited for me to come back on the line and could envision a love like this in her own life.

"He's just processing with you, Debra. He can't do it with anyone else. He feels so many obligations and is pulled in many different directions. He's going to have a huge shift in the winter." I trusted her guidance. Sometimes her timing was off, but she had been right on the money regarding Ari and me thus far. "Let his objections roll off your back. Just love him and reassure him." She did not waiver.

CHAPTER 11

The Star of David

I was thrilled by the sexual exclusivity between Ari and me. I was committed to him. Our love felt solidly grounded. I thought about what he had told me regarding his first marriage. According to him, Marcie was having an affair almost the whole time they were together. I knew it was painful for him. I reflected on the theme of betrayal in his life. In the deepest recesses of my heart, beyond all insecurity and doubt, I knew that he was faithful to me, and I trusted him. Our bond was unbreakable, and communication happened organically between us, even when we were far apart. But why all the drama? Why wasn't this beautiful soul mate fully available to me? I picked up my journal and wrote him a letter.

"Ari, I am not Marcie. I am not your mother. I am not Celeste, nor am I Katrina. I am me, and I love you with all of my heart. You are my True Love and the man I want to share my life with. If I walked away from you, I would break my own heart and regret it for the rest of my life. I am scared too, and I don't want to lose you. I am trying to allow the fullness of my feelings for you because I would only betray myself by not doing so, even though this makes me feel vulnerable. I love you. You *are* the man I've waited for all of my life. And lucky for me, I didn't marry anyone else, or I wouldn't be here now and would have missed out on the greatest love I have ever known. I will never betray your love. Trust God, for our Holy Relationship is in His hands. Let yourself feel your feelings too, and if you love me, don't deprive yourself of that joy. Feel it fully. Express it. It is the most precious thing we can share. I am here for you. I will not leave you or betray your trust or your love. I love you. I love you always."

Ari phoned while I was at Juan Les Pins beach with Nadine a few days later. It was a pleasant surprise to hear his voice. He was lively and kinetic, a man with a busy mind. He was in Holland with his mother and Sarena, visiting Willem. He would be traveling the following week to meet with his German investors. He said we might go away for a few days together soon. His life was so changeable and dense with obligations that it was hard to imagine creating this window of opportunity. But the last time we were together, I had felt another shift. He was more playful and confident. He knew his way around my body, and I melted when he touched me. Our interaction was so comfortable and so natural. There would be deep regret if I walked away.

"I'm a traitor," he had said on more than one occasion. He stunned me into silence when he made broad-stroke statements like this. Did he think that suffering was tantamount to happiness? He seemed more motivated by a promise to a long-dead commitment than finding joy and harmony in a relationship. Did he believe he deserved to be happy, that there was such a thing in love? His guilt seemed to stoke his indebtedness, but his imprisonment was his own doing. Could he see that?

Ultimately, I wanted a relationship that transcended the ego's fixations. But first, those fixations had to be acknowledged, forgiven, and blessed. I had been working on healing my issues and patterns for years. I felt that true forgiveness was neither an intellectual nor emotional pursuit, although it was of the heart, the spiritual heart. I imagined true forgiveness as a release, an expansion of the soul, a reminder of our connection to Source. Could my relationship with Ari become this? Was this the relationship destiny I felt deep in my being?

Ari called me the day after he'd visited his brother. "Debra, Willem is feeling fine!" I could sense his relief but was somewhat surprised by Willem's turnaround. We laughed and flirted. He was looking forward to seeing me and "doing everything." He couldn't be explicit because he was in his private car and didn't want Thomas to overhear, but he did not attempt to hide his joy. "I am *there,*" he whispered playfully.

"You *should* be here. When am I going to see your gorgeous face?" I teased.

I hoped to see him before his weeklong trip to Barcelona with his family. He said he didn't want to go but had canceled it last year and felt obligated.

A few days later, he was in my waiting arms. He could only stay for a couple of hours but called me once he was back home. He was exhilarated. He had just spoken to Willem, who had gained ten pounds. He was hopeful that Willem could beat the odds, and we prayed for a miracle. He thanked me for a beautiful evening and apologized for the brevity of his visit. I told him to stop worrying and to cherish our feelings for one another. There was enormous spontaneity and joy between us, so much to be thankful for. I was content.

* * *

ARI PICKED ME UP EARLY THE NEXT WEEK, and we drove to Fréjus for a delectable seafood paella lunch. He was back on the guilt yo-yo.

"Four months ago, our relationship was so pure," he lamented as I filled my fork with a small mound of the sweet, aromatic, saffron-yellow rice.

I wanted to stave the conversation, weary of carrying a torch for our relationship. "You're layering so much guilt on it that you cannot see the gift of love here," I said gently. He looked at me, letting me continue. "We don't know what the highest good is, Ari. All we can do is be honest with ourselves and each other."

"I am worried about your expectations, Debra," he countered.

"Our relationship is no accident, Ari. We can hardly profess to know God's plan." Did he ever think about the magical way we had entered each other's lives? What were the chances that out of the blue, he'd shown up in Delaware, U.S.A., at the same time that I was in the *unlikely* position as a chiropractor giving massages in a fancy hotel? And on a three-month handshake deal that was so far an *eighteen-month* adventure that we would be eating gambas and rice at La Villa des Fleurs, talking about a relationship of equally impossible odds, debating the rightness of it?

The conversation went back and forth like this throughout our lunch. I hardly ate because I was talking so much. I was exhausted and irritated. Here we were, alone together and wasting precious time on this conversation. I didn't know what he wanted me to say. Did he want to go back to just being friends? "I don't know what our relationship will look like ten years from now, but it is built on honesty, trust, respect, compassion, and love. No matter what it transforms into, those components will always be here, Ari." I held his gaze deeply, sincere about what I was saying, tired of having to defend what was happening *now* between us.

He agreed. "Life goes quickly, Debra." I knew I had temporarily quelled his doubts but that they would return, as his perspective had not yet shifted.

"Read your *Course in Miracles* book," I reminded him, toying with my now lukewarm rice.

"I need to put the time aside to do that," he said earnestly.

It was a big undertaking. I could appreciate his desire to "make time," but this could easily be a life path. "You may never get that opportunity, Ari. Just open the book as time allows and let yourself be guided. If not, twenty years will skate by, and you may regret having never done it." I knew he never would, but I was happy to continue sending him a weekly text. Something was better than nothing. And where the *Course* was concerned, a little went a long way.

Ari was very playful on the ride home, sliding my dress up to caress my bare thigh or holding my hand. He made several phone calls from the car, laughing and relaxed, free to be himself, at ease in his big whirling world of people, places, and things.

He had been thinking about everything I'd said and mentioned psychotherapy. I said it would help him understand some of his behavior patterns and where they originated—in most cases, the mother and father. The point was to understand, acknowledge, and release them, not to condemn but forgive the past. Easier said than done, I grinned, thinking about my own adult journey. He was listening. The endlessly ringing phone interrupted us again, but he was calmer. Someday it might all fall into place for him; he would be able to hear it.

When we arrived at my place, he stepped in for a few minutes, and we kissed and hugged. "What are you doing tomorrow?" I teased, knowing he was headed to Barcelona.

"I'm coming here for a massage, and then I will make love to you *twice*." He kissed me again tenderly, and then he was off.

* * *

ARI'S TEXT INFORMED ME he was "in Barcelona, hugs." The day was unfolding with a palpable difference. I felt myself entering a different level of consciousness that felt somehow magical. My emotions were toned down, low, ebbing, and I felt my mind, my presence, moving inward, deeper. There was a sense of utter stillness and a peaceful, vibratory excitement. I could see more clearly, sharply; there was no haze or space between or around anything. Everything was fluid and connected.

I had been reading about a few of the individuals influential in bringing *A Course In Miracles* into the world. Intuitively I realized my trip to France was orchestrated at a level of Love I didn't understand. All the actors in the play were here to receive me when I arrived: Theo, Nadine, Gwyn, and Ari's whole world. My bond with him felt strong, deep, and reverent. He was my King; I was his Queen. I felt I'd known him forever and that France was just another moment in time where we came together with eyes to see, remember, and honor each other. I would get wafts of the smell of his cologne, as I had earlier after his text to me. They would come out of nowhere, linger for a few moments, and then disappear. How was that possible? In these moments, I had no doubts about anything. I knew there was an essential purpose in our coming together. His mother saw it in the tree I drew. She had said I would spend the rest of my life with this man. I knew there was no separation between us.

I was lying on my sofa, my mind quiet, surrounded by books in a deep state of calm, taking in what I had read. My gaze drifted toward the ceiling, and I noticed a faint blue outline of a star circumscribed by a circle. Casually, a thought slipped into my mind: *It's the Star of Jesus*. It appeared as a faded blue neon glow like the tube-shaped necklaces children could buy at a carnival. It hovered for several minutes, angled toward my patio doors. It wasn't connected to the ceiling and hung suspended like a star in the sky. Then it disappeared.

Arising from the couch, I typed "star of Jesus" into Google search. As I hit the enter button, I said aloud, "there was no Star of Jesus. It was the Star of David, wasn't it?" The first choice Google presented was "the Star of David is the Star of Jesus." There was my answer as if someone had been listening to me! I didn't know much about it, as I had never been interested. Christianity had always felt heavy and laden with the idea of sin and guilt.

I couldn't imagine an infinite Universe structured around the concept of one Son, Jesus, and billions of groveling humans making sure they didn't make mistakes to piss off and garner the eternal wrath of a temperamental Supreme Being.

It was interesting then that I was so attracted to *A Course In Miracles*, its words, but not its message, spoken in the same "language" that had threatened me most of my life. Once I got past the semantics, I realized that Jesus' message was one of infinite Love. The terms, ideas, and constructs expounded in the *Course* were expressed purely and congruously to what I believed was an unfathomably benevolent Creator, the essence of all and everything, including us. We were all sons and daughters of God, and Jesus was our brother, our self-same heart. There was no separation. That was an ego construct. In those moments when I surrendered to the Divine within myself, I discovered that Love is all there is.

I thought about the star hanging from my ceiling, and I smiled. I wondered why I would have needed to come to France to study the *Course,* given it had originated in the States. Why did I find it now? Maybe it was just time, the next part of my spiritual awakening, and France—the fantastic stage for my fairy tale—was also a divinely crafted spiritual sabbatical.

Metaphorically, I wrestled with holding onto and letting go of Ari, which reflected my state of trust or mistrust. As far as I was concerned, the love relationship was the most difficult. I found myself trying to rise above and separate myself from the human desire to unite with the object of my heart's desire. From my understanding of the *Course,* the challenge was not to make an "idol" of the object of my affection nor rise above the basic *need* for love, but to maintain my center and self-worth; to not give my power away to something that seemed outside of me, beyond my control.

This was often an extraordinary effort, as I repeatedly slipped away into Ari. The *Course* addressed the "special relationship" very directly as a constant reminder that the ego must relinquish this illusory relationship to the Divine so it could be purified and made holy.

Believing the concept to my core, I genuinely wanted the highest good between Ari and me. I would tell him that only we knew what that was for ourselves individually. Could I abide by whatever his decision was about us? Did I secretly believe that I knew what was best for him, that I was using these concepts to bring him closer to me under that perception? Did I constantly have to put myself under his nose so he would remember me? And even though the sex was delicious, was that also a way of binding him to me? Was I using the *Course* as bait?

These were the ideas I struggled with almost daily; deciding if my actions were the *right* actions and taking responsibility for these actions and my reactions. One thing I knew for sure: Regardless of the level of consciousness of my behavior, I did not have the intention of manipulation or dishonesty. And I did want to remain present with my *motivations* when approaching a love relationship. The only thing I could do was continue to invite truth, trust, honesty, and integrity to govern my actions. I was open to whatever perspectives were shifting inside me, but it wasn't always easy.

And what about Ari's guilt? He never really got deep. I believed he was capable, but maybe he was afraid. I didn't think he'd ever really had anyone to listen to his feelings without calling it complaining. From what I could gather, he'd likely grown up listening to his mother's laments and maybe even Marcie's, most definitely Celeste's. His guilt might have been a way to stop the onslaught of criticism that pelted him like a hard rain. As long as he donned the armor of self-denigration, maybe they would leave him alone. And when he couldn't take it anymore, he would run away, disappear into his crazy schedule, so he could keep running. Was he terrified to stop because of what he might find inside himself? I put my journal down. Therein was the weight of the world, I thought heavily. I prayed. "God, let us feel our Oneness with You and all that is Light, Love, and Truth."

* * *

THE FOLLOWING WEEK, Nadine and I went to the Netherlands for the Sail celebration, a festival of ships that originated in 1975 to commemorate the 700th anniversary of Amsterdam. More than fifty ships from all over the world were moored there. Many were historic, and some were replicas of ships hundreds of years old. They strung for miles along the eastern harbor in IJhaven and Oosterdok, their colossal masts and sails soaring majestically into the blue sky. National flags in bold colors snapped and fluttered sharply in the stiff port breezes. I smiled, gazing at the Dutch flag waving proudly in red, white, and blue.

We walked for miles and took a dinner cruise on a simple, flat, open tour boat. After two hours, our captain had to turn around and head back, as the harbor was so crowded that boats were bumping into one another!

Afterward, Nadine and I headed to watch a stunning fireworks display. We "oohed and ahhed" as flashes of colored lights sizzled, popped, and exploded in brilliant cascades over our heads. Before we left, I bought a few souvenirs for Willem, Faye, and Theo. The next day I would visit Willem in the hospital while Nadine visited with family and friends.

* * *

MOUNTING FEAR WAS EVIDENT in Willem's eyes. Faye was there, and I had become a little uneasy around her. I felt she was jealous of me, as she likely didn't understand why I was such a frequent visitor for Willem.

She later drove me back to my hotel and asked what I thought about him. I mentioned the fear in his eyes. "That's because he thinks you hate me!" she nearly shouted. I was stunned. It came out of nowhere, and I couldn't even compute what she said. Why would I hate her, and why would a dying man be afraid of that?

Suddenly I was in a conversation about jealousy. She purported that Willem was projecting his jealousy onto her. I suggested that the other half of this picture might be her jealousy, which she staunchly denied. According to Faye, Willem didn't believe that women could have male friends who were "just friends."

I recalled the drive from Le Mans to Amsterdam well over a year ago. Willem was overly curious about my relationship with Ari (long before our romance), and some of his questions had been inappropriate. I told him that Ari confided in me. He said that Ari must trust me because he rarely confided in anyone. I made a mental note to remember and honor that.

My choice to visit Willem was more out of allegiance to Ari. Neither Willem nor Faye knew the specifics of my relationship with him, so they were understandably confused. I discussed only our trusted friendship, and by the time she had dropped me off at the hotel, Faye was satisfied.

I see-sawed between utter glee and intense distress about my romance with Ari, and it was painful not to be able to share the truth with anyone here. Why had I fallen in love with a man whose life was so complicated? How did I reconcile the glory and the anguish of it all? I continued to ask for the highest good, and Ari kept moving toward me. In a few days, I would be back in Holland with him, stealing away in the same hotel Nadine and I had stayed in for the Sail festival.

* * *

IT WAS ALMOST MIDNIGHT when Ari arrived at the hotel. "Debra, you came to me!" he exclaimed, opening his arms wide to embrace me, kissing me with a mouth I wanted to disappear into. We played and caressed. "I love to make love with you," he sighed contentedly. I told him I loved him, over and over.

"I can't handle all the love you give me," he said, a sentiment he often expressed.

"That's because you're resisting it and thinking it means expectation and obligation," I offered playfully.

"Maybe so," he replied. I could hear the reflection in his voice.

"I only want your honest expression, Ari. How could I ask for love at your expense?" I asked, cuddling closer to him. I felt him relax deeply as I stroked his hair, and he quickly fell asleep.

The following morning we talked about Willem. Ari had visited him the night before and said he didn't look good because of the chemo. I told him they both needed to talk about their feelings to resolve some of their childhood pain and that the closure would heal them. Ari became fidgety, attempting to change the subject. It was so hard for this family to talk about feelings.

Later, I spoke to Willem on the phone, and he became emotional. He wasn't ready. I consoled him and told him to be gentle with himself. *Two resistant peas in a pod*, I thought to myself.

It was late when Ari got in. He had spent the evening with some business associates. He had a headache because one of them had been smoking a cigar all night. He was exhausted, and his stomach hurt. I massaged him lightly, hoping he would doze off early to get some rest, but we stayed awake until after midnight. Lying in Ari's arms the following morning, I whispered, "I'm sad I won't get to wake up with you tomorrow morning."

"That makes two of us, Debra. You see, that's why it's bad—"

"Shhh...," I cut him off, rocking him. "Just let it be, Ari." What would he have done if I had agreed with him? I was reluctant to entertain that conversation because of where it might lead; I didn't want our love story to end.

Later as we ate breakfast in our room, he fixed his eyes on mine. "You're something else, Debra. Never a dull moment with you." His face was radiant, his smile soft and genuine, eyes lit with the light of love that I knew was the reality of our coming together. I beamed, holding his gaze deeply. "I haven't told Otto about you because he would be jealous." Otto was his most trusted friend. He was an accountant, a single man, who took an occasional opportunity with a woman. "Bed and breakfast," Ari said, laughing lightly. Otto was probably just like him, longing for real love, someone he could put his heart and trust in, scared to death of intimacy. Like all of us, I grinned to myself. "Do you think Rochelle would double date with us?" he asked demurely.

"You mean the four of us?" I raised my eyebrows in surprise. Did he want Otto to be a witness to our love?

"Yes, it would be fun to have some laughs," he said, carefully examining my expression.

"I don't know if she's coming back," I answered honestly. I didn't doubt Ari's propriety, but I didn't want to implicate Rochelle for "bed and breakfast."

Ari called me just before boarding his plane. He was exhausted but happy. He recalled the day we drove back from Fréjus and how I had pulled up my dress to give him a visual on the ride home. "No one has ever done that before, Debra," he said with mischievous delight. I was glad I'd given him something playful to think about.

I felt completely at ease with him sexually, something I had always longed for but never experienced with a man before. That was my barometer for love. Sexual intimacy was measured entirely by my heart. If there was doubt in one, there was doubt in the other. I trusted Ari on a level that went way beyond my thinking mind. It transcended all of my objections, judgments, and fears. With him, *inside him,* I was home.

* * *

IT WAS GOOD TO FEEL THE HEAT of the Riviera. I was glad to be back in France. I appreciated my tiny apartment with its French doors that I kept wide open all day to let in the glorious sunshine. Ari called me, and we chatted briefly.

"Debra, I let you down," he started.

"I don't feel that way *at all*, Ari. I was elated to share two beautiful nights with you!"

"I wanted to be able to take you to dinner and spend more time with you," he said, no doubt longing for some normalcy in our relationship. He had come in late after long meetings on both nights we had spent together in Amsterdam.

"I know you have a busy schedule. It's all okay," I said, content with our last visit. "I'm looking forward to the next time we are together. I want to love you without demands or expectations." The truth of that rang deeply in my heart.

I told him about my upcoming trip to Corsica with Nadine and Erik. He was glad I was filling up my time with travel, but I could hear a twinge of disappointment in his voice. I knew he wanted to be with me and take me to places in the world that he enjoyed. It was something we both longed for. I wanted to make love to him for the rest of my life.

"My dearest Debra, I give you the biggest hugs and all my love!" he saluted and hung up the phone.

CHAPTER 12

Two Feet In

Corsica was a much-needed trip for me. Mostly, it took my thoughts off of Ari and the mind-racing that usually went with it.

Nadine, Erik, and I departed Nice and landed in Calvi via cruise ship in the late morning. We drove the coast to Piana to see the famous "calanques," the exposed striated edge evident in certain parts of the island. The calanques were composed of layered limestone, dolomite, or other carbonate strata, making the island appear as a giant black-and-white striped layer cake bobbing high atop the sea.

"I'm so glad you are doing the driving, Debra," Erik said with a chuckle from the back seat. "As much as I appreciate these beautiful cliffs, I'm afraid of heights. I don't think I could drive on these roads." I liked Erik. He was easy-going and curious, enjoyed traveling, and had helped to plot out the sights we would visit on our trip. He didn't come to France often, but when he did, the three of us always went somewhere new, and it was exciting to explore places I'd never seen.

"You bet, Erik! As long as the Corsicans don't mind if I'm cautious near the drop-offs. We don't have roads like this back in New York, especially on Long Island, which is virtually flat. Even up in the mountains on the east coast, most roads are wide and paved, at least from what I've visited."

"It sounds a lot safer," Erik said, keeping his eye on the road. "I'd love to visit New York one day. Everyone knows about the city, but there isn't much talk about Long Island."

"The ocean beaches are beautiful. It's a little-known fact amongst outsiders, but that's fine with me," I said, recalling the crowds jamming the shoreline during the hot, humid months of July and August. "We've got such a large population that the shores are anything but desolate in the summer season."

"I've always wanted to go to New York too!" Nadine chimed in. "It's my dream to visit someday, and if there's time, I'd like to visit the beaches of Long Island. I've seen many pictures and videos, but I want to experience it for myself," she said longingly.

We drove along, chit-chatting and gaping at the spectacular heights. The scenery that hugged the coast was refreshingly different from the lower-lying coastline between Nice and Cannes. The sheer, plunging yellow-rock cliffs were stunning and dangerous, and there were no guard rails. The ofttimes rubbly roads were edged by a border wall less than a foot high. A reckless vehicle could easily careen off the narrow winding roadways at any time of the day or night, bouncing off of rocky, treed crags, tumbling straight into the vivid blue of the Mediterranean Sea far below.

Nadine and Erik would lean away when I was driving on the drop-off side, hugging tight to the car. Erik would sit behind me when they were on the drop-off side, and Nadine would lean toward me, almost in my lap. It was a hilarious ride as we held our breath and laughed our heads off, taking in the craggy, majestic scenery that left us breathless, humbled, and more than a little nervous.

Unsympathetic to our touristic plight, impatient delivery trucks would often flash their lights behind us or squeeze dangerously past us in either direction. The twisting road narrowed so dramatically in some areas that it was impossible for two-way traffic. At one point, an oncoming driver insisted I back up to let him pass. He was on the drop-off side, and although it may have been proper etiquette, I white-knuckled the steering wheel as I slowly proceeded backward. "Typical French," Nadine said, shaking her head. Although she was not French, I had heard those exact words uttered from many a Frenchman's lips.

We stopped briefly in Porto for a quick lunch and then headed to Piana. We parked at one of the scenic overlooks and walked down to the beach. There were various natural rock formations along the path and small human-made cairns, upon which we added a token stone or two. We sat on the beach at Erik's request and meditated for a little while. I felt the sun and the gently lapping shoreline stilling me while simultaneously re-energizing my physical body. Afterward, we drove to the outskirts of Corte to meet Véronique, Nadine's sister-in-law, a travel agent who had arranged our stay in Corte.

We followed her through Défilé da la Scala di Santa Regina in the misty darkness on route D84, a breathtakingly scenic, narrow roadway built in the nineteenth century that meandered through the rocky granite thousand-foot-high gorge gouged by the Golo river through the untamed Corsican wilderness. We wound our way slowly in the dark, oblivious to the sheer magnificence of Corsica's highest peaks looming before us, its plunging cliffs toppling into the unseen white rushes of the winding river below. I felt a pang of disappointment to be missing these superb views as we would not be heading back on this roadway, instead making our way east to d'Orezza, to taste the iron-laden water for which it was famous. Nadine and Erik were relieved. There would be plenty of white-knuckle landscape over the next few days.

As I drove, I leaned forward close to the steering wheel, keeping my eyes on Véronique's taillights waxing and waning in the heavy fog. I wondered what she was keeping *her* eyes on as we proceeded along the largely unlit roadway to our hotel on the river.

The next day, we made our way to Bergeries de Grotelle in hopes of seeing Lac de Melo, a spectacular glacial lake in the pristine Vallé de la Restonica. Nadine was intimidated by the steep, rocky climb, so we forfeited the adventure, opting for a short walk from the parking area to the lower banks of the river Restonica.

After, we headed to d'Orezza, marveling at the sensational views on some of the most magnificent mountain roads I'd ever driven. We stopped at a high point and could see the west coast of Corsica from where we were on the northeastern part of the island. Later, we returned to Corte to meet with Véronique and her husband for some of the best lasagna I'd ever had in Europe, laden with beef, pork, veal, and sumptuous cheeses. I enjoyed my first taste of Muscat, a fragrant, sherry-like wine aperitif indigenous to

Corsica, and chestnut cake, a sweet and savory cross between cake and bread, its dense, rustic flavor a first-time delight.

The following day, we tumbled out of bed early for the long drive to Bonifacio, located at the island's southern tip. We checked into a grossly overstated three-star hotel with sagging mattresses that we had to throw on the floor for support. A loud, malfunctioning air conditioning unit did little to obliterate the street noise below, and we showered in a stall missing a shower curtain, but we laughed and made the most of it.

We had come for the beautiful scenery and rich stratified rock formations, ledges, and caves epitomizing the port town. We took a boat tour, visiting the calanques and entering one of the striated caves. Erik and I walked down and then up "L'escalier du roi d'Aragon," a 187-step plunging staircase carved at a forty-five-degree incline into the limestone cliff centuries prior. Descending from the Pointe du Timon, the site of the Citadel of Bonifacio, to the beautiful sandy and rocky shoreline beach at the base of the cliff, the stairway overlooked the strait of Bouches de Bonifacio southward to the Island of Sardinia.

Heading out early again the following morning, we set our compass northwest to the tiny-pebbled beaches and crystal-clear waters of the well-protected bay of Propriano at sea level on the west coast, forty miles from Bonifacio. We scrunched along barefoot on one of the beaches. "The tiny pebbles are like a micro-massage for our feet!" Erik exclaimed, happily digging his feet into the shoreline as we strolled along the pretty beach.

We set out for Ajaccio, the port Capitol city of Corsica and the birthplace of Napoleon Bonaparte. Ajaccio's white sandy beaches sprawled for miles, and its turquoise and pale blue waters were some of the prettiest in Corsica. We didn't have much time for the beautiful resort city, as we had to catch our boat back to Nice later that afternoon. We snapped some pictures of Napoleon's monuments, took a quick stroll around town to buy a few souvenirs, ate another fantastic lasagna with chunky garden vegetables, aromatic basil, and gobs of fresh cheese, and headed for our boat in Calvi.

Later that evening, we enjoyed an Indonesian chicken dinner at Nadine's house, which Erik had lovingly prepared. "How did you learn to cook like this, Erik?" I asked, reaching for the "sambal kacang" sauce he had prepared.

"My mother is Indonesian. I grew up eating this kind of food," he said cheerily.

I stuffed another piece of the tender chicken into my mouth. The homemade sweet and spicy peanut sauce clung thickly to the succulent chunks of white meat, and I smacked my lips as I hungrily dabbed it all over the sticky jasmine rice and tender-steamed green beans. I could have eaten it like soup!

* * *

ARI PHONED LATER THAT EVENING. "How do you feel, Debra? Do you need a massage?" he teased me. Did I ever! He needed one as well. We set our sights on Zurich, and I hoped we could meet there soon. I had seen him only two weeks prior, but I missed him, frustrated by the space inherent in our relationship.

"You are his refuge, Debra; Ari trusts you. You're taking his absence too personally. He is having trouble keeping it all together. He's overwhelmed, and he sees what he does not have. He has no comfort, joy, or safety," Concetta reminded me over the phone. "Things are happening that you don't know about." She paused. "He's scared and feels obligated. He had children with Celeste. And the loss of his brother will cause deep suffering for him, more than he even knows. There is a ping-pong game going on in his head. He's trying to take care of business to be with you. You have to keep steady. Things will shift, and you will be guided. He has no one else to talk to about this. Your relationship with him is so strong. No one in the Universe can compete with you for his love. You don't need to worry about Katrina; she is not an issue. She is a true friend to him." Concetta paused again, receiving the message that was coming through to her. "This is the beginning of the end of his relationship with his old life. He's shifting, and his wife feels it. Her radar is up. It wasn't up with Katrina because she wasn't a threat. He's feeling emptiness without you, which he's never experienced before. You make him *feel.* You opened the locked door."

"Wow," I breathed, moved to stillness, the intensity of her words bathing my heart, touching the vulnerability deep within, like little fingers of light stroking the part of me that was just as frightened as Ari was.

"The obstacles will help him move," she continued confidently. "They are part of the reason he's shifting. He needs to know that you miss him and adore him. Tell him that you will take a plane on a moment's notice. He doesn't understand his feelings. Give him time; he is trying to work things out. Trust. Be patient. Things *will* shift."

With all of Concetta's enduring guidance, how was it that I could slip back into the unconsciousness of my cogitating, doubting mind? I was intensely grateful for her ability to bring forth the deep, unjudging wisdom from an unfathomable, wordless wellspring that communicated utter unconditionality, indelible presence, and infinite patience as I navigated the greatest love I had ever known.

It was the scariest of places for me, dredging up guilt, hypervigilance, and feelings of unworthiness, erupting from a deeply self-judgmental conscience that came from believing I had to play by the rules. Fingers could be pointed from any direction, hurling daggers of condemnation. "What you are doing is wrong, wrong, wrong!" they would sing like a great cosmic chorus of vultures, plucking at the quivering strings of my exposed heart. How could I be true to myself as a person of integrity who unwaveringly followed her deepest directive? Was there an answer that spanned two seemingly disparate perspectives?

"Why are you questioning yourself when all you feel is love for him?" Concetta asked. "They brought you together, so why would they want you not to be? You asked for your heart's desire." I was making this an issue. "They" didn't see it as one. "You are listening to society's rules," Concetta continued. "You are not living in the moment of your truth. You've never had this feeling before. The guilt you feel has nothing to do with reality. You are choosing it; they are not giving it to you. The gift is *now*." Her guides had shown Concetta an image. "When you open your heart to Ari, it's shooting stars." I heard the breathiness in her voice as she shared this with me. Yes, it was all that and more. It was true that I was closing myself off. "Love and fear cannot live in the same place. You are creating an end for something that has just begun." Concetta's words hovered in the air; I could hear the pangs of frustration in her voice.

"I am just as conflicted as Ari is," I said.

"No one is judging you but you. They would be very saddened if you chose not to grab that star. It would be a big mistake to let go. Ari would be devastated if you walked away. This love is frightening and amazing, joyful, and terrifying for him. He *truly* loves you. You wanted a man with a sense of duty, obligation, and responsibility, but it extends outward, and you can't expect him to be less in other circumstances." That was true. I respected Ari for his sense of commitment to everyone in his world, including me. He had always ensured I was taken care of long before we became intimate. He saw it as his responsibility to see that I had everything I needed in my paradise on the coast of southern France. Concetta continued steadily, "you don't understand what marriage is. You are more 'married' to Ari than Celeste is. The love in your heart is what true marriage is. Ari stayed with her because of children and material things." Her guides showed her a picture of quicksand. "Theirs is not a true marriage."

"Society would definitely argue that point," I said soberly.

"You know in your heart that you love and trust him. The old wounds you are living are those *you* are choosing. Ari *is* your heart's desire, and there should be no question. This is your chance to live fully and with love. You are being presented with the opportunity to trust and move forward. Everything will be worked out. Give it the time to do so."

I wanted to stay in a trusting space where my love for Ari could flourish. It was hard to stave off his guilt and my own, which sometimes felt like two freight trains colliding. I was thankful for the guidance I received, which resonated deeply as the truth in my heart of hearts.

"You and Ari are so connected that he picks up on your conflict. I'm surprised you don't read each other's minds," Concetta chuckled.

"Sometimes we do," I offered quietly.

"You can shift out of the doubt," Concetta said gently but firmly. She wanted it too. I sometimes felt like Joan of Arc, carrying a torch for all the women in the world with sensitive hearts. Hearts that were broken open, longing to receive a love that proved what we sought could be found in the flesh of another who hungered for the same. Before he'd met me, was there a place inside Ari that longed for the richness, fullness, and expansiveness that our relationship offered? Did he recognize my coming as such, like I could for his presence in my life? He didn't have someone like Concetta to guide him, draw on the wisdom of the ageless, the timeless, the otherworldliness, the heart of cosmic consciousness. Maybe he didn't need it. His heart would see him through. His was a remarkable, formidable spirit, gentle but utterly pursuant as he followed his passions, with only his gut to guide him. "He is in a spider's web. You have to shift to help both yourself *and* him." Concetta's guidance was unwavering. "Freedom is in his future."

I wished I'd had her certainty. Could I just let go and allow life to live itself through me?

* * *

ERIK WAS STILL IN TOWN. I invited him, Nadine, and Theo to a dinner of shrimp parmigiana with angel hair pasta, a veritable stick-to-your-ribs comfort meal. I'd bought a new, bold floral tablecloth splashed with large magenta peonies and bright green leaves, with napkins to match. I unquestionably enjoyed having guests in my home. I felt warm and happy. I played some music and bustled around cooking and preparing as I waited for my guests to arrive, my comfortable friends who were almost family. I smiled as I thought of them sitting around the table in lively conversation, gracing my space with their presence and laughter.

Nadine and I would be booking our flight to the States soon. I was excited to bring her to meet my family and friends, connecting the two worlds I called home and showing her New York. She had never been there, and it was her long-held dream that she would one day be able to visit. The Universe was working diligently on making all of our dreams come true. We were vehicles for each other's delight and expansion.

Notwithstanding all the upcoming adventures, my mind continued to plague me, and I thanked God for Tina's objectivity. I'd been in a tailspin for days, questioning everything despite Concetta's incredible reading. All of my issues were rearing their ugly heads, and I felt very out of control internally.

Tina pointed out that all of the issues I had concerning Ari were surrounding the core experience I'd had in childhood: my father's alcoholism was emotionally life-threatening to the child inside me, *and I could not die that death again.* The issue was so deeply obfuscating that I was cutting myself off from my own love and *heart,* and I couldn't—*wouldn't*—allow myself to "feel" Ari's love for me, the loss of which would be unspeakably devastating. I burst into tears, letting the tension bound into the cellular memory of my being drain from my body, unwinding the cords gripping my chest, throat, shoulders, and aching brain. I nodded in tearful recognition as the "thlunk" of her wise arrow plunged accurately into the soft, fleshy bullseye of my heart. I let the tears bleed out of me as she spoke, feeling numb and relieved.

The following afternoon, Ari came to my apartment. Soon we would be flying to Holland for a couple of nights, and he wanted to take me to dinner while we were there. He asked me again if I planned on returning to the States to live. "I am staying *here*, Ari," I said firmly. It was interesting how we each had our tracts of doubt. I told him to open his heart to receive my love.

"What about your heart, Debra? Is it open?" his voice gently questioned.

"It is. I am letting your love in," I asserted. Was I? We talked about knowing each other, and he said that he was sometimes closed emotionally, that it was part of his character. "I disagree. I think your real self is very open, trusting, and sensitive, and that you learned to shut down because of the hurts in your life."

"I feel fear in this relationship," he said, his voice revealing his vulnerability. He was quiet, awaiting my reply.

"I do too, Ari. But I'm trusting God." We both had so much to lose and gain as our hearts surfed the emotional turbulence that could be briskly whipped up on the winds of doubt or wiped away by a tender kiss. "The more you let the relationship grow, the more you will open up and trust me," I said confidently, feeling my commitment to him solidly within my center.

He seemed content with my reply. "I look forward to letting the relationship grow, Debra," he said and mentioned other things growing, lightening the conversation. We both giggled.

"I wish I could read *A Course In Miracles* to you every night," I said reflexively, longing for a future that promised freedom for our union.

"There will come a time when you can do that, but not right now. It is still new for me," he said. I appreciated his honesty. These were the guiltless moments when I felt most blessed.

Inevitably, the emotional see-sawing would begin, plunging the conversation into the doldrums. "Debra, there is no future for us."

"You don't know that," I countered, exhausted by his conclusions. "You shouldn't look so far into the future," I continued, reminding myself to heed my advice. It was painful, but I encouraged him to share his feelings with me, remembering what Concetta had said about the ping-pong game in Ari's head and that he only had me to help him process. It was a challenge, but I did my best to be patient. "Neither of us knows why God brought us together. Maybe you could look at us as a gift," I said gently. "No matter what happens for us, I will always love you and be here for you," I said, letting what I knew to be true define the moment.

"We have such a high-level relationship, Debra. I will always be here for you too," he sighed.

"Our relationship is based on respect, trust, and honesty. I appreciate your sense of responsibility and obligation," I said.

"I feel so split," he said soberly. I could hear the gravity in his voice. I knew Ari was struggling intensely with the guilt he felt. It was understandable that these feelings made him feel like he was living two separate lives. "I never share my emotions with anyone," he said tentatively.

I rested my head on his chest. "I'm here for all of it."

"Debra, how does my heartbeat sound? I have a heart murmur," he said, redirecting the conversation. Since Willem had been diagnosed with cancer, he had become more vigilant about his health.

"I can hear that," I said, my head pressed against his thorax, listening to the heart I loved beating in my ear. From what I understood, heart murmurs were common, and some were transient depending on other factors, like blood pressure. He hadn't seemed concerned and had just received a clean bill of health from the doctor during his MRI follow-up, so I wasn't alarmed. "That's because you had a broken heart. I'm here to fix it," I said lovingly, squeezing him tightly.

Later, he called me to say goodnight. I told him to let all his troubles go and to read one of the books I had given him before he went to sleep. I told him how wonderfully satisfied I was after his visit. I knew how much he adored pleasing me. "I feel marvelous," he remarked. "I'm going to take a bath and go to sleep."

The next day I hoped to see him again. I was a bit tense, awaiting the final decision, knowing plans with him could change in a moment. I let myself hover in the tension without letting it grab hold of any particular place inside me.

He called in the afternoon just before three o'clock and invited me for tea in his guesthouse. The staff had set up a massage table he had bought for the premises, and I no longer had to lug mine around.

I gave him the "old" massage I had always given him before our romance began. "Do you remember what happened on April 9th?" I teased him. He didn't. "That was the first day we made love."

"I haven't had a *real* massage since April 9th!" he exclaimed.

"You don't have to make it sound like the end of the world," I laughed.

"I made love to you for four hours," he bragged.

"That was the best sex I've ever had," I said, drawing out the words for emphasis. It was true. My body opened like a flower to his touch. I felt adored by him. Safe. I massaged him for two hours, as I had done many times. He called me later that evening before bed. "Well, hello, marathon man," I teased.

"We should be in the Olympics, Debra!" His tone was relaxed and playful.

"I always wanted a gold medal."

"I will give you one!" he heartily exclaimed.

"My gold medal is hanging between your legs," I said. We both laughed, thoroughly enjoying our sensual banter.

"The weekend was fantastic for me," I wrote in my journal, happy to have spent part of Saturday and Sunday with him. I was fulfilled. "I continue to commit to him because I know it will be right for me no matter what happens. I have both feet in the door. I love you, Ari! I stand beside you," I wrote.

I closed my journal and exhaled deeply, expelling the love I felt for him into the space around me. I recalled his words to me on Saturday. "Debra, I will always support you in whatever you do. I will stand beside you, behind you, in front of you, in every way. I will *always* be your friend."

I knew there would be more doubts, more questioning, the gripping sensation of insecurity voicing its ever-presence beneath the surface. But it was true; I had two feet in. I had shifted, stepped across the threshold. I wanted to be Ari's wife, which is the direction I would move in. Brick by brick, I was building a bridge. I was enjoying our "now." But I also knew that he would always be my friend and that whatever happened between us, we would be happy. It was our collective desire. It could only, unerringly, be so.

Ari called me at 9:30 a.m. and sang me a slightly out-of-tune Happy Birthday. "I miss you so much, Debra." I let myself settle into his soft voice. With him, I felt safe, seen, and beautiful. The prior evening, he'd sent me a text: "Let me be the first to wish you a happy and great birthday. All my hugs."

Theo and his kids had tied three dozen colored balloons to my bushes and given me roses. For lunch, Gwyn and Nadine took me to Chateau de la Napoule, a fortified castle from the fourteenth century in Mandelieu. It was one of my favorite places. We sat outside along the edge of the wall to enjoy the beautiful sea lapping gently just below. I rolled my eyes in reverence to the chef as I savored my Moroccan chicken, my taste buds rejoicing in its effervescent, lemony succulence.

I couldn't have been happier. The early-autumn day was warm but not overpowering. We celebrated over lunch as the sun glinted off our wine glasses, lighting up the beautiful pink of the Côte de Rhone rosé. I was undoubtedly the luckiest girl in the world. I had friends that made my heart sing and loved a man whose touch melted me like butter. I was in love with life, *my* life, this beautiful French Riviera dream in which I had awakened. I clung to these moments, aware of their fleeting preciousness, capturing them as best I could in my memory, my journal, the words always falling short of the sights, sounds, smells, and textures that came to life every morning as I opened my eyes.

Shortly after arriving home, I received an enormous bouquet of gorgeous, long-stemmed vanilla-colored roses. Nadine gasped. "From Mr. Sorensen?!" I nodded, my heart bursting, longing to tell her we were in love.

Just before midnight, Ari called again. He wanted to be the *last* to wish me a happy birthday.

* * *

ARI CAME OVER TWICE the following week. "I want to take you to Italy with me for a couple of days to wake up together," he said as we lay in each other's arms. "We can share joy and laughter, and I will kiss you with all my love." I hugged him tightly. He was exhausted from an arduous business deal he had just completed with a group of American investors. We made love, and he fell asleep with our lips touching!

I knew our relationship was causing a tremendous moral dilemma for him, as it was for me. I had not been the first woman outside of his marriage. "If I did it to Celeste, I could do it to you," he had once said. He didn't trust himself, but I knew he would be faithful to me. He had never been in love. He had also said *that* to me.

There were days his guilt reared up strongly, and he would declare, finger pointed to the sky, "I will never leave my wife," as if it were a battle cry.

"How do you know what the future holds?" I asked him at one of these moments.

"I made a promise," he said disparagingly.

His words stabbed at my chest. It was the Achilles' heel of our relationship, repeatedly bobbing to the surface like a cork, unsinkable, buoyed by the deep waters of his entanglement, guilt, and the facts at hand. Was he willing to die by the self-prescribed sword he held precariously over his head? It was not for me to decide. All I could do was choose for myself and let my heart love as it wanted; pure, exposed, and vulnerable. "I love you, Ari." I steadily held his gaze.

He beheld me and smiled, kissing me gently, making his own choices. "I love you too," he said softly. His tone was quiet, defenseless, shorn of self-contempt.

Later that evening, I prayed for our relationship. For truth, trust, and the highest good. I prayed with the power of a lover's heart and holding Ari's heart within my own I prayed for his prayers to be that too.

CHAPTER 13

You Were Invented for Me

I hadn't heard from Ari in nearly a week. I knew he was in Croatia with his family. I wondered what he was feeling and thinking. I missed him but felt very grounded in myself, worthy. I AM, I thought to myself, feeling connected and at peace with the world. I felt a joyful presence, hearing each bird sing its unique song. I listened to the ticking of my clock and the sound of my pen scratching paper as I journaled. I heard a car horn in the distance and the low droning of my refrigerator. I saw different colors and textures all around me, alive and loving me. I could feel Ari, near and far. I had not given up "me" for "him." I sensed my "self," felt my love for him glowing in the center of my chest, strong, accepting, without desperation. I was unattached to anything being any particular way.

Stillness enveloped me, bathing the world in shimmering light. I contemplated desire and longing. I could disengage from these emotions when I remembered who I was beyond form. Although I knew Ari was a soul mate, a fellow traveler, I could experience us as separate individuals, even in our joining. I could experience the gift of sharing love, knowing it comes through us—to us, as inexhaustible and eternal. There is only gain by loving. My commitment to Ari was ultimately a commitment to myself, a promise to let myself love fully, freely, and completely. I could spend the rest of my life with him or without him and let the honesty of each moment choose its eternity. Whatever was real between us could not be threatened.

I arose from my bed, where I'd sat writing. Placing my bare soles on the cold tiled floor, I walked into the living room and let the afternoon sun warm my feet as I stood in the sunlight streaked across the carpet through my wide-open French doors. I stepped outside into the full mantle of the brilliant Riviera sunshine. I looked lovingly at my flowers, rimming the edges of the patio in radiant color, their velvety, petaled faces filling me with deferent joy. I stretched my arms high into the bluest blue sky, arching my back and letting my spine elongate as I sucked in a sweet breath of fresh autumn air. I was in love—a love like no other.

Ari came over that evening at five o'clock. I had wanted to give him a massage, but we both became quickly excited and went straight to the bedroom. This evening could be leisurely, as he had time to relax.

"I drew a tree for your mother when I visited her," I said cheerfully.

He raised his eyebrows. "She asked you to draw a tree?"

"Yes, so she could read things about my life," I offered.

He propped himself up on his elbow. "What did she see?"

"She saw me with an older man I would be with for the rest of my life. She asked me if I knew who he was. I told her he was close," I said, remembering how much I wanted to tell her it was her son. "It's you, Ari," I said, holding his gaze as his eyes deepened.

"Really? I'm the one for you?" he asked. Taken by his innocence, I realized why I loved him so. He didn't take what we had for granted. Anything or everything could change instantly, and we both knew it.

"Yes...you are," I said definitively.

"But I enjoy my freedom," he said, still holding my gaze.

"I would never take that away from you. I need freedom, too," I said.

"Are you sure I'm not too old for you?" he asked.

"Not at all." I pulled him close and kissed him. I liked the maturity of an older man. There was a confidence, a willingness to share himself as he was, the wisdom of his years, his observations about life. He didn't want or need to change anything about me, and I felt it through and through. For a man, maybe that came in later years. I hadn't seen it so much with men I'd dated who were my age. There was a striving that didn't exist with Ari. We accepted each other as we were. Our obstacles were external and far away for now.

"This is the best time we've had yet, Debra." He relaxed into my embrace.

"We're only just beginning, Ari," I whispered contentedly.

"Your belated birthday present will be ready in November." He had mentioned it a couple of times. I could hardly imagine what it was. It made no matter to me. He was my gift. "When you're back from your trip to the States, I will take you to Italy." I smiled. He said this nearly every time we were together. We had talked about Portofino a few times, and I knew he wanted to make it happen. Maybe he, too, was carrying a torch for our love.

I felt less enamored, less electric, more comfortable and grounded in his presence. I imagined a long-term relationship with him would feel like this, drawing on a deeply bonded friendship and mutual respect.

* * *

WE DISCUSSED HIS ONGOING DILEMMA with the American lawyers when Ari returned the following week. He was a little embarrassed and frustrated by all the delays. He didn't understand the ways of the lawyers in the U.S. and felt there was a lot of "overkill." Yes, I thought, that must be frustrating for a European man. After all, he and I had consummated our work agreement on a handshake.

I was delighted to have seen him three weekends in a row. He shared a dream with me that was unsettling for him. He was in a room with a thin man and a woman. They were all undressed. The woman was wearing sexy undergarments and headed toward the bathroom, but what struck him was the man. He had no penis, and there was a big burn scar in its place. He was appalled and could not figure out who the man and woman were or what the dream meant.

"Maybe the man represented the part of you that feels guilty about having sex with me," I said.

Ari pursed his lips. "Sometimes, I think about going back to our old relationship."

"I love you, Ari. I accept you, and I understand what you are saying," I said, allowing him the space to say whatever he needed.

"There are no secrets between us, Debra." It was true, but his circumstances were painful for us both. All we could do was take things one day at a time.

"You don't know what the future holds," I said. It was my placeholder for things to change.

"Neither do you," he said gently, countering my response. Of course, neither one of us knew. I just knew I wanted him to be mine. He paused, shifting gears. "Your birthday present will be ready in December," he said, pulling me towards him.

"I'm so excited!" I exclaimed.

"Why is that Debra?" he asked.

"Because it's from you! Although by then, it will have become a Christmas present!" We laughed heartily.

* * *

THE FOLLOWING WEEK, Ari called me from Olympia. He and Brock had begun the Tour du Péloponnèse, zooming around the gorgeous coast and historic landscapes of the beautiful Greek peninsula, their posse in tow.

I knew Katrina was accompanying him on this trip. She had for many years. She was part of the enormous "tribe" that dangled from his mainframe like a thousand separate tentacles, connected only by their association with him, the king of his self-created empire.

I was envious. I wanted to join Ari in something meaningful. I trusted they were just friends, as Katrina was now dating another man, but I wanted to share something with him publicly among people he respected and trusted. I didn't want our love to be secret anymore. Concetta said I must be patient, but would our union ever be seen by the world?

Ari phoned the next evening to say goodnight. It had been raining in Péloponnèse, making driving more challenging. All in all, he was having a good time. I missed him but was looking forward to chorus practice and hiking over the next few days.

I awoke the following morning after a dream, feeling him near as if his very breath were on my cheek. Unexpectedly, I felt a tiny wall encircling my heart. I started to cry. Why did I choose this situation? Was Ari *really* the right man for me? I felt our coming together was so divinely guided. Would he ever leave Celeste? Was I naively refusing to accept the statistics about a married man? Did I have to walk away?

Our additive guilt was sometimes too much for me to bear. Didn't Ari see a way out? Or was he *unwilling* to get out, to extricate himself from the self-created entanglements he seemed to loathe and cherish simultaneously? It would be "too easy," he had once told me. Was he just too afraid to take a chance, a stand? I *knew* he loved me. I *knew* I was his heart's desire. I also knew he had never been in love. Is that what he'd meant when he said it was too easy? Was there not enough strife, struggle, or guilt inherent in our relationship to allow him to extricate himself from his present circumstances? If it was "too easy," was it then invalid? Was he carrying a torch for guilt? Was I?

I'd recently joined the International Women's Club of the Riviera (IWCR). I went on a couple of hikes and adored the coastal countryside, the "pays de cotier." I bought all the necessary gear to go on the "randonnées." Ari said it was a "snob club," but I didn't care. I had already made a couple of friends who were down-to-earth and fun. Some were originally from France, but many were expatriates from other parts of Europe.

A few women were visiting the coast for a week, and I was happy to take them to some of my favorite places. In the old commune of Saint-Paul-de-Vence, we window-shopped at the plentiful shops and art galleries that epitomized the popular, affluent village and stopped to eat lunch at a small outdoor café where a group of older men were playing boules in the dirt courtyard.

Afterward, we drove up to Tourrettes-sur-Loup, where Gwyn lived and one of the first places I'd taken Rochelle. I never tired of the charming village perched high atop a rocky spur of the surrounding gorges of La Brague river. We indulged in a tasty scoop of "violet" ice cream, an exquisite, lavender-colored confection crafted from the abundant local flower.

Heading back down to the coast, we stopped in Mandelieu, so the ladies could visit the Château de la Napoule, where I had lunched on my birthday with Nadine and Gwyn and took a walk on the beach nearby. Later, we dined al fresco in Antibes, exchanging lively conversation over a delightful, fruity Côte de Provence rosé and a tasty platter of cheese, dried fruit, and salami, recounting the day's adventures.

* * *

FIVE DAYS LATER, I arrived late in Amsterdam and checked into the quaint Hotel Amstelzicht near Rembrandtplein, where I had first stayed when I visited Holland. I awoke in the morning to the roar of a sanitation truck making its daily rounds. My *Course In Miracles* lesson for the day said, "I will receive whatever I request." I decided to let go and let everything unfold without trying to effort my way through a plan.

After a breakfast of fruit and yogurt, I stepped out into the chilly November day to purchase some massage oil for Ari and a beautiful bouquet of crimson daisies and hydrangea for Faye and Willem. I had brought along some candies from the local confectioner in Nice. French chocolates were superior to any I'd had in Europe, including Switzerland or Belgium.

It was a quick tram ride to Stadionplein, where Thomas waited to take me to the hospital. Ari arrived at the hospital shortly afterward with Honey, who embraced me in a huge hug. I politely kissed Ari's cheek, and he exclaimed, "Debra, you know my whole family!"

We had a lively visit, but Willem was very emotional by the time I'd left. He had pneumonia and was on morphine, making it difficult to speak. His body had become frail, and I wondered how long he would live. Faye seemed more relaxed around me, and I hoped she understood that I was just a friend to Willem. I wanted to see him on my return from the States.

After my visit, Thomas dropped me off at the train station in Amstelveen, just outside Amsterdam. I indulged in some delicious sushi while waiting for my train and was back in the hotel by three o'clock. Two hours later, Ari called me on his phone from the other side of the door. In seconds we were in each other's arms, stumbling to the bed. He held me tightly afterward. "Debra, when I make love to you, I give you *all* my love." I could feel the shift. It had been happening over the past couple of months. And what his lips couldn't always say, his body could.

"I love you too," I sighed as he held me close, rocking me.

Afterward, we enjoyed a late romantic dinner at a nearby gourmet restaurant and gazed out the window at a cobbled footbridge arcing elegantly over a narrow canal. Dinner conversation was varied, and Ari told me again that he would take me to Portofino in December. I smiled. Portofino had become his clarion call. It didn't make a difference to me where we went. "I am in the presence of an exceptional woman," he said softly, his eyes penetrating deeply into mine.

He phoned Thomas two hours later to retrieve us. It was hard not to kiss him goodnight as we arrived at my hotel. I stood on the curb, and he smiled sweetly, waving from behind his closed window as they pulled away. I wondered what Thomas was thinking. Was he able to pick up on the vibe between us? Still in the car, Ari called me to say goodnight. He couldn't offer much more, but I teased him, saying I could feel his "transcendental communication."

* * *

IT WAS THE DAY BEFORE MY TRIP back to the States. It was already late, and I doubted if Ari, having met with one of his finance people from Paris, would be able to stop by before my trip. I shrugged; he would make it happen if he wanted to be here. He did.

I gave him a full massage. He felt incredibly pampered. "I'm going to miss your laughter, your hands, your sense of humor, your texts, and your pussy." We giggled. "I'm selling off my golf courses in France because I need more time for myself and to spend with you." We lingered, contentedly entwined, enjoying the warmth of our attachment. Sex was so much fun with him; my heart and soul felt incredibly free and alive, completely unselfconscious.

The shift between us was palpable, and I trusted Ari completely. I would miss him, but I was excited about bringing Nadine to New York for an extended Thanksgiving Holiday. I knew I would return home into his waiting arms. It was *clear* to me now. We were invisibly connected by a golden string, inseverable. I felt unspeakably lucky and divinely blessed to live a life where I felt loved and appreciated. Sometimes the heavenly orchestration blew my mind. My simple request had turned into a full-blown fairy tale. "You were invented for me, Debra," Ari said. Perhaps I was.

* * *

CHRISTMAS WAS QUICKLY APPROACHING. I would be spending it in Holland with Nadine and some of her family. She and I were still giddy from our whirlwind trip to New York. Her dream had indeed come true.

We'd stayed in New York City for four days and crammed as much as we could into our brief stay: The Empire State Building (Nadine was both thrilled and terrified on the eighty-sixth-floor outdoor observatory), a visit to the New York Helmsley Hotel, Rockefeller Center, and the gorgeous architecture and stained glass windows of St. Patrick's Cathedral, dinner at Patsy's (where we spied Liza Minelli), the Broadway play *Mama Mia*, a fantastic helicopter ride that swept up the East River from the South Street Seaport to Grand Central Park, and back down along the Hudson River taking in all the beautiful sights and bridges. It was late fall, and I was breathless as we hovered high above Central Park, agape at the trees in red, orange, and yellow tufts like broccoli heads far below us.

We took a subway from the South Street Seaport over the East River to Brooklyn Heights. We stood on the windy Promenade, ogling back at lower Manhattan's iconic, soaring skyline, its mirrored facade shimmering like a gigantic constellation of quartz crystals. We took taxis and walked for miles. We stayed near Times Square with its famous looming marquis and traversed Grand Central Station under Orion's ethereal gaze from the ceiling high above. We ogled at the art, arches, and architecture of the New York Public Library—as otherworldly as the Sistine Chapel, ambled Central Park, took pictures of the carousel, and dined in the opulent, windowed dining room at Tavern on the Green. We strolled around artsy SoHo and the Village and took the Circle-Line cruise around the Statue of Liberty. We ate lox and bagels, New York pizza, and Peking duck in Chinatown, and noshed on "street food" like roasted chestnuts, gyros, sugared peanuts, and potato knishes. Nadine tasted her first hotdog, and by the look on her face, I knew it would be her last.

We returned to my parent's home on Long Island, where I grew up. After a few romping days of visiting some of my closest friends (Tina, Concetta, Rochelle, Shane, and a few others), Mom, Dad, Nadine, and I drove down to Delaware, where my sister lived, for the Thanksgiving Holiday.

While there, Nadine met Derek and Anthony, and she and I took a quick day trip to Philadelphia. We walked around the Old City, saw the Liberty Bell, visited Independence Hall, and lunched at City Tavern (circa 1754), where the waitstaff served us dressed in period style.

It was great fun having Nadine with me for Thanksgiving. She had never seen a raw turkey. It became a photo shoot before, during, and after its journey into and out of my sister's oven.

Nadine enjoyed my little family, and it was nice to have them meet someone from France who had become a good friend. It was the happiest Thanksgiving I could remember, and the first time I felt assured about my return to France. I missed Ari but felt secure in our love. I knew we only had eyes for each other. I had everything my heart desired, the way I always dreamed it would be.

CHAPTER 14

The Impossible Dream

Nadine and I each had a three-seater for the plane ride back to Nice. I stretched out comfortably and slept solidly for a few hours of the overnight trip home.

My heart was humming with contentment. I had seen Concetta for a Tarot reading before leaving New York, and the future seemed bright for Ari and me. She saw us getting engaged and married! She had maintained that he would "see-saw" throughout the experience of separating from Celeste and told me not to judge this process but listen patiently, stand beside him, and be his strength; I was a catalyst for his ability to leave.

* * *

DECEMBER WAS UPON US. Nadine and I gave our deposit to the bus company for our five-day trip to Rome in April. We were excited. Neither of us had ever been to Rome.

I loved my life. How lucky could one girl be? It was a beautiful fairy tale, and everything always fell into place; I had good friends, exciting travel, and was deeply in love. Precisely what I had dreamed of, I felt I had "arrived" into my beautiful life. I had been studying *A Course In Miracles* for over a year, and my sense of connection to a higher source allowed me to stay grounded within myself, knowing things would always turn out for the best.

Concetta had no good news about how Ari's family would conduct themselves as he and I moved forward with our relationship. Was I ready for this? The drama would surely be enormous, as there were strong egos on both sides of his family. Neither he nor I wanted to hurt anyone, and we took our promises seriously. I had never fallen in love with a man who had first been a friend, and we'd had ample time to get to know one another. I had been in France for over a year, our friendship solidly forged when destiny sounded its romantic thunderclap.

Our mutual admiration bordered on reverence. "Sometimes I wish we could go back to how it used to be," he had said more than once. "I don't ever want to lose our friendship." That spoke volumes to me of what my presence in his life meant.

I wanted the "happily ever after," but my feelings also made me realize how much I feared commitment and was frightened of making a mistake. I didn't want to get into something that ultimately was not right for him or me. Could I make a lasting commitment to Ari? How much space did I need?

* * *

THE DECEMBER SUN SHINED warm and bright. My French doors were opened to let in the fresh air. I pulled out the dead summer plants that were brown and drooping in my garden. Ari arrived a couple of hours later to spend a few precious hours with me. I flung my arms around him. "I missed you!" I trilled. "I love you. I want you. I *need* you!"

"You need me?" he raised his eyebrows slightly, straightening his spine.

"Of course!" Didn't he know that? I was crazy about him. Every inch of me ached for this man who delighted my senses.

In moments, he was lying on his back, me on top. "Kiss me," he whispered. I bent closer, and he enveloped me firmly. His words tumbled out urgently, spilling over, too long contained. "Don't ever leave me, Debra."

"Oh Ari, I could never leave you!" My words gushed forth as I embraced him, any remaining doubt, resistance, or judgment released like a cork from a champagne bottle. The moment was decisive, shrouding us like an umbrella as we clung to each other.

"Hold me…" he entreated softly. "You do love me, don't you?" his voice implored. I could barely believe he still questioned this.

"Don't *ever* doubt my love, Ari. I love you with all of my heart. You are the *only* man for me." My heart was quiet, and I felt its warmth expanding, pushing outward, filling me with joy. Words I'd waited all my life to say, I could say guiltlessly now, surrendering the heart I could share with another who felt the same longing, having wondered, too, if he could ever dare to believe it would happen.

The afternoon was leisurely as the late-day sun streaked through the dainty lace panels adorning my French doors. I made some ginger tea with honey, and we sat in my bed, slowly sipping the steaming, spicy brew. We talked about Theo, and Willem, who was perishing quickly. He was worried about their aging mother. Ari, the patriarch, wanted to ensure the well-being of everyone in his world.

"Debra, I have to do a speech for a charity I donate to in the Caribbean. I will be there for a week and would love to have you join me."

My heart sank. That was the week of my concerts with the chorus. We were recently down by two sopranos, and I had committed. I had to decline. "I'm sorry, I can't. My performances are that week." I held my breath, awaiting his reply.

He flushed briefly with what I thought was indignance, but I knew he understood commitment. "It's okay, Debra, he said softly. We accept each other with things as they are." He smiled. "There is a lot of respect between us. There will be another opportunity."

I was relieved that he understood. It was the first time I had ever put myself first. In prior relationships, I would have reneged on my commitment without a second thought. It felt right. I could hold my head high, knowing I had not given my power away. What was even more affirming was that he didn't expect me to. It made him want me even more. Something had shifted. I felt healthy. Whole. Intact.

The next evening Ari phoned. He was in Holland with his mother. "How's Willem?" I asked. I knew he was deteriorating, having endured chemo and radiation treatments.

"Not good, Debra," he said, downhearted. He didn't think Willem had much more time. He was taking his vitamin drinks and could still get to the restroom independently, but he wasn't eating much.

"I'll call Faye tomorrow to see when I can visit him," I said, knowing it could be my last opportunity. I would be spending the Christmas holiday with Nadine and her family, and we would stay in Haarlem at her sister Sofie's house for a week, less than half an hour from Amsterdam by train.

***

I WAS EXCITED ABOUT MY TRIP to Holland. I had already been there almost a dozen times and had always enjoyed my stay. Nadine and I had plans to visit other friends of hers while we were there.

Ari had returned from his visit with Willem. He stopped by my apartment. It was a very emotional time, and he looked tired. We planned to meet in Amsterdam on Christmas eve. "Will you tell Nadine you'll be with me?" he inquired softly.

"No, Ari, I'm not going to share that with her." I had no intention of telling anyone in France about us. Until we could be public about our relationship, I wanted to be sure he was protected. Period. Not even Theo knew.

"Are you embarrassed to tell her…?" His voice trailed off.

"Are you *kidding?!"* I was aghast. "I want to tell the whole *world* about us! From high up on a mountaintop." After all these months, was he still questioning the love that poured forth from me like a fire hose with the nozzle cut off?

Searching for the proper translation, he often said, "I cannot hold your love." And then the guilt would inevitably come. He didn't want to "deceive" me and hated to keep me hanging. He thought he was selfish, a terrible person who was hurting everyone.

Concetta had said he would continue to vacillate wildly. His guilt was intense, reminding us of the stark reality that would have to be overcome. Neither of us knew what the future held. I wanted us both to be happy. My journal pages bulged with endless rumination about the rightness and wrongness of our life together. It was the thorny stem of a beautiful rose.

I thought about my chorus performance the night before in Cabris. Singing was a bright light in my life. I cherished our holiday performances in beautiful centuries-old churches in the breathtaking Alpes-Maritimes. Our voices would float upward, grazing the stone walls, rolling around the curves of the cathedral ceiling, then back down, creating a soft, round tone that always left me feeling exhilarated and at peace.

Our chorus was a lively bunch of roughly two dozen mostly retired French, British and American voices, of which I was the youngest. Our chorusmaster was a seventy-year-old Scotsman raised in London, an accomplished sound technician with a punchy personality and perfectionist ear. I grinned as I recalled auditioning for Baxter in his living room while he accompanied me on his piano. He would bang brightly on the keyboard during rehearsals, halting abruptly when we were off-key, his face twisting up as if he had bitten a sour pickle. "No, no, no!" he would scowl in his clipped British accent, his thick curly eyebrows knitting together like a fluffy white shelf, as we stood cowering. "Let's try it again!"

Grouchy or not, he always picked music that challenged us and delighted our audiences. We adored Baxter and practiced hard. A dinner celebration always followed our performances. My mouth watered thinking about the pheasant, risotto, and "soupe de chataigne" (chestnut soup), that I had indulged in at l'Auberge du Vieux Chateau after our last performance. My life, and my heart, were filled with good fortune.

A few days later, Ari dropped by my apartment to pick up the karaoke mics we hadn't used on his prior visit. Carefully, he climbed over the low wooden fence surrounding the complex with two dozen chiffon-colored roses. I gushed at their lemony delicateness. "I should bring you roses every time I see you, Debra," he said lovingly.

Holding hands and crooning, we sang Christmas songs like "Winter Wonderland" and "White Christmas." We belted out Dean Martin's "Everybody Loves Somebody Sometime" as he held me close and rocked me.

Ari was eager to give me my Christmas gift. "Thomas will take you to see Willem next week while you are in the Netherlands. I will see you after Sarena's birthday party. We can spend the night and exchange our gifts on Christmas Eve morning." I could hardly wait. It didn't matter what it was; there was nothing I needed. What mattered was that it was from *him.*

* * *

NADINE WAS STILL BASKING in the afterglow of our trip to New York, as was I, and now she graciously returned the favor by taking me to stay with her family for Christmas in Holland. I had previously met her sister,

Sofie, and brother-in-law Luuk on earlier trips, and some of their friends, as many of them were eager to come to Nice for a French Riviera getaway.

Luuk lit a fire in the sitting room fireplace every evening as we settled in to sing and play guitar. Many of the songs were Dutch folk songs. Some were French; only a few were English. We sang Christmas songs, and they occasionally joined me in the English version.

A few days before Christmas, Nadine and I went south to Maastricht to visit her friend Delphine and stayed overnight in a nearby hotel in Vrijthof Square, where we visited the Basilica of Saint Servatius. The beautiful thousand-year-old Romanesque church had evolved from smaller structures and churches over the centuries, built initially to house the crypt of the Armenian missionary St. Servatius, who allegedly died in the year 384 A.D. Inside, I lit a candle for Willem.

***

THE AFTERNOON BEFORE CHRISTMAS EVE, I checked into a beautiful modern Japanese-style hotel in Amsterdam. Ari would likely arrive late and tired from a lively evening with his "first" family. I took a bath in the oversized tub and settled into the comfy king-sized bed to await his arrival.

He came in just before midnight complaining about them as he wrenched his tie loose, tossing his bulging leather briefcase on the bench at the foot of the bed. He placed a gift bag on the dresser. Gushing, I flung open my arms. "Is that my gift?"

He kissed me deeply. "You can't open it before Christmas Eve, Debra," he teased. I knew he was bone-tired, and it didn't matter if we made love; I was happy to have him in my arms for the entire night.

The next morning I awoke excitedly. It was Christmas Eve, and I was with the love of my life! We were going to exchange gifts. I beamed as I lay next to him, kissing him awake. We briefly made love, enjoying the morning sun streaming through the window. "Are you ready to open your gift now?" he asked eagerly. I was. I had gotten him two beautiful lavender silk ties. I had never seen him wear lavender before. The color was unique but still conservative enough that he could wear them as business attire. He was pleased and kissed me tenderly. He was keen for me to open my gift.

He set an oblong package as large as a loaf of bread on my lap, wrapped in decorative red foil, with a large red fabric bow.

I undid the wrapping, revealing a smooth, striated cherrywood box lined in regal red silk. In the middle, perched in molded folds, was a beautiful designer watch from Geneva. It had a fur band and a ring of diamonds arranged around its classic rectangular-shaped face. Ari carefully observed me as I looked at it with awe and curiosity, inspecting it slowly in my hands. "It's a Spider, Debra, the first of the series. The band is mink, with two carats of diamonds around the face. They will only make twenty-five or thirty of these," he said proudly.

"You're covering me with diamonds and fur?" I teased. We laughed. I didn't expect such an elaborate, unconservative gift. It was sexy and playful, just like our relationship.

"I have a meeting this morning, so I have to leave you soon," he sighed, pulling me toward him. "Do you like your gift?"

"Of course I do. It's from you!" I purred contentedly, pressing my hips into him.

He was in a bit of a rush for his meeting. He quickly showered and dressed. After a few more kisses, he scolded me playfully. "Debra, I'm going to be late. I'll see you when we're back in France." He hurried out the door. I felt the usual tug on my heartstrings after he left. I ordered some breakfast and ran the water for a bath. Suddenly, I spied his briefcase on the bench where he had put it the night before. *Shit.* I knew he would need it for his meeting.

"You forgot your briefcase," I texted him.

He called me right away. "I've never done that in my life before, Debra."

He didn't have time to turn back and retrieve it. He was nearly at his meeting. We decided I would leave it at the front desk for Thomas to pick up. I pondered the significance of the event in my mind.

Later that afternoon, when he was alone, he called me playfully to tell me it was my fault and that I had "distracted" him. Was it? His briefcase was his life, the heart of his power, and he had unwittingly left it with me. He had proudly shown me his briefcase collection many months before. On some level, had he been ready to surrender his heart to something greater than the next irresistible financial windfall?

By mid-evening, I was singing Christmas carols in Dutch at the town square near Sofie and Luuk's home, sporting my new furry gift proudly around my wrist. I sight-read from a printout, and it felt intoxicating to be mouthing new sounds to tunes embedded in my psyche. I listened to my voice as it mingled with the others, filled with the hope and joy of the Holiday season. I had everything I could ever want. Love. Friendship. Travel. A growing sense that all would be well.

With bright eyes, I looked forward to the New Year. Ari and I were getting closer and more comfortable with each other. Relaxed, I could abandon my self-consciousness, letting my love for him gush forth.

* * *

DAYS LATER, BACK HOME IN MY BED, I was awakened by a call from Ari. He was headed to Geneva Airport from Zermatt, Switzerland, home of the towering Matterhorn, to pick up Izabella and bring her back to the family's chalet. He was tired, as they kept him up late. We talked about my visit with Willem, and he asked me if I missed my family. I did but I had no intention of moving back to the U.S. He commented about the restrictions of our relationship.

"Our love is authentic, Ari. It's the situation surrounding it that is challenging."

"Can you handle it?" he asked, catching me off guard.

"I don't know." It was true. I didn't know how I would handle whatever was shaping up as a future. How could I? How could either of us?

My answer seemed to stun him into a cavalcade of self-deprecation. "I feel so guilty about what I'm doing to you and everyone in my family."

I could hear his despair but stopped him short. "You're not *doing* anything to me, Ari. I want to be here," I rallied, digging into my dwindling reserves of patience.

"Love can perish, Debra," he said solemnly. I couldn't respond. What did he mean? I loved him intensely but was feeling vulnerable.

To add to my loneliness, I knew I would likely be spending New Year's Eve alone. Nadine was still in Holland, and seeing Willem wasting away during my last visit had been heartbreaking.

My mind fast-forwarded to Willem's wake and funeral. All of Ari's family would be there, both sides. I wouldn't be able to touch Ari or comfort him. No one would comfort me. There would be a chasm between us as vast as the ocean.

***

NEW YEAR'S EVE MORNING was crisp and sunny. By mid-afternoon, I was inspired to take a walk to La Brague, the river near me that spilled into the Mediterranean Sea near Antibes. I stood on its bank, observing the tiny yellow leaves of early winter wafting unhurriedly down to its surface. I was at peace, feeling the Divine alive and well within me.

I wanted time to stop, and to enjoy my own precious company. I had decided to spend the evening alone, perhaps burning a candle and setting an intention of what I wanted to ring in for the upcoming year. I sat down on a large log to send Ari a text of my experience: "I am walking along the river, and tears of peace and joy are flowing. I feel God in every breath, every step. This is my wish for you, too, all the days of your life. Thank you for all of the gifts you've given me, especially the gift of your love. Forever yours, Debra xo."

He called later to thank me for the most beautiful text he had ever received. He told me that he and Celeste would see Willem on New Year's Day. I knew this was making him extremely tense. That, and the end-of-year tax wrap-up for all his companies, had him justifiably on edge. "Everything will be alright," I consoled him gently. "Did I tell you I love you today?" I asked, lightening the conversation.

"No," he said, drawing out the word, feigning disappointment.

"I love you today," I said playfully.

"Today," he echoed, suddenly less playful.

"Tell me you love me one more time this year!"

"Yo te quiero," he offered in Spanish, still quiet.

"Tell me in Dutch!"

"Ik houd van Jouw," he said twice.

"Ik houd van Jouw," I returned, my heart full to the brim.

"I'll be in the Netherlands all next week, Debra. Maybe you can join me," he said, the lightness returning to his voice. I couldn't wait to see him again.

That evening I made a tasty dinner and decided to write down what I wanted to manifest in the coming year and beyond. Sitting on my sofa,

I made a list. My first item was "to be in a loving, totally available marriage partnership with my True Love and make a home with him." I flinched slightly, feeling like I was trying to force the hand of God and somehow was betraying Ari. Would I ever be married to him? I wanted that with all of my heart.

Nearing the stroke of midnight, I stepped outside, read my list aloud to the starry heavens, and folded the piece of paper into a tiny square, placing it on the cement patio. I bent to light it to consecrate it before the mighty creative Source and give my deepest desires life. As the edges of the paper started to smoke and curl, turning brown and black from the flame, I suddenly felt anxious, and my palms went damp. I had an overpowering urge to extinguish the flame and rewrite what I had written about my True Love and replace it with Ari's name. "It's okay," I said aloud, comforting myself. "The Universe knows you mean Ari."

"Everything is okay, Debra," Valentina reassured me over the phone. "You're just being honest about what you want in a relationship. There's nothing wrong with putting it on paper."

"I wish I could relax and let myself be in love. I'm so tired of self-judgment. Maybe a good night's sleep will help. Thanks, Tina. Happy New Year."

"You're welcome. I love you! Happy New Year, Debra."

I'd remained inexplicably restless up until the time I went to sleep. But something had shifted for me before I'd left for New York six weeks earlier. The understanding that washed over me had been crystal clear, and I knew I wasn't going anywhere. I had never committed my heart in this way before. In earlier relationships, I'd always had a foot out the door. When I returned from New York, I had felt it in Ari, too, in his eyes and his embrace. Unspoken. Unshakeable. Despite his guilty tirades, he wasn't going anywhere either.

* * *

THE FOLLOWING MORNING, I lay in bed thinking about the little ritual I had performed the night before. I was still anxious. Why? I hadn't done anything wrong; it was a beautiful dedication to the life and love I wanted to experience.

I stretched and rose from my bed, padding to the kitchen to prepare a cup of coffee. I scooped some grounds into the French press and set a pot of water to boil. Maybe I would call Tina to help shake off my uneasiness. I opened the door to peek outside. The air was chilly and damp, and the sky was white with winter clouds.

The phone rang. It was Theo. I glanced at the clock. It was early for him. "Hi, Theo, what's up?

"I have terrible news, Debra."

My mind went black as he spoke. "*What*…?!"

"Yes, he died…from heart complications…," Theo stammered.

"No! It's not possible, Theo! Ari died? *Died*?? Are you *sure*??" I pleaded.

"Yes, I'm sure…."

"You mean *Willem* Sorensen, right?!"

"No, Debra! *Ari* Sorensen. Ari Sorensen is dead!"

I reeled, clutching the phone, grabbing my forehead as the air stuttered into my lungs. My windpipe choked shut as I started to sob, my face contorted, stunned with grief. It was a mistake! Ari was healthy! I was going to meet him in Amsterdam next week!

In moments Theo was in my living room. We embraced, weeping desperately, gripped by shock and disbelief. "I have to call Thomas! I have to hear it myself!" I said, pulling away.

"I'm afraid it's true, Debra. Mr. Sorensen died last night," Thomas said, his voice sickened. Theo sat numbly on my red sofa, tears streaming unimpeded down his face as I paced wildly, staggering like a wounded animal, shaking as I beseeched Thomas to tell me that Ari was alive.

Thomas's deep, sorrowful voice flooded my ear. "I'm sorry, Debra…" he trailed off quietly, his voice breaking, trying to contain the deluge of emotions that threatened to topple him at any moment. He had been Ari's driver, a trusted confidante for many years; a humble, dependable man, sitting behind the wheel of a luxury vehicle he could never afford to buy, absorbing confidential business conversations and family disputes. A man who, each day, went home to his own life, his own story, and thoughts about things. "There will be a service within the next few days. I will call you with the details." His voice was laden with grief.

Collecting myself to the gravity of this man's devastation, I croaked softly: "I'm sorry for your loss too, Thomas."

"Thank you, Debra," he mumbled and hung up the phone.

I stood frozen, paralyzed, my whole world destroyed. A great tidal wave had slammed me to the shore, shattering my heart in one fatal blow. Theo didn't know about Ari and me. I could no longer hold back the truth that exploded inside my chest. I gaped at him as the words erupted from my lips. "Ari and I were in love, Theo!" I trumpeted, my words punching the air. "We were in love, and now he's gone!"

Theo's jaw dropped, dumbstruck as I gaped at him. "I knew it! Every time Mr. S. mentioned your name, it was as if he was singing it!" In a flickering moment of respite, I locked onto his liquid eyes, sharing what should have been a happy truth with someone who knew and adored Ariel Sorensen with all his heart and soul. But it was too late. I hung my head, letting the tears flow, drowning in desperation. As I raised my arms, Theo sprung up off the sofa. Tears wetting each other's shoulders, standing solemnly draped together, we wept.

Part Three

The Clock Struck Twelve

CHAPTER 15

Shattered

The sofa smelled faintly of cigarettes where Theo had sat. Staring dumbly out to the patio, my body numb with shock, I dialed Valentina's number. How was I going to break the devastating news, convey the inconceivable?

"Hi, Debra, what's up?" she singsonged.

My emotions rose sharply at the sound of her voice. "Oh, Tina!" I cried, "Ari is dead!"

"*What*...?!"

"He died last night."

"Ari *died*?! How—"

"Ari is *gone*!" I blared, cutting her off, howling my misery into her ear.

Tina was silent for a moment registering the gravity of my words. "Oh, Debra, I—I'm so sorry...," she stammered. "What...*happened*?!" Overcome with emotion, my mouth refused to speak as another wave of tears drowned me speechless. Tina said nothing further, as there was nothing she could say. We wept together as we surrendered to our sadness, joined as one an ocean apart.

"Ari had to guide Willem," my sister said sadly. "One day, you'll feel only the love in your heart, without the pain, and you'll have that forever." I let that sink in, let the tears flow. She hadn't known about my romance with Ari. It had been challenging to keep my unbounded love for him bottled up inside me. My sister's words were like a gentle hand stroking the magic lamp that was my tender heart, and I could finally let the infinitude of my love burst forth and be known to her.

"I loved Ari so much!" I cried, my tears cascading in great heaves, covering my cheeks and lips, and swelling my eyes. My sister listened quietly as the wave of my emotion quickly rose and fell, settling temporarily into the restless surf from which it was birthed. "What made you say Ari was guiding Willem?" I asked softly, dabbing my eyes with a tissue, remembering Concetta's very same words earlier. Concetta, who had guided me through it all. Her abiding wisdom had steered me through the storms of my oppressive self-doubt and torrents of guilt—both Ari's and mine—keeping me steady as I endeavored to walk the razor's edge of stillness, feeling and living the love inside my heart within an ever-turbulent swell of emotions. She had shown me the lighthouse—the love that was myself—that had drawn Ari to me in what seemed like a lifetime ago.

"I don't know," my sister said pensively, "it just came to me. Being who he was, he had to be a helper to the end." It was true. I had shared so much about Ari. I had wanted everyone to know the magnitude of the man I loved with all my heart.

"Thank you for that," I said, feeling close to her, sharing the realness and rawness of the moment.

I was exhausted. Grief quaked through me, banging me against the craggy rocks of a murky shore. In great surges of ragged disbelief and gripping fear, wave after wave, it came, squeezing my guts, heart, throat, and brain, choking me as I collapsed helplessly into swells of tears. There was nowhere to run, no life raft to cling to that would save me from the storm thrashing within. How could I live without Ari? *How??* Why was this happening to me?

I hadn't eaten all day. Staring at the contents of my refrigerator, a wave of nausea swept over me and I gagged, shutting the door and opting for a glass of water instead. I sunk down onto the sofa and picked up my journal, writing and sobbing, putting it down, picking it up again. There was no relief in writing the words. I read and reread my entry from the night before. Ari had still been alive when I'd written those words.

Thomas phoned to provide me with the details of the service and the cemetery where Ari's body would be laid to rest. I asked him about Ari's mother, and he said she was strong. She would have to bear the death of her two sons, one right after the other, as Willem was holding on by barely a thread. Thomas said Brock was taking it the hardest. I was not surprised. My heart sank as I thought about his grief. I sent him a text, but I knew he wouldn't call. I couldn't even imagine the turmoil now that Ari's two families would be forced together, suspended in the same vessel, yet inexorably separate, like oil and water, unable to dissolve the walls that kept them apart.

I called Nadine and then Gwyn with the sad news. Nadine cried softly, offering her condolences. "Oh, Debra, I am so sorry. How could this be? I thought Mr. Sorensen was healthy!" she gasped as I recounted the heartbreaking story. I told her that Ari and I had been in love. I felt relieved to tell her the whole truth, but it was overwhelming for her head and heart to manage all at once. "Oh my God, why didn't you tell me?" she cried.

"I'm sorry, Nadine. I couldn't. I felt I had to protect him. No one knew except for Tina and Concetta in New York," I said sadly.

Nadine's voice consoled me. "Please don't be sorry, Debra. I understand," she said as we cried together. She was happy that he and I had shared our hearts before he left this life.

"Oh, my dearest Debra, I am so very sorry," Gwyn said quietly, her voice laced with tears. She paused, listening compassionately, as I told her of my grand and beautiful love affair with Ari, speaking the truth of my heart.

"Oh, Gwyn! I can hardly stand it. It hurts so much…," my voice trailed off into tears.

"Ari must have loved you with all his heart. What an incredible gift you gave to each other. I'm saddened that you have to bear this, but you will be okay. Is there anything I can do to help?" she asked softly.

"Thanks, Gwyn," I said, feeling incredibly safe in her loving presence. "I'm going to need a lot of moral support over the coming weeks."

"Absolutely, my dear. I will speak to you soon. And remember, Ari hasn't really left you. I know that's so hard to feel right now, but you do know it's true, don't you?" she asked tenderly.

"Yes, in my heart I know it, even though I haven't 'felt' him reach out to me yet," I said.

"Give him time," she said gently.

That evening, I lit a tea light and placed it in the little outdoor lantern I had bought months before. It was a ritual I would perform nightly as an offering. I felt Ari could somehow see its tiny flame from high above, like a lighthouse on a foggy coastline, and would remember how much I loved him. I had a sense of crushing guilt about his death. Was it my fault? Had our last conversation led him to believe I wouldn't love him *forever*? My insides twisted sharply, imagining him clutching his chest, thinking I wouldn't love him *today. Or tomorrow. Or the next day, week, month, year, eternity. "Ari, oh my precious Ari! Why, why, why did you leave me? You were my True Love!! No one ever loved me the way you did!"*

My heart shrilled and shrieked, imploring his return. Up and down I went, perched in a tiny boat on the ruthless surf of my emotions. I hated death; hated some demon inside me that had killed Ari; hated the vengeful God who waited until I was deeply in love, only to yank the rug out from under me as I tumbled and crashed into the cement wall that caged my broken heart.

Each time I tried to lie flat, I would cry. I stacked my bed pillows so I would be propped up. Desperately needing comfort, I gripped my amethyst crystal and nestled myself in a semi-seated position amongst the pillows, praying sleep would come. Maybe I would awaken tomorrow morning, and all of this would have been a terrible dream.

In the morning, pressing Ari's picture to my chest, I sang him "The Rose" by Bette Midler as I danced and cried in my living room, reliving every word, every promise that would cradle the seed of my love through the winter into some far-away springtime, when I would be rebirthed as one who would love again.

I sank to my knees, letting the love, the longing, and the anguish flood from my tired eyes unrestrained. I remembered the words Rochelle had leveled at me so many years ago, long before I'd met Ari. "You won't let yourself fall deeply in love because you are afraid it will be taken away." And so it was. The chance we take with true surrender is the other side of the dastardly coin, the potential of the equal and opposite of a love that fills us to bursting beyond life itself, a loss that is unbearable, threatening to shatter us to extinction. Utterly broken, bleeding, annihilated by the impermanence of form winging its way through our heart of hearts, we clutch the feathers that fall lifelessly from a bird who has flown.

I walked back to La Brague, where I had sent Ari the beautiful text seemingly moments—lifetimes—ago. Leaves see-sawed back and forth as they floated lazily down to the river's surface, their brilliant red, orange, and yellow bodies capturing the sunlight, pulling it down to the crystal-clear water below. Each has a life of its own, I sighed. Like *everything*, if we are paying attention. I thought about a book I might someday write. How grand and beautiful it would be, a testament to the power of love, a fairy tale I could read and reread to the hungry, innocent child inside me, like a bedtime story, once upon a time.

A tiny little glimmer of light, barely perceptible, otherworldly, pulsing like a distant future under a heavy blanket of dark clouds, whispered its peace to me. "One day, I'm going to be okay," I thought, sighing in a single breath of respite. Ari would be guiding me from *inside* of myself. He was indelibly, eternally, a part of me now. No one and nothing could rend that from me. Though fleeting and incredibly premature, some other knowing had beckoned from a place of unknowable grace.

Walking home, I stopped to pick up the Nice-Matin. Ari's obituary was in French, of course. All the names were in there, even Giuseppina's. It was a bitter pill. I was the unnamed widow. The woman who had his heart. The woman with whom he shared his emotions, his body, his joy, and love; all of this—like me—a secret.

Brock called as I walked. "Oh, Brock, I'm so sorry for your loss. Your father loved you so much."

"Thank you, Debra." His voice was nasal and small from crying, clobbered by the gut punch of Ari's sudden passing.

I wanted to hold him, give him words of comfort, and share something that would make him feel that his father was still here, perched like a great eagle, his wings spread wide to envelop us all with his mighty, loving embrace. "Your father wanted all of his family to be together in harmony," I offered slowly, remembering what Concetta had said months earlier. "Feel your feelings, Brock," I said gently. "Your father is watching over you." He sniffled, and I felt him holding his breath, halted by his emotions. Feeling feelings was not a comfortable place for the Sorensen men.

"I feel him around me, everywhere I go," he said, his voice momentarily brightening. "At least now there are no phones ringing in the background," he deadpanned, attempting to lighten the burden with humor—typical of his personality. *His father would have done the same*, I thought with a smile. Brock would be okay. He was strong.

"I spoke to your father the night before he died," I offered. Brock seemed taken aback. "Really?" His voice was laced with curiosity and mild disbelief, oblivious to my part of Ari's world.

"We were very close, Brock." The words poured softly out of the hole in my heart. I longed to tell him about his father and the love we had shared. I wanted him to know his father was happy, in love, and had someone he trusted who adored him.

Brock paused. "I know it's important for you to say goodbye to him too, Debra. I'm sorry it took me so long to get back to you. I will see you at the service." I knew he had questions, but he wouldn't pry. Concetta had said he would be jealous if he knew about his father and me. I wondered if that were true.

"I will be there," I said, happy he had followed through.

Faye had just told Willem about his brother's death shortly before I'd called. She handed the phone to Willem. "Hello, Debra," he said in a tiny voice.

"Oh, Willem, I'm so sorry!"

"Thank you..." he stammered.

"Ari is waiting for you. Don't be afraid!" I paused. "He told me he loves you."

"I cannot believe he is gone..." Willem's voice started to break.

"Ari is safe and happy. Let him guide you, and follow the Light. I loved him so much, Willem!" It was excruciating not to blurt out the truth about Ari and me, especially to his brother. It had been the same with Brock.

"Willem is sad, but he knows Ari is at peace," Faye translated as she started to cry. "I must go and take care of my husband now."

"You are his angel, Faye. Thank you so much for sharing your lives with me. I'm happy to have gotten to know you all," I said, heavy with gratitude and grief.

"I am too, Debra," she said warmly and hung up the phone.

Valentina believed I'd brought Ari and Willem closer. Concetta told me that Ari wanted me to help bring his family together. I sighed. I knew it was true. The bubble had burst, but I was now an unextractable part of this family's journey, the story of Ari.

Thomas was bringing Honey to France the day before the services. I wanted to see her too, this diminutive, superstitious woman who had seen the truth in the tree I drew for her; the tree whose limbs were my arms, its arboreal roots burrowed into my weeping heart. The mother of the man who had changed my life. My Knight, my *King*, the beloved who had broken my heart open, releasing the white dove that wanted to fly, to sing her heart's song. I longed for his mother to know her son had joy, peace, and love—that he had been *alive* with passion.

Ari had once said to me, "Debra, you take all my troubles away!" I was a haven for him, and I felt blessed by his trust, honesty, respect, and growing ability to be vulnerable and to be himself around me.

Since he had died, I'd pored back over my journals. As lovers, we had seen each other on only sixteen occasions over the past nine months, and during this momentous time had offered each other the most precious of gifts, our unbound hearts. He had kept all his promises, and now he was gone, leaving a gaping hole that threatened to swallow us all up as we stood teetering on its volcanic rim, recoiling as we peered down into the unfathomable depths of roiling grief.

"Live your life, Debra," Ari would say to me often. His voice echoed through the chambers of my heart, pushing out against the walls of my very containment. Ours was supposed to be a fairy tale, not a tragedy! I was a widow. I could die and not care. I closed my journal and let my tears fall on its cover. I was lost. Unsafe. Forgotten. Needy and vulnerable. Afraid of what would happen or not happen. Who was going to take care of *me*? I wanted my loss to be recognized and to feel part of the great circle surrounding Ari and his memory.

The idea of sharing our love story thrummed like a low tone, pulsing in the hidden crevices of my broken heart. I wanted to immortalize, to *sanctify* our union. To forever celebrate a love that soared and played, to share our glory with the world. I wanted the world to know his heart, to experience the truth of who he was and who he and I had been together. Was staying too much for him to bear?

I remembered the night he had clung to me, imploring me not to let him go. And now he had flung himself into the heavens without me, leaving our lifetime behind. I missed him desperately. Ari, the man who would never be again—*this* life, *this* tapestry, *this* preciousness. Had I loved him enough? Would I ever love like this again, or would I die in sorrow? "Oh, Ari, *why did you go?* Our love had barely begun!" I cried.

Later, Faye and I spoke again. Willem was asleep. He knew Ari was with God, and this was bringing him much peace. She shared that Marcie would not be at the funeral. That saddened me. I had forgotten about the conflict between Marcie and Celeste and the constant argument Ari had with Celeste about the financial support he continued to provide to his first family. *Shouldn't bygones be bygones?* The man had died. Surely everyone should be entitled to closure, to say goodbye. It seemed a punitive perspective but rather matter-of-fact to Faye. I told her that Ari was committed to his brother and that I spoke with him after almost every visit to let him share his pain. I wanted to offer her my insight and let her know he had wanted to heal the rift.

It was only mid-afternoon, but I was already exhausted. I continued to sleep propped up at night and wasn't getting much sleep. Ari's service was two days away. There were many faces, some I wanted to see, like Brock and the race crew. I wondered if Thomas, Otto, or anyone else knew about Ari and me. Theo said I would know; I would see it in their eyes. I wanted our love to be known, not hidden away to wither and die.

Celeste would find the books I had given Ari and the inscriptions I'd written inside. I wondered how she was feeling, what she was thinking and if she knew about us. Was she devastated? Angry? Did she realize she had lost the best thing that had ever happened to her?

I had let myself love him deeply, dearly, and completely. I had no remorse. We earned each other's love through respect, kindness, honesty, and trust. There was no higher love than unbridled authenticity. My words fell staggeringly short, but I was thankful I had my journals to help me remember our moments, big and small, chronicled in ink scrawled across many pages.

I had told Ari it would take courage to leave Celeste. Was that true? Maybe it took more courage to stay. Who was I to say what was right? Perhaps the reasons were not for me to know, but it didn't change the reality of our love, which was not diminished by anything else, standing firmly on its merit. I cherished him. He cherished me.

Ari lived his life his way and went out at the top of his game before he could change his mind or guilt himself into staying. He had lived his life to the fullest and reminded me I could do the same. I remembered when he'd told me France was the most beautiful country in the world. Our love was written in the stars, and it was here that our love was born unto the earth, here that my heart called home, here in my bed that we'd made love, consecrating the beauty and light of our sharing. I felt a warm glow, filling me up with his memory, our eternal love cradled with indescribable knowing, and I knew he was right here with me, joined forever in a place where love is never forgotten, where Love is all there is.

* * *

MANY PEOPLE WOULD ATTEND ARI'S SERVICE, including the owners of a small magazine, *Opstand*, that he had taken under his wing. Lars and Margaux were staying with Theo for a couple of days, and I would join them for dinner. They were a lovely couple who told me through tears that Ari had many ideas for their magazine and wanted to bring it to prominence. They were shocked, heartbroken at the loss of someone who had touched them so profoundly, and intended to write an article about him, the visionary businessman and friend they had come to know. I was happy to share my experiences, and although there was sadness at having to suppress the private reality that Ari and I shared, I was grateful to spend some time with people he had impacted so much.

I bought two dozen multicolored roses for the dinner table, and Dean Martin was crooning softly in the background as I wanted to "invite" Ari to the dinner table with us. It was a touching evening.

Lars and Margaux gave me insights into his dynamic personality and tireless ambition. We shared the common traits we all saw and admired in him through our stories and remembrances. I told them that Ari and I had deep respect and trust for each other and recounted my work with him in his home office. They were delighted at the idea and could appreciate my desire to help him organize his workspace. It seemed we all sensed he was present as we humbly dined by candlelight on pasta with tangy mushroom marinara sauce and crusty, warm French baguette. I knew Ari would be happy that I was taking care of his friends. Things could have gone a different way, taken a different path.

Tomorrow was the funeral. I knew it would be a long, emotional day. I drank in the momentary respite as I enjoyed the presence of my guests, happy to savor the memories of a man who had made his indelible mark on so many.

CHAPTER 16

The Rose

Thankfully, I had slept well but was awakened by a sound from my cell phone at 4:00 a.m. and couldn't return to a restful sleep. I was still in shock and knew I would have to keep a lid on my feelings, which now included significant trepidation. My palms were sweaty at the thought of seeing Celeste. Would she confront, expose, dismiss, or embarrass me somehow?

It was a cold, dreary morning, and I hoped it wouldn't rain. Many people would surround me; some I knew, others I didn't, but my heart would be alone. Among Ari's entourage, the only person who knew about us, as far as I was aware, was Theo.

Theo had dropped Lars and Margaux at Ari's house in Cap d'Antibes for the final viewing. He and I returned later to retrieve them for the service. Lars said the scene was a cross between "The Godfather Three" and "Dallas," with men in black and sleek Mercedes stuffing the wide, flat stoned driveway. He told us it was a good idea that we hadn't come into the house and said that Ari didn't look "good." I squirmed. As if anyone dead could look "good," but I knew what Lars had meant.

The thought that Ari might have died in anguish left me feeling raw, deepening my despair at the incontrovertible tragedy unfolding slowly and painfully before me. To make matters more excruciating, he had a bruise on his head, perhaps due to falling from his bed. I forced myself to avoid the imagery that wanted to land squarely in the center of my being. I clung to the thought that he was no longer suffering, no longer inhabiting the body I had stroked, kissed, and adored.

We made our way down the busy side streets of Antibes and stopped at a local coffee shop before heading to the cathedral where the service would be held. I wrapped the thick, camel-colored woolen shawl I had purchased in Florence tightly around me to stave off the January dampness. The four of us trod in silence, our heeled shoes click-clacking against the pavement as we solemnly made our way to the cathedral.

I spotted Thomas straight away, standing just outside the entrance, and hurried over to hug him. I could see he had been crying, his bulky frame shrunken from his surrender to grief. I scanned the sizeable crowd, recognizing faces from the race crew, the race car drivers, some of Ari's CEOs, and many I didn't know. Katrina was there with her boyfriend, Bram. We shuffled inside and slid into the pews. Everyone in our section cried, letting the tears flow shamelessly down our cheeks. I had never experienced so many men in tears.

The pallbearers walked in carrying Ari's casket. I jolted as another wave of emotion ripped into my heart, the procession trailing behind them: Celeste, wearing a floppy, black velvet hat; Izabella, her pancake white face shrouded by a long black lace veil, a black shawl around her slumped shoulders, her mouth frozen open in tortured demise; Natasha, unreadable, devil-may-care. I gazed intently at the three of them, reading their eyes and behaviors, remembering the family I had experienced at the luncheon long ago. Next came Brock, his face puffy from crying, his ego punched out of him as the weight of the hour bore down. Honey, Sarena, and Zachary were solemn but contained. Giuseppina brought up the rear, her face molded into an expression appropriate for the occasion.

After the young priest opened the service, Brock offered his tribute in Dutch. Nods and tears from the Dutch mourners signaled me to the gravity of his words, and he had to pause often to stave off the emotions which threatened to overcome him. Celeste spoke tearlessly as she read off the page, her soliloquy translated into English as she spoke. She paused, glancing up at the unmoved crowd, her amber eyes darting about, set in the same countenance as her picture in Ari's office.

Celeste continued in words that fell steadily, like rain on a tin roof, pelting but not penetrating, far away from the essence of the heart of the man I knew. Izabella's intermittent sobs stabbed the heavy silence as her mother's words punctuated the leaden curtain of air hanging motionless from the arched ceiling high above us. I closed my eyes, trying to erect a barrier between her monologue and my emotions. I wanted to run, but there was a tiny shred of comfort when I rested my gaze on the wooden box at the foot of the altar.

People clustered loosely about as hugs, kisses, and condolences were offered all around in the stone courtyard of the cathedral. Numbly, I stumbled to a timely placed shuttle which carried us to the cemetery where Ari's body would be laid to rest.

Theo drove to the cemetery, where he would wait for me to complete the ceremony. He was distraught, jaw set, his lips pursed thinly across his squared chin, as he stepped out of his car to hand me two white, long-stemmed roses to toss onto the casket. He wanted no part of the drama or "that bitch." Theo minced no words when it came to Ari's French family, especially Celeste, who, from his perspective, likely "killed him," figuratively or literally.

I stood in the long line of black-bedecked mourners with Lars and Margaux as we waited to hurl our roses and say our last goodbyes. Ari's Dutch family were the first to leave and would not be there to receive our condolences at the end of the procession. I wasn't sure why—something about the heavy rush hour traffic and guests getting lost—but I was sad that I wouldn't get to connect with them, especially Brock, whom I hadn't seen since the end of the races more than a year ago.

As I approached Celeste, her expression in the cathedral still pinned to her face like a mannequin, I took a deep breath and extended my hand. "I'm sorry, Celeste." She cocked her head ever so slightly, eyes questioning, receiving my hand. Did she not remember me? "Debra," I stated, somewhat surprised. "I'm so sorry," I offered again, holding her gaze. Her body straightened as she slid her hand from mine, but she said nothing.

Zachary stood quietly next to her. I mumbled the same sentiment and got the very same reaction. Thankfully, the line's momentum kept us moving, and I was grateful that nothing had erupted from our exchange.

Izabella and Natasha were already split off from the receiving line, laughing amongst themselves. I felt an eerie cold come over me as I silently walked past them.

Returning to the safety of Theo's car, I plunked down onto the passenger seat. Muscle by muscle, I felt my body slowly unclench, releasing the tension that had gripped me for the past week. I sighed deeply. I hoped I would never see Celeste, Zachary, or those girls, again.

We drove home on the A8, now somewhat heavy with late afternoon traffic. Up ahead was a long, black Mercedes limo. As we passed, I glanced into the window and stared in disbelief. Inside were Izabella and Natasha! What were the chances? I was surprised they had left the cemetery so early.

The scene assaulted my sensibilities. They were laughing. Natasha lit a cigarette and tipped her head back to exhale a long trail of grey smoke. She waved her hand, holding the cigarette in a gesture that looked like a dismissal. I shuddered, remembering what Concetta had said to me. If Ari and I were to come together publicly after his divorce from Celeste, she and the children would "fly the coop." It wasn't hard for me to imagine. It made me deeply sad.

We went to a local restaurant in Antibes, where some other mourners had gathered at the bar. Otto was drinking whisky. I made my way over to him. "I'm so sorry you lost your best friend, Otto. You made Ari laugh the most," I offered sincerely, remembering how Ari had wanted us to double date with Otto and Rochelle. I knew Ari desperately wanted to contextualize me in his world, and Otto was certainly the ocean bed where he could safely sink an anchor.

Otto grinned at me with sparkling eyes. He told me about a car-racing rally through Suriname where Ari had stuffed the donation box full at the local church and purchased an entire fruit stand, letting the local children descend upon it. Ari had given the children watches too.

Extending my wrist proudly, I showed Otto the watch Ari had given me for Christmas. He smiled, his bushy mustache curtained around his mouth, covering his upper lip. He said he had heard a lot about me. I didn't ask him for details, nor could I procure them from his kind expression.

Thomas was standing alone at the bar, drinking a cup of coffee. I offered him my final condolences. "You and I lost a very dear friend," I said gently.

He nodded through tears. "I'm sure I will see you in Amsterdam soon," I continued quietly, thinking about Willem and the next round of grief.

***

I HADN'T SLEPT WELL, and my mind churned in low gear all night, recounting everything that had transpired, shooting an arrow into an unknown future. Where was I going to go? Was this the end of the line for me? Where did I belong now?

Bitterness rankled deep within me as I reflected on Celeste's starched tribute and the ceremony that had felt so contrived, emotionless, and phony. Of course, I was utterly slanted to one side. I didn't know the back story, the thirty years of history that preceded my arrival into a fairy tale that sprung to life like a children's colorful pop-up book. And now the corpse, and the story of my beloved, lie buried in the ground, covered in dirt and roses.

Why did this man who was larger than life have to leave us all? Like Humpty Dumpty, he had fallen off a colossal wall, and the broken pieces of his mighty empire lay in a jagged heap. Could anyone put them back together again?

I was numb, tired of unearthing painful memories that could only proceed backward. Ari had been gone for only a week, the longest week of my life. My tattered emotions left me shaky and off-balance, blistering the surface of my broken heart. I held my breath, searching for the solid ground within me. When would I get to exhale?

I'd had a dream about Celeste. I was at the end of a long line of people, standing shoulder to shoulder. It may have been Ari's house in Cap d'Antibes. She wanted to speak to me, and I was nervous. I expected the obvious question, but it didn't come. She was very businesslike—softer than at the funeral—and I felt she was trying to convey to me that she wasn't so bad by her gestures and willingness to speak with me, as if she were showing me her side, her role in Ari's kaleidoscopic life.

In the dream, she focused on tending to the houses they owned. People were reporting to her, and we went outside. She pointed to a house in one direction, and I pointed in another. Our conversation was guarded, but I awoke feeling less cynical about her. I remembered Ari had told me months before how she fulfilled this part of his life, the external persona he showed to the world. Of course, it made perfect sense. So, what was *my* role in coming into his life? Was I pointing him to a new "house," a different trajectory?

What did it matter? He was gone. I longed for the impossible, to feel Ari's arms around me. To taste, touch and smell him, lavish him with love, surrender to his. I was so wary of the future. Still not sure that the Universe wouldn't wrest me from safety and hurl me back into the nothingness from which I came, ship me back part and parcel to the U.S., severing the foreverness of my once-beautiful dream.

Every day, with Dean Martin's voice crooning in my living room, I sang and danced and cried, clutching Ari's picture to my chest. We came to life to *feel*, and I'd been turned inside out. What would happen to me? Was it time to go? How would I feel knowing Ari was gone when I looked out over the endless blue sea? Would I want to stay?

Ari had given me so much. He had healed so much inside me. He loved my body and the woman who inhabited it. I'd had the best sex ever. Gone were the little voices that told me I was inadequate, drowned out in my complete abandonment to his touch, his kiss. He cared for me without judgment or expectation, without the twisted distortions of alcoholic fatherly demons I had known in my youth. He was consistent, always the same man to me, not a Jekyll one moment, a Hyde the next. I felt safe with him, trusting. He gave because he was a giver. He didn't expect anything in return and hadn't made me feel guilty. Through him, I had learned to love myself better, something I could hold onto for the rest of my life, reflecting a deeper worth I hadn't yet discovered.

* * *

THE FOLLOWING WEEK, I went with Nadine to visit Ari's gravesite. The cemetery was expansive and confusing. Ari's humble slab was propped plainly in muddy dirt tamped down and bordered by unkempt grass among the rows and rows of chiseled stones. It seemed so small and inappropriate for a man larger than life. My mind envisioned King Tut's tomb, and I frowned. The simple granite offering before me didn't do his memory justice.

The evening before I had written Ari a tribute. I unfolded my little papers and sang him "The Rose" as warm tears trickled down the cool skin of my cheeks. I read him "The Invitation" by Oriah Mountain Dreamer, its brazen first line halting my thoughts and grief, forcing me into the bare moment in which I stood and breathed. Holding the pieces of paper in chilly fingers, watching the little tufts of breath as they gently puffed out of my mouth, I read the words that couldn't reassemble his form as they trundled into the cold air, disappearing like tiny bubbles of sound vibrating themselves into silence.

I refolded the papers and stuffed them into my jacket pocket, staring at the stone and the dirt, the mound under which Ari's stiff cadaver lay unmoving. A few small bouquets from recent visitors, hardly fit for a king, had been placed against the granite, surrounded by rings of wilted flowers from the wreaths of days before that lie withering, like the body of the man beneath them. I couldn't feel him there and decided I didn't need to return here to retrieve my memories of him or us. I sucked in a drag of the damp, white-grey air and bestowed one last glance at the dead and dying flowers; their pretty colors could not convince me of the spectacle of death. I gathered myself around me, my love for Ari contained safely within, and headed back to the warmth of Nadine's car.

* * *

I HAD SLEPT WELL, believing I was off somewhere with Ari, some other dimension out of time. Today I was going to join Gwyn at her friend Renata's for *A Course In Miracles* meeting in French.

Originally from Poland, Renata had come to France as a child with her family, fleeing the communist regime threatening to destroy so much and so many. She'd had a tumultuous life, especially concerning matters of the heart. She had been married with children, divorced, and fell deeply in love with a creative man who drank too much and lost his battle with cancer.

Renata was a generous soul with an open, unjudging heart. I was happy to be at her meeting for a change of scenery, surrounded by others looking deeply within to reveal the truth of who we all are. I was raw, feeling Ari's loss as we meditated in her living room, peppered with little candles and the cleansing smell of sage.

We began with the "Manual for Teachers," section 3, page 7, in my English version of the text, and took turns reading paragraphs aloud from our books. I was brought to tears.

> [A teacher of God] cannot meet everyone, nor can everyone find him. Therefore the plan includes very specific contacts to be made for each teacher of God. There are no accidents in salvation. Those who are to meet will meet, because together they have the potential for a holy relationship. They are ready for each other.[1]

I sat silently, letting the tears wet my cheeks, as each of the others read their paragraphs in French. When it was my turn again, I let the words bathe my heart, feeling the rightness, the privilege, and the holiness of having come together with Ari. Paragraph four read:

> Each teaching-learning situation is maximal in the sense that each person involved will learn the most that he can from the other person at that time...The second level of teaching is a more sustained relationship, in which, for a time, two people enter into a fairly intense teaching-learning situation and then appear to separate...These meetings are not accidental, nor is what appears to be the end of the relationship a real end. Again, each has learned the most he can at the time. Yet all who meet will someday meet again, for all relationships are destined to become holy. God is not mistaken in his son.[2]

The weight of the book on my lap comforted me; my eyes rested on its thin pages of scritta paper. I let the perfection of Jesus' words seep into the spongy warmth of my heart, anointing my pain with a Love that I could only allow and never completely understand.

Later, I confided to Renata that I feared the judgment of those who would point to Ari's marriage, as if, in that fact, our love could be expunged and burned to the ground. "Love is *always* right," she said softly in her eastern European accent, taking my hand. I felt bruised and vulnerable, yet I could feel peace underneath the sadness. I wanted to leave to be with Ari, and I wanted to live too. I wanted to stay here, in France, where my heart belonged.

* * *

I SPOKE WITH FAYE THE FOLLOWING EVENING. Ari had left no will! I was shocked. Speechless. Celeste could get half of his entire estate! The family was staggering in disbelief. I felt anger clamp its hot little fingers around my throat, wrenching my guts into a virulent froth that threatened to choke out any neutrality that had started to scab around my negative perceptions of Celeste. War would be waged from both sides. Lawyers would be perched on the collective edges of outrage, trumpeting righteous indignation in contractual scrivening as they dug their claws into a mountain not of their own making.

Where was *A Course In Miracles* now? How could I feel "love" for Celeste when all I could conjure were hellish grievances? I sucked in a breath, releasing it slowly, hoping it would carry these thoughts out of my mind. I was disturbed and unnerved by all the personalities that populated Ari's family. Fortunately, he had sheltered me from all of that. I didn't have the constitution for fighting. I wanted to dissolve the miscreants of my ego, not fortify its errant perceptions.

I reflected on the paragraphs I had read at Renata's. In time, it would all become clear. For now, I had to let Life expand through me as I allowed my heart to be as it was in the momentousness, or monotonousness, of each day. I had to embrace the nuances of grief that could still hold peace, and love that could still allow the entitled presence of the shearing volatility that threatened to whittle me to the bone, to render me utterly, outrightly, unreservedly human. I had loved and been loved completely. One day I would be ready to love again. My heart would pine to burst from its container, and I would have the courage to stab my mighty walking stick into the fertile ground.

* * *

AFTER ARI DIED, it was as if the clock had struck twelve. The carriage turned back into a pumpkin. Mice scurried everywhere. I was thrust out of the magic kingdom, skinning my knees on the mighty staircase as I fell flat on my face. I would have to relinquish my rental car, vacate my apartment, uproot myself in the throes of deep grief, and move forward. I knew Ari wasn't "gone," but I couldn't connect with him because of the biting anguish that made me feel like I would implode or explode at any moment. I couldn't eat and could barely sleep. Lying down made me feel like I would drown in my broken heart, and I had to keep my head above it. Avid journaling, *A Course In Miracles,* and close friends who knew the truth were the only things that kept me afloat in a wildly rocking emotional boat.

Inevitably, I would need to work. Now that Ari was gone, I would have to find a way to pay for my life in France or leave. That idea made me incredibly sad. It was painful to stay, but leaving was out of the question. There were opportunities, but none inspired me.

I had met an American chiropractor named Parker many months earlier, who had a practice in France near Monaco. He offered that I could provide massage therapy to his patients. He had a friend named Ronnie in the Netherlands who was looking to expand his chiropractic practice in Amsterdam. I loved Holland and had envisioned having a second apartment there, but I did not want to leave France.

I would have to move if I didn't find work right away. I was running out of money quickly, and I had difficulty presuming things would work out. I didn't trust that the Divine was on my side. Was relief—or even happiness, within my reach?

* * *

NADINE AND I WENT TO HER FRIEND Yvette's in Bar-sur-Loup for a walk. I could feel Ari's presence around me as we traipsed the meandering streets. Later, we lunched on delicious fondue at Yvette's lovely house. Her home was beautiful and bright, painted in warm and cool pastels, with deep windows letting the sunlight stream everywhere. I felt comforted. Like Renata, Yvette had offered me a place to stay while I figured out my next steps. I was deeply grateful for their generosity. Yvette was active, and it would be fun to walk with her and spend time in nature. Renata was a wise old soul and offered deep insights into life. I was relieved to have choices but still felt uneasy. Was this Life's way of taking care of me?

As Nadine's little car descended the dark, hilly roads, I contemplated Yvette's offer. I would have a private bedroom and bath. I would also have the opportunity to practice speaking more French. I would be closer to Gwyn in Tourrettes-sur-Loup, and Nadine would likely be a frequent visitor. I could still attend ACIM meetings nearby and drive with Gwyn for chorus practice.

Nadine pulled up in front of my apartment to drop me off. I fished around my purse and coat pockets for my housekey but couldn't find it. I hoped I hadn't left it in the lock. It wouldn't be the first time, but it was better than paying fifty euros to replace it.

I recalled placing my handbag and keychain momentarily on the roof of her car to remove my coat before I got in when she had picked me up, so it had to be somewhere. I hadn't taken it out at Yvette's. I got out of the car to look under my seat, and Nadine came to help me. "Look!" she laughed, pointing to the roof. I gaped at my keys lying against the smooth surface of the roof rack.

"Impossible!" I said as she held them up like a prize, jingling them in the chilly night air. It had to be a sign.

"Only you, Debra!" she said, laughing and shaking her head. It was indeed a miracle that they had remained perched on the roof for the jostling roundtrip journey and that neither she nor I had seen them when we got out of, or back into, her car at Yvette's. It seemed I had my answer. I would stay with Yvette.

CHAPTER 17

Moving On

Theo found out that the race car collection had not been registered in Brock's name. I felt sick to my stomach, stunned. Celeste would take everything. I was oblivious to the workings of the family "business," but my heart went out to Brock. Life had dealt us all a gut-wrenching blow.

I didn't want to think about things I had no control over, so I started packing. Although I lived in a furnished apartment, I had accumulated many belongings over the past two years. I looked at my tired eyes in the mirror under the bright bathroom light. I had been crying for nearly a month, and I was exhausted. I hated to leave the place I called home. My rental car was gone, and my things had become a burden, but I couldn't let them go. Eckhart Tolle was right. One of the biggest illusions was the word "mine." If this were someone else's stuff, I could leave it all behind. A thought flashed through my mind: *you cannot find your safety in people, places, or things. They are all impermanent and will disappear.*

Yvette called a few days later to tell me I could only stay for three weeks. Another blow. I was sure my rocking boat would tip over. Gwyn assured me that I would be okay, that I had chosen a hard lesson, and that the Universe was supporting me even if I couldn't see it. *No, I couldn't see it.* What was the lesson? I'd watched two brothers teach me about loss. And, though Willem was still breathing, I knew now what people's hearts endured when someone they loved died.

The loss of Ari was crushing. My grandmother died when I was sixteen, but I hadn't understood life then. It didn't include death. I'd watched my mother grieve and observed *her* pain, which made me deeply sad, but I wouldn't feel the loss of my grandmother until ten years later when, one snowy Christmas Eve, I realized what I had lost. The tears spouted forth, vaulted away for all those years, and then, like the melting snow, seeped back into the soil of my resilient heart, planting a seed that would erupt in a far-away future.

* * *

THEO DREAMT THAT ARI was standing with his hands stretched out in a welcoming gesture, laughing and crying at the same time. A man dressed in black approached Ari, but Theo could not see who it was. He thought it might be Willem. He related that he rarely had dreams like this, and when he did, it meant something.

Later on, Thomas confirmed. Willem had indeed died the night of Theo's dream. I had some peace that Ari and Willem were now together, and neither was suffering. I spoke with Faye to offer my condolences, and she gave me the details for the viewing and services. Willem would be cremated, and his remains sprinkled over the dunes by the seaside. My heart was heavy. Another sad goodbye dug into a wound still festering in my heart.

* * *

THE FOLLOWING DAY I WAS GLAD I had decided to go to chorus rehearsal. Hattie, an alto, offered me her house in the mountains of Monatroux for a month while she vacationed in New Zealand with her boyfriend. She had a little Siamese cat named Loki and said I could use her car. I accepted her offer. I would stay with Yvette for three weeks and then move into Hattie's place.

I lit a tea light and placed it in the little lantern on the patio for Ari, as I had every night since he had died. It was just after midnight. I sat on the bed in my apartment, writing there for the last time in my journal. It was so hard to believe I wouldn't be coming back anymore. My heart was laden with sorrow. I missed Ari with every cell of my being, expecting the phone to ring, him waiting eagerly on the other end. I was grateful for the benevolence extended to me, thankful I would have a roof over my head for the next couple of months. I knew I had to go. The Universe had a way of pushing me into or out of things, and although my mind knew it was all for the highest good, my heart just wanted Ari to come back.

Willem's service was a week away. I wasn't looking forward to the tsunami of emotion that would surely arise as I plunged into the Sorensen world again. Theo would not be there; I would have no life raft to cling to.

I turned off the light and nestled under the comforter, feeling the softness and warmth of the bed beneath me and Ari's presence to my right, where he had held me in his arms and made love to me, shared his emotions with me, sipped tea with me in the afterglow. I had been a lighthouse for him, drawing his ship into the port of my heart, where he had laid down his mighty anchor.

In the morning, I danced my last dance with him in the place I had called home for two glorious, magical years, weeping softly to Dean Martin's mellow voice serenading me in my living room. "Goodbye, sweet home, sweet memories. Goodbye, my beautiful Ari, my angel, my Knight, my King. Thank you for your love, your passion, born with me here in this holy nest, where we laid and entwined our hungry hearts. I am forever, unequivocally, yours."

Theo arrived with the rental van and would drive me to Yvette's. I said a silent thanks. Theo. Always there. A helper soul and a man who had become a good friend, equally stunned by a loss neither of us could yet grapple with. I would be leaving the comfort of his camaraderie too. I knew the Universe was guiding him and that he would be okay. He was strong, resilient, full of sparks.

He smiled, marshaling a toothy grin. "Ready?"

"Sure," I mustered with a sigh as I opened the lace-paneled doors wide so we could load the truck.

I slipped the key into the lock for the last time and turned the key to the right, sliding the bolt across into the wooden doorframe. "I'll be there in a minute," I said to Theo. I wanted to offer my last goodbyes, feel the patio beneath my feet, drink in the dark, pointy leaves of the oleander bushes, the slender arborvitae curtaining my view of the street, the now withered winter gardens encircling the precious space that had offered me everything I had ever dreamed of; a fairy tale come to life. I closed my eyes and placed my attention in the center of my heart. "*Thank you.*"

* * *

THAT NIGHT AT YVETTE'S, I lit a candle in my lantern stationed outside my bedroom window. The sun had shone brightly all day, and the temperature was warm. I looked around at my new surroundings as I sat on the firm bed, my journal propped on a pillow on my lap. The bedroom was a pretty shade of blue pastel, with a blue and white quilt on the bed, white furniture, and dainty white trimmings. There was a clear vase filled with dried lavender. I smiled. Very French. The scene was surreal. I had been carried here on the current of a new day. Everything *was* working out. Life had not abandoned me and was rising solidly to meet my hesitant feet, one step and one day at a time.

Yvette knocked softly at my door to check in and say good night. "Tu es à l'aise, Debra?" she inquired sweetly.

"Oui, je suis confortable," I replied.

"Alors, dors biens," she lilted.

"Bonne nuit, Yvette. Merci pour tous."

In two days, I would be in the Netherlands to say goodbye to Willem and the Sorensen family. It would be a somber but fitting end to a spectacular dream, the final act in an extraordinary fairy tale, and a sad farewell to a pageant of people, places, and unforgettable occurrences. I closed my journal, placed it on the nightstand beside me, and gazed at the lantern flickering outside in the dark. "*Thank you, Ari. For everything.*" I snuggled under the covers and closed my tired eyes.

* * *

THE WEATHER IN HOLLAND was chilly and damp. I braced myself as I walked into the funeral home. Brock, Marcie, and Honey were there. I was relieved to see them, as I hadn't been able to offer anyone but Brock my condolences about Ari. Faye welcomed me with a big hug.

Willem was laid out as thin and small as a child. I felt a pang in my chest. Honey stood next to me as I struggled to accept the sight before me. "You are a good person," she said ruefully, squeezing my hand. Pain swirled in her dark eyes. She had lost both of her sons in the same month. I wished

I could comfort her with thoughts of my beautiful love story with Ari. On some level, I was sure she knew.

"Thank you," I said softly, wishing I could convey the grandeur of the past two years into her soft, petite palm.

Later that afternoon, I met with Ronnie, the chiropractor in Amsterdam. I wasn't ready to work. I was incredibly exhausted. Moving to Holland would have been an enormous commitment for me.

I decided to have a massage. The energy inside my body felt torn and jagged. The massage smoothed it out, reassembling me into a coherent whole. Tomorrow was the funeral. I wanted it all to be over, to run back to the sunny skies of the French Riviera and my memories of Ari.

* * *

I TOOK A SEAT AT THE BACK OF THE CHAPEL. All the familiar faces were there—most of the race team crew but none of the drivers other than Brock. Tears were flowing freely, silently. My emotions pressed firmly against the dam that threatened to betray me as my grief for Ari overshadowed my ability to feel the loss of Willem. My gaze reached across the respectably-sized crowd to Faye in the front row, and our eyes locked. She knew. I know she knew. We had both just lost our loves, a magnitude in which pretense could not be feigned.

Celeste walked in with Natasha. I startled, sucking in a short sharp breath. They took a seat next to Faye. I'd been told Celeste had never visited Willem throughout his battle with cancer and had not attended the wake.

Her appearance could be interpreted from various viewpoints. It took a lot of courage to show up here, as these were Ari's people, but she and Faye shared the bond of the brothers, and, for today, it appeared bygones would be bygones.

* * *

MY FLIGHT BACK TO NICE was three hours late. I'd been suffering from a chest cold which made me cough frequently, and I hadn't slept well. I didn't feel like making idle conversation and sat quietly in my seat, avoiding eye contact, staring out the oval window at the clouds below.

Grief smothered me like an elephant seated on my chest. "*I have a broken heart,*" I announced quietly to myself. I bowed my head, letting the tears fall hard. Part of me wished I had never come to France; the loss was unbearable. Was the story over? I hadn't realized how much I'd been waiting for the other shoe to drop, and the experience of Willem's funeral thunked to the floor like a heavy boot. I was glad I had seen those I loved in Ari's circle. I would probably never see any of them again.

* * *

IT WAS LATE. I GLANCED AT the orchid on top of the white dresser in my blue bedroom at Yvette's. It would be blooming soon. The dark green stems were about six inches high, with little bulges at the tips indicating more growth. I had purchased it promptly upon my arrival in France, its lavender blooms erupting proudly from long sturdy stems like birds perched on a tree branch, and I was delighted it would be flowering again. The stalks had appeared just before Ari died, promising a happy future. Was there still a happy future ahead? I couldn't imagine loving anyone as much as I'd loved him. And, if lightning struck twice, in another fairy tale far away, our love would always be here, like a copious banquet, a benchmark for two hearts with the audacity to love.

It was Valentine's day. I had been in France for precisely two years. I was compelled to write. I let everything have its expression in my journal as I recounted the love story that gushed from me like a fountain. On some days, it felt as if Ari had never come; on others, it merely felt like he was traveling, and I'd see him in a couple of weeks. When my phone rang, I would jump. It was always "him" on the other end. Reluctantly, I changed my ringtone. I cried the first time it erupted with the new sound, but I resisted the urge to change it back. My life felt so insignificant. What was my purpose here? Why had something that had felt so right come to this? Could I ever trust life again?

* * *

YVETTE HAD BEEN A GRACIOUS HOSTESS, and now I was moving up to the mountains of Montaroux to Hattie's. Gwyn arrived early, and we stuffed her little car with my belongings and headed for the hills.

When we arrived, Hattie and Alfred were ready to go and instructed me on the workings of the house. Heavy drapes covered the windows of the chilly home to keep the heat in or the cold out—I couldn't tell which. All the heating was on timers. There was a kerosene heater for the living room, which would help warm the daylight hours, but it was smelly, and kerosene was costly. The fuel would be at my expense.

After the two had gone, Gwyn and I unburdened her car of my belongings that bulged like a great wall behind the front seat. Some of my possessions were at Yvette's, and some were in Nadine's storage unit, although I had given many items away. It was cumbersome to have to tow everything around with me, but what choice did I have? I didn't know where I would ultimately end up and didn't want to have to replace anything I could potentially use.

An amusing thought blossomed in my head and made me burst out laughing. "What are you laughing about?" Gwyn asked, breaking into a sunny smile, her round eyes sparkling.

"Here I am, having been the lover of a multi-millionaire, and I have a set of plastic drawers for a lingerie chest!" We whooped with delight. I was relieved to have told Gwyn about my love story with Ari. Our sneakered feet crunched against the white pebbles of the driveway as we carried the remaining boxes and bags into the chilly house. We ate a simple lunch, and she left in the afternoon. My heart sank as I watched her pull out of the driveway.

Alone with my thoughts once more, grief rose abruptly. I settled on the couch and pulled a scratchy woolen throw over my legs. Loki leapt up onto me. His youthful fur was silky smooth, and I was comforted as I stroked the back of his warm, purring body curled up on my lap. *What now?* I thought, gazing tearfully at the kerosene heater several feet away. I was raw. It would be a long, damp winter up in the misty mountains.

My dwindling reserves of money were soon to run out, but the thought of performing a massage on anyone other than Ari depressed me so much that I would start to cry just thinking about it. My massage work had gotten me to France but, more importantly, had given Ari a *reason* to bring me here. Ultimately, we had to come together to experience the most incredible love either of us had ever known, and now that he was gone, my desire to provide massage had gone with him. They had become part and parcel. Aside from Brock and the team, I had only provided sporadic chiropractic treatment and wanted no part of touching anyone. My well was empty; I had nothing to give.

My tears fell silently as I petted the cat, letting my thoughts and emotions be present. I was so tired of trying to figure out the future. Deep inside, I knew something would show up and that I would be ready when it did.

CHAPTER 18

Carried by the Wings of Grace

Several of the choristers lived in and around Montaroux. On one particular evening, I was invited to Poppy and Jacob's to meet a friend of theirs who had recently left southern Australia and was temporarily lodging with them.

Darla Hetterly was originally from the States and had worked in Beijing as a high-level event planner. She enjoyed many years in the East, but her passion was to make essential oils, and she had relocated to Melbourne, where she'd started growing herbs and flowers on a small piece of property that had a couple of dwellings where she could live, including a small shop to develop her craft.

She had long, greying hair that hung thick and frizzy around her strawberry-shaped face, well-lined from years of cigarette smoking. Her voice was pleasant and slightly husked from her habit. As she spoke about her experiences, she reminded me of Concetta, straight-forward and astute in her contemplations and life philosophy. She had sustained deep losses through a raging fire that had recently demolished her premises in Australia and had suffered the death of her beloved sister years earlier. She was no stranger to suffering.

"Everything burned," she said sullenly, her lips pulled tightly across her face.

"I'm so sorry, Darla," I said, my heart filling with compassion. "I can't imagine how devastating it must have been to lose everything you owned."

"Some losses change our lives forever, like yours," she said. "Some we can figure out; others leave us shaking our heads, down on our knees. But for whatever reasons they happen, it's what we do with the new seeds that arise from the ashes that show us we can reclaim our dignity and fortify ourselves through the very purging itself." She paused. "An alchemy of the soul, so to speak. Humans excel at starting over," she said, smiling somewhat wryly.

I nodded my assent. I could feel the weight of her sadness, but her depth and wisdom intrigued me. We'd both suffered damages that had left a gaping hole in our hearts, and perhaps we would help each other heal.

Other friends were coming to visit me, and I stayed relatively busy. Erik was in town, and he and Nadine drove up from the coast to take me to lunch. We headed up to Mons and were delighted by a gorgeous view of Cannes, and the Iles de Ste. Marguerite and St. Honorat, far, far below in the Mediterranean Sea.

I saw Gwyn every weekend at chorus practice. Niccolo, her boyfriend, offered to translate my CV into French. Pauline, another chorister, offered to deliver my resume to the director of an exclusive health spa in Monaco. Her husband Sylvan, a lawyer, was trying to help me get a European passport through my Irish lineage so that I could work in France. Hattie's son Torin was friendly with the Four Seasons Resort owner and offered to forward my CV to him.

People from the chorus introduced me to their circles, and I felt a great uprising of love and support around me to help me get back on my feet. I still wasn't motivated to do massage or chiropractic work, but I needed money. I wanted creative work, something that felt purposeful and joyful. I had no idea what that was. I needed a car, and I needed a place of my own.

I drove Hattie's car to the coast to retrieve the rest of the belongings I'd stored at Yvette's. Afterward, I drove to Theo's, and when he embraced me, I started to cry. It felt so good to be hugged by someone who had been a mainstay in my life in France and loved Ari as dearly as I did.

Lars and Margaux had written a captivating article about Ari in their magazine, *Opstand*, which Theo had given Nadine to read. When I arrived at her house, she handed it to me. Ari was dashing, dressed conservatively in a tawny wool suit, smiling and relaxed in the full-page photo. The article chronicled Ari's life and quest for greatness, his accomplishments as a businessman, a father, and husband; a generous, tireless man filled with passion for his life and work. Overcome by emotion, I burst into tears. Nadine held me as I cried.

We went to lunch at a simple seaside restaurant on the strip of St. Laurent. The blue of the sea filled the spaces that had once again cried a hole in me. I didn't want to go back up to the mountains. My heart was not there.

* * *

I HAD BEEN SPENDING QUITE A BIT OF TIME with Darla, who had now moved into her own house. I told her the truth about Ari and me. "I know," she nodded calmly, having guessed it from my voice and the picture I'd shown her of him and me standing at the foot of his private jet. "I feel like I know him through you," she offered. She would not be the first to tell me this.

She picked up the magazine folded open to Lars and Margaux's article and studied Ari's photo. "Surinamese men are much gentler," she said softly. "I can see Chinese blood in him too." She pointed out the nuances of his facial structure that made her believe this was so. I could see it as well. Was this the flash of recognition I'd had when Karen, the concierge from the Hotel du Pont, had left that message on my answering machine in Delaware more than two years ago, and I had seen the face of a Chinese man in my mind? I had read that the Surinamese culture was a diverse blend of people from all over the world, including the Netherlands, India, Africa, China, Indonesia, and others who settled and integrated with the indigenous people who lived there.

"We were so in love, Darla. I know it doesn't matter now, but I still don't know why it was almost impossible for Ari to leave Celeste. He had so much guilt over it," I said, shaking my head slowly.

"Ari probably wouldn't have been able to leave Celeste because they had children," she said plainly, pulling deeply on her cigarette and blowing the smoke out through her mouth and nostrils, looking like a medicine woman—or a human dragon.

Darla presented me with a perspective I wouldn't have deduced on my own. She had lived in and around Brazil for nearly a decade and then in Asia for seven years, where she had worked closely with a Chinese man.

"It's a question of honor," she said, sipping her tea, as dark as coffee from the three teabags submerged at the bottom of a tall, flowered mug. "I'm sure he never felt for anyone like he did for you. He'd probably been able to compartmentalize his life in many ways until he started having deep feelings for you. It must have been a physical stressor for him. He likely couldn't figure out how to find the balance." She looked off into the distance. "Celeste would have taken everything she could from him," she said pejoratively, exhaling another trail of grey smoke.

We sat on her back patio, eyes fixed on the little firepit burning just a few feet from us. I watched the smoke drift up and away as I adjusted the wool blanket draped across my lap.

"In a Chinese marriage, the bond that holds the parents together is the children," Darla continued. I didn't know if this were true or not, nor if Ari had Chinese heritage—as I had no reference point for either—but I felt that Darla offered wisdom that would help me to heal the questioning and give me an understanding I wasn't able to proffer through my own inquiry. "You had Ari's heart. He gave and taught you so much. There are very few people in the world like him. He planted a seed in you. You will take what you learned from your experience with him, and somehow you will use it in your life or your work." She spoke with detached certainty as if she were prophesying an unknown future. "Keep him close on your journey," she smiled, "he is still with you. Talk to him."

Darla told me that when she'd lost her home, herbs, and beautiful gardens in Australia to the conflagration, she'd invited her deceased sister into her story so that she didn't have to go through it alone. "It gave me strength," she said ruefully, recalling a tragedy that still kindled much pain.

Later that evening, I prayed. I needed Ari to help me get through his death and the tumult of finding a new path, as I had no idea how the grieving process would unfold.

My days continued to seesaw as I struggled to remain at the fulcrum. I felt I was a burden, a failure, relying on so many people to help me recover. I visited Ari's grave with Nadine, compelled to return. I laid my red rose on the cold mound as I spoke to him through teary eyes. "Help me get through this," I whispered. "I need you." I wanted joy. To feel whole again. I sometimes felt I was being punished, that God didn't want me to be happy. I was ill again for the third time, sick of grieving, my emotions, and the cold winter air.

I'd been having many dreams since Ari had died. Celeste, Brock, my mother, father, and sister were frequently in them. In one particular dream, he and I were flying in his plane. My mother was in the opposite row, facing us, doing a crossword puzzle. Ari was complaining about Celeste's criticism. I wanted to comfort him, so I hugged him and put my head on his chest. My mother looked at us and said gently, without judgment, "Why are you doing that? he's not here anymore." I awoke feeling terror.

Renata had called to see how I was faring. "All of your behavior, all of your dreams, are centered around one thought. There is only *one thing* you want. You cannot make him come back," she said tenderly. I started to cry, tearfully nodding my understanding on the other end of the line.

"Nothing is wrong, Debra," Tina said to me. "You *are* being supported. There have been so many signs. The guidance is here for you. You're going to be okay," she declared confidently.

The Universe continued to support me through the blessing of many friends with indelibly important roles, holding and healing my tender heart and taking their places beside me as they held my hand for a while. A fellow chorister had brought me her guitar as a loaner. It had a beautiful, round, warm tone that brought me joy. Another had brought me the want ads, and I scheduled an interview with a kinesiologist looking for a massage therapist in his center. I had already started providing private massages again, and it was a surprisingly good experience. It had taken me many weeks to feel emotionally strong enough to do so.

That evening, I cradled Ari's picture and danced to Dean Martin. I felt him filling me up with light, love, and guidance. It was the first time I did not cry.

* * *

HATTIE AND ALFRED HAD RETURNED from New Zealand, and I needed another place to live. Hattie contacted a neighbor, Stewart Dawson, whose house was vacant most of the year, as his family lived in Wales and only visited for a couple of weeks in spring and summer. They were amenable to me living there until the middle of June as long as I paid the utility bills. I was thrilled. It would buy me more time to save money to purchase a car and figure out my next steps.

The house was quaint, with southern exposure, a large central terrace that looked out over a valley, and a smaller one off the main bedroom. I was thrilled to have a place of my own again. I offered to weed the premises and establish a flowering garden showcasing the main terrace in return for free rent. Gardening was my bailiwick, and I knew the project would bring life into my veins, digging my hands into the soil and making the home's exterior as pretty as possible. The homeowners had happily agreed to this exchange, so I rolled up my sleeves and got to work.

The daytime temperatures were warming, and soon the ground would be ready for planting. I cleaned the home's interior from top to bottom, washing, sweeping, vacuuming, and dusting everything I possibly could to freshen the place, which had been vacant for several months. It took four full days.

Heavy drapes covered the windows like Hattie's place, but I opened them to let the light stream in. To my delight, my orchid was coming into bloom, and a couple of flowers had already sprouted bright lavender petals from its spiky sheaths.

Weeds and tall grass had grossly overrun the gardens around the house's perimeter, and dandelions filled the large, white-pebbled driveway on the north side, especially near the entrance. I knew it would take a couple of weeks to get all the weeds out. I certainly had my work cut out for me.

Nadine came to visit with a friend and stayed from early afternoon until the evening. We ate a simple dinner of curried chicken and rice I had prepared earlier. "Wow, Debra, this is a nice place!" she exclaimed, gazing appreciatively around the modest home. "And you don't have to pay rent?"

"I am beautifying the premises," I chirped, happy to have a big task with an end goal in sight. My structured personality adored projects which included physical might and organization, especially gardening outdoors in the fresh air.

We sat contentedly on the sofas in the living room, sipping our red wine. It felt good to have other people in the house, filling it with laughter and enjoying the simple pleasure of coming together.

* * *

I'D SET UP A MASSAGE TABLE in one of the guest bedrooms to provide massage therapy services. Hattie had introduced me to some of her friends, and my schedule was full. I was exhausted from all the physical work, but I was happy here. Life had been non-stop since Ari had died, and I'd dropped twenty pounds. I wanted to start hiking again. Getting to know some of the ladies in Hattie's group would be fun. I had no friends close by and needed camaraderie.

I missed Ari very much, but the gnawing had mostly become an ache. I felt healing seep slowly into my core. White butterflies showed up as I weeded the gardens, and I sensed Ari's presence around me. Butterflies didn't usually appear until April. I knew it was another sign. I would be okay.

In a recent dream, Ari was sitting comfortably in a high-backed chair. I was sitting on the floor at his feet, and we held hands. I questioned the validity of what we'd shared, wondering if it was as magical as I'd believed. He rushed in. "Don't *ever* think that what we had wasn't real, Debra." When I awoke, I distinctly felt "someone" blowing gently into my right ear. The sensation persisted. I knew it was Ari. I smiled, but I also wanted to die. It was so painful to live without him.

Later that afternoon, while gardening, I saw two white butterflies twirling about each other. "Oh, Ari!" I cried. "I miss you so much!"

I felt tired, angry, and drained. I'd worked so hard since Ari had died, moving all over the place, struggling to survive. I was emotionally and physically exhausted. I was still singing with the chorus, but I heard my voice laced with sadness, like a bird in a cage. I wanted to feel joy again. I felt so unsafe. I cried and cried, but the relief was temporary.

My love for him was spilling, gushing, streaming out of me with nowhere to go. The amount of time I was engulfed in sorrow was lessening but losing him still hurt as much as it had the day he died. I feared I would grieve the rest of my life, terrified I wouldn't survive. Love had pointed its rosy finger at me, and I had exclaimed, "YES! YES!" jumping onto its thorny hook, letting it reel me in, swinging both feet into the boat, making a commitment my heart had never promised before. Once my haven, it now had a gaping hole in its hull and was sucking me to the ocean floor.

Losing Ari was like losing a limb, I thought. Shocking. Terminal. Unbelievable. Unacceptable. Gone from sight but still there when my eyes were closed. When would the pain be over? Were these feelings normal? Was I progressing, digressing, regressing? My monkey mind swung from vine to vine. Sometimes beneath it all trickled a quiet stream, glittering with light, letting me believe all would be okay. But when? *When?*

* * *

THE DAWSON FAMILY CAME for a week and were delighted by the new gardens beautifying their comfortable home. I would stay in the house for another two months.

I contemplated obtaining a visa to work in France, but I was afraid I wouldn't have the energy it took to complete the stack of paperwork to make it happen. I would be required to go back to the United States to process it at the embassy in New York City and I was reluctant, afraid my application would be denied and the dream would be over.

* * *

AT THE END OF APRIL, Nadine and I took a bus tour through Rome that we'd scheduled before Ari died. It was a delightful reprieve from the raucous debate ricocheting around my heart and mind.

Everything in Rome was colossal; the statues, fountains, arches, columns, and churches were masterful and grandiose. We saw all the sights Rome is famous for, including the Pope, who drove by the massive crowds in his Pope mobile when we attended his Wednesday morning address in St. Peter's Square at the Vatican.

We visited St. Patrick's Church and were awed and humbled by the stunning scenes on the walls and ceiling of the iconic Sistine Chapel. We marveled at the monstrous dome and inner ruins of the Colosseum and visited the crumbling, once magnificent Forum. The Pantheon, a former Roman temple dedicated to all the pagan gods of Rome, was now a Catholic church. Our jaws dropped as we drank in the stunning, verdant landscapes and fountains of Tivoli Gardens at Villa d'Este, and we were utterly dwarfed by Trevi Fountain, the largest Baroque fountain in Rome and one of the most famous in the world.

We climbed the steep slope of the Spanish steps and viewed the slender obelisk piercing the sky in the center of Pincio Park. We ate our fill of delectable Italian food: pungent cheeses, homemade plates of pasta smothered with creamy carbonara, and leathery, unctuous salamis, but I was spoiled by French cuisine.

* * *

OUR TOUR GUIDE HAD SPOKEN PRIMARILY French, and Nadine had often translated for me. I missed her and our regular walks by the coast, as I now lived more than an hour away. I wondered what the future held and if I would return with a visa. I didn't want to go back to the States, as my heart was decidedly in France.

Having recently purchased a car from a cousin of Niccolo's, I'd acquired the freedom I needed to get around on my own. I had paid work in Monaco, thanks to Parker's patients, and although the drive from the mountains was long, it was well worth the money I received per massage.

Sometimes I would meet up with Nadine afterward, and it felt good to be down on the coast. The ride from Nice to Monaco on the A8 was as stunning as ever. Driving through the frequent tunnels high above the sea across rocketing bridges and viaducts always took my breath away. None of the places I had been in my life had my heart like France. She sang an ancient song like a siren deep inside me. I longed for her beauty, timeless shores, and vivid colors splashed around me in brilliant hues and textures. I couldn't bear the thought of leaving, even for a short time.

Having stalled long enough, I downloaded the necessary forms for a visa and began filling them out. I struggled with choosing a flight to New York. My resistance loomed like an unscalable wall before me; I couldn't see what was on the other side. I felt the tension in the muscles of my body wound tightly to my bones. It was so hard for me to let go, to let things flow.

* * *

CONCETTA HAD DONE A PHONE READING for me two weeks before my flight home. Ari was indeed watching over me. He mentioned what she thought was a poem about a "rose." Tears of acknowledgment trickled down my cheeks. "The Rose," I said. "It's a Bette Midler song. I sang it to Ari after he died and at his grave, and I would dance with him in my living room."

"He wants you to know he weeps at being separated from you and misses you terribly. He didn't know he was leaving," Concetta said gently. "He would have married you if he had the opportunity." There was certainty in her voice. I knew it was the truth. "He wants you to live your life. He still loves you and will *always* love you." She stopped, moved by the emotion that was washing over her. She paused, and her voice brightened. "He wants you to savor life. Loving someone else will not diminish what he shared with you. He doesn't want you to mourn him. He will see you soon."

Her guides had more to tell me. "They want you to see the bigger picture," she continued. "There is a whole new adventure for you on the horizon. You chose a life that is incredibly full, exciting, and constant. Let your heart open to that." She paused. "Focus on the gift of gratitude. You will develop very deep friendships, and life will get lighter."

CHAPTER 19

The End of an Era

I sat quietly on the airplane from Frankfurt, Germany, to JFK. I usually flew direct from Nice, but the prices were steep in June, so I chose a stopover flight. I peeked out the little window over the wing and wondered if I'd ever be back. I could hardly bear that thought. I felt so lost. I didn't know who I was or how to define myself; I couldn't reach my core. I missed my apartment in France. All my flowers would have been planted and blooming by now, their colorful little faces smiling at me like Heaven itself.

Nadine and I had enjoyed dinner together on my last night near her place in Vallauris. I would miss her the most. She and Theo had been anchors for me and made me feel like I had never lived anywhere else, and now, there was nowhere else I wanted to live.

I had made an appointment months earlier to see Richard Harrington, a well-known psychic medium on Long Island. Tina was also going to have a reading. I was a bit nervous and hoping Ari would come through. I would not be disappointed.

Richard started the recording. "There is a male with the first initial 'A' here," Richard said as he indicated the presence over my right shoulder and somewhat beside me. "He is holding a large bouquet of red roses."

"That's Ari!" I beamed, feeling excited and peaceful at the same time. Wherever we had lain, Ari had always been on my right, and he had "blown" in my right ear after my dream at the Dawsons' house a couple of months earlier.

Ari had a lot to say to me through Richard. "He would have died a lot more traumatically if you hadn't come into his life. You completed him. You were the only woman he was ever faithful to, and you made a deep impression on him." He paused. I let his words sink into my heart. "He was not the same person to others that he was to you. You got to know the real Ari. You gave him unconditional love and never made him feel guilty or manipulated." Concetta's readings echoed many of the same sentiments. I'd felt the truth of her words like a salve to my heart, bolstered by Richard's insight. "He died in turmoil, but not because of you. It was his time." I was relieved to hear this. I had been carrying so much guilt, feeling that Ari's death was my fault. Richard continued. "He cleared your father issues, your ex-lover issues, and your abandonment issues," he said without going into detail.

"Wow, that's a big accomplishment." I blushed shyly, feeling somewhat exposed, as Richard's words touched those tender places inside me. Concetta had said more than once that my childhood issues had not been at play in this relationship. Indeed, I also believed they were not. I felt safe with Ari. Safe to be wholly myself. There was no power struggle between us.

"Ari wants you to know he is saving a dance for you and that he'll sing for you." Richard smiled, amused. "Well, maybe singing is not such a great idea. Singing wasn't his forte." I sat bolt upright in my seat and clapped my hands together. I could hear Ari laughing, his sense of humor shining through. There was no way Richard could have known about my dances with Ari, nor his singing to me! True, his singing was not tuneful, but he sang directly to my heart, and it hadn't mattered in the least. He'd sung *to me.*

"He has cleared a lot of karma with his family since he died," Richard offered thoughtfully. I could feel the impact of this communication, both through his words and Ari's loving presence in the room. I was happy to hear this. I had been deeply saddened that Ari had suffered so much with his family and was delighted to have been the one person he trusted to share his emotions with.

Richard's reading brought immense closure. What was most comforting to me was that Ari's presence in the room with Richard and I felt the same as his presence with me since his passing; that I had been able to call him to me, that it was not a figment of my imagination. I sensed that I'd made significant spiritual progress since Ari had died. I felt he had helped to thrust me ahead, that I had completed lifetimes of work by coming together with him to forge a connection that remained deeply in place. He had indeed never left me! I felt his presence as a constant companion and light around me. I could have him in my life for the rest of my life. With deep gratitude, I felt greatly loved. I had been given a unique privilege, a magnificent gift.

A couple of days later, Ari came to me in a dream. Seated on a couch or a car seat, he said with all the love in his heart, "I would have fallen in love with you *deeply*." He said it over and over, slowly. I felt this statement was of utmost importance to him and could feel the intensity of his emotion behind it. The look of love on his face reflected an incredible peace and power of presence. "Debra, I *loved* your kisses," he crooned as his head swayed back and forth. I awoke in rapture, the luckiest girl in the world.

* * *

I HADN'T TOLD EVERYONE ABOUT ARI. I wasn't sure how that knowledge would be received, especially by my father. I sat next to him on the couch. "Dad, Ari and I were in love," I said quietly, holding my breath, awaiting his reply.

He looked at me for a few moments, processing the gravity of the statement before speaking. "I suspected something when I saw the pictures of you and him," he said softly, without judgment. I had shown him pictures from the races and the one in front of Ari's plane. Yes, I'm sure someone who knew me well would be able to tell there was more to the story. I hadn't suspected my father was one of those someones. "I knew you had deep feelings for him by how you spoke of him." He had done the mathematical calculation, weighing the tones and the words that I thought had carefully guarded my secret. My father was intuitive in his own right, a brilliant civil engineer well-recognized in his trade who always trusted his inner authority. "I knew he was a good man because of how he treated you," he said with a smile, a respectful gaze lighting up his thoughtful eyes—another accurate calculation.

"I miss him so much, Dad. Going back to France feels like going back to an empty house," I said sadly.

He nodded with deep understanding. "I know how that feels," he said, his eyes reflecting his inner thoughts.

"I know you are no stranger to loss," I said, looking into his eyes. He had lost his mother to ovarian cancer when he was thirteen. She had dwindled for many months, and they were finally forced to put her in the hospital. When it came time for her to pass, he, and his older brother, John, had never gotten to say goodbye to her.

Suddenly my father became uncharacteristically emotional as tears sprung from his eyes. "I don't know what I would do if your mother went first...." I squeezed his hand. "And I lost Carol too...," he said, his voice halting in a stifled sob as he choked back the tsunami that threatened to obliterate a well-defined shoreline. I was still holding his hand, holding the space for his feelings. He had used alcohol to numb these feelings for so long but had spontaneously stopped drinking almost ten years before my trip to France. "That's why I keep it all up here," he said, now composed, tapping on his right temple. "Because it's—"

"Safer?" I offered gently, smiling. He nodded. It felt good to have him share his emotions with me. "I love you, Dad," I said, present with the tenderness of the moment. I was still holding his hand.

"I love you too, honey," he said, looking at me with deep appreciation.

My sister Carol had been born severely retarded, and by the time she was eighteen months old, my parents had put her in a facility that offered full-time care. It was devastating for them, but they wanted to give me a normal life. I was three years old then and had no conscious recollection of Carol, except for the images of her empty yellow bedroom and the placement of her crib, a memory my mother confirmed as I shared this with her decades later. No, my dad was no stranger to loss.

"I never wanted to keep this from you, but I didn't want you to judge me," I said innocently. He wasn't. It had been incredibly healing for me to share this moment with him. His guard had briefly dropped as he opened his heart in a fleeting respite from his mind that sat like a watchdog, unleashing the legitimacy of his feelings. It was the greatest gift he could ever have given me. I felt close to him as we held hands, meeting on the common ground of our hearts. I couldn't recall ever having had a moment like this with him. There was no greater gift than the strength of the realness he offered me.

***

RICHARD HARRINGTON HAD TOLD ME to be aware of flashing red lights. Ari had indicated to Richard that he would come to me this way. It was three months, and nothing had transpired. As I lay on my back meditating one evening before bed, a deep, red, irregular light rose softly into my awareness. Tiny white lights twinkled in front of it like stars. I watched them for a while and rolled over to go to sleep. As I did, I saw softly shimmering pinheads of red light, ebbing and surging, almost as if I were looking at a fiber optic Christmas tree, but they were arranged in a circular pattern, like a wreath. I had never experienced such a vision and was delighted that Ari had kept his promise.

My visit to the French Embassy was approaching, and I had received my submission package back from the translator. I had recently started a temp job at a university student services clinic nearby and was happy to be reconnecting with an old friend who worked upstairs. I told her about my love for Ari and the magic we shared. I still missed him. It had been almost nine months since he had passed. Some days I felt the memory of him slipping away. In others, he was palpably around me.

I had dropped the watch he had given me for the second time. The clasp was simple and unreliable, with a row of holes punched into a leather band where a golden ball-type fastener on the other end could be pushed through. Hardly the type of security for a watch with its worth. This time, the watch had landed on the hardwood floor of my bedroom in my parents' house, and the glass face had shattered, embedding minuscule shards in the tiny gears. I'd found a jeweler who specialized in fixing this type of mechanism, and I reluctantly handed it over to him. He repaired it, but it stopped frequently, and after a couple of visits to him, it never worked the same way again, and eventually, it stopped altogether. I was deeply disappointed, but it was no surprise to me. I knew I had to move on at some point. I was sad. My life felt small and without impact. I needed a change. I needed to feel alive again.

It was my birthday, and I asked Ari to reach out to me in some significant, unmistakable way. I had a fun celebration with friends, and my sister gave me a beautiful necklace. It was an open circle studded with tiny diamonds that hung suspended from a slender chain.

I felt loved. The day's celebration had filled me up, and I had received e-cards from Gwyn and Niccolo, Nadine, and Erik, my "family" overseas. I knew Ari must have been with me somehow, even if I couldn't feel his presence. He did not forget my request.

While asleep in the wee hours, I stirred, feeling a hand cupping the back of my neck. I knew immediately that I was being "touched." There was, of course, no one else but me in my room. I knew it was Ari but was still afraid because I had only experienced him in the dream state. "I know it's you, Ari, but I'm afraid," I said aloud. His touch lingered for a moment more, and then he was gone. I drifted back to sleep and awoke in the morning ecstatic. I'd just had a once-in-a-lifetime experience that I would never forget. How was it that I could ever doubt his love for me?

Before his birthday visit, I had seen a pair of white butterflies twirling about each other. White butterflies always signified his presence. They had first started to appear in Montaroux when I had moved to the Dawsons' house. The two tiny white creatures twirled around each other for a few moments and separated. Immediately, a third white butterfly appeared and started fluttering with one of the others. Maybe there *is* another perfect mate for me, I thought happily.

I had moved on to another temp job in a local vitamin company that employed thousands of people. My visa for France had been denied. I was no longer sure it mattered. I knew I had to return because my car, and some of my personal belongings, including an additional massage table I had purchased for Parker's office, still had to be dealt with. I needed to be on French soil to see how I felt about living there again. I scheduled a two-week trip but sensed the fairy tale was over.

The temp job in the vitamin company had turned into a promising full-time position in the company's international division. I liked the job, but over time found out that it wouldn't offer the travel I was hoping for, as that belonged to the well-seasoned sales directors.

I wanted to travel the world, especially Europe. I experienced a deep ache that told me my real opportunities weren't here in the States. Work was consuming. I was putting in extra hours because I wanted to learn the industry faster and felt hampered by what I considered a steep learning curve that had to be quickly mastered. My bosses were happy with my performance, but I was unfulfilled. Regardless, I would wind up staying for three years.

***

MY TRIP TO FRANCE CAME AND WENT. I stayed with Nadine and took care of business while I was there. I had to sell the car I had recently purchased, which Gwyn and Niccolo had been minding, and give away the remainder of my possessions, which I had been storing in the Dawsons' garage. A friend of Nadine's bought the massage table for personal use.

Nadine and I indulged in a "pizza quatre fromage" at Santa Lucia on marina Baie des Anges. It had a thin crispy semolina crust coated with fresh, chunky marinara sauce heaped with gooey lumps of Roquefort, cantal, goat, and mozzarella cheeses—a delectable favorite of mine that I would miss for a long time to come.

Being on the coast filled my senses with the delights I'd experienced while living there. I still missed Ari, but I enjoyed my trip and my friends. I could hardly believe how quickly the months had flown by since my departure nine months prior.

Theo hadn't answered my calls or emails. Nadine said she didn't see him much anymore. I wondered how he was faring and was distressed that he hadn't connected with me. Maybe he had changed his contact information? I hoped nothing bad had happened to him.

When I returned from France, I checked my French phone for the text messages I had received from Ari. I had saved them all. They were gone! I panicked. It must have happened when I switched the SIM card. I quickly remembered I had written them down in my journal and was relieved. I was not ready to let go.

Tina and I went to see Richard Harrington for a second time. He shared much of the same information he had on the first visit. Ari was "there" for me, and I was thrilled to connect with him again. "He said you helped him make the transition and changed his mind about women." Richard smirked as he looked at me. I asked for a concrete sign. "Pay attention to the butterflies," he said.

I clapped my hands together in glee. "Ari *is* my beautiful white butterfly!" I squealed. "He always shows up for me!" My heart brimmed with delight as I recalled the first time I had seen butterflies in the mountains of Montaroux, well before their season.

"When have you ever seen a butterfly in the winter?" Richard asked with a wink.

* * *

THE SPRING WORE ON AND TURNED into early summer. I still missed Ari acutely from time to time, but I felt ready to open my heart to another. A few men from other departments at the vitamin company were attractive, and I was hopeful.

As I prepared for bed one evening, I looked over at Ari's picture, ever present on my nightstand. "I'm ready, Ari," I said, feeling my love for him without pain. My sister had been right all that time ago. It had been eighteen months since he'd passed. I could think of him and simultaneously feel my desire for another. He had opened my heart like no one ever had in my life. I wanted a fairy tale with a happy ending and to experience what I knew was possible with a man. I would not settle for less.

Maybe there was promise at the vitamin company, but I had one hard fast rule about work and relationships: do not mix business with pleasure. I had dated an older man I had worked with when I was barely twenty, and although it ended amicably, I drew a line between my job and romance. It was a safe bet and a great excuse when a man wanted to date me. I could roll it out like an elevator pitch without guilt and only minor objection on his part. We all understood it was not a good idea. I didn't need to prove this to myself again.

* * *

THE FIRST TIME I HEARD TRISTAN'S VOICE on the other end of the phone, I thought, *wow, if this guy looks like he sounds, he must be gorgeous.* He was slated to become one of our company's new regional sales directors, and I had coordinated his flight from Wisconsin to New York to meet our department head. He had the gift of gab and gratitude—a winning combination. We had spoken several times already, and he felt like a friend. I was looking forward to having him join the team.

***

"DEBRA?" HE ASKED, striding quickly toward me, looking like he would smother me in a bear hug.

"Tristan?" I blinked, knowing the voice, but stunned by the slim, bald man with huge dark eyes and tiny ears rapidly approaching me. I was taken aback by his appearance, which defied the voice I'd heard over the phone; all I could do was thrust out my hand.

Awkwardly, he shook it. "It's so nice to finally meet you!" he said, pumping my hand up and down.

"Yeah, same here!" I managed, still dumbfounded. I was in shock, without knowing why. Was there a fantasy brewing somewhere that had just been shattered?

Tristan was always the first to arrive at the office and the last to leave. He was passionate about his work. Everything between us evened out, and I eventually became accustomed to his appearance. He was fun. Everyone loved him. We all went out after hours frequently. Tristan drank a lot.

That year, I'd had a lively Christmas party at my place, and we all drank too much. After the other guests had left, I could see Tristan was wobbling, so I offered to let him stay. We both slept in my bed. I was still dressed when I awoke groggily the next morning. I gazed over at him and looked into his soft dark eyes. The line I had drawn in the sand disappeared from view as I pulled myself toward him and laid my head on his bare chest.

On a typical night, Tristan and I were dining at our favorite local restaurant. He had ordered one bottle of red wine, as usual. Once we returned to his place, I knew the bottle of vodka would come out. After our first glass, he excused himself to smoke a cigarette. I took the opportunity to guzzle a couple more glasses with the crazy notion of diminishing his intake. I sat there, bloated but perversely triumphant, as I waited for him to return.

"Wow, I didn't think we drank that much," he chuckled, filling our glasses again. The waiter returned to take our order. "We'll have another bottle of red," Tristan chirped. I was dumbstruck. It had *never* occurred to me that he would order a second bottle.

***

AFTER I BROKE UP WITH HIM, Tristan's behavior became erratic and malicious. He sent seething texts, then apologetic texts, and even climbed up to my second-floor balcony in the middle of the night with a bouquet of flowers in his hand, yanked from the garden we had planted at his apartment. He stood swaying outside the screen door, dirt-caked roots dangling—a pathetic shadow imploring me to take him back.

Even though we had kept our romance a secret, life at the office was excruciating after that. I loved Tristan but didn't budge. He became hostile. I became withdrawn. He rebounded into another relationship at work. What had happened? How could I go from loving a man like Ari, who adored me, to a man who attacked me like a rabid dog? Had I just settled for the first man who came along? Worse yet, had I been the other half of this wounded relationship dynamic?

Half-heartedly, I started reading *Codependent No More* by Melody Beattie. At the time, my perspective was on understanding (and fixing) behaviors, especially the behaviors of others, but it was a start. I didn't actually see myself as codependent. Still, I was willing to look deeper at my childhood, aberrant attraction to men, and unhealthy behaviors in a romantic relationship.

One morning at work, I gazed at the laminated world map tacked to the fabric panel of my cubicle. My heart plummeted as I raised my hand to touch it. I hung my head and surrendered to the tears pouring from my eyes. My dream of traveling the world had gone up in smoke, and I had broken a cardinal rule by dating a man at work, which backfired miserably. *I don't want to be here anymore,* I thought, deeply regretting the past year. Pulling myself together, I finished printing out a report for our department head, Amil Chowdhury, a man I respected and adored.

The company was recently acquired, and significant layoffs swept through every department. Ours had been no exception. Tristan was one of the people who got fired. I had just found out when I returned from lunch. I was stunned but relieved. Numbly, I gathered up my report and a notebook and headed to Amil's office.

Arising from his seat, he motioned for me to come in and uncharacteristically closed the door. "I'm not supposed to tell you this," he began, his eyes locked on mine, his voice softer than usual, "but HR is coming for you in five minutes." I gaped at him in disbelief as his eyes filled with compassion.

I hurried back to my cubicle scooping up anything I thought mattered, and threw it into a small cardboard box. A woman from the Human Resources department arrived. "I have to say goodbye to everyone," I said, my eyes starting to water. I ignored her objections as I made my way around the department, offering hugs through teary eyes to incredulous coworkers as I said my last goodbyes.

The Human Resources lady trailed impatiently behind me: "Debra, you must go now."

I saved my boss, Jen, for last. She had found out only that morning that I would be let go. Over my time there, we had become close, wishing we could pursue a friendship that neither of us thought appropriate, as she was my boss. "I'm so sorry!" she said, stepping outside her door. She raised her arms to embrace me, our cheeks wet with tears.

"Well, at least now we can be friends!" I said, laughing and crying. In time, this would become a happy reality, but it was the end of an era. The Human Resources lady escorted me to the door, and I walked out, letting it close behind me for the last time.

Part Four

The Reckoning

CHAPTER 20

Hello Stranger

The newly renovated TWA Hotel at John F. Kennedy International Airport was elegantly fashioned in mid-century modern panache. Everything in the spacious lobby was decorated in red and white. Balconies of broad, forward-tilted windows illuminated the whitewashed scene below, with color splattered boldly in posters capturing famous people, places, and things from years gone by.

I spotted Jonathan right away, and my heart skipped a beat as I hurried toward him. His face brightened into recognition as he waved back. We'd been planning our rendezvous for the past couple of weeks as he coordinated his arrival from the west coast to New York City, and I was excited to see him again. "Hi, Debra! Thank you for coming to pick me up," he said, leaning forward to give me a warm hug.

"Of course. It's so good to see you!" I beamed as we embraced.

He smiled and gazed appreciatively at our surroundings. "Isn't this lobby amazing?"

"It's spectacular! I love the retro décor," I offered, taking it all in, exhilarated to be in his presence.

"I'm starving. Let's get something to eat," he said, pointing to a parked airplane visible through the large windows. "That's where we're having lunch," he said, eager to explore the newly renovated aircraft that now served as a restaurant.

Dragging his scuffed suitcases behind him, Jonathan Hulley admired the expansive perimeter, a traveler in love with his travels. He strolled, chin up, head moving slowly like a periscope on his slender neck, as we made our way through the bustling scene toward a long red carpeted hall leading out to where the "Connie" stood.

Stepping outside, the wind promptly whipped our hair away from our faces. Stretched before us, the glamorous 1962 Lockheed Constellation L-1649A airplane, recently remodeled into a cocktail lounge, lavished proudly atop the asphalt, completely visible to the guests from the spacious airport lobby.

As we approached the airstair, we stopped to take photos. Out of nowhere, a woman appeared and offered to take our picture. She was dark-skinned, with short-cropped, light pink hair and big-rimmed glasses that offset her pretty face. "Do you guys want me to take a couple of photos of you?" she inquired, making her way toward us. "I'm Yvonne," she said, extending a friendly hand.

"That would be great!" I chirped, delightedly handing her my cell phone. We finished our introductions, and she motioned for us to stand in front of the stairs. I sensed that Jonathan was apprehensive, but he moved into position beside me and put his arm snuggly around my shoulders as we posed for Yvonne. Was he worried that I would share the photos?

"Let's get some action shots," Yvonne offered and directed us to ascend the stairs. We paused to look back at her in various poses on the steps so that she could capture the moments.

"Wow! thank you so much!" I gushed, quickly scrolling through the pictures she had taken. *We look like Jackie and JFK himself!* I thought, imagining a grand life to come.

"Oh, you're so welcome!" she smiled broadly. "Enjoy your stay."

A pleasant young man dressed in a 1960s flight-crew uniform escorted us to our seats, which had been reupholstered with light brown leather to replicate the style of that period. A tiny white pedestal table sat in front of us on the red carpet. We settled in and ordered some snacks.

We sipped our Chardonnay as we chatted about FARM, eating flatbreads with bean sprouts and avocado dip. Jonathan playfully smeared some onto my fingers in a moment of spontaneous flirtation. "Hey!" I protested, wiping the mess with a napkin. I wanted him to lick it off. Would he have? Would I have had to dare him? Was he attracted to me like I was to him?

He had been quite engaged with WhatsApp messages over the past few months as we got to know one another, typing my name wrapped in heart and flower emojis, singing me little snippets of songs as he hopped about the country. One evening he even sent me a little teddy bear emoji before bed. "Oh, I love it!" I typed.

"It told me to tell you it loves you too," he replied, followed by a heart and another teddy bear. Apparently, our relationship was not strictly business.

I hadn't been this excited about a man since Ari and had nearly given up hope of finding "the one" for me. The antics with Tristan had clobbered my heart, and a couple of short-lived romances over the past decade made me question my ability to be in a healthy, sustainable relationship.

A good friend had shared a YouTube video of Jonathan months before I'd met him, teaching others about a company called FARM and their regenerative agriculture software technology, Regenaware. I was riveted as I searched his eyes deeply, letting his voice and features drip into my consciousness, waiting for recognition. "*This is my guy!*" I whispered breathily, alone in my living room. I just *had* to meet him! Maybe I could assist him somehow, and we would serve the world together. I thought it was a good idea and sent him an email. He politely declined, but I had gotten him thinking about it.

Over the ensuing months, I created a concise educational document about regenerative farming and sent it to him. He appreciated the effort and started to share it with others. I wanted more. He was getting busier, and my intuition told me it was time to try again. He agreed. "Let's see where we go with each other," he said. I could hardly contain myself, certain this was the beginning of something long-awaited. I would pick him up at JFK airport the following month, as he had business in New York City. This would be a perfect opportunity for us to get to know one another more and discuss possibilities for working together.

And now here we were, having lunch over a glass of wine! "Let's take a selfie!" I tittered gleefully as I picked up my phone.

"I'm not a selfie kind of guy," Jonathan countered decisively.

"Why not?" I asked innocently.

He shrugged. "You're not going to post it anywhere, are you?" It seems my intuition had been correct.

"Why would I do that? It's just for me," I said, shaking my head. Jonathan made no motion to partake. "Fine, I'll take one of myself," I sighed. I was stung but decided I wouldn't make a mountain out of a molehill. As I prepared to snap the photo, he leaned in. I was ecstatic. We looked like the perfect, happy couple. Could I become the woman of his dreams?

After the Connie, we strolled around the lobby, admiring the retro décor as Beatles music serenaded us from overhead. "Would you like another drink?" Jonathan offered.

We headed toward a freestanding oval-shaped bar in the sunken lobby lounge. As we sat down to order, we spied Yvonne. Jonathan motioned for her to come and join us. She delightedly obliged, ordering a Margarita. We sipped our drinks as Yvonne told us about her daughter in college in California.

"My daughter is in her first semester," Yvonne shared. "She tells me she's lost and doesn't know what she wants to do with her life."

"What are her interests?" I asked, eager to give my insight. I was well acquainted with feeling lost.

"She's a creative type," Yvonne said proudly. "She likes art and poetry, but she doesn't have a direction and is unsure if college is what she wants...," she trailed off pensively. "I worry about her. She doesn't have any friends out there and is becoming depressed."

"You need to start imagining a positive outcome for her situation," Jonathan offered. "Try to avoid dwelling on negative thoughts," he said definitively.

"It's tough to do that. I'm so far away from her, and I feel I can't help her," she said, gazing down at the floor.

"That's just your inner dialog running an old tape," Jonathan continued, his eyes intent as he leaned closer toward Yvonne.

"She's not focused and is becoming more and more down. I can hear it in her voice," she said, her lips pulled tightly across her face.

"You can change those thoughts," Jonathan continued with an air of absolutism. "Start seeing her in your mind's eye as choosing opportunities that light her up. Put your attention there. Nothing bad is *happening*. It's the feeling you're experiencing that is causing you to worry. It's up to you to choose positive thoughts," he said gently.

Yvonne brightened. "I never really thought about it like that."

I squirmed enthusiastically in my seat, relishing this line of thinking. "And remember," I added, "she is being guided. She has a path and a purpose, as we all do. You can help her see this instead of reinforcing her difficulties. Remind her of her strengths, talents, and ability to make choices or change her mind." Yvonne's eyes were dewy. Her shoulders dropped slightly as she slowly nodded her head up and down. "All of her feelings are valid, as are yours," I continued. "We all know life can feel harsh, especially when we're overwhelmed, not knowing what direction to head in. Trust that she will be okay and will grow through her pain. Where she is now is part of helping her to discover who she is. She isn't failing, and *nothing's wrong*; she's on her path." I put my hand on her shoulder.

"You're right," Yvonne said. "I've been through many ups and downs in life and have come through, so she will too." She readjusted herself on her barstool. "Where did you find this girl?" she asked, smiling at Jonathan.

"We're doing some work together," he said, looking at me. He didn't appear particularly impressed. I, however, was entirely taken by our conversation. I envisioned he and I like airport prophets, traveling the world, raising the spirits of those who felt drawn to hear it. Maybe it was like any other day for him, striking up a conversation with another stranger in a string of endless faces, places, and airport lounges. Wasn't he attached to any of them?

I recounted the first in-person conversation we'd had in another hotel lobby in New York City six months earlier when I'd decided to attend one of his presentations. "While I'm with a group of people at a meeting or a dinner, I'm completely interested and immersed," he said. "When it's over, I move on. I never really miss anyone or anything," he offered, his luminous eyes detached but present in the moment. Appreciative of the flow of things, he moved accordingly, letting the current of life carry him along. That wasn't to say he wasn't fiercely passionate about FARM. The mission grounded his efforts, propelling him forward, but he didn't need to control the specifics of his direction. I marveled at that idea, having forced so many things in life. I was growing tired of my resistance.

At the time, I found myself compelled to share with him. "My dad died recently, and I have a tightness in my chest, something I can't digest." I was still grieving his loss, though I sometimes felt he had gone long ago.

Without apologizing for my loss or taking his eyes off me, he said softly, "you can choose to change your mind about your dad and the grieving process." I thought it odd that he hadn't acknowledged my feelings. "The western world focuses so much on loss when that person hasn't really gone. Communication becomes easier when you learn how to tune into their energy. My dad died ten years ago, and I feel his presence with me all the time." His eyes illuminated as he connected deeply with the idea.

Something in me had shifted; I was buoyant. This wasn't a new idea for me. Maybe it was just the way he had conveyed it. I studied him as he spoke. Sophisticated and slim, his long golden hair hung attractively around his face. He was uncommonly "self-contained," his personal space circumscribed tightly around him, and though polite, he didn't need my presence to change anything; he was the focal point of his life.

Since that time, he had become warmer and more engaged. We were comfortable around each other, and he was friendly, flirtatious, and incredibly magnetic. Was I reading too much into things? Hadn't the universe brought us together for a reason—a soul mate with whom I could travel and serve the world? Why else would he be here? He had shown up out of the blue, as Ari had when I decided I wanted to go to the French Riviera.

The sound of Yvonne's voice escorted my senses back to the present moment. "Is that one of those old black and white photobooths, like when we were kids?" she asked gleefully, pointing to a small rectangular chamber with a thick red drape covering its entrance. The three of us hurried over and crammed ourselves into the little booth. "Say cheese," she snickered as we wiggled closer together on the narrow bench, making a little bit of history.

Later that afternoon, Jonathan and I drove to Kate Surinoff's Riverdale apartment in the Bronx for the night before heading out to Saddle River,

New Jersey, for a meeting the next day. I was delighted that the three of us would spend some time together. I had met Kate briefly while attending Jonathan's presentation in New York City, and months later, at another gathering, we struck up a friendship. Keenly interested in regenerative and organic farming practices, she was a loyal supporter of FARM and their Regenaware technology.

We pulled into the narrow driveway and parked behind her building. Kate was already at the door when we arrived at the front steps. As Jonathan and I walked into the small foyer, she flung her arms around us, one at a time, her pretty face glowing with delight.

"I can't believe you're here!" she gushed, leading us down the narrow hall to the small kitchen. It was a modest, sparsely furnished space with three bedrooms and two bathrooms. Several folding chairs were arranged around a small table in the kitchen—Kate was a self-proclaimed minimalist.

Jonathan settled himself into the largest room, just off the kitchen. "Do you two want something to eat?" Kate asked.

"I've got a meeting in the city tonight, but thank you anyway," Jonathan said. "Kate, do you think I should call for a car or take the train?"

"It's probably better for you to take an Uber. There's no direct train," she said.

Kate and I went out for Thai food after Jonathan left. I enjoyed her presence. She was a lively, cheerful soul, always looking forward to the best outcomes. She confided that she had initially thought Jonathan and I were a couple. "When you and Jonathan were talking, I felt the energy between you. I was so happy at the idea that he might have found someone," she recounted with delight. "I still feel it," she said with a smile.

She had known him a long time. I trusted her. Her perspective was very optimistic, and I appreciated her fresh, unjudging outlook on situations and people. "I like him, Kate. He's got many qualities that I want in a partner. I haven't felt this way in so many years."

"I don't ever remember Jonathan talking about a relationship; he never seemed to be focused on that," Kate said reflectively. "It would be wonderful if you wind up becoming a couple!"

Jonathan returned late in the evening. We prepared some ginger tea and sat around the kitchen table, making small talk.

"Is there a man in your life, Kate?" Jonathan inquired cheerfully.

"There is," she offered, her face lighting up. "We started dating only a few months ago, but I like him."

"Did you tell him about FARM?" Jonathan asked, sipping his hot tea, his eyes intent on hers.

"Michael is more interested in traditional investments," Kate said, still smiling.

"FARM is a very significant part of your life," Jonathan offered as if nothing else mattered.

"I'm not going to pressure him about it," she said courteously. Kate wasn't one to force things. Jonathan nodded and turned to me.

"What about you, Debra? Is there anyone special in your life?" he asked.

"No…I…I'm not dating anyone right now," I stammered, caught off guard. Didn't he know he was the one for me?

Kate had seen my reaction. "What about you, Jonathan?" she asked, politely reciprocating.

"Dating is difficult, as I'm never in one place for very long. Besides, I'm focused on FARM right now," he said decisively. Of course, he didn't know how I felt. I hoped things would change if he spent enough time with me. I wanted to travel with him. Undoubtedly, spending time together would be the recipe we needed to cultivate a deeper relationship—one I wanted with all my heart.

The next morning we made fried eggs and toast, and I treated them to energy work on Kate's massage table that we had set up in Jonathan's room. He and I would be returning to her place once we finished in Saddle River. After the treatments, we headed off into the midday Bronx traffic toward the George Washington Bridge.

Jonathan was scheduled to meet over dinner with Libertine Newsome, a long-time FARM benefactor, and one of her friends Alistair Chase, a brilliant engineer and technology mogul during the tech boom and early Silicon Valley era interested in helping FARM to standardize their Regenaware software for international distribution. As we drove along, I breathed in Jonathan's presence, listening to his conference call, his lilting voice serenading my ears. He was hopeful about the meeting but open to the hands of fate. Cool, calm, collected, and confident, he had a sixth sense that guided him.

We walked into the charming, chateau-style hotel lobby attractively appointed in a European-American flare that I remembered oh-so-well from the Hotel du Pont, its elegant, sophisticated superior. "I've got a dinner meeting with Libby and her friend Alistair," Jonathan said as he checked us into our rooms. "I'll see you in the morning."

The valet drove me to a nearby café. Jonathan, Libby, and Alistair would be dining at the small restaurant in the hotel, and I needed space to chill out, have a glass of red wine, and eat something small but satiating.

I sat in the back seat of the Tesla, its wide, slanted windshield offering an unencumbered view of the dark business district landscape around me. The driver fawned over the oversized screen of the navigation system covering the entire midsection of the console, clucking this and that about the virtues of Tesla. I wasn't paying much attention, imagining myself seated at the dinner table next to Jonathan with a white linen napkin draped elegantly across my lap.

Later that evening, I heard his voice through the thin hotel room wall, leaving messages for people in other countries. Jonathan rarely settled anywhere for long, although the U.S. was home for now. Nearly everything he owned was packed heavily into a couple of well-worn suitcases and a leather carry bag, which frequently graced his shoulder. I believed in him and his mission, floored at his ability to move tirelessly from one place to another. I thought of Ari, tenderly recounting the stories of his briefcases as beloved travel companions who had never let him down. It was a life I yearned for. Ari had given me a taste of something magical. I wanted more, and I wanted it to last.

* * *

I RECLINED ON A COMFY LEATHER CHAIR in the hotel library, imbibing a steaming cup of espresso as I waited for Jonathan to come downstairs. "Good morning," he smiled, gesturing toward the little birds outside the hotel window, splashing about in the birdbath. "I've just checked us out. Are you ready to leave?"

"I am," I said, arising from my chair.

Bags in tow, we made our way toward the parking lot. He opened the rear passenger door of my car and took off his jacket to put it on the back seat. "Oh, look, we're both wearing the same color sweater!" I exclaimed happily. Jonathan was sporting a cashmere, lavender-colored pullover. I had on my favorite lavender cardigan, which flared slightly at the bottom. He smiled softly, saying nothing. He had seen me in that sweater when we'd met at JFK. He settled into the passenger seat beside me as I backed out of the narrow space in the covered hotel parking lot. "Is Alistair going to move forward?" I inquired hopefully, contemplating the twenty-mile drive back to the Bronx.

"He wants me to return in a couple of weeks. There are people he wants to connect me with." His eyes sparkled with possibility. This would be his last push before the holidays, and if Alistair championed their technology development, FARM could have significant distribution of Regenaware in under two years.

"That's fantastic news!" I exclaimed, anticipating a rosy future for FARM.

Jonathan fiddled with the carry bag on the floor behind his seat, extracting a simple set of earbuds for an important conference call with a couple of bankers in New York City interested in financing the production of the Regenaware technology. "If this conversation goes well, I might meet with these guys in the city later," he said.

"I'll keep my fingers crossed," I said with a smile.

Arriving at Kate's, I maneuvered my car down the slender driveway and parked in the back. Jonathan's conference call had gone well, and we would take an Uber to Manhattan, returning to have dinner with Kate before I brought him back to the airport.

I stepped out and closed the car door. "Oh my God, look!" I tittered, ecstatic that I had a witness. I stood agape, eye level with the smooth glass rooftop, ogling my keys in astonishment. *Impossible!* Twice in a lifetime? Jonathan leveled a silent glance at the roof and then at me, calculating the unlikelihood of the situation. "And what's even *more* amazing is that the same thing happened to me when I lived in France!" I gushed, feeling I had won the lottery twice. It had to be a sign. Jonathan walked around the car and raised his hand for a high five, an incredulous smile playing at the corners of his mouth.

Later, we took an Uber into the city from Kate's, sitting side by side in the back seat. I felt a comfortable familiarity as I relaxed quietly next to him, watching him scroll through his phone as he snacked contentedly on a power bar. Without lifting his gaze, he casually handed the bar to me.

"You're sharing your saliva with me?" I teased, gazing at his teeth marks on the bar. Were we mixing business with pleasure again?

He chuckled. "I thought you might be hungry."

After enjoying a tasty Vietnamese dinner in town with Kate later in the evening, we headed to JFK airport. Jonathan would be back in two weeks to meet again with Alistair and other interested parties to give them a deeper look into FARM and Regenaware.

"I'd love to join you," I offered, excited at the opportunity to explore our working relationship and a friendship that I hoped would take a romantic turn. He thought that was a good idea, and we set a tentative plan. I beamed at the thought of spending more time with him. I was smitten. Could this be my new fairy tale?

We pulled into the valet area of the TWA Hotel, where he was staying that evening before his early morning flight. The valet hoisted Jonathan's heavy bags out of my SUV, plopping them onto a luggage cart. As the valet placed my small suitcase on top of his, I was hopeful. Jonathan looked at the young man and said abruptly, "no, not that one. She's not staying." I looked at him, holding my breath. "We're done here," he said coolly, making a short, sharp, slicing motion across his neck with his flattened hand. His gesture assaulted me, and I stood riveted to the pavement. Registering my reaction, he offered to buy me a drink at the lobby bar.

What had just happened? I had already observed that he wasn't particularly emotive but he had never been cold. Was this an indication of things to come, or had he just been tired? "Sure," I mumbled, feeling the power drain out of me. I knew I should have gone home, but I didn't want to leave him.

His back was stiff, and I offered to give him a chiropractic treatment as he checked in at the front desk. "Room 555," the clerk smiled, handing him his room key.

"Cool, thank you," he remarked, swinging the cart toward the elevator.

Numerology fascinated me. "Five symbolizes flux and change," I offered, tagging along beside him. The number five presented itself frequently in my life related to Jonathan. In doubles and triples, they appeared on speed limit signs, license plates, grocery receipts, and the sides of buildings.

But change wasn't necessarily stable, and I wondered where my relationship with him was actually headed. I wanted the beautiful love story that had been cut short when Ari died suddenly. Jonathan wasn't as warm as Ari and didn't tend to me as Ari had. Ari was upfront; I always knew where I stood with him. I didn't feel the same security with Jonathan; he was quiet. There was no "us;" it was just "him" and "me," two distinctly separate entities. Maybe it was just too soon to tell.

I adjusted Jonathan's spine on the bed. He stood up and opened his arms to hug me. "Thank you, Debra. I appreciate you driving me around and look forward to working with you on some of the educational documents we spoke about." He was going on vacation for a couple of weeks and would contact me when he was ready to return to New York.

"My pleasure. Enjoy your vacation; it's well deserved," I said, mustering a reply. I was tired, and it was late.

Jonathan rarely took a vacation, immersed in his work with FARM. I appreciated the kind of person it took to dedicate their life to a great cause, a decision that came from a profound sense of purpose and commitment to doing the right thing. Deeply intuitive, he was following the directives of his heart.

And what about my heart? It was infinitely easier to fall in love with a man who knew who he was and what he wanted. I preferred to be the brilliant tail of the comet streaking along behind him. Was there anything intrinsically wrong with that? "Behind every great man is a great woman." Isn't that how the saying went? Wasn't that its own glory?

He and I stayed in touch over the next couple of weeks as we anticipated his return. I provided him with another writing sample as I researched up-and-coming technologies in the regenerative agriculture industry. "This is stunning, Debra!" he replied to an attachment I had emailed him.

I desperately wanted our working situation to pan out, for him to see my capabilities and value, so I searched for places we might stay around

Saddle River. He appreciated my efforts to find lodging but didn't consider any of them a fit. "The perfect place will present itself to us," he said confidently.

And so it did. We were invited to stay at Alistair's residence in Saddle River. My mind raced with possibilities. There was nowhere else I wanted to be but by Jonathan's side.

CHAPTER 21

The Big House

Jonathan and I pulled up to the wrought iron gate of Alistair's home, and I lowered my window to press the button on the call box. "Hi. Come on in and pull to the right." His voice was friendly and unpretentious. The gate opened slowly inward, and we rolled down the shrub-lined driveway, breathless. Even in the dark, we could see the magnificent house elegantly backlit by small spotlights placed strategically on the well-manicured lawn.

"*Holy shit,*" I gurgled under my breath.

"Awesome...," Jonathan uttered, smiling broadly, gazing up through the windshield as we drove to the parking area.

Alistair was casually dressed in khakis and a long-sleeved collared sports shirt. His dark auburn hair was neatly combed in place, and he exuded a simple warmth that was welcoming and familiar.

The stylish panorama of the handsome home dazzled our senses. The walls were richly covered with raised cherrywood paneling, and curved archways straddled the length of the entryway hall. On the left side of the foyer sat a marble-topped Bombay chest crowned by an ornate gold-framed mirror. A carpeted staircase in colorful Persian floral swept gracefully up to a second-floor balcony on the right. I was agog at the sight of it all. This was going to be home for awhile. I sighed, looking at Jonathan, who undoubtedly felt the same way.

Alistair led us down a long second-floor corridor that rambled from one end of the main wing to the other. I felt as if I were in a small hotel. He stopped midway down the interminable hallway and pointed to a bedroom on the left. "Libby's room is here," he gestured. He offered us the choice of two rooms on the right. One was robin's egg blue and had a short hallway entrance. The other was a soft peach color. Both had walk-in closets the size of small rooms, a bathroom with a separate shower and soaker tub, a large main room with antique furnishings, and a king-sized bed.

Jonathan looked at me inquisitively. "You want the blue one, don't you?" I winked. Yes, he did. He eagerly wheeled his bulging suitcases inside. It didn't matter to me. I was thrilled to be staying in this residential utopia.

My beautiful bedroom was nearly half the size of my entire apartment. I was brimming with joy and excitement, tingling all over. Every cell in my body was convinced this was a taste of my future, and I would be sleeping contentedly in the room next door to the man I wanted to love with all of my heart.

After settling in, we made our way to the kitchen downstairs. There were three staircases in the house, and it would take me several days to get my bearings. Alistair offered an oaky cabernet sauvignon, and we chatted around the granite-topped center island that spanned the length of the Tuscan-styled kitchen. "Let me give you a little tour," he offered proudly.

We followed him down another long hallway that led back to the foyer where we had entered the stately home. He showed us three more rooms. The spacious, central living room was the largest, with fabric-inset walls and ornate white cornice moldings. A large marble fireplace occupied the far end of the room. Pearl-white damask sofas created two distinct seating areas flanked by satin-covered armchairs and glass-topped end tables. The room's perimeter was softly lit by slender brass wall lamps, showcasing attractive artwork and expensive ceramic statues, and a plush area rug in rich jewel tones sprawled unapologetically across the wood floor.

To the left of the living room was a small, pink-carpeted parlor with long windows and elegant seating slathered in rose-gold velvet brocade. A sparkling crystal beaded chandelier hung regally like a tiara in the center of the storybook room, which looked out onto a large brick patio bordering the pool.

Alistair's library was to the right of the main living room and served as his office. The small bright room was encrusted with cherrywood bookcases and a thick-legged mahogany desk with various files, papers, and books strewn about its surface. Behind the desk was an antique curio cabinet filled with a rare collection of vases. A small settee and a couple of armchairs faced each other in the center of the welcoming room.

Libby had just arrived. A long-time friend of Alistair's, she was a friend through thick, thin, and a couple of failed relationships. I liked her a lot. I sensed her depth and trustworthiness and felt comfortable in her calm presence. I was looking forward to getting to know her.

Alistair decided to commemorate the occasion. Disappearing into his wine cellar, he returned with a vintage bottle of Dom Perignon and an elegant carved-leather case containing a delicate set of long-stemmed crystal champagne glasses. I basked in my outlandish fortune. It felt good to be here, part of something greater than myself.

We listened respectfully as Alistair recounted the story of his tragically deceased twin brother, imbuing in him the desire to serve others. "Here's to Max," he said, tearfully raising his glass. I was touched by his wish to leave a legacy for his beloved brother.

It was getting late, and we were all hungry. We piled into Alistair's Rolls-Royce Phantom and headed to one of his favorite restaurants. Darren Torino, Alistair's assistant, fluttered in as we were ordering. He was handsome with thick sable hair cut short on the sides and had round doe-shaped eyes. He used his hands frequently when speaking, and I was glad he'd sat next to Libby and not me.

Overcome by the delectable menu, I opted for the handmade black truffle risotto with a mushroom cream sauce. I was hoping to cook while Jonathan and I were visiting, as I didn't want to make any assumptions about the expensive dinners Alistair would be treating us to. I couldn't afford to reciprocate at these prices.

Later, we watched a movie in Alistair's cozy den. I glanced over at Jonathan. Everything so far was adding up for me. I was attracted to him physically, but he was also intelligent, classy, cultured, and worldly, qualities I craved in a partner. I wanted to be part of his world, wanted him to show me all the places that took his breath away. Unlike Ari, he wasn't tied down by endless obligations; life was on his terms. His global vision to implement

Regenaware worldwide was intoxicating, and I felt I had been waiting all my life for a man like him to arrive.

* * *

THE FOLLOWING MORNING was sunny and crisp, typical for early November. I gazed out the kitchen window at the long, heated swimming pool below, rimmed by a brick patio leading out from the lower level of the house. "Are you going to join Jonathan and me for a swim?" Alistair inquired.

"Absolutely!" I wasn't going to miss out on anything while I was here. I had brought my swimsuit, hoping for an occasion like this.

I clambered up the stairs to my bedroom and tore through the clothes in my quilted Vera Bradley overnight bag. I had no expectations about the possibility of a pool in this magnificent home, but I had made some well-calculated assumptions. Slipping into my swimsuit, I donned a plush white bathrobe hanging in the closet and quickly descended to the lower level of the house.

Jonathan and Alistair were already in the pool when I arrived. Stepping out onto the cold terrace, I took a deep breath, draping the robe and towel over a cement bench next to the pool steps. The morning sun glinted through the tall oak treetops, dappling the water's surface. In the far corners of the pool were two stone elephant statues, trunks held high, spewing a narrow stream of water that arced into the pool in spattering bubbles. I gazed beyond the brilliant red hedges surrounding the pool. A chipped wood path meandered around the back property, dominated by old, mighty oaks and tall pines. *Heavenly.* Even more heavenly that I was about to step into the pool with Jonathan.

Alistair stood in the little hot tub near the pool's steps. In the deeper end of the pool, Jonathan was dog paddling lazily, his long golden hair twisted into a bun behind his head. "The water is amazing, Debra! Come on in," he warbled, luxuriating in the scene we were privileged to.

"The main part of the pool is set for eighty degrees," Alistair said.

"Ahhh!" I gushed, lowering myself into the water. I paddled my way over to Jonathan at the other end of the pool. "This is amazing!" I chattered, drunk on the fresh November air, cold on my face, as my body shivered, adjusting to the lukewarm water.

Alistair gazed contentedly at Jonathan and me, bobbing at the other end of the pool. We swam over to the hot tub and climbed in. "It's 102 degrees in here," Alistair said as I settled in, tiny bubbles frizzling around my skin as I pressed my back against the hot water jet. We sat on the submerged ledges of the tub, Jonathan facing Alistair. *Our little office in the pool,* I grinned to myself.

"Jonathan, when do you anticipate the rollout for Regenaware? Alistair asked.

"That depends," Jonathan said, tilting his head as he glanced thoughtfully into the distance. "The prototype testing will be done by the middle of next year, and we've already demonstrated scalability through advanced simulations testing. Still, we've had to go through the motions of running it as a full-scale agribusiness and agtech model in all twelve global climate regions and subregions, completing two growing and harvesting cycles," he said, moving his feet lazily around in the water.

"Excellent progress," Alistair said. "Where do you see the most potential for the Regenaware technology?" he asked, submerging himself further into the warm water.

"We've been working with twenty countries representing the twelve different climate types globally, but the first adopters will likely be in Europe and Canada," Jonathan said.

"What about the U.S.?" Alistair inquired.

I shifted my legs and moved my hands quietly back and forth under the pleasantly hot water. I was eager to hear what Jonathan had to say.

"The U.S. could probably benefit the most since their overall global standing in sustainability is quite low due to a high level of greenhouse gas emissions from the agricultural sector. Organic farming is also low as an overall percentage of farmland use, and the U.S. has notoriously high land usage for animal feed and biofuel production." I could tell Jonathan had given this speech many times before.

Alistair paused. "I want to reach out to some of my government connections in the agricultural industry. If we can get just a few of them on board, we could forge an inroad to some of the larger farming conglomerates here."

I listened intently, absorbing as much as possible; ideas were formulating in my mind. I'd always wanted to be part of something that could positively impact the planet. I reckoned that I might be part of the administrative end of things, educating, writing, or coordinating. I was bored with my chiropractic work and wanted something different, something new, to be a part of a movement that had a bright green future for me.

***

EVERY MORNING ALISTAIR, JONATHAN, AND I would meet in the pool at 8:30 a.m. Alistair was a man of routine. *Successful people usually are,* I mused. He rose early, watched the news, worked out in his gym, ate a simple breakfast, hit the pool for a quick swim, showered, and was ready to work by 9:30 a.m. By day, the five of us would convene around a large table in the downstairs sitting room that gazed out over the pool and patio. Many evenings, long after everyone else had stopped working for the day, Jonathan could be found sitting at his laptop in a late-night Zoom meeting or sending emails.

Alistair had an exhaustive list of contacts. There was plenty to do and many meetings with influential people, either by conference call or in person. Alistair had scheduled meetings in New York City, so he, Jonathan, Libby, and I took a train from Allendale. Later, we would meet with Darren and his friend Yosef, whose family was interested in supporting FARM.

It was a chilly, damp day that threatened to rain or snow at any moment. We trudged the twenty-minute walk from Pennsylvania Station to the Harvard Club for lunch, where Alistair was a member.

I welcomed the blast of warm air from the heaters above as we whisked into the iconic Harvard club restaurant lobby set in deep reds, golds, and rich brown mahogany. We checked our coats in the modest cloakroom, and Jonathan donned a tie, a required formality at the conservative nineteenth-century club. As we entered the wood-paneled dining hall for a buffet lunch, my eyes bulged as the maître d' escorted us to our table. Dozens of tables adorned the impressive dining room, and massive candelabra chandeliers dangled regally from the high ceiling, illuminating ornate Persian tapestries, balconies, and portraits wrapping the periphery.

"This place is stunning!" I gasped.

"Amazing!" Jonathan chimed in, his cultured eye drinking in the fine mahogany paneling and lavish period décor.

Alistair grinned. He was a generous man, eager to show us a little piece of his world, a patriarch, as Ari had been, who took care of everyone in his company, ensuring we were all having a good time.

Silverware clink-clanked noisily in the large, uncarpeted ballroom, and waitstaff scurried around refilling coffee cups and water glasses of wealthy patrons and their guests. As we ate our sumptuous buffet lunch, Jonathan and Alistair talked about FARM and Regenaware. Alistair intended to expand the technology in the United States and had many contacts. He was accustomed to getting what he wanted in the business world and had birthed many endeavors into significant financial gain.

I sliced into the filet mignon on my plate, covered with au jus, and slid a tender, succulent tidbit into my mouth. "This filet is *outstanding!*" I oozed, trying to become part of the conversation.

"The food is always excellent here," Alistair acknowledged. "I've never been disappointed."

Libby nodded. "We should come for breakfast sometime. The club is known for its popovers, an absolute delight." She was unpretentious, and I felt she and I were forging an honest friendship. Many mornings we sat drinking coffee and chatting on the large comfortable sofa in the den while Alistair and Jonathan conducted meetings in the main living room or held conference calls downstairs in our makeshift office. Well-educated and evolved, Libby had a depth I appreciated. Our conversations often revolved around love and relationships, and it was nice to have another woman in the house.

Redirecting the conversation, Alistair told a couple of jokes and a humorous tale about one of his most embarrassing moments. He looked playfully at Jonathan, enjoying a plate of chicken with roasted vegetables. "Jonathan, what was your most embarrassing moment?" he queried, raising a morsel of almond-crusted salmon to his lips. I squirmed in my seat. Was he going to ask me next?

Jonathan leaned forward, smiling. "I've never been embarrassed," he said. The hairs on my neck stood up in contumacious protest. I examined his eyes, which were focused on Alistair. *That's impossible,* my mind objected. Never? Had he just deprogrammed himself from feeling this emotion? I thought back to our conversation with Yvonne in the airport lounge. But why was I suddenly feeling shame?

"Hmph," Alistair remarked quietly, unaffected. Hadn't anyone else found Jonathan's comment unfeasible?

We'd had time to spare before we met with Darren. Alistair walked us to the cozy library in the club, which smelled of old paper and leather. Bookshelves stretched from floor to ceiling, wrapping the room in a literary blanket. Small desks with simple lamps were placed around the softly lit room between comfy leather chairs where someone could read or plug in a laptop.

He led us to another room where men and women sat around simple wooden tables in groups of four, playing bridge and chatting casually while others read the Wall Street Journal or the New York Times. *Wow, people actually play bridge?* I thought. This was a world very unlike my own. "My mother plays bridge," Jonathan offered, his voice soft in reflection.

"I never really got into the game much," Alistair countered lightly. These men did not talk about feelings. Besides, it was a business trip. I wanted to know more about Jonathan. I probably could have asked him more questions, but for some reason, I didn't. I wanted him to offer, but for some reason, he hadn't.

We chatted for a little while before heading to the main lobby to meet Darren and Yosef, who had already arrived. Darren was visibly upset that we hadn't invited him to lunch. The real issue may have been that he was romantic with Alistair. He turned to Alistair. "Why didn't you tell me you were having lunch?" he whined, feebly concealing his hurt and disappointment. "You knew I was free until this meeting." Alistair stammered an excuse, attempting to move the conversation to the matter at hand.

I ogled the enormous lobby, its sweeping mahogany walls embellished with portraits, sprawling tapestries, and wild animal heads. Libby, Darren, and I reclined on a soft brown leather sofa facing the others, sitting on well-appointed armchairs a few feet from us. Although they were close, I could barely hear Jonathan's quiet voice over the din in the high-ceilinged lobby. I chatted with Libby, seated next to me, and repeatedly glanced at the gargantuan elephant head that stared down at us from its lofty perch on the elegantly furnished wall.

"Yosef seems genuinely interested," Jonathan shared as the five of us walked back toward the train station. "He knows a couple of people he wants to put me in touch with."

Darren had business in town and wouldn't be joining us for the train back to Alistair's, who offered earlier that he felt strained about their relationship. They were up ahead of us, but I could hear snippets of their conversation. "Why didn't you just call me and tell me to meet you there?" Darren's voice trailed off as they rounded the corner.

* * *

"IT'S NEVER A GOOD IDEA TO MIX BUSINESS with pleasure," Jonathan said definitively as the train rocked his body gently back and forth. *True*, I thought, but would I be the exception for him?

"He wants me to increase his salary," Alistair said, "but he's only working for me part-time."

"You need to decide which relationship is more important," Jonathan countered, the warmth gone from his voice.

"I'm not sure I want to *be* in a relationship," Alistair replied, letting the idea be spoken aloud. "It is complicating my life. I want to focus on Regenaware."

"You need to cut it off then," Jonathan stated coolly, his eyes devoid of emotion, letting an invisible ax fall as he flattened his hand in a slicing gesture across his neck, as he had with me that night at the TWA Hotel. I bristled. What right did he have to make that decision? *And what about Darren's feelings?*

It was decided. Alistair would tell Darren the next day when he came to work that their relationship would be strictly business. I shifted my weight uncomfortably in my seat. Would Alistair have come to the same conclusion without Jonathan's input? I gazed at Jonathan sitting opposite me, checking his cell phone, unperturbed, already moving forward. Alistair rehearsed what he would say to Darren, and once satisfied, we were talking about Regenaware again.

Alistair stared at his car parked a hundred feet away as we descended the steps of the train platform. "Why are the lights on?" he puzzled, half to himself. "You've got to be kidding. I left it running…?" We were in disbelief as we climbed in. "I just filled it yesterday!" he exclaimed.

The car had burned through nearly a tank of gas. I burst into laughter. "So much for people who are environmentally conscious!" We laughed all the way to the gas station, with barely enough fuel to pull next to the pump. The situation amused me so much that I repeatedly erupted into uncontrollable laughter, and each time Alistair caught my eye in the rearview mirror, he laughed too. Jonathan turned to look back at me, and although he was smiling, I felt my laughter annoyed him. I shook it off. "Alistair, you sure make for a lot of excitement!" I said, delighting in the hilarity of the situation.

Later that evening, after Alistair and Libby had retired, Jonathan and I shared a cup of ginger tea in the kitchen. "It was so nice to hear you laugh and have fun," he said, eyes beholding me gently. "I've never been in a situation like this," he continued. "I'm normally alone when I travel. It's so nice to have you here to help me." Was he being honest? I hadn't been able to get a handle on him, which perplexed me. He could be hot and cold. There was a disparity I couldn't resolve. Did he genuinely appreciate me?

I recalled his voice message less than a month ago. "You sound like you might be that personal assistant we talked about," he had teased. "One who can write informational documents, provide healing work, and help with other things we've yet to discover."

"I am," I had purred in reply. Now that I was here with him, I wasn't so sure.

"And what about you, Jonathan? Don't you ever tire of going from place to place, living out of a suitcase?" I asked the man standing before me.

"It's been a great run, and I've met so many amazing people along the way, but… I'm ready to be done," he said softly. I could hear the honest reflection and the fatigue in his voice.

"What's next for you?" I was curious.

"I'm not sure," he said, sipping his tea pensively. "I might set some roots down and work on the technology side of things with Alistair." He took another swallow of his tea. I sensed his excitement for the future but could see he was tired. He was looking forward to resting over the holiday season. I wondered what my role could be with him and FARM.

It was late. "Would you like a treatment now?" I asked him.

"You're not too tired?" he asked, sipping his tea hopefully.

We headed to the small gym upstairs, where one of the massage tables was stationed. I was tired, but I wanted to touch and be near him. Jonathan enjoyed it when I did my energy work on him. The others in the house had also taken to it, and it became something we all looked forward to. "Lie face down," I instructed as he removed his shoes. He eagerly climbed onto the table and sighed deeply as he settled in. Yes, I supposed this was a rare treat for him. I felt privileged and content.

I could separate therapeutics from my attraction to him, but my fantasy of being his partner was growing in a way that seemed beyond my control. I wondered what would happen between us. We hugged each night before retiring in the evenings, and I would lay my head on his shoulder. Sometimes I said, "I love you." It was genuine for me. "I love you too," he would say. What did he mean when he said it? I couldn't read his intentions.

On one particular evening, as he and I stood at the kitchen island hugging, he'd let his hand subtly graze my lower back as he released me. I was confused. He hadn't made any romantic overtures, but it didn't take much for me to believe our friendship might head in this direction.

CHAPTER 22

The Way to a Man's Heart

The next day we waited for Darren to arrive. He had been busy networking all morning, meeting with a couple of acquaintances interested in supporting FARM, and learning about Regenaware. Alistair had placed a lunch order for takeout, and when Darren arrived, they disappeared so he could break the news about their changing relationship while we waited for the food to be delivered.

Twenty minutes later, they returned. I could see Darren had been crying, and his hands were perceptibly shaking. We ate lunch, making light conversation, and I knew he must be reeling inside.

Later that afternoon, I treated Darren in a beautiful upstairs sitting room far down the hall where another massage table had been placed. He cried quietly as he lay on the table, attempting to contain a barrage of emotions he'd had to hold back since lunch, trying to integrate what had happened into his nervous system. "We were getting along so well," he said, tears running down to his ears from the corners of his closed eyes. "He just sprang it on me before lunch. He doesn't want to see me anymore except to work together." He sat up, letting his tears flow. His nervous energy overwhelmed me, and I felt a dam was about to break inside him. We needed to get back to work. "We'll talk some more later," I said and hugged him reassuringly. "They're waiting for us downstairs."

Alistair, Libby, and Jonathan were working quietly around our makeshift desk, the late-afternoon sun streaming in through the French doors, which opened to the patio. Alistair pecked away slowly on his keyboard, composing an email introducing FARM and Regenaware to his contacts. Like a pianist, Jonathan raced adeptly over the keys of his laptop. His focus was exacting and almost unnatural. "I've never seen anyone type so fast!" I exclaimed. He stared at me blankly. This was not the same man who had texted me the teddy bear emoji on WhatsApp.

Darren took a seat and began stabbing his keyboard. Libby leaned quietly over her phone, her dark curly hair piled atop her head in a giant bun, as she tapped and swiped, her glasses perched on the tip of her nose. I sat down at my computer and opened a document I had created for Jonathan to edit as the five of us clustered around the table, working silently.

Alistair looked up from his email. "What should I say about the Regenaware technology?" he asked. "Should I get detailed or just mention that it is a groundbreaking opportunity that could revolutionize the agricultural industry?" He looked at me, and I chimed in.

"Maybe you could say…."

"Shhh!" Jonathan hissed, dismissing me with a gesturing hand. I was stung. Suddenly I felt small and insignificant.

"I want them to see the magnitude of the potential. I need a sentence that will grab their attention," Alistair continued, still looking at me or perhaps through me.

I rallied again. "How about something like—"

"SHHH!" Jonathan chided me. "Let him finish," he snapped, his voice low. I could hardly believe he was speaking to me this way.

"I'm just trying to help," I mumbled, unable to conceal the hurt stabbing me in the chest.

Alistair ignored the scene as he stumbled aloud, searching for the most impactful words. I knew I could help him, but I sat quietly, deflated. This was the side of Jonathan that I didn't understand. I knew he was accustomed to working alone, but my enthusiastic participation didn't warrant his response. It wasn't fair or appropriate, but I didn't push it. I had been too eager to please him, and sadly, this wouldn't be the first or the last time I gave my power away to him.

I didn't want him to send me home. As in my early relationship with Ari, I was insecure, believing that any false move would generate a plane ticket from France back to the United States. My romantic feelings for Jonathan didn't allow me to think objectively, and I let this moment, and many others, slide.

***

I HAD BEEN BURNING THROUGH my vacation days at work, bridging weekends so I could spend as much time as possible with Jonathan and the team in Saddle River. It was difficult for me to pull away and return to New York when all I wanted to do was to quit my job and be with him.

Consistently, I would return with food to prepare. I didn't want Alistair to think I was taking advantage of being a guest. I enjoyed cooking and delighted in their appreciation of my culinary efforts, but I also knew I was going overboard. I felt taxed by giving too much, and Jonathan was not matching my efforts.

Tonight we would have my carb-free turkey meatloaf. I prepared it by grating up different vegetables for moisture and bulk. I slathered it with mustard, browned it amidst a pile of freshly sliced mushrooms, and topped it off with a tomato-based gravy which added sweetness and balance. I roasted carrots with brown sugar and curry and tossed a colorful salad with a homemade tahini dressing. I enjoyed cooking in Alistair's gourmet kitchen, as I didn't have this luxury in my apartment back home. I took full advantage of it, and the meals became more and more elaborate.

"This meatloaf is delicious, Debra!" Alistair remarked appreciatingly.

"I'll have another piece of this amazing creation," Jonathan smiled as he reached for a second helping. We were a family, I'd thought. Unaccustomed to mixing business with pleasure, I didn't know how to separate the two.

The kitchen had become somewhat of a compulsion; I prepared lunch and dinner whenever we dined in. The splendid home was warm and inviting, and Alistair was a gracious, unimposing host. He hadn't seemed to mind me taking over his kitchen. One morning he said to me as we stood alone in the kitchen after breakfast, "I like having you here." I felt valued. According to Libby, who had known him for many years, he wasn't given to saying anything he didn't mean.

"If Alistair doesn't feel that the Regenaware opportunity is something he's interested in, he'll get up and walk away from the table," Libby had said to Jonathan when they'd first met at the hotel weeks ago. "That's how he does business. He doesn't give anything a second glance. He knows what he wants and what he doesn't. He has a sixth sense about these things," she said knowingly. Jonathan was thrilled when Alistair not only remained for the dessert course but was eagerly making a list of people he wanted Jonathan to speak with upon his return.

***

JONATHAN AND I PADDLED AROUND THE POOL the following morning while Alistair soaked in the hot tub. "Debra, look at how the sunlight is hitting the water from the fountains," Jonathan said dreamily, observing the water droplets glittering like tiny diamonds as they spritzed the water's surface. He appeared to be more interested in "things" than people. Warm one minute and cold the next, his demeanor could be exasperating. I was starting to feel somewhat diminished in his presence and was afraid to say the wrong thing, although it didn't change my feelings for him. Part of me wanted to walk away, but a bigger part wanted to believe the growing fantasy I was creating about our imminent love affair.

At this point, I was not attending any of the networking meetings. I had repeatedly heard Jonathan's speech about Regenaware, and some of the technical explanations were out of my reach. I was content cooking and working on educational documents about the regenerative agriculture economy.

One chilly morning, I made tea for Jonathan to drink on the train to New York City, where he was attending a meeting. I put it into a slim metal thermos, and he thanked me, placing it in his shoulder bag. When he returned hours later, he placed it on the counter nearly full.

"You didn't drink your tea?" I asked, puzzled. Tea was a staple for him.

"It was too hot. I nearly *burnt* myself," he said emphatically.

"I'm sorry." I was crushed. "Why didn't you take the top off to let it cool?" He hadn't thought about that. Neither had he thought to thank me for the effort.

***

I WAS PLANNING A SPECIAL DINNER for the weekend. Libby was still staying at the house. I enjoyed the times when Darren wasn't present. Whenever he cornered me alone, he wanted to talk about his relationship with Alistair and his troubles in general. I didn't want to get into it. I liked Alistair, and my heart went out to Darren, but I didn't want to straddle the line.

Libby was excited about the meal. I enthusiastically discussed my menu ideas with her as we sat on the comfortable sofa in the den, drinking a second cup of morning coffee. I would buy a pork roast from the butcher near my home. I had a delectable spice rub in mind for the meat and would cook scalloped potatoes and a couple of vegetable sautés that I thought would be delicious accompaniments. "Do you want me to bring anything?" she asked. "You shouldn't have to go to all that trouble yourself."

"I want to show Alistair my appreciation for having me as a guest," I said.

"I can be your sous-chef," she offered, giggling.

"Wow, that will be a first. There will be a lot on the menu, and I'm sure I will need another pair of hands." I felt close to her, and my respect continued to grow. "I have feelings for Jonathan," I confided.

"I know," she smiled, tipping her cup to her lips.

The floodgates opened as I shared the intensity of what I felt for him. "I can't figure him out. His behavior toward me is hot and cold, and I get mixed messages. I want him to be happy with my work, but he doesn't show his feelings or guide me, so I feel somewhat insecure. I don't know if he's glad I'm here or not."

"Are you kidding? Of course, you're valuable to him, or you wouldn't be here," she said, placing her hand on top of mine. "Give him some time. He's not used to having someone like you in his life. Besides, being objective is hard when you have feelings for someone. He'll come around. Just let him lead. You don't need to fawn over him so much. Let him come to you."

That was good advice and hard to follow. My energy and efforts streamed in his direction, and I found it challenging to focus on myself. Jonathan was a man accustomed to traveling—and living—alone. Whenever I was successful in pulling back, he would come toward me, and one evening he even made me a cup of tea. Maybe Libby had been right.

***

NO ONE HAD INVITED DARREN to the dinner, and I didn't press it, deciding to let the chips fall where they may. Besides, it wasn't my responsibility. It seemed to me that Alistair was more comfortable when Darren wasn't around socially, and I wanted to relax and spend time with the others.

Donning my simple black apron, I glanced at the kitchen clock. The meal would take a few hours to prepare. I had already cooked the roasted acorn squash soup and baked the scalloped potatoes in advance, so I needed only to assemble the salad and sauté the vegetables. I arranged the meat in a large roasting pan and slid it into the oven.

Gradually, the house filled with the delectable aroma of garlic, fennel, and other spices infusing the pork as it sizzled in the oven. Libby prepared the salad, grating carrots and beets for a garnish. The men were working downstairs, occasionally surfacing, following their nose into the warm kitchen, anticipating the repast we would soon be enjoying.

"It smells amazing in here," Jonathan remarked, inhaling deeply. "Do you need any help?"

"No, thank you," I chirped happily. "Libby and I have it all under control."

Jonathan made himself a cup of ginger tea, drizzling in some honey. Every morning we sliced a bunch of the pungent root into a pot of water, boiling it until the liquid was yellow and spicy. It sat on the stovetop to be reheated as needed throughout the day.

"What time is dinner?" he asked, intending to schedule his meetings around our meal.

"In about two hours," I said, glancing up at the clock.

"Sweet!" he clucked, heading back downstairs.

Libby and I scurried around, coordinating the elements of our repast.

"Thank God for this warming drawer!" I crooned, placing the steaming casserole of potatoes inside.

I pulled the sizzling meat out of the oven and placed the pan on the stovetop as I prepared to make the gravy. Libby rallied around me, picking up the slack. I adored her company, grinning warmly as I watched her mincing garlic, her glasses ready to slip off the end of her nose.

"Come and get it!" I singsonged to the men downstairs, poking my head down the stairwell.

Jonathan glanced at the pork sitting on a large white platter. "Wow, that looks and smells delicious!" he said, eyeballing the crispy browned fat of the roast.

"You should do the honors," I beamed, handing him a serving fork and a long carving knife. I envisioned many meals like this in our future, traveling about, inviting friends to wherever in the world we were graced to be, laughing over large goblets of fine red wine—a beautiful fairy tale in the making.

Jonathan had finished carving the pork, and everyone settled in eagerly around the table as I served the soup. Alistair poured the cabernet sauvignon that he had retrieved from his wine cellar. We toasted to friends and Regenaware.

"My, this soup is delicious!" Libby said, spooning the creamy orange puree from her bowl.

Jonathan rose to fetch the pork from the kitchen, placing it in the center of the table. Libby took a photo of us. Alistair and Jonathan took the first bites of the pork, crusted brown with sweet and savory spices. "Wow," Alistair said, looking straight at me, "this is the best pork roast I've ever had." I was thrilled.

"Yet," Jonathan offered, teasing. I was hurt. His comment felt mean-spirited and withholding. He hadn't shown much appreciation in general, and it was beginning to weigh on me.

"Give her some credit, Jonathan!" Libby scolded him. "Debra went to a lot of trouble to prepare this meal."

Jonathan approached me in the hall later that evening. "That pork could have been served in *any* restaurant, on *any* menu," he offered emphatically. Was that an apology? Maybe he did have a conscience after all.

I went to the kitchen and assessed the contents of the fridge. "I think I'll make eggs with lox tomorrow," I said offhandedly to Jonathan, who was now preparing a cup of tea, planning to finish some work downstairs. "Would you like to join me?"

"I can't make that decision now. It depends on how I feel in the morning," he said.

He had caught me off guard again. "As you wish," I shrugged my shoulders as Jonathan headed downstairs.

Libby had posted the photos she'd taken of our little feast. "Oh, how nice. I didn't know it was *tonight,*" Darren replied late in the evening. He had attended a play with a friend but said he would have changed his plans *had he known.*

***

THE BACKPEDALING BEGAN THE NEXT MORNING as Jonathan and Libby replied to Darren's messages. "*Surely you would have been invited had we known you were free,*" and "*you can come to lunch to enjoy the wonderful leftovers.*" Neither Alistair nor I made any comment. I couldn't bring myself to lie; I hadn't wanted Darren there. Libby later recounted how she had made the apology through clenched teeth. I didn't know why she posted the pictures in the first place, but there was something else brewing that I wasn't aware of.

"Are you still planning on lox and eggs for breakfast?" Jonathan inquired.

"Yes, I'm getting tired of eating granola every morning," I quipped.

"I think that's a good idea. May I join you?" he asked.

"Sure," I said, somewhat surprised.

I arranged our plates with salad greens, avocado, and warm asparagus with spicy ginger sauce and draped the lox on top. Jonathan poached a couple of eggs and spooned them over the lox. We ate alone at the card table in the den, making light conversation. "Another amazing creation, Debra," Jonathan said as we finished, picking up his plate to lick it off. I flushed as I watched his tongue polish the plate clean. "Compliments to the chef," he said, playfully locking onto my eyes.

He picked up my plate and repeated the ritual. His gesture flustered me. Did he have a point? Was he just an incorrigible flirt, smitten by his own flirtatiousness? Could I have been *any* woman sitting beside him? What was it about him that hooked me so completely?

That evening, we sat in the den watching another movie. I glanced appreciatively at Libby, Alistair, and Jonathan, wondering how our path together would unfold. There was so much to be accomplished to implement Regenaware. I snuggled on the couch, letting my thoughts carry me away.

CHAPTER 23

The Dance of Unworthiness

Monday morning came quickly. Jonathan and I made a cup of tea and headed downstairs to work. Alistair was already at the desk, sorting through a mountain of business cards. "I need to make a contact list," he said, looking at the pile, then at me. "Would you help me…?" Sure I would. I began creating a spreadsheet where we could put all of the information.

Whirling in an hour later, Darren plopped his briefcase and laptop on the table. The first order of the day was more backpedaling about the pork dinner. Jonathan did most of the backpedaling; I couldn't bring myself to engage. I wondered if the drama was all in a day's work for Jonathan, as Darren was garnering substantial support for FARM through interested friends and contacts.

I happened to be wearing the Eiffel tower necklace I bought when I lived in France. Darren was wearing a shirt patterned with a tiny Eiffel tower motif. Jonathan noticed and tried to inject some levity. "You and Debra are both wearing Eiffel Towers!" he exclaimed.

Darren squinted at my neck from across the desk. Jonathan pointed his finger close to my necklace, and I grabbed it playfully. He pulled his hand away and flicked his finger discreetly, but I saw the gesture. Darren didn't notice, but Jonathan hadn't tried to hide it from me. My body flooded hotly with shame, and my throat squeezed shut with anger that threatened to scorch me. I scrambled desperately to hold onto my composure as the power drained out of me into the earth. I wanted to run, to scream, to flip the table. Humiliated, I sat riveted to my seat, stewing in my pain. This was the same man who had licked the breakfast dishes only yesterday! Why did he trigger so much shame in me? Did he even care about my feelings?

As if on cue, Libby arrived. *Thank you, God,* I thought to myself. She was a grounding force for me, one I desperately needed right now. I collected myself, recovering slowly from the blow I had just received, feeling the blood return to my stunned body. She sidled beside me in her chair, reading the details from Alistair's business cards while I typed them onto the spreadsheet.

Most of the morning centered around Alistair's email efforts, and we made considerable headway. From what I could gather, Darren was still feeling jilted. I went to the kitchen to make myself a cup of tea, and Libby joined me. We sat in the den, and she told me what was on her mind.

"Darren told me I don't need to be present at all the meetings," she said, her hands encircling her teacup.

"Why?" I asked.

"He mentioned something about me being an observer with no information to bring to the conversation," she said, pursing her lips. "He thinks potential supporters and business liaisons might be uncomfortable talking about money or other specifics around me."

"Why does that matter to him?" I asked.

"I'm not sure. Maybe he doesn't want me to know the details of the people he's bringing to the table," she said.

"Did you discuss any of this with Alistair or Jonathan?" I asked.

"No, I don't want to make it a big deal. Maybe I'm just reading too much into it," she said, sipping her tea, "but I do enjoy the meetings. I learn so much," she sighed.

I could appreciate Libby's concern, but I couldn't argue with Darren's point of view. Typically, everyone at the table contributed to further FARM's mission through financial support, a particular service, or a product. The conversations could get pretty technical, and it might be awkward if some of us were not part of the discussion. Jonathan had alluded to that early on, and it was another reason I had stopped attending the meetings, not wanting to rock the boat. Had Darren caught wind of that?

Alistair had a late-morning meeting with a couple of old friends interested in hearing about Regenaware. He donned a red tie, and we wished him luck. In the large living room, Jonathan and Darren were setting up for a meeting with a gentleman from the Department of Agriculture, who had a keen personal interest in regenerative farming, and the ability to move things forward. Libby had some errands to run, and I puttered around the kitchen, making a salad from a leftover roasted chicken to serve for lunch later.

The house meetings would sometimes last for two hours. When it was well underway, Libby returned and decided to join Jonathan, Darren, and their guest in the living room. Moments later, I heard her footsteps pounding toward me from the long main hall. She wheeled into the kitchen, slapping her notebook emphatically on the stone island. "I've had enough of this bullshit!" she announced.

"What the hell happened?" I asked, taking hold of her arm.

"Darren saw me coming and waved me away," she gestured.

"Why would he do that?" I asked.

"I don't know, but I'm done with them all!" she harrumphed, starting up the stairs to the bedroom hall.

Anxiously, I followed behind her like a puppy as she marched down the hall to her bedroom. "What are you going to do?" I asked, not sure I wanted to know.

She grabbed the pink chiffon scarf that Jonathan had given her over the weekend and chucked it onto his bedroom floor. I cringed. She stormed back into her room, stuffing her clothing into an overnight bag.

Jonathan had bought the scarf after a meeting in New York City. He'd stayed an extra day to see a couple of sights. The pretty scarf was studded with beautifully colored gems that sparkled in the light. Libby was delighted, and I'd snapped a photo of her with the scarf swaddling her neck.

He'd also bought a gift for Alistair, an elegant replica of nineteenth-century champagne glasses in a polished teakwood case lined in blue silk. The glasses were fluted crystal, rimmed in silver at the edges, and perched on long etched sterling silver stems.

He had made a great fanfare of bestowing the gifts after our pork dinner. They were thoughtfully wrapped, and I could see he had taken pride in selecting them. He was well-bred and generous, and I'd never had to pay for anything when he was around.

Libby started down the hallway, bag over her shoulder, then spun around. "Better yet, I think I'll hand it to him personally," she huffed, scooping the scarf from the floor.

"But he's in a meeting," I pleaded, trailing her back down the stairs, the scarf clutched to her chest. She dropped the overnight bag at the front door and turned on her heel.

"Libby, please don't do this," I gasped as she gently wrenched her arm from my grip.

"I'm not going to be treated like this," she averred. "You probably won't see me for a while." She smiled weakly. "I appreciate all your work, holding this team together with your love and support."

"I didn't do anything more than anyone else," I said quietly, not wanting her to go.

"Don't sell yourself short, my dear. You deserve so much better. I hope Jonathan is paying you well." Actually, I wasn't sure he would pay me at all. We hadn't discussed it since he'd first agreed to move forward. She turned toward the hall, the jeweled scarf tucked under her arm.

"Can't you just wait until their meeting is over?" I whimpered as she firmly unclamped my fingers that had re-entwined themselves with the sleeve of her jacket.

"I'm sorry you have to witness this," she said, chin in the air, and started toward the hall. I watched her as she strode confidently down the long corridor, holding my breath, dread filling my heart. I wished I had her moxie. She wasn't thinking about consequences, only the action it took to stand up for herself. I hadn't done this once with Jonathan, and part of me was there with her, cheering her on, having the guts to do something I couldn't.

They were all standing, and I heard her proclaim something to Jonathan. I looked on from afar, flummoxed, as she thrust the scarf into his arms. A few words were exchanged between them, but I couldn't make out what was said. I slunk back into the kitchen, my heart ticking like a stopwatch in my chest. Her footsteps grew louder as she returned down the hall and marched toward the front door. I corralled her there.

"I'm so sorry. Be well, Debra," she said, flinging her arm around my neck in a quick, tight squeeze.

"Please keep in touch with me, Libby," I whispered sadly, but I knew she wouldn't. I watched her pull away, disappearing down the long driveway. My heart dropped into my stomach as tears began to roll down my cheeks. I was shocked. I wondered about Jonathan, Darren, and the gentleman who would undoubtedly have a story to tell at his dinner table.

I clomped heavily up the stairs and stole quietly into her vacated room. I plunked down on the edge of the bed, letting my tears flow freely. I could smell her perfume punctuating the stillness. I walked to the window and put my hand on the deep crimson brocaded satin drapes as I looked out over the manicured courtyard, breathing her in, her presence still vibrating in the molecules around me. I would miss her. She was somehow inextricably tied to Jonathan, though they had met only weeks ago. Some big plan was playing itself out here, that much I knew. But what?

I walked downstairs to the kitchen. Alistair had returned from his meeting. "What's the matter?" he asked, reading my expression.

"I'm not sure," I mumbled, still dazed.

"Where is everyone?" he asked calmly.

"Libby just left. Jonathan and Darren are still in a meeting with the DOA guy," I said, walking into the den. I wasn't accustomed to high drama and needed space. I heard voices and footsteps approaching from the other end of the hall. The meeting must have concluded. My legs felt weak, so I sat on the sofa to collect myself. Jonathan and Darren whisked into the kitchen. "What the hell happened with Libby?" Jonathan demanded, looking directly at me. I stared at him wordlessly. *You tell me, Jonathan.*

Darren waited his turn. "Did I do something wrong? Is Libby mad at me? I was inviting her into the meeting, and she stormed away. Then she came back and threw her scarf at Jonathan. What's going on? Did she tell you?" he implored, his brown eyes round and blinking, his words tumbling out in a single high-pitched stream, riddling me like bullets.

The air hung heavily in the room as three sets of eyes fixed steadily on me, awaiting a reply. I didn't think it was my place to get into the details. I wanted to defend Libby, but what was the truth? What really went on in the discussions between the others?

I requested a private meeting with Alistair and Jonathan. Darren was growing more agitated. "How come no one wants to tell me what's going on?" he protested.

The three of us trudged up the stairs to Jonathan's room. I heard Darren grumbling his dissent as he banged noisily around the kitchen. The three of us sat on upholstered armchairs in Jonathan's large bedroom, clustered at the foot of his bed. "Libby is upset because she feels like she is being disrespected," I offered cautiously, not wanting to betray her confidence.

Jonathan raised his eyebrows, somewhat surprised. "What do you mean?" he asked, his gaze disconcerted, hands stuffed into his pockets.

"It has something to do with her attending the meetings. She doesn't feel welcome," I said, choosing my words carefully.

A look of concern washed over Alistair's face. "Of course, she's welcome. Who gave her the idea she wasn't?"

"I don't know," I repeated, refusing to offer an opinion with only information from her perspective. "I would like to say this, though," I said, looking at Alistair. "You've known Libby for many years. With all due respect, if it weren't for her, you wouldn't even know about Regenaware. You've only known Darren for a couple of months. I think you need to speak with Libby."

Jonathan chimed in. "Darren is bringing some key people to the table. We're not doing anything to undermine Libby." I looked deeply into his eyes, sensing his honesty. Maybe it was just a communication issue. I'd had a few of them with him myself.

"I don't know all the details. It's none of my business. It's between the three of you—or the four of you. Libby has supported FARM for many years, Jonathan, and she is why we are at Alistair's house today," I countered as respectfully as I could.

I didn't feel he was taking that into account and was uncomfortable with the conversation. I wanted resolution and for things to go back to normal. Sadly, I didn't think they would.

We headed back down to the kitchen. Libby had been pelting Alistair with texts. She told Jonathan she never wanted to speak to him again. "You need to reach out to her, Jonathan," I said, knowing she didn't mean what she had written in her texts.

"Don't *tell* me what to do," he leveled at me, his lips tense as he jerked open the refrigerator door for a bottle of water. "This is the second time she's done something like this," he snorted, thwacking a banana peel emphatically into the trash. "Never in all my years have I experienced such a display."

"I'm not telling you what to do," I said, shaking my head. *He was clueless.* "Women need closure. She wants you to make things right."

Alistair convinced Libby to come back. Darren continued to dog me with the same questions, and I deferred. Jonathan disappeared to the basement. After a while, Alistair—and thankfully Darren—followed suit. I sat numbly on the sofa, trying to make sense of everything. The spectacle had affected me, and I couldn't regain my center. I felt weak and wrung out. This wasn't my drama, but I was smack dab in the middle. My mind gnawed at me. Why was this happening? What was the lesson for me, for them? After everything that had transpired, was Jonathan truly the man I wanted to share my life with?

Libby returned later in the afternoon, tail between her legs. She, Alistair, and Jonathan disappeared for a long time into the living room. I was left with Darren, who continued to probe me for answers. "Please! I don't want to talk about it, Darren. It's between you and Libby." He stopped asking questions, but I could tell he wasn't satisfied.

We reconvened in our downstairs office, Libby sitting close to me. Her eyes were clouded with shame, and she looked defeated. Alistair and Jonathan seemed content, and I wondered how their conversation had gone. The five of us worked together for a while, mostly in silence. The emotional undercurrent in the room nearly wiped me out, so I retreated upstairs. Darren appeared minutes later. I flitted about the kitchen, trying to wrap my head around a dinner menu.

"I'm looking forward to your roast pork," he chirped. I knew where this was going. "I still don't know why you guys just didn't let me know about the dinner. I could have changed my plans. Why didn't anyone call me?" His words stabbed my tired brain, pecking at me like a dead carcass. *Drop it already!* I thought, yanking open the refrigerator door.

"Do you want to help me prepare the meal?" I asked, hoping to redirect the conversation. I knew he wasn't going anywhere until after dinner.

I heard Libby ascending the stairs. I knew everyone's footsteps by now. I left Darren preparing the salad and cornered Libby in the front foyer. "What happened? You don't seem resolved about this."

"Jonathan explained things to me about the meetings. I guess I just misunderstood," she shrugged, somewhat dejected. Had all that commotion been for nothing? I wasn't so sure. My feelings for Jonathan clouded my mind, and it was hard to be objective. "I guess I have to straighten things out with Darren," she sighed. I felt close to her, and it hurt me to see her suffering.

Darren finished preparing the salad. Not ready to talk, Libby avoided him and went to her room. Alistair came upstairs and turned on the evening news. "Where's Libby?" he asked casually, parking himself on the couch. "Is she staying for dinner?" I didn't think she was. I couldn't imagine her suffering through idle chit-chat. She later confided that she would leave for the night and return the following morning to work. I hoped so.

The four of us sat around the square wooden table in the den. Darren was victoriously enjoying his pork. For me, the thrill was gone. I missed Libby's presence. "Maybe we should text Libby a photo," Jonathan offered, genuinely wanting to include her. *Really?* Did he think she would be thrilled to see a picture of Darren chomping on a pork chop that should have been hers? I didn't respond to his comment. Thankfully, no one took a picture.

Darren left soon after dinner, and I felt the tension slowly release its stranglehold on my nerve-wracked body. Alistair had retired early, likely wiped out by the emotional upheaval.

Jonathan and I stood at the kitchen island, waiting for our ginger water to boil. "I don't know if I have enough work for you to do," he said with sincerity. I looked at him inquisitively. "I know you want to quit your job," he continued. "I don't want to disappoint you." He looked at me with what felt like genuine appreciation. His directness brought momentary relief, and I sighed.

"It doesn't have to go like that," I said, thinking that the present structure was good enough. "Let's just let it evolve," I offered. He didn't answer. Did he agree? I had a difficult time figuring out what direction he was going in. Our timing and communication were different. I was more structured, and he seemed to flow with a different priority, which I hadn't yet figured out. I was somewhat frustrated by his ways and couldn't tell if he was satisfied with our work together. His sometimes-cold response, or lack of response, often left me unsettled.

Later as we washed the dinner dishes, he surprised me. "I have a couple of ideas about a project you could help me with," he said earnestly, without offering any other details. "Let's talk about it tomorrow morning."

"That sounds good to me," I countered, wondering how long it would take to figure this man out. "I'd like to give you a treatment and maybe a massage tonight," I offered brightly. He happily accepted, and we decided we would end the evening that way.

He headed to the downstairs office to make a couple of phone calls. We met later in the kitchen. "It's late. Are you sure you're not too tired?" he inquired.

I was exhausted, but I wanted to touch him once more. "It's my last night here," I said softly, missing him already, feeling the incredible pull I always felt when I was near him.

We walked upstairs and padded softly down the hall past Alistair's room to the gym. I placed the little bottle of massage oil on a workout bench near the massage table. Jonathan took off his socks and lavender cashmere sweater, laid them on the bench beside the oil, and climbed onto the table.

I stood on the left side of the table and placed my right hand on his lower back, allowing the energy to flow into me. I let my hands be guided, touching him lightly along his spine, neck, and head. I rested my palms on the backs of his knees, directing the energy into his recumbent body.

The stillness filled me with peace. It had taken nearly my whole career to allow the intangible healing Love that wanted to use me as its conduit. I had denied its stillness, its undefined yet powerful simplicity. Because of my romantic feelings for Jonathan, the experience felt more weighty, a "true but false" light, dimmer, and somewhat earthbound by my attachment to him.

I picked up the bottle of oil and squeezed some into my palm. The smell of sweet almonds filled my senses, and I breathed it in deeply. I applied the oil in broad strokes to his back and around his shoulders and ribcage. Suddenly, I felt the impulse to run out of the room. The feeling rose swiftly, grabbing my chest, my throat. I swallowed hard, fighting the uninvited brooding that turned into a dark memory.

"Rub my back! Rub my legs too!" my drunken father giggled, kicking his feet like a swimmer, lying face down on the bed as my mother and I kneeled beside him, rubbing slowly and rhythmically back and forth as if scrubbing laundry on a washboard, waiting for him to pass out after the evening's long tirade.

I hated Friday nights. Every week like clockwork, my father would sit at the kitchen table drinking Manhattans, his eyes becoming glazed and more vacant with every drink. Pounding on the table, he would tear into us, "I'm the one who makes this house run! You're a piece of shit!" I would sit facing him, flinching with every blow of his fist on the table, his obscene words reverberating in my ears and heart, slicing my self-worth to ribbons, leveling me impotent and insecure in this absurd weekly ritual. He was nasty when he drank, name-calling as he stabbed his finger at me from across the table. My mother's back would be toward us, head bowed, and I could see her body heaving, crying as she tended to his meal cooking on the stove.

I was the oldest of two girls, Carol having been long gone. My younger sister might have been curled up in a ball on her bed, too young to understand what was happening. And just *what was* happening? Why did adults have to hurl their demons at their children? Even though I was young and terrified, I knew we hadn't done anything wrong. How could two preteen kids have done anything incredibly *wrong*?

Or my mom, for that matter. She was a good-natured, sensitive woman who catered happily to my father's needs and her family. She was an artist. There were murals on our bedroom walls and days she spent with us creating arts and crafts or leaning over us, guiding our hands as she taught us how to crochet or sew on her Singer sewing machine.

There was the big morning-after fallout on Saturday and the resurgence of life in our veins by Sunday. Monday was back to work, back to school, and back to normal, where Dad was his typical hard-working, fair—but strict—self.

We played board games, badminton in the backyard, barbecued on hot summer nights, and laughed at jokes told over the dinner table. The tension would mount slowly over the week, and then it was Friday all over again. I don't know why my mother put up with my father's behavior, worshipping a man who had dashed her on the rocks, week in and week out, not being able to say no. Why couldn't she stand up to him? Why didn't she rescue herself, rescue us all?

"Turn face up so I can massage your feet," I said tiredly to Jonathan, who lay draped contentedly, arms dangling off the table. I had recovered from my urge to bolt but was decidedly spent. The day's antics with Libby had effectively wiped me out. I stroked Jonathan's feet as firmly as I could, an effort I barely had the energy to make.

I let my mind wander to our time in the airport with Yvonne as we offered her our guidance. I remembered how I felt as I observed his intense focus, feeling the light and the vibration of Love surrounding us. To my eyes, he was like a messiah, directing a laser beam of compassion toward her as he spoke. I had been awestruck, ready to fall from grace. And now, with all the theatrics happening here in Saddle River, was I unwittingly resurrecting the shame from my unresolved past?

I moved Jonathan's feet closer together, my mind in a trance. Before I knew what was happening, I leaned over and kissed the top of one foot and then the other. He jerked abruptly as if I'd jabbed him with a pin. His body stiffened, but he didn't open his eyes. At once, it was utterly wrong, inappropriate, possessed. I cringed, repulsed by my actions, my body trembling with self-disgust. I had crossed a forbidden boundary. *What am I doing?!* My mind spiraled out of control, and my breastbone crushed inwardly against my pounding heart. I wanted to run again but remained planted, my legs leaden with the inertia of instant remorse.

The air felt dense, like a heavy blanket of shame and regret I'd draped over my shoulders. Jonathan's eyes were still closed as he lay on the table. I could only imagine what he was thinking. Clearly, he had been startled, and I'd never seen him jump at anything. "Okay, you're all done," I said in a tiny voice, squeaking out the words I was nearly choking on. Jonathan sat up without a word, perching himself on the edge of the table, staring straight ahead, his gaze unfocused, silently collecting himself from my intrusion. "You should put your socks on so you don't slip from the oil," I said mechanically, feeling like my voice was coming from somewhere outside of me, the sensation of his skin still on my lips. I couldn't believe this nightmare I had birthed into form. I wanted to crawl under a rock.

"Why? It's good for the floor," he said, smiling, sliding his feet back and forth playfully on the shiny wood. I was shocked. He had let the incident slip by without a single word. The whole scene was ridiculous, a parody, a blithering facade. Didn't he want to call me out on my behavior? Didn't he want to know *why* the hell I had done that? I was desperate for him to say something, *anything*. I wanted him to let me off the hook, but not by ignoring what had happened. I wanted to face it head-on, laying my feelings out for him, no holds barred.

We returned down the hall and hugged briefly outside our bedroom doors. "Goodnight...I love you," I said, the words tumbling out of my mouth, but he didn't return the sentiment. It was the truth, my truth. I didn't know why my feelings for him were so strong, but I meant it with all of my heart as I had with Ari.

But Jonathan wasn't Ari. He wasn't anything like Ari, and I couldn't assimilate a clear picture of him. Sometimes he came across as hollow or scripted, with parroted replies, as if he were a collection of "personas" enclosed within a container named Jonathan, an undefinable man. It was exasperating. I just wanted an honest conversation with him to know how he felt. How do you *feel*, Jonathan? *Do you feel anything at all*??

My heart was heavy as I lay awake in my bed. Why couldn't I have been truthful with him, apologizing for my behavior instead of engaging in this unconscious dance of inauthenticity? I desperately wanted honest communication, but ostensibly, that wasn't going to be initiated by him.

CHAPTER 24

Goodbye, Yellow Brick Road

It was my last morning at the house. I hated to leave. I had the feeling I wasn't going to see any of them again.

Alistair soaked in the hot tub. Jonathan and I paddled our way to the other end of the pool. I wanted to drink him in. I searched his eyes, looking for clues. It was business as usual, and I felt he wasn't holding the previous evening's indiscretion against me. It was interesting how he didn't appear to need closure, able to move forward without dissecting or analyzing a situation. Maybe I just hadn't known him long enough.

I wanted him in my life and was willing to redirect my amorous feelings. I believed we were supposed to be together, but I struggled with his flow and pushed too much. I felt that his ambiguous responses were a way to create distance. He hadn't done that initially, even though I always thought he was somewhat elusive. Maybe that was the wrong word. He was not compelled to answer to anyone, being secure within himself, guided by a strange timing that was not always linear. He trusted the process of life, something that I struggled with. I knew things always worked out in the end, but it was the present moment I had a hard time with. I could look back, seeing they had, or forward and hoped they would, but the "now" felt too unpredictable, too unknowable, uncontrollable, and dangerous to the future. I couldn't linger there for very long.

We floated over to Alistair and joined him in the hot tub. Jonathan sat cross-legged as we chatted. I hadn't seen him do that before and thought maybe the previous night's energy work had helped him. He hadn't admitted to a knee problem, though I'd inquired.

"I've sent out over a thousand emails," Alistair said proudly.

Jonathan was impressed. "How many responses have you received?"

"A few, maybe fifty or so," Alistair estimated. "I've got meetings lined up for the week that are promising and more emails to send. I need to compose a follow-up. Shall we get to work?" he asked, clapping his hands together.

We hoisted our bodies up and out of the pool. I didn't like the cold weather but enjoyed the brisk air against my hot skin. Like a little kid, Jonathan made a bunch of wet footprints, water dripping from his swim trunks. He playfully shot me a glance as I wrapped my white terrycloth robe around me. "What time are you leaving?" he inquired.

"Probably late morning," I said as cheerfully as possible. Leaving was going to be tough. I knew I wouldn't see him for quite some time as he was headed to Hawaii for the holidays. He didn't know when he would return to the east coast, but he anticipated that his work would bring him back quickly, especially given the unfolding situation with Alistair.

"I have a Zoom meeting at 9:30 a.m.," he said. "I don't know how long it will run. It might take more than an hour." I guessed it could last longer, having been in these meetings before.

"I'll probably say goodbye to you before you make the call. I don't want to get stuck in traffic. I have to work in the afternoon," I said as we headed upstairs to shower.

A half-hour later, he and I were in the kitchen together. Alistair was already downstairs working in the office. Darren and Libby would be along shortly.

Jonathan stood at the counter eating granola with almond milk. He put down his bowl and walked over to me with outstretched arms, grinning broadly. "Thank you for everything," he said, enfolding me as I rested my head on his shoulder, hugging him close. "Thank you for your hard work, energy treatments, and amazing cooking," he continued cheerfully. I felt energetically bonded to him, wanting to rest in his arms forever. I didn't know where things were going, and he didn't offer. Documents were pending, and I clung to the idea. It was all I had. He disappeared into the large, elegant living room down the hall.

I went downstairs to say my goodbyes to the others. Libby had yet to arrive, and I hoped I would see her before I left. Darren warmly embraced me and thanked me for the meals and my energy work on him. I was impressed by his ability to shift gears with Alistair. I could tell Darren had genuine feelings for him. At least he would get to work with him, as Alistair had decided to enlist Darren as his full-time personal assistant. I wished I could do the same with Jonathan. "Are you going to come back?" he inquired genuinely.

"That depends," I said, glancing over at Alistair, sitting at his laptop, pecking out an email with his index finger. *His accomplishments certainly aren't a reflection of his email skills,* I thought, smiling. "I would love to be part of the team," I said, excited about the possibilities.

"You're always welcome here," Alistair said, arising from his chair. He gave me a quick hug, and I said one last goodbye as I headed unwillingly up the stairs.

I hastily packed my overnight bag and brought it to the main foyer, where I had first entered the impressive house. I had an appreciable stack of items to take home, including my roasting pans, myriad spices, teas, vitamins, and granola.

Nervously, I thought about the book I had wanted to give Alistair when I first learned about his brother. "What book?" Jonathan had inquired as we'd driven to Alistair's for the first time.

It's a spiritual book about what happens when we cross over to the other side. I want to share it with him to give him some closure," I said.

Jonathan was silent for a moment. After their first meeting with Alistair, Libby had mentioned Max's death to him. "I'm not sure that's such a good idea. He didn't mention his brother's passing to me directly, so what would be the premise of you offering this book to him? We don't even know what he believes," he said, weighing in factors I hadn't considered.

"True. Let's see what happens. I've given it to a handful of people who have received a lot of closure from reading it." I was all about closure. I felt life had too many loose ends, and if I could tie a few of them back together, maybe it wouldn't have to be so hard.

I sat on the sofa in the den, the book on my lap. I had already written a heartfelt note to Alistair on the inside cover weeks ago. I read it once more, feeling into the words and my intuition about sharing it with him. Alistair had indeed told us about his brother. I'd been carrying the book around in my overnight bag, waiting for an appropriate moment if one arose. I didn't intend to give him the book at this point, but the thought still nagged me.

Just let it go, Debra, I thought to myself. I stood up and headed to pack my car. I walked down the long hall and looked into the living room at Jonathan, sitting cross-legged on the floor, his laptop in front of him on the round mirrored coffee table. I would miss him intensely. My legs felt heavy as I walked back and forth, loading my belongings from the foyer into the car, every inch of me resisting this moment.

I headed upstairs one last time and gazed into the luxurious bedroom I had called my own for a while. "Thank you," I said aloud, standing in the doorway. So much had happened in the past couple of days. I walked over to the window and looked at the manicured yard, sadness tugging at the edges of my heart.

Sighing, I pulled myself away and hurried back down the stairs. I thought again about the book for Alistair. Something wouldn't let me leave. *Leave! No, give it to him.* The words played a tug-of-war in my head. I dismissed them aloud. "It doesn't matter! Listen to Jonathan."

I tried to quiet my chattering mind. The air around me was still. I felt a strange mix of peace and apprehension prickling beneath my skin. I wanted Alistair to know for sure that his brother was perfectly okay. I wanted to give him something, to thank him for the pool, the Harvard Club, the vintage champagne we toasted with on our first night, and all the evenings we sat on the cozy sofa in the den that would never come again. Why did I have to second-guess everything? Maybe I just wanted him to remember me.

I opened the zipper of my overnight bag and took out the book. I stood for a moment, gazing at its shiny cover. Ignoring my fluttering heart, I tucked it discreetly under my arm and went down the hall and back up the stairs to the bedrooms.

Alistair's room was at the far end of the corridor. I arrived at his closed door, collecting myself. Slowly, I put my fingers around the doorknob and took a deep breath, my heart pounding rapidly as I stepped over the threshold. I reached over, placed the book on his bed, and quickly exited the room, softly shutting the door behind me.

As I descended the sweeping staircase that led directly to the foyer, I could hear Jonathan's voice in the living room. He was still in his meeting. My body trembled. I was having second thoughts. So many emotions were flooding me, and I couldn't think straight. Had I done the wrong thing?

Walking toward the living room, I waited for Jonathan to see me. Still cross-legged, he turned to me, our eyes locked in farewell, and we waved a silent goodbye. I felt genuine appreciation from him at that moment, but my heart was breaking. Something in his eyes was different, as if he were looking at me for the last time, capturing me like a photograph. I knew the dream was over.

* * *

PEERING THROUGH MY WINDSHIELD, I beheld the extraordinary home for the last time. I gazed fondly at the beautiful mahogany entrance that had welcomed me weeks before, straddling the slate-covered porch flanked by ornamental stone flowerpots. I admired the magnificent, corniced gables of the resplendent home as I lingered, saying goodbye and thank you, wondering what Alistair would think when he found the book. I pulled away slowly, turning my car to head back down the winding driveway that led to the wrought iron gate. The gate opened slowly, unfolding its arms, bidding me farewell.

I drove through the affluent neighborhood, gazing at the elegant homes rising over well-maintained hedges or hidden down long white pebbled driveways, through the town, and onto NJ-17, past the Mercedes-Benz, Maserati, and Lamborghini dealerships. Merging back into the mainstream, I felt as if I had been lifted out of a fairy tale. The next day I sent Alistair a text. I hoped he didn't mind that I had left him the book. He didn't answer.

Jonathan hadn't responded to my emails. We had completed our document on carbon sequestration and regenerative farming practices, and I was now beginning another project that necessitated his input and guidance. I felt uneasy about his absence, but it was nothing new. Sometimes it took him days to respond.

The following evening I headed to Delaware. It would be good to spend the Holiday with my family. I needed to break the spell. I was overwhelmed by everything that had happened in Saddle River and now had to rely on the others to keep me in the loop.

* * *

THANKSGIVING CAME AND WENT. I hadn't told my mother or sister all the details of what had transpired. More days passed. A week passed. The tension was mounting, and I was obsessed, playing the whole scene repeatedly in my mind. No matter what Libby had done, what I had done was worse. Jonathan trusted me, and I had failed him.

Anxious, I fell into a state of total despair. I prayed that I would hear from Jonathan. The shame, guilt, and remorse I was experiencing were compounded as the days wore on, and I grew desperate.

Christmas was nearing; I would be returning to Delaware for a week. I hadn't been sleeping well. I still hadn't heard from Jonathan. I felt abandoned and devastated. Why did I sabotage something I wanted with all of my heart? Why did I get into these trances of impulsivity that felt so ordained but overrode common sensibility? Why was I wired for the fairy tale?

I had been banished from the land. That's not how the story was supposed to go. I was sure the Universe had delivered Jonathan to my doorstep, a valiant white knight who galloped to the center of my heart only to run me through with his iron lancet. My feelings of shame and guilt were unshakeable. *What was so terribly wrong with me?*

Several days before Christmas, I got a voice message from Jonathan. I held my breath as I listened. "Hello again, Debra," he began. *Please let me off the hook;* my mind begged the voice on the recording. He apologized for taking so long and was now in Kauai. He needed to take some time to sit with all that had happened, including the incident with Libby. As non-judgmentally and matter-of-factly as he could likely muster, he told me what I knew was coming. He thought kissing his feet was inappropriate. Alistair thought putting the book on his bed was inappropriate. "I brought you in there…," he paused. I winced with each phrase as if someone were digging a glass shard from my fingertip. "I *don't* want to move forward," he continued. It was the clearest he had ever communicated. His words skewered me, the statement impaling my heart like a giant sword from which I hung.

I remembered that night at JFK and the slicing motion he had made across his neck. I placed my hands over my chest, reminding myself to breathe. I was sickened with shame and hardened with remorse, my entire body gripped, turning to stone. I wanted to crumble, to die. How could so much pain come from a heart that wanted only to love? I was utterly disillusioned, so sure I was meant to be with him. Was my compass broken? What did I have to go by save for my intuition? I hung my head. "It's not fair!" I cried.

Jonathan's tone lifted halfway through the message. He wished my family and me a happy Holiday and said he looked forward to seeing me again sometime. I felt a glimmer of hope through the ebony cloud of despair that had thickened around me.

I composed myself and replied. I apologized for crossing his boundaries and Alistair's. I apologized for breaking his trust. I apologized over and over, beating myself with my own words, shrinking my light, exalting his, groveling at his feet. What was I worshipping in him? What was I loathing in me, and why? *I had to die at your feet for you to be clear?* Surely there must be some good in all this. I told him that too. I believed everything happened for a reason, even if we couldn't see it, even if circumstances denied that belief. I told him I loved him. I meant it with all of my heart.

My sister came by to have breakfast with me at a local diner. I couldn't contain what was happening to me any longer. I didn't know how much to share. I didn't want her to judge me. When it came to matters of the heart, she was much more practical than me. She knew that things hadn't worked out with Jonathan, that much I had told her.

We sat on my mother's bed with the door closed. "There's a lot more to it than I told you," I said, letting the whole story spill out of me in every direction. I told her about Libby, the scarf with the jewels, and the scene with Jonathan when she shoved it into his incredulous arms. I told her about Alistair and putting the book by his pillow. I told her about the drama with Darren, the pork dinner, and all the emotions I was attempting to juggle; the undercurrent that I alone appeared to be managing that Jonathan was utterly oblivious to, erupting around him, refusing to be ignored. I told her about my last night there, the massage I gave him, what I was feeling at that point, and the thoughts flooding my mind, overwhelming me. "I kissed his feet," I said, holding my breath, waiting for her to reprimand me.

"Awww!" she exclaimed, feeling the place it came from in me, knowing me and my heart like only a sister could.

Tears fell from my eyes. I was awash with guilt, but relieved the truth was out. It was the climax of my experience with Jonathan. A pinnacle or a nadir; I didn't know which. Everything I had done culminated in this crazy final act in a bizarre play, blazing toward it as I barged blindly through every boundary, every barrier. And there at the mountaintop, I had laid a gleaming chest of gold, the gold that was my heart, at Jonathan's feet, giving it all away. "Take it all. I am nothing. You are everything," my words, deeds, and actions seemed to say.

"I *don't* want to move forward," he had said. His words had paralyzed me. I imagined myself in a ball at his feet as he wedged his foot under me and shoved me off the cliff. I plunged and bounced off its sheer, jagged walls, breaking and tumbling, smacking into a broken heap, vanquished on the valley floor. He dusted his hands together, peering over the edge, and turned to walk away.

My sister and I sat in my car in front of the diner. I played Jonathan's message and then mine. "You give your heart too soon," she said gently. "I know you want the fairy tale, but sometimes you have to step back from the situation and look at what's going on. Yes, maybe there's a lot of fun and camaraderie between everyone, but at the end of the day, he's there to do his job." She sounded a lot like my father. I couldn't argue with her logic. I nodded silently, letting the tears stream down my face.

"Maybe it's for the best," she said. "I know how deep your feelings are for him," she continued gently. I held her gaze, letting her words cover me like a warm blanket. I was waiting for her to give me an answer, looking toward her logic to predict a happy ending that I could not extract from the story that had spiraled helplessly out of control. "I don't think it's over yet. Give him time," she said softly. I let myself hold onto that idea. It became the little bit of hope that I would cling to for months.

"I'm starving. Let's go inside," she said, examining my expression to see if I was done processing.

I nodded in agreement. “Yeah, me too. Thanks for listening. This is so difficult. I do love Jonathan.”

“I know,” she said, putting her hand on my forearm. “You’ll be okay.”

CHAPTER 25

Alone with Myself

Christmas came and went. I was glad I had been with my family. It took the edge off the rawness and the waves of shame and remorse that rose and fell like an unrelenting tide inside my body and mind. Now, all I had to do was wait, to let time heal the wound that had gouged my heart.

Worry was the order of every day. The passing of time wasn't helping. Daily, I analyzed and over-analyzed, journaled, meditated, and prayed. I tried to make sense of it all but couldn't. Why had this happened? Had I truly needed to fall in love with another unavailable man?

I reached out to Concetta, whom I'd kept in touch with spottily ov the years since Ari's death, and she agreed to "read" Jonathan's pictur Unfortunately, she fell ill, and it never came to be. Likely, her reading wou have been very telling and very precise. I knew that I needed to get closu another way. I also felt it was going to be a long, circuitous path. I sighe was still in abject shock and couldn't make room for the thought t everything happened exactly as it was meant to, and I would be okay.

Disillusioned and gripped by anxiety and fear, I struggled to ge stable ground. I was fragile, terrified the rug would be yanked out f under me. Hadn't it already been? What else could possibly happen? W Jonathan make a public announcement declaring my mental and emot infirmity? I felt that everything I had said and done, even my loving would be rejected and hurled back at me. I would be a laughingst shamed, humiliated, and expelled from humanity.

The rest of the world seemed happy, full of the zest of life, as I sat idly by, a nobody, licking my wounds, the skin of Jonathan's stiff feet still stinging my lips, my psyche, my soul. I felt like a puny child who knew nothing about anything, my nose pressed against the glass of life, like someone who had crawled under the door into a room where she didn't belong. Invalid. Forgotten. Inept. Had the stork mistakenly dumped me onto the wrong planet?

I felt my chest would collapse as I shifted under the weight of an unbudging, invisible elephant. Sadness and regret plagued me as I turned the situation against myself, foundering under a blanket of disdain and utter disgust. Would I die in this life without ever having loved again? I could forgive everyone their trespasses and felt their bad behavior was all my fault. A self-imposed scapegoat, I was ever willing to absorb their pain and my own and to accept that somehow this was what God wanted too, to teach me a lesson about my undeserving nature, taking away the littlest crumbs of any good I had done, throwing the baby out briskly with the bathwater.

My ego bellowed in my ear, and I wanted to hide. I was afraid to be seen, afraid to be alive. Nothing anyone said to me made any lasting difference. I had fucked everything up. I couldn't see the light, and the practicality of life and love seemed to elude me at the very bedrock of whomever I was.

Whenever I thought I'd seen the rightness in a romantic situation, I had strode mightily forward. There was always a crash, one that I never saw coming. Like a burgeoning wave, it sucked me under, drawing me blindly to its dark center, slamming me mercilessly to the heaving shore. As I spluttered for air, it would grab me by the ankles, dragging me back into the frothy surf. I was powerless to it, a force much mightier than me, forgetful of its revolution as it swung around to resurrect its ugly head in another story, another place in time. I had no explanation.

What was this recurring nightmare, this pitiful face of shame? What purpose did it serve? Was there a hidden memory I was trying to resolve through blind repetition, an invisible anchor chaining me to a past I didn't even remember? To *what* did I cling? Why couldn't I awake from the dream that compelled me like Sisyphus, rolling a stupendous boulder up a hill whose crest could never be reached?

Again and again, I couldn't see the forest for the trees, thinking I could melt the bulging iceberg under the surface, its frozen entanglements paralyzing me at the surface of the still water. How did I heal this devastation, the shackles that bound my heart? What was I here to learn from this unbidden, ominous force that lashed me to its prow, driving me to an inner oblivion? What was the answer to this lifelong plight, this pattern which demanded unrelenting obeisance from me? Who were the ghosts that rode me bareback in the dark night of my soul? Was I such a burden, an imposter from whom any mortal man would surely cringe in horror? *What,* dear Lord, wasn't I getting?

I had met my ultimate opposite in Jonathan, a man whose highest priority was self-preservation. Buoyed and driven by an acute sense of purpose, he was likely oblivious to even a tiny fraction of my plight, nor had he cared to find out. I was emotionally volatile around him, never consciously at ease. He could be cold, dismissive, and withdrawing, and neither of us had offered our best. How did I heal this? Where did I begin? I didn't have faith in myself anymore. I wanted to know *why* I kept repeating a cycle that surely needed no revisitation.

Before that fateful day when Jonathan had told me he didn't want to move forward, I'd had a dream about him. In one part of the dream, I was on a ship, in a gift shop. I held a small statue of a ceramic guinea pig lying on its back with a hole in its belly big enough for a plant. Inside were two live guinea pigs. They were sleeping, and their teeth were interlocked, one male, one female. A man was standing near me on my left, but I did not turn to look at him. I took the female into my arms and noticed that the male wasn't moving. He was dead. I looked at the man next to me and burst into tears which had become wracking sobs as I cradled the statue. I knew I was crying *his* tears. I was sobbing as if I were him, feeling *his* pain. A few moments later, the dead guinea pig came to life, and I experienced an exquisite sense of joy and relief. I awoke before dawn, feeling intense love for Jonathan as a *boy.*

I sensed that the dream was giving me information I somehow needed to know. I recalled his face at the hotel in New Jersey, where he had stooped to pet a little dog in the lobby, and in the hotel library, where he had pointed to the tiny finches splashing in the birdbath outside the picture window.

His devotion to FARM is for the animals, I thought; it's how he gets to save them. Had something tragic happened in his youth? Something that had prevented him from crying his tears? Were they stoppered up inside, walled off somewhere dark and foreboding? Why did I have this dream?

***

THE WINTER WAS COLD, but the light started to come in as a tiny glimmer of hope poked its shimmering finger through a cobwebbed crack in the doorway of my rigidified mind. Different resources slowly trickled in; a great stream of healers, spiritual teachers, friends, and way-showers arrived at the appointed hour.

I started to learn about self-love. I had thought I loved myself, but I never really knew what that meant. I turned my attention inward for the first time, not to the weakness but to the still strength that whispered deep within my chest.

Through Gaia TV, I discovered a lecture series by Dr. Joe Dispenza, a chiropractor whose extensive knowledge of neuroanatomy and the human brain changed my life. His guided meditations taught me to focus my attention in a new way by directing my attention through my heart. I drank in this new learning, eager to heal and cauterize the wound in the center of my being.

My friend Zoie gave me a Tarot reading a few weeks after the new year. "Flirting is Jonathan's pattern on some emotional level—a bit manipulative, but he's not even aware of it. He's magnetic, charismatic, and a truly enthusiastic, joyful person. People are drawn to him. He hooks them in, and then they are dropped. You're not the first person to get hurt. He has broken many hearts. Both men and women are attracted to him." She paused in reflection. "He had feelings for you. He has something to get off the ground and can't have distractions. Love confuses and frightens him. Nothing is going to get in his way." Zoie was emphatic. "He is a boundary person," she continued. "Keep it strictly business with him. Focus on yourself. Jonathan helped you wring out some old karmic patterns, and what happened with him is helping you move into a new paradigm. Do a meditation where you bring him into the light, thank him, and then say goodbye. Watch him walking away."

Her words stung, but I knew she was right. I had to let go of him. "You need to react differently," she continued. "Be confident that you are on target when you 'read' someone. You have been basing things on old experiences. Watch what you put out. The Universe will always mirror you. Too much clutter from old programs blocks your greater expression of joy and love. Surrender. Open up to possibilities. The new is coming, and it's all good! You are moving into your light. Focus on Debra. Don't cling to Jonathan. Don't suck him back in. If he comes back, he will be a different person too—but don't let it matter. This is going to be the best decade of your life! Everything is under Divine timing. Don't push the Divine. Let it unfold."

I needed to fall in love with *me*. "When we are truly in love with Self, we have fallen in love with God," Zoie had said. How would I go about falling in love with myself? How would I become my own beloved? Perhaps I could follow Jonathan's lead. I had seen him brush a stray hair from his face lovingly like a mother would stroke her infant child. Was I worthy of my adoration? Could I become the one who would comfort and hold herself through raging inner storms? Could I become the beautiful one who would bequeath herself the same love she had laid at another's feet?

As I continued to meditate and contemplate, I found peace in the moment and a warm glow around my heart that settled me into myself. I knew I was on a healing path, but my mind wanted to understand *why* I acted and reacted the way I did and how to free myself. Just what *was* it that got me stuck?

Could an epiphany bring the release I was subconsciously seeking? Would the *knowledge* of the inner workings of my romantic patterns point me toward resolution? Or was it purely the neurological "unwiring" from the *feeling*, regardless of the situation—remembered or not—that released the emotion from the physical body to bring resolution? Were these lodged emotions draining all of my energy, leaving me incapable of creating and living my dreams? Were the feelings of shame, guilt, remorse, overwhelm, lack of confidence, and confusion generating a simple, automatic life? Was I in a "trance of unworthiness," as the great meditation teacher Tara Brach termed it?

I envisioned being in love, traveling the world, and joyfully pursuing a path that inspired me. So what was in the way of me getting there? Was it because I didn't know precisely what my purpose was? Were my talents really in line with my desires? Did I have a passion that could be channeled into something that sustainably mattered to me?

My mind was an inveterate spin doctor as questions exploded there, begetting each other in a frantic scramble for my attention, like a three-year-old tugging at her mother's sleeve. What was I addicted to? The longing? The fantasy? What did it offer me? If recollection was only fifty percent accurate, as I understood from Dr. Joe, the other fifty percent was made up. What did I make up that kept me a prisoner? And if I got what I thought I wanted, would I be happy? Was I pursuing *myself*? Was it *my own love* I had been looking for?

Thankfully, there were respites from the cauldron of my mind. Radiant days where the light shone in brightly, and I could breathe. These moments felt altered, and the air and energy around me felt "new." I was aware of the love inside me, expanding and brimming over into my surrounding environment as if I were experiencing a future version of myself. The awareness didn't last, and in a matter of hours or moments, I could be right back in the swill of darkness that loomed ever-present like a black cloud I would disappear into and lose myself.

That night, as I slept, I was gripped with fear. My mind was latched onto very dark thoughts of persecution that revolved around the events in Saddle River. Suddenly, I felt the warmth of Jonathan's presence around my left ear. "I love you," he said, startling me from the dream, and then he was gone. I knew it was a visitation. I had had them with Ari, little experiences that crossed over from another dimension into this one.

On a soul level, I knew that Jonathan didn't want me to suffer. I also knew that everything was happening for a reason, for my healing, part of a much larger plan to remember my purpose and desire to love and be loved. I knew that I chose this specific lifetime and the scenario in New Jersey to help me evolve to a higher capacity to love myself *first.* Only then could I be in a healthy love relationship. I *had* to fall deeply head over heels for Jonathan, or the severance wouldn't have generated enough momentum to have the breakthrough I felt I was headed for. I didn't know it yet, but I was careening headlong into *myself*, where the answer to all my patterns of loss lay ready to be released. The die had been cast long ago and far away.

I had indeed been under Jonathan's spell. Like most of the men I had instantly fallen hard for, I functioned out of the perspective of saving them when what I subconsciously wanted was for them to save me. They neither needed nor wanted my saving. I had only recently become aware of this. It made me feel weak, needy, and impotent as a human being. I had no enthusiasm for my life. The passion these men had for their lives baffled me. Where did the internal drive come from to tend to something every day, work toward something, love the path, love their life, and love themselves?

Jonathan epitomized this paradigm. I was envious—another pitiable emotion that made me feel small, ineffectual, and bankrupt, stalling my entire nervous system. Unconsciously, I had been looking to tap into the energy of these men to help me find my own. I had let their cause become my cause, let them become the battery *and* the vehicle for my undirected life force.

Completely hypnotized by Jonathan, I allowed all of his talents and strengths to eclipse mine. In my mind, he was a brilliant genius with a perfect, staggeringly successful life. I lowered myself to the level of a servant, compulsive pleaser, and caretaker to try to gain his love, approval, and adoration. Was I looking for him to give up *himself* for *me* or merely desperate for him to show me my own heart?

What did I *truly* want from a man? Recognition? Approval? Love? Devotion? Was I looking for a knight who would carry me away to an idyllic life where I had everything my heart desired? Did I want him to relinquish his will, allow himself to be vulnerable, break open, break *down*? Or did I want to control him? Did I need a man's energy, support, capability, and strength, or did I need to feel important to someone I thought was important in the world? And just what was I missing out on by not having a man—who didn't desire me romantically—in my life? What kind of life did I think I would *have* with him in it? And why, when a glimmer of possibility shone its light toward that to which I wanted to run, did my feet tug ineffectually against immovable cement boots as I fell grasping desperately at the shallow roots of salvation, leaving me helplessly tethered to an oblivion that rendered me utterly powerless, where my very self was squandered into the particulate eternity of the abyss?

It was a lose-lose situation. I was starting to see my pattern very clearly in romance, a stark contrast to how I was at work, home, or with family and friends.

I was exasperated. My friend Kate was there to listen and offer support. I had shared the whole gut-wrenching story with her shortly after I had returned from Saddle River. I was thankful for her patience in navigating the raging storm tearing at the fabric of my self-esteem.

"Be kind to yourself, Debra. You know you deserve an amazing man to love you. You need a giver, not a taker. Ask for more love and shift your intention to *receive* that. When I did that, Michael showed up. Things with Jonathan happened because you strayed too far from your core. You didn't love yourself. In that respect, him cutting you off was a gift from your Higher Self!" she said lovingly.

I nodded in agreement. "On a deep level, I know that's true, Kate, but I feel so much anguish. I alienated someone I care about. I don't trust myself, and Jonathan may never trust me again either," I said sadly.

"That's just your fears talking," Kate said tenderly. "Whether you perceive it or not, the experience of joy and misery *are* under your control, unlike Jonathan or any of your other relationships, past or present. Once you understand this, what happened in the past won't matter. At some point in your interaction with Jonathan or the people from New Jersey, they won't even remember how or why they acted the way they did! It's okay to move on. Trust me. Everything will work out for you," she said reassuringly.

I had wanted Jonathan's love so badly. He was my white knight; only the damsel he was rescuing was FARM, not me, an inanimate lover to whom he was entirely and unswervingly devoted.

My mind was relentless in its pursuit of a solution. Was self-worth within my reach? Did I want freedom, or did I just want to dream about it? Could I endure being seen? A fixed point on a map where I could be judged, humiliated, stripped of dignity, annihilated? What was it that made me think I was so hideous a creation? Was this hell? The ego? Some evil I would not, or could not acknowledge, lest it explode out of some tarnished, forbidden lamp burrowed inside of me like a possessed black cloud, a satanic genie who would cast me into the black heart of misery? What was it that I was afraid of? What ridicule, what punishment awaited me for every wrong I had ever done? Was I going to wither and die of embarrassment and agonizing self-regret?

This fear kept me shackled to my insignificance, desperation, and insecurity, so I dreamed of some imagined, happy future in which I thought well of myself and was free to be me. It lived somewhere "out there" on the other side of the looking glass. Until then, I was bound to mediocrity, another trance that required no incredible feats, just washing the dinner dishes before bed. No challenges, no demands, and no rewards. Either way, I was in a trance.

New Jersey had been one of those trances, and, painful as it was, I had still wanted it. I hadn't the courage to tell Jonathan the truth about how I felt. I was indirect and metaphorical. I couldn't bear the thought of him telling me that his feelings were not reciprocal, giving him no choice but to reject me once and for all. I couldn't handle that. So I died a slower death by misrepresenting my intentions, allowing him to flick me away with no remorse, no second thoughts—a simple goodbye with one hundred percent assuredness of self.

Oh, that I could aspire to this level of self-esteem! I envied him because he knew, trusted, and chose himself. I hadn't done this, which had cost me my integrity. Could I ever heal enough never to betray myself again? Was Jonathan a mirror for this too? I couldn't live like this any longer. How would I ever be able to love myself if I didn't even like myself?

The boundaries with Jonathan had gotten so blurry. He was a boundary person Zoie had said, but I knew this all along. It was circumscribed all around him through actions, communications, and body language. I had intuited all these things but had ignored them, *plowed over them.* I didn't do this intentionally; it was a compulsion, an obsession born of childhood needs that did not get met by my father or even my mother. Years of immersive spiritual and psychological soul searching had turned up many deep understandings, and yet I was driven by some hidden agenda that would take over like sleepwalking, an automated trajectory that was not grounded in truth or love, a travesty doomed to fail, imprisoning me in my own life.

My attraction to Jonathan had only been fatal to me. Undeniably he hadn't seen it coming. Or maybe he did and thought it would blow over like a little black cloud. Instead, the winds stopped blowing, and he got drenched in a scathing rain, pelting him out of his illusions. He'd had no choice but to let go of me.

With all the years of diligent, fruitful intention work I had undertaken in the name of my liberation, why did I feel my progress did not match the magnitude of the effort? I likened it to using an ice shaver on an iceberg or trying to move a mountain with a teaspoon, one tiny scoop at a time. At this rate, it would take me millions of years to evolve.

Why couldn't I be normal? I woke up in fear almost every day. I was running out of energy, trying to drag myself to the next best thing. Life was way too short for these shenanigans. There *had* to be something I was missing. Where did salvation lie?

* * *

MANY WEEKS PASSED, and I hadn't heard from Jonathan. Why would I? In his mind, the situation was done. He had moved on and cut me off. His sense of self-worth was firmly intact, and he knew how to take care of his needs. I was the one clinging to the past like a deranged life raft, my salvation always "out there" somewhere.

At some point, I began to forgive myself, him, and the situation. Things started to feel lighter. Everything had happened for a reason, some of it beyond my understanding. The Universe was orchestrating a resolution. There was a rightness in coming together with Jonathan, Alistair, Libby, and Darren. I was free in those moments of clarity, and I could free them too. I'm not sure why those moments didn't turn into lasting acceptance. Perhaps they never would.

On one of those days, I reached out to Jonathan with love in my heart. I wanted him to know that my personal cataclysm had brought me clarity and release. I wished him Love in all its unbounded forms. It didn't matter whether or not he responded; I didn't need his approval for my existence in the world.

The feeling didn't last. Days later, I spiraled down, not knowing what the future held for me in any way. I wanted desperately to know that my existence in the world mattered and that I had a purpose to fulfill. I felt utterly at peril, not knowing what ideas to believe. Would I ever be in love again? Had I permanently ruined my relationship with Jonathan? Would he ever trust me again? Would *I* ever trust myself again? What part of me kept resurfacing to bowl me over when I wasn't looking? Why didn't those blessed moments of enlightened thinking last? Why did I continue to revisit the situation, like a broken record hung up on a scratch? Was I addicted to pain, addicted to instability?

I had been watching an interesting series on the evolution of our planet, which brought up a lot of fear about a recurring childhood nightmare regarding aliens. A "male" and "female" figure stood before me in the dream, gazing at an organ that looked to my nine-year-old senses like a brain. They had large black eyes and no other discernible facial features. They were dressed in body-contoured suits, their attention fixed on the "brain" into which they inserted long metal probes. I always awoke in terror after this dream, and it left me with a strange sensation that I couldn't translate to earthly terms, a feeling like I could look at the whole world at once, but one in which I felt eerily detached and alone. I spent years trying to figure out the symbology of this dream, to no avail. I had two other recurring childhood nightmares that had to do with my father and the upheavals I was experiencing due to his drinking. All three dreams would occur in succession.

From a metaphorical perspective, I could see the connection to my life of the others, but not the alien dream. Life moved on, I grew up, and I forgot about it. The television series had resurrected the discomfort, and it was on my mind.

Thankful for my yoga classes, which I attended from home due to Zoom capabilities, I took my "alien problem" to the mat. As I did the poses, I felt as if my heart were manacled by cords of darkness, surrendering to a plight I could not see with my body's eyes, wanting release, wanting to go "home." I felt as if no one, nothing, was helping me or guiding me, and I was sinking into a terrifying blackness. At that moment, Jonathan cheerfully reached out to me on WhatsApp, thanking me for everything and telling me he hoped to see me the next time he was in New York. He had also sent me a link to an inspirational video, thinking it was an excellent way to "reconnect."

I felt great relief. I was tired of judging myself so severely and taking the world personally. Misinterpreting the word "reconnect," I thought things were looking up, but he wouldn't communicate anything further. Interestingly, he had "rescued" me again. I knew we were connected on a level neither of us remembered, and he didn't want me to suffer.

Later that day, I drove to the bay, less than a mile away. It was raining. The sky was gray, and I watched the dark, choppy waters slap against the bulkhead. Two geese floated fifty feet from the shore, facing the current, pelted by the steady rain. Although they weren't "moving," I knew they were working hard to move forward against the current. Treading and bobbing, unresistant to the forces of nature, they looked the same as they would on a much kinder day. After some minutes, they took off noisily into the strong wind, flying low to the water's surface, continuing on their journey.

It was a timely metaphor. I felt so stuck in the quagmire of "me." Sometimes the work was too hard, and I struggled to pedal forward as life's current threatened to drag me back to the shore. Did I have the strength to flap my wings and lift myself out of the water? Could I envision and create a greater possibility for myself in life and love? I felt stymied, listening with excruciating silence for the still, small voice to whisper to me: "come this way. Here is your calling. I will guide you." Where was that voice? *Where?*

Part Five

REWRITING THE FAIRY TALE

CHAPTER 26

In the Arms of the Angels

I had listened to a short hypnosis session with an internationally famous therapist whose confident voice told us we are "enough," that we are "loveable," and that many people's core issues stemmed from the one belief that they *weren't* enough. I listened to the meditations every night for weeks to reinforce these ideas. I tapped further into childhood remembrances, where fears of abandonment and rejection clamored for release. It was slow going, but now was the time to jackhammer them away. Armed with the idea of loving myself, it was a path I was willing to pursue.

So much help was pouring in. Had the still, small voice heard my plea? Was life finally saying "yes" to me? Did I matter? I needed to say "yes" to life, to love *my* life. Jonathan was a great example of someone who loved *his* life. He wasn't perfect, but he was an ideal example for me, bringing me one of the hardest lessons of rejection that I had suffered to date, refusing to accept my misaligned behavior as the truth of who I am, and passively *forcing* me to come to terms with the dark patterns of self-abandonment and self-criticism that I had battered myself with for so many years.

I had recently and reluctantly pulled *Codependent No More*, by Melody Beattie, out of my collection and started to reread it, this time dropping my pretenses, my obstinance, bringing my open heart to the honesty of its pages; all of my obstacles, challenges, the beauty, and the beast in me. I let them all have a seat at the table. I wanted to reveal to myself the value of my life, to bless and relinquish the painful journey that had brought me to this moment. I realized deeply that I had never actually been rejected by life because I was *here.*

Was it time to write my book? Time to tell the beautiful story of Ari, the incredible love of my life who showed me I was *enough*, was *lovable*? I had the time now. Like a swooping sabbatical, things had changed drastically with my career, and I could legitimately bring it to life. I always sensed I would tell my story about him and my awakening in France. My friends knew it too, and they were excited that I might finally bring it to fruition.

Would this be how I would love myself into wholeness? By liberating myself from the clamoring voices and errant compulsions that frequently ruined my romantic life, leaving me splattered on the pavement of self-imposed crucifixion? Yes, I wanted that with all of my heart. I was an ordinary woman with an extraordinary desire to know who I was and why I was here.

One day while watching an episode of Matias DeStefano's Initiation Series on Gaia TV, I had an epiphany. He was speaking about "light" and "dark" forces, describing how the soul requires a diversion or distraction to be able to "find" itself—typically through crisis or another precipitating factor—which is basically *by design* in the journey to knowing oneself. I understood this to mean that those dark forces or things on the *outside*—surrounding us as situations, problems, emotions, or patterns *around* us but *not us*, were compelling us to look "out there," believing we don't have or aren't what we already need; that something is missing or lacking, that there is something we have to do, accomplish, solve, or conquer to become ourselves.

The paradox is that we *are already* ourselves; all those things are just distractions compelling us to "seek" and "not find" ourselves, preventing us from remembering who we already are. Like an obstacle course, we aren't the course or the obstacles themselves, but the one moving along or within the obstacle course *encountering* the obstacles. The obstacle course will never become who or what we are; *we* are the only thing that can be *us*.

Had that been why, to consider writing a book, I'd had to buy books to show me how? Methods, structures, exercises—someone else's ideas—a distraction that kept me from expressing what was *already within me?* Was this how I stifled my creativity in life, through endless searching? Ultimately, these distractions would keep me from what I feared the most: *being me*—the me who could be rejected. "Just write!" a little voice inside me offered. Would I? *Could I?* What if I were talentless?

And was it the same with love? Did I want love, or just the path to love, the chase of some imagined ideal? What would it feel like to have an actual being who adored me as is without having to become more before I could have love? Did I have to become that person for myself?

I had to stop putting all my eggs in Jonathan's basket; he wasn't in love with me. Why was I trying to change that? What if he suddenly wanted me? What would I do? Did I trust him? Trust him to stay? Was I merely in love with the fantasy of the man I thought he was? Was I *addicted* to this fantasy? Would the real Jonathan be less exciting than the fairy tale—the *fiction*—that seemed to offer more than the reality? Jonathan wasn't even Jonathan. It was *my version* of him that I was in love with. The emotionally thoughtful, tender-not-cold Jonathan. The man who was crazy about me, *connected,* romantic, passionate. The man who wanted to share his journey with me. The *real* Jonathan didn't make me feel *safe,* a critical element to a successful relationship. He had already abandoned me more than once. Why couldn't I accept that? If he were a person I wasn't in love with, I would have moved on long ago! Yet, here I was, waiting for him to come running back to me as if he couldn't live without me!

Where did the confusion lie? Was it simply the alcoholic personality dynamics of my childhood father that confused me, that didn't provide a stable emotional foundation for me to decipher fact from fiction when it came to romantic relationships? Was this just my way of keeping myself helplessly and *safely* single? Had Jonathan represented all the unrequited love I was trying to sweep into a pile and shove under the carpet? Was chasing him another way to keep me from living—and finding myself?

In my understanding, Matias implied that darkness is a tool to help us create new possibilities, that it showed us how to evolve, and that darkness and light were inextricable parts of us all. When we learned to honor them both, we could create new realities. Was writing that new reality? Something I could do for myself, by myself, and through myself? Could the goal be *me*?

I awoke the next morning at dawn to the sounds of little birds outside chirping the day into being. The sound of their peeps and shrills brought peace. "*It's going to be okay, Debra,*" I reassured myself. I thought about what Matias had said. Why did we have to install so many obstacles before receiving the big epiphany about who we are?

It was almost sunrise, so I hopped in my car and drove to the bay near my home. "Oh, you birds!" I exclaimed. They were ever exuberant in their song, heedless of my past, my presence here at the shore, as I sat staring at the choppy water, waiting for salvation to arrive in a life I felt destined to change. How would I write this life? What *mattered?* What was my gift to the world? Was there a permanent bliss awaiting my arrival, or was life like these bobbing waters, endlessly up and down?

Soon others would be awake, and my attention would be distracted. Sometimes I wished it could just be the birds and me. But then my craving would set in, and I wanted something more. Was I entitled to a happy life, allowed to love what I do? Would anyone see the beauty in me? Could I find it in myself? Would others run if they knew the truth about my light and dark mind?

Matias had suggested we must go down to go up. How far down did I have to go? What if there was no bottom? What made me believe that if I *got* to the bottom of my life, I'd suddenly be able to get to the top? Was writing a book going to save me, give me the life I was dreaming of? Who was I writing it for? Could I be devoted? I had always thought my life would be devoted to the man I loved. Could I be devoted to myself, my book? Where would the energy come from for that?

I wasn't always unhappy, just loaded with questions. Nor was I crazy; I simply didn't know how or where to find my sustenance. Maybe it was something I was born without. Others seemed to have endless energy, confidence, and interest in their projects. Where did these people get the reserves to achieve greatness? Did they have to go through all this processing first? What answer would take all my questions away?

My life was good, I reminded myself, and I was deeply thankful for my friends and family. I was in excellent health, ate well, and lived in a lovely apartment near the bay. My work as a chiropractor had been gratifying, yet

I felt there was something more. I couldn't put my finger on it. Was writing the "something more" I was seeking? Did I have something valuable to say?

"Just write!" the voice had said. How was that going to pay the bills? The thought of striving would rise out of the surf, and I would feel separate and unloved again. When I brought myself back into the present moment, I had peace, and the only thing I needed was the birds and the gently lapping water. It was then that I loved being me, with the ability to convey what I was thinking and feeling onto the page.

What if only God got to see what I wrote? If God was All and All was God, did it matter if other people read my words? Was it God, or me, who needed me to write? Did God want to be an author through me? I had always been an avid journaler; could I start writing using my laptop? Write an actual book?

The next morning I sat at the bay. I had made an important decision. I would write my book, which would be about my time in France. I would do it every day for thirty days, no matter what. I had to see if there was something to it. I wanted to share my magnificent love story, and my beloved Ari, with the world. The book would include my spiritual journey, my awakening—a beautiful, magical story made manifest. I would write it first for me. I would write it for my heart, the heart that wanted to love. Maybe others would read it too. It was time to stop giving all of my attention to Jonathan. He certainly wasn't giving any to me. I had to love myself. I had to try.

* * *

I AROSE AT 6:30 A.M., earlier than usual. I felt a sense of excitement, an exuberant fluttering in my chest, heart, and throat. An hour later, I was parked at the bay, contemplating my decision from a few days ago. I got out of my car, took a deep breath of the salty air, walked to the passenger side, and got in. I placed my laptop on my lap and set my timer for an hour. Opening a new document, I started writing about my arrival at Nice Airport all those years ago.

As I typed, I felt an intensity building around my chest, a warm, focused peace. I was in the zone. I smiled, feeling connected to myself in a new way. Suddenly, I gasped. Two American bald eagles landed on a telephone pole twenty feet above me! I was breathless. I had never seen an eagle on Long

Island, let alone this close. And two of them! What were the chances? It felt very ordained.

Was it my dad sending me a message? I believed that souls we once loved could touch us from the afterlife. He'd always cherished his beat-up royal blue cap with an eagle decal and wore it almost daily. Had it symbolized freedom for him?

I'd parked at the end of this street many times before. I felt awed by the eagles majestically perched overhead. I was able to take some pictures and a video. One of them flew away, but the other remained. Was this gesture, this decision to write, a claim to my freedom? My father had always loved my writing. Was this the ultimate thumbs-up from him?

Immense gratitude filled me with preciousness and love for my dad, whom I believed was sharing this moment with me. I sat silently, feeling the rise and fall of my breathing as I lingered momentarily. Like anything started anew, there would never be another "first day." This was the beginning of my journey as a writer. I wanted to hold onto it.

I was putting *my* dream first this time, using *my* voice and talents to bring *my* story into the world. I didn't have to chase someone else's dream to find my desired fulfillment. It had been inside me all along. I had never really thought about being a writer, although this wasn't the first time I'd thought about writing a book. I merely hadn't put two and two together.

A couple of days later, one of the eagles returned to sit on the same telephone pole! I knew it was a sign. I had chosen something that would undoubtedly impact my life in ways I couldn't imagine. France had shown me this kind of magic too.

I thought about my dad. He had not been spiritual in this lifetime. He was an engineer with a mathematical mind. He was a deep thinker, in awe of nature and the infinity of the Universe, but life, in its awesomeness, still came down to math and physics.

As a young man with a deeply analytical mind, he had explored western philosophy and read works by Plato, Socrates, Spinoza, Descartes, Immanuel Kant, and even Hegel's dialectics; none provided the definitive conclusions he sought. Science appeared to be more satisfying. He was intrigued by the life work of great men like Einstein, Carl Sagan, and Steven Hawking, who were deeply fascinated by the cosmos.

In my teens and young adulthood, my father and I would have lengthy conversations about the meaning of life, especially from a scientific perspective. But my breakup with Shane after graduation from chiropractic college had catapulted me into severe personal upheaval, plunging me into an abyss of self-searching that ignited my spiritual journey. Divine territory was not where my father pitched his tent, and those scientific conversations could no longer provide the answers my heart was longing for.

Every day I showed up at the bay to write. My sessions usually lasted for ninety minutes or so. After just one week, my motivation started to flag. Why was I writing this book? Was it to show my dad I could succeed? Was it an attempt to become valuable to Jonathan so he would want me back? Did I want to go into the deep, dark tunnel of my past to extricate a journey worthy of the effort? Was the fantasy of a finished book better than the reality? Could I handle the day-to-day monotony, whether or not I felt like writing?

The next day an eagle flew by overhead! I still had many questions and felt my mind churning, even when I slept. I started thinking about everything that had unfolded during my time in France, my stunning romance with Ari, and the tragic loss of that magical love.

I wanted to write this book. I had to allow the questions to rise and fall, to keep going, regardless of the ebbing and surging of my desire. It was just a choice, one that demanded grit. Both would have a path. Which path did I want more? I had to stop ruminating about what would or wouldn't happen and simply *choose* to write. "Just write," I reminded myself. Perhaps the eagle, if it were a sign of my father's presence, also wanted me to write.

Amidst all this newness, I'd had another dream about Jonathan. Oddly, he was sitting in my father's spot on the couch at my parents' house. There was a pure white cat at my feet, and I bent to pick it up and walked over to sit next to him. I looked at her, and she now had grey spots. I noticed that Jonathan and I had our legs crossed at the ankle. I was pleasantly surprised.

The dream held promise for me. I thought the grey spots on the cat symbolized the necessary imperfections that were inherent to all relationships. It certainly didn't make it any easier to move on. Perhaps that decision would come from something more profound than a "sign."

I was learning to love myself better. I continued listening to the meditations about being "loveable" and "enough" and Dr. Joe's teachings about the connection between heart and mind. I was starting to heal, beginning to locate the heart of myself. With all that had happened between the men I longed for and me, I knew one thing to be true: It took courage to love and seek your own heart.

My book became an everyday reality, a journey I would not abandon, regardless of where it took me. My new book coach, Lynn Komlenic, had shown up through the recommendation of a friend, and I knew she was the best choice for me. She was a spiritually conscious, heart-centered person, and I trusted her. We were kindred spirits and had studied many of the same teachings. Our philosophies were similar. She was the person who would take the journey with me and could help me successfully bring my book into the world.

"The book will write itself, Debra," she had said confidently. We both believed I must allow it to flow through me, and we embraced the perspective that I was remembering what was already buried deep inside, waiting to come forth. I was confident I had a companion to help me through what I knew would be an up-and-down journey laden with joy and doubt, someone who would see it through to the end.

* * *

I AWOKE DISTRAUGHT AFTER A LATE-NIGHT conversation with my friend Kate. She said it was essential to let our feelings be known and practiced this in her relationship with Michael. If there were times she felt she had betrayed herself, she and Michael would talk it out. It always seemed to bring them closer.

"How can you love Jonathan more?" she had asked me gently.

My ego roared. *More??* I couldn't possibly love him any more than I did.

I recalled the first time I had hugged Jonathan. I'd held him a long time, in an embrace that seemed to have waited hundreds of years. I inhaled his clean, fresh smell, his sweater warm against my chest. "I love you," I said, the words tumbling out, not needing or wanting a reply.

"I love you too," he had said, equally unencumbered.

All those months ago. So much water under the bridge, so much I'd misread, such a horrific fall. I desperately needed *closure*. I didn't know how to ask for it then. The realization shocked me, arriving in great sheaves of tears, my voice erupting from a deep well inside me, begging for relief. I didn't recognize the sound of me, an aboriginal, convulsing plea released from a yawning pit of despair from which I could no longer escape. Reeling into my bedroom, I clutched the high post of the footboard, clinging, legs threatening to collapse. I hung there howling, washed away in all that old pain, afraid to let go, afraid to hold on.

Spent, I flopped down onto the bed and curled into a little ball, my arms wrapped around me as I consoled myself. Kate's words haunted me. "Love Jonathan more." What did that mean? How could I love him any more than I did? I was *dying* inside. *More…?!*

Later, I parked at the bay, gazing into the gently lapping water. In a moment of unbounded clarity, I realized what Kate had meant. I would love Jonathan more by loving *me* more!

A white butterfly cruised by my open car window. I decided to reach out to Jonathan to give both of us the opportunity for true healing and release and sent him a beautiful voice message, telling him that I didn't have closure about our time in Saddle River and asking him for the gift of a conversation. We could move forward or move on. Maybe he needed it too.

I beamed. It felt right; I was taking my power back. Things were going to be all right. It wasn't my fault if he didn't respond, but I had to trust my feelings. This was my journey to love myself, and my only compass was my heart. So many people reflected that for me, and I was filled with gratitude, ready to receive.

Twenty-four hours, and no response from Jonathan. I waited. The power I felt I had reclaimed ebbed from me once more. *He doesn't care,* I thought. *What made you think he was going to change? You chase, and he runs. It's what he does—it's what you do. They're patterns,* I reasoned, still shaking my head. The little voice returned, louder now. *You asked for closure, but you don't get to decide how that happens.*

I could barely stand all these little epiphanies poking me reluctantly awake. I wanted to stay in the dream. Slowly, I felt my power return. It felt good in the center of myself. Why, then, did I keep striving to find the answer outside? Every time I'd acted on a compulsion, even when I'd felt so warmed by its intention, there was a fall, and my mind tripped over it. I struggled. Why couldn't I resolve this? Why couldn't I let go of Jonathan? Clearly, the voice said that closure would come just because I had asked.

It was then that The Council entered my life. Lynn introduced me to their channeled messages which came through a woman named Sara Landon. Their teachings were profoundly healing, like *A Course In Miracles* had been in France. As a collective of non-physical higher-consciousness beings, The Council offered an expanded perspective of the human experience as a reminder that life is meant to be joyful and blessed; that abundance and prosperity are our inherent birthright as we are divine beings of Love and Light expressed in physical form; that there is a benevolent Source greater than us orchestrating things on our behalf, and that we are the creators of what is possible in our lives, with the power to draw to ourselves the experiences we truly desire.[1] Their teachings encouraged me to shift my focus from lack and limitation to abundance and possibility and to allow myself to experience the feelings of my imagined desires, as this would draw my destiny closer.

***

JONATHAN STILL HADN'T ANSWERED MY TEXT. Mired in feelings of remorse and self-judgment, shame started to hijack my emotional landscape. How dare he ignore me! I was inviting him to vent too, so we could start over or move on. Did he want to brush it under the rug as if it had never happened? Didn't he want a resolution? Apparently, only one of us needed closure.

I plummeted. What did I want from him? Why did he show up when I was willing to love again, ready to take a chance on another human being? Why did things fall apart so quickly before we'd even really begun? I'd felt so raw and vulnerable around him, but I realized that part of his role was to show me what loving yourself looked like. Was that the only reason he was here? Why couldn't I accept that he didn't have feelings for me? Yes, he had hurt me, but why couldn't I move on? I was stuck.

My work with Lynn gave me hope for myself. She was patient and kind with my emotional vacillations, which frequently tripped me up. As a fellow student of The Council's teachings, she was committed to following the

Light and listening to the directives of her heart. She helped me "feel" into my heart center to ask myself what was best for me.

"Our joy is derived from our relationship to ourselves, Debra. What would it look like for you to be fully sovereign? Drop into your heart and listen. Ask questions and trust that the answers will come. Ask yourself, 'what does my heart want me to know right now?' or 'what would feel good to my heart?'"

"I'm just learning to discern whether the messages are from my heart or my head," I said eagerly. "It's a relatively new experience for me. I'd never separated the two until recently."

"Be patient and allow yourself to feel into it. The wisdom is behind the feeling. Our quality of life is defined by the quality of the moment. You will build trust in yourself by allowing instead of ignoring your emotions."

"I often forget to do that, Lynn. I'm learning to listen to my heart more, but trust is hard. I find myself thinking and worrying about the future. I feel tension around my heart center when this happens," I said.

"Part of the lack of trust comes from thinking. Instead of thinking about your feelings, feel them. Real intelligence is in the body. Get on your yoga mat and let your body move you—meet yourself in the moment. Doing this will increase your peace and confidence because you will connect with yourself instead of just going through the motions. In this way, you become the authority in your life. You are not your thoughts," she said confidently.

"I want to have peace around whatever is coming up for me. I know the anxiousness is because of my resistance toward my thoughts," I said.

"Exactly, Debra! Ask yourself how you can build a relationship with your mind that is harmonious, loving, acknowledging, and respectful. It's not about shaming the mind. Thank your mind—there's something it's trying to tell you."

"I need to remember to do that, Lynn. It's a natural reaction to push away painful thoughts and emotions, and I often forget I'm not my 'thinking.' I get lost in it," I said introspectively.

"I completely understand, Debra. Sovereignty is practicing who we are. We can live a life without guilt, shame, and other negative emotions. It takes practice. Allow the I AM presence to come through and follow the Light. Ask yourself, 'What is it that I want?'"

"I want to feel safe," I said. "To trust. To have freedom from self-judgment."

"So, whatever arises, can you give it to the Light?" she asked.

"I can try," I said tentatively.

"Remember what The Council says: 'Everything is happening for me. I have everything I need and more.' The highest vibration is Love. What actions and behaviors would bring more love, freedom, and safety? Ask yourself, 'how can I come to a level of acceptance?' Stay in your creative power, and move away from ideas of 'what's wrong.' Let go of forcing and efforting. Your heart is where *Life* lives. Ask, 'what would bring my heart more hopefulness?' Give things the space to transform."

The truth of her words bathed my heart, and I sighed deeply. "Thanks, Lynn. I feel peaceful now."

"Be gentle with yourself, Debra" she said. "Just continue to ask."

***

AND SO I DID. I WAS GUIDED to Matt Kahn, a spiritual teacher and transformational leader whose teachings helped me embrace the emotions that merely wanted to be seen, heard, and loved by me. The adult me, loving the little girl me, who needed so desperately to be acknowledged and soothed, undenied her human needs and desires. In Matt's book, *Everything is Here to Help You,* he explains:

> Through the eyes of the Universe, those we are meant to heal have us feeling uplifted instead of exhausted. And when feelings that were once uplifting suddenly create a sense of exhaustion, that is the Universe suggesting that we have shared enough space with that person for the time being. Instead of attempting to push past this energetic boundary, the Universe reminds us how we would be better suited to rest and integrate the exchange that has occurred.[2]

Yes, my relationship with Jonathan had exhausted me toward the end. Or, rather, my emotions toward him had exhausted me. Even though I couldn't see or understand, our parting had to be of the highest order. I felt a lot better after reading Matt's words. Energetically, I knew it had happened on the last night in New Jersey when I gave him the massage. I was exhausted and should have gone to bed. I had overridden this impulse and suffered deeply for it. All of my energy had been driving in one direction.

Everything else was showing up serendipitously in my life, so why didn't I trust that my love partner would too? Herein lay my Achilles' heel. There were many times when I'd felt utterly defeated by my skepticism. Yet, bit by bit, things were starting to shift. I could look at all the other areas of my life and see how things flowed, as I had less grip on the outcome. I had all the tools to make this book happen, and others would show up when it was time to move to the next level. In these precious moments, I knew everything was Love, and everything was happening "for" me. Nothing that happened could be wrong. It was the path back to God. The journey had already been completed, and I was merely waking up from the dream.

A Course In Miracles says, "you see only the past." We could only look out at what had already occurred. So the only choice I had, was *how* I would experience the journey. Happily, without resistance? Or as if being dragged by an oxcart? That was the choice. I knew which one I had to make.

CHAPTER 27

Unbreakable

I had fallen in love with Jonathan before I met him. Does love at first sight ever pan out? Jonathan hadn't been the first. Would he be the last? *The last of what*? I pondered. A big, fat illusion? Would I ever find the love I had always dreamed of? How was I supposed to honor myself and my deep feelings for Jonathan, and honor him at the same time? Could there be one answer to both questions?

I was exhausted from seeing only his perfection while abhorring myself. Could a truly evolved person have passive-aggressive tendencies? He had been so able to cut off his feelings and be critical. Why was I even in love with him? Was he just a perfect embodiment of my father's emotional unavailability? What was I attracted to? Why was the thought of him leaving me so devastating, and yet I had never actually *had* him? What was the illusion, the promise of salvation, that he held for me? And if I just let him go, focused on something else, would someone just as dangerous come along, knocking me off my perch into a stormy sea again? How would I *ever* be able to create a healthy relationship?

If codependency is an addiction to another—which I believed it was, how would I ever truly love a man? Since the entire emotional spectrum is necessarily part of being in a relationship, how could a codependent, who never *saw* a fully healthy romantic relationship, create one? Where was the template? What did healthy conflict look like? "Fixing" would always be a great temptation. Perhaps that was the compelling addiction obfuscating the "now."

My closure wasn't going to come from Jonathan. I had to give myself the closure I desperately sought. I had to get the "Jonathan story" out of my head and onto the page to move forward with my book.

I started writing it, switching from the "France story" that was well underway. It took three weeks and tens of thousands of words. It was a book unto itself, and I was exhausted after finishing it. I still didn't have closure, but at least the story was written down and chronicled for a later time when I could revisit it. Maybe it would become part of the book I was presently writing.

Potentially, my book could be about transcending my patterns with men, finally liberating myself from something hidden that had governed my entire romantic life, and being free to create love from a self-loving place. I didn't have to make that decision now.

I wanted to allow the journey of my book. I was feeling more centered. The work I had been doing with Lynn and The Council was paying off. I was starting to "feel" my feelings as sensations around my heart—my physical heart, instead of "thinking" about how I felt. I began to understand that this was how a person fell in love with herself. It was an actual sensation. It was the Self I had been seeking. It wasn't in my head; it was *in my heart.*

Exhilarated, I could feel the feeling expanding *from* me—*as me.* This was new. It felt like something I'd been waiting on forever, but I hadn't known what to look for. Why didn't anyone put more emphasis on finding this place *inside* yourself? I could feel the difference between my heart "feeling" and my head "thinking!"

My energy was renewed, and I buckled down harder with my book. The pages were accumulating. Tomorrow was Jonathan's birthday. I wasn't going to reach out to him. My incessant reaching out was part of my pattern, and I knew I would feel deflated if he didn't respond. There would *always* be an excuse to connect, and I had to let him reach out to me. I knew he had given me the greatest gift. His rejection of me was my salvation. I realized the problem was not him; it was me. I'd had only one place to go to, and that "place" was me. And in that place, I found the courage, energy, capacity, and tenacity to write every day. In the process, I became a morning person, waking up daily at 5:30 a.m. and giving myself two hours or more to write. I knew now there would be no turning back. I would publish my book. It was a promise I made to myself.

With unflinching persistence, the highs and the lows continued to exasperate my heart and mind. My ego would retaliate if I stayed too high or too confident, and I would get sucked down so fast it would make my head spin. Was writing my book just an excuse to have something to do?

When anger surfaced, I didn't know how to handle it, so I pushed it down and turned it into tears. Praying and EFT tapping[1] would lessen it, but it always returned with a vengeance, creeping under my skin, tightening its vice grip around my chest until I felt I would implode. I second-guessed myself, and the pain, shame, and guilt would come rushing in to feast on my heart like hungry piranha.

This was the part of the pattern that kept me huddled and cowering in a corner, fearing for my life, and was the thing that always made me quit. I needed to give my anger a voice when it arose. How could I do that in a safe way, one that wouldn't destroy me? If I was angry, I wanted to feel angry, not sublimate it, deny it, or make it wrong.

I wanted to tell my story. The real story. Now that I had finished the account about Jonathan, I knew it had to be part of the book. The contrast between him and Ari was stark. Sandwiched between his son Brock and Jonathan, Ari showed me the beauty in myself. Brock and Jonathan had shown me the beast. I was the hunter. Men didn't want to be hunted. I'd been loath to my receptivity, seeing it as a weakness.

Concetta had said my relationship with Ari was not based on my pattern. I wondered what she would say about Jonathan. I often wondered why he needed to show up, but deep down I knew why; my pattern didn't change from anyone else who'd come before. I wouldn't have had the profound shift occurring in my life if my encounter with Jonathan hadn't been so blitheringly painful.

Neither he nor Alistair had asked for the emotional or spiritual intervention I offered in Saddle River. I had to allow people their path without seeing a deficit I could fix or fill *unless they asked* and to pay attention to what I saw happening rather than reading between the lines of what I thought was missing. Hypervigilance may have worked in a regularly unstable home environment when I was a kid, but it wasn't appropriate here. I needed to base my actions on the situation and nothing more. I had crossed boundaries and suffered shame and embarrassment from behaviors born of unconscious agendas. I needed to wake up.

And where was my deceased father in all this? Was he guiding me? I couldn't *feel* him around me in the background of my life, although I had felt his huge presence visit me a couple of times. His energy was gargantuan, knocking me over with the unfathomable Love that it brought, making me sob with grief. I missed him so much at times. I knew he was in a state of formless omniscience, but I hadn't had a soulful relationship with him while he was here. Our relationship had been based on our personalities, and I didn't know "who" he was now. I wanted his everyday presence to feel warm and safe like Ari, whose guidance was undeniable.

I felt guilty that I didn't have full closure with my dad and was sure he could sense that, wherever he was. I wanted a deep connection, to talk to and rely on him. Undoubtedly, he wanted me to heal. This pattern needed to be laid to rest. I prayed for healing and the closure I didn't know how to get.

One day I made a list of everything I could remember that was good between my father and me. He said he used to put me on his lap and sing to me as an infant. There were things on the list like days at the beach, a trip to the game farm, playing badminton, and the tears that streamed down his face when I graduated from chiropractic school. Friday nights were just one thing—the same thing—repeated over and over, gouging a deep groove in my psyche and sense of worth. Yet, from where I stood now, I knew I had always been loved.

I spoke with my mom at length, and we reminisced about all those good times. "You were our Christmas present," she said, her voice gilded with happy reflection.

My father wanted our family. He'd always thought everything out. I was planned. There was never a threat of him leaving me or abandoning me. Those feelings were a calculation by a young child of an alcoholic parent about what could happen but never did.

After I wrote the list, something shifted, and I felt happier. I walked the little labyrinth in the park in my neighborhood. I was working on forgiveness—for my father and myself.

Jonathan continued to loom large, like a float in a parade, a grotesque caricature of my internal polarization, yet I was still waiting for a miracle with him. Emotions continued to rise, and I clung desperately to the practices that helped quell the great storm that still threatened to swallow me. I listened to "mindfulness" meditations on shame and other painful emotions, which enabled me to be present with my feelings.

Late one morning, while practicing yoga at home via Zoom, I saw an image of my mother falling to her hands and knees when she walked in the front door after taking my sister Carol to the hospital for the last time. She told me I had seen this scene where she'd been overcome with grief. I imagined myself a three-year-old, gaping helplessly as I beheld her anguish, both of us overwhelmed by uncontainable emotions—hers for Carol, mine for her—and I had an epiphany: Psychically, I had taken on some of her grief to unburden her.

I sobbed hard as I lay face up on my yoga mat, releasing the past in great heaves of emotion as my yoga instructor read a beautiful quote by Teresa of Avila. I envisioned another image of my mother and me, as children and adults, standing in a circle with Carol in the middle. We had one hand extended to touch Carol, and the other was on the shoulder of the four versions of us in the circle, making a wheel formation around Carol as the hub. I imagined the child and adult forms of us sending Carol love and her sending love back to us. It was incredibly healing and satisfying. After yoga, I was raw but present and content, and joy seeped back into my weary bones. Something had been released.

I thought of how this incident in my life pertained to Jonathan and all the other men I'd chased who had abandoned me. It made perfect sense. When I loved someone intensely and they left me, it triggered the emotions I had experienced as a child. When Carol left, she never came back, and she died at the age of sixteen. I remember visiting her with my family once when I was still a young child, but I had no recollection of her, only a memory of a sandbox in the hospital playground and an empty bed in a row of beds that might have been hers. So for me, not only did the men that I loved *leave* me, but I would also never see them again as if they had died. It was too much to bear. My reaction matched that intensity and felt perilous to my sensibilities—a double whammy. Because of this separation anxiety, I could cling to their memory for years before being able to move on and truly let go.

I prayed to be released from these entanglements, these neurological wirings, and for them to become alchemized into wisdom so I could heal and move forward. I also realized clearly that what had happened in Saddle River was for all concerned, that *all* of our interactions were for the highest good, and that the writing of my book would bring healing on some level, known or unknown. Ultimately, writing my book was my gift to myself. Only I could free myself from the past to create a healthy future.

The next morning, I fleetingly smelled Ari's cologne as I lay in bed. I smiled, intuiting that he was paying a visit. I was incredibly thankful to feel his presence in my life and had the sense that he, too, was guiding me to a resolution. After all these years, I could still miss him as I tuned into him from my heart, accessing the deep feelings I had for him. Sometimes I still cried.

I appreciated the guidance that showed up when I needed it and started to trust that I would be okay. My heart only wanted to love and be received. I imagined myself as a detective, unraveling all of my inner workings to heal a fractured view of love. What was the key that would release me from this?

Around this time, I was also reading the memoir *Daring* by Gail Sheehy. It was written with so much grace, and I could feel her rise to greatness as a woman. I wanted this for myself, feeling I had been waiting decades to live, buried under mountains of inertia and false starts, waiting for something or someone to be the answer to that which I sought. I never realized my talents were waiting for me to use them as instruments to find and heal myself by directing them *through* and *for* myself. I estimated that I could have written several books by now if I had been paying attention.

As I read through my journals, a path unfolded before me as I stepped into my life. I was not inserting myself into someone else's creation; I was giving power to my own. I had long ago forgotten what that felt like. Many poems, songs, paintings, and drawings had gone by the wayside. There would always be a reason not to pursue it, but I would ultimately only be denying myself.

My birthday came, and I received cards from family and friends that touched me deeply. I realized we had to live, shine, and feel our hearts to give each other the privilege of loving more. I wanted to bring the story inside me to life and create a magical new one by infusing it with who I was *now*.

That evening, I felt a presence, as if a hand was placed between my shoulder blades as I slept. I wasn't afraid this time, unlike my birthday all those years ago when Ari had come to visit. Had it been him?

* * *

EVELYN, A NURSE PRACTITIONER I'd met long ago in the early years of my practice, had resurfaced out of the blue, answering an email I had sent through LinkedIn three years prior. Intuiting our reconnection happened for a reason, I called her. She provided profound remote therapy that operated through many strata of the physical, emotional, and psychospiritual healing realms.

Each week Evelyn would perform a two-hour session, releasing all kinds of microscopic foreign invaders in form and formless from my body, mind, and soul. I always felt renewed and rejuvenated after her work, but something earth-shattering happened on one particular day.

As Evelyn worked, reading and clearing every possible infliction throughout all layers of my being, the "alien" dream suddenly popped into my mind vividly. I realized the "probes" they had stuck into my brain had not been my brain at all; it had been *my heart!!* As a young child, I had no idea what a brain or heart looked like, and I'd envisioned a big potato on a steel table. I had never experienced this before, and suddenly I could "see" my poor, contracted heart, lashed and bound with luminous red threads.

I had always perceived my heart was somehow physically contracted, constricted inside my chest, even during significant moments of feeling love and expansion. There had been an inexplicable limitation as if it could only expand so far. As Evelyn continued her treatment, without knowing what was happening, I felt the threads break, release, and dissolve as she quietly declared that all "non-human" interference be gone.

"Oh my god, Evelyn, I need to tell you what's happening!" I said through tears as I recounted the dream.

She cried with me, sensing my release. "I can feel it too, Debra," she said gently.

I was in a state of deep, trance-like consciousness. "My heart is *mine*," I declared softly, almost in a whisper, tears rolling down my cheeks as I lay on my bed, feeling the weight of the world lifted from me. "My heart is *mine*." It was the most powerful healing I had ever experienced.

Later, I performed an EFT tapping session to release any fragments or remnants of whatever had occurred decades ago that Evelyn had helped me to release. At last, I was free of whatever had bound my heart.

* * *

I STILL FELT UNCOMFORTABLE when I thought about my father, sad that we didn't have a substantial relationship. I thought he would disapprove of the structure of my life and the men I was compelled to chase if he were alive. His was more a human memory than an essence I could tune into. I'd never felt a complete release of the past after he died, and I continued to experience self-judgment. Why didn't he make himself known? Could the presence have been him the night of my birthday?

And what about my book? Would I regret exposing myself? Would I look like a silly fool, groveling over men who didn't give me—or my emotions—the time of day? Would Jonathan read it? Would he even understand the emotional psychodynamics, or would he toss it away, as he'd done to me? Would I ever be able to see him for who he was and accept him without the glorification I had laid upon him like emotional chainmail?

Interestingly, I still felt my book was alive and well, but I needed miracles. Was there a realization on its way to me? Was I doing a good job? Was I afraid of my power? Would I still be writing this book if everything had been going well with Jonathan? A book about my love story in France?

That night I had another dream about him. We were at a large gathering in what seemed like a hotel setting. Libby, or someone like her, was there. Jonathan was sitting at a table, writing in a notebook, and I knew it was his "story." When I inquired about it, he said he needed to write it himself—I shouldn't take it personally. Many people wanted to help him write it, but only he knew the specifics. He did not hide the notebook, and I told him I could help him if he liked. He was in alignment with that idea.

Libby and I searched for a "symbol" or the right "color" Jonathan wanted for his book. We entered different rooms. All the rooms were white and had a yellow, orange, or bright green light glowing in the corner that was too bright to look at. I remember feeling exhilarated as if something long desired was finally going to happen. We chose the yellow light. I returned to Jonathan, and we sat on the floor, arms touching, talking excitedly. Something was different and new about our interaction. He was receptive to me, and we were both in our power.

I awoke invigorated, believing the dream was symbolic. The white walls indicated "purity." The lights were brighter than usual, and we couldn't look at them directly. To me, this meant something beyond the ordinary and unknowable could occur. He and I were aligned throughout the dream, especially when our focus was unified in his book. In the dream, the past was gone, but the history of our coming back together was not. I wanted to write a new story with him and forgive the past.

A few weeks later, I dreamed about Alistair. He hadn't answered my apology texts after the whole episode at his house. It was a simple, brief dream. We were at his home, chatting as if nothing terrible had ever happened. He was smiling, and I was content, like when I'd been a guest. I awoke from the dream smiling and felt that everything would be okay. Maybe something unspoken had finally shifted.

CHAPTER 28

Reawakening

Approximately a month later, I heard some great news about FARM related to a significant contract that would launch their Regenaware software package into the public arena of regenerative agricultural practices. I was thrilled. I wanted to reach out to Jonathan to congratulate him, as his efforts made this happen. Would that be a mistake? He had never answered my text to him months ago. Would he reject me again by not responding? I didn't care as much one way or another.

I started typing. I congratulated him for all his hard work and tenacity. He didn't need or want accolades. That much I knew about him. He was on a mission and was starting to realize a dream come true. I hit the send button.

His nonresponse was no surprise, but I felt I had done the right thing and had no expectations. I reflected on a Council transmission I had recently heard. They gave a listener advice about rewriting old memories by telling herself a new, more loving version of her "story," which planted a seed. How could I rewrite my stories to find the love and forgiveness for myself that I was looking for?

I had made a recording months ago that detailed the qualities of the man I was seeking as a partner. I had been praying to shift my pattern, and hearing my voice on the recording gave me hope. I let my thoughts drift away from Jonathan.

I awoke to a message from Jonathan to Kate and me on our shared page the following day. He hadn't posted there in over a year! I did a double-take. So did Kate, who had texted me privately on the side. He thanked us for our support and wished us happiness in the coming year.

He sent a few more messages over the next several days. I was jaded; was this how he wanted it to play out—sweeping the past in one big brushstroke under the rug? Could *I* do that? It wasn't my style to walk around the white elephant in the room. Could I observe from my heart and let go of needing things to be any particular way? Could I endure a superficial relationship with him, living in the outer valences, the emotional shallows? Was it time to move on?

Nearing the end of the first draft of my book, I felt an enormous sense of accomplishment, but things still felt unfinished with my dad and Jonathan; I wondered if I had to accept these aspects as facts of life.

Jonathan's behavior was decidedly the coldest I'd endured, and I questioned his capacity to be compassionate. He was polite, allowing, and believed in the magic of creation, but his heart did not feel round and full. The idea that I had given him so much power saddened me. Why did I even need to go through this with him? Why couldn't I draw on my relationship with Ari? Why did I revert to my old pattern? Did I have to hit the bottom of myself to find the love hidden there?

And now that Jonathan and I were back in each other's orbit, so to speak, I felt guilty writing a book that he knew nothing about. Was I living a duplicitous lie? Should I tell him about the book? Of course, I would protect everyone's identity, but a significant part was still about him. How would he feel if he knew? Would he understand that he had given me the greatest gift in his rejection of me? Would he reject me again? I felt a bit out of control now that he was back in my life, afraid to re-enter the labyrinth of the unknown.

Feelings of guilt and distrust plagued me, and I was becoming anxious. I wanted to run, to undo the text I sent him weeks prior. Was I headed for another fall? I decided I needed to write something different. I would write a new ending to the "Jonathan story." Our conversation would be sincere, without pretense. He would acknowledge that he'd hurt me, confess that he'd had feelings for me, and take responsibility for all that had been his. I would take responsibility for all that had been mine. After I wrote it, something shifted palpably, *physically* for me, as if it had happened! The story was complete, scrawled across a half dozen pages. The gift had been received. Maybe The Council had been right about rewriting the story. "You can leave now if you want, Jonathan," I said aloud.

Less than a week later, he was back. He'd posted a link to an article about FARM acknowledging his accomplishments with them. I was overjoyed for him and reached out immediately. So did Kate. We shared a happy moment, and suddenly nothing that had happened in the past mattered, and I felt exquisitely aligned with them both. I had another choice. I could accept what was, with all its apparent flaws and limitations, or long for the past to be corrected, which it probably never would. It didn't feel honest to make either choice right then. My heart didn't want an either/or. I wanted to be happy. Perhaps the closure was finishing my book and giving myself the completion I desperately wanted and needed.

I felt I was getting sucked back in with Jonathan. I had been so ready to let go. The new "story" had brought closure but was now starting to erode by his appearances. I wanted whatever happened to feel good to my heart; an honest, receptive relationship. Were we perched too far at opposite ends of the spectrum, unable to meet in the middle? Did he want to be in love? I was learning to love myself now, which was absent when I met him nearly two years ago. I was no longer willing to give myself or my power away. No, he would have to come to me with an open heart, a heart that desired itself to be planted as a golden seed in the heart of another.

While searching for a book in my nightstand drawers, I came across a journal more than twenty years old, sitting untouched for probably as many years as I rarely went back to read what I wrote. I cracked it open and winced at the harsh words I had written about my father. He had already stopped drinking half a dozen years before, but the anger and pain I had felt then were seethingly apparent. I needed to do something to get closure and knew my father somehow needed this too.

My search turned up another book I had purchased long ago, *The Wounded Woman: Healing the Father-Daughter Relationship*, by Linda Schierse Leonard. I felt a hardness under my sternum, and I said aloud, "Ugh, I've been through this already. Do I really need to reread this?" I didn't remember if I had or hadn't read it, nor its impact on me, but I sensed it held something I needed to know and believed my father had guided me to find it, so I started to read.

With the same half-baked arrogance with which I had initially resurrected my journey into *Codependent No More,* I was somewhat tongue-in-cheek about *Wounded Woman.* The book was written forty years prior, and I thought its concepts might not generate a shift in perception worth the time investment.

Meanwhile, I struggled with how to get closure with my dad. He hadn't known about my journals, but would have been deeply hurt if he had seen what I'd written. There was so much pain in my past reflections, and I wanted it to be healed.

I started journaling, not knowing what to write to bring the closure I sought. Would it be healing, like what I had written about Jonathan? Should I write him a letter? Initiate a dialog? I quieted my mind and took a few calming breaths.

"Dad, I don't know you," I wrote. "Who are you? I only knew your personality, the parts you showed me, and only through my interpretation, my filter. And because we diverged, we stopped talking in a way that had previously brought contentment through common ground. I wish you would visit me in a way that feels real and healing. I can't go back and 'unsay' all the horrible words I hurled at you on those pages, and I can't access the depth of feeling I know I have for you. I'm sure you know that I am thinking about you. It's hard to perceive your energy now because we did not connect on a spiritual level." I paused. "I'm sorry I hurt you," I continued, feeling the emotion rise warmly through my chest and throat as tears started to fall. "I'm sorry I put words of anger and hate in my journals about you. I was in pain, deeply disillusioned. I thought you didn't like who I was, couldn't see the good in me, and didn't want to know the 'me' I was desperate for you to see. Surely there was a time when I was 'daddy's little girl.' When did that change? Why did that change? Why did you drink and hurt us? I loved you so much that sometimes the thought of you not being on the earth would make me cry."

I continued, letting the words flow, trying not to judge what was coming through me. "I remember the day you fell and our conversation just before that. You had gotten so weak from the dialysis over the past year. You looked at me and said, 'you probably think I'm a burden. I don't want to be a burden to anyone.' I couldn't answer; my throat was frozen. Inside I felt you were a burden sometimes, but I could never tell you that. I couldn't comfort you and tell you that you weren't either; the words would not come out of my mouth. I'm sorry if that hurt you. I know it doesn't matter now because you have omniscience that is only a glimmer of remembrance in my heart. I know you are experiencing all the joys and bliss of being out of the body and that you are aware of my knowledge and consciousness as I envision the realm you are in."

Closing my eyes, I let the questions come forth. "What are you doing? Why don't you come to us? We all still need closure. I know mom talks to you, but do you answer? Do you show her a sign that you've heard her? And what about my sister? I think she misses you more than I do because I don't know what part of 'you' I miss. I don't feel you around me like I do with Ari. I wish that you and I could have known each other in a way that felt loving when I felt so unloved by you. Maybe you felt unloved by me too. I always remember how surprised you were when I told you that you were the most important man in my life. I think that in many ways, you overshadowed me, and I tried to figure out a way to make you see me as a success; that even if you didn't understand me, you could still be proud of me, even if what interested me wasn't something that interested you. I know you were here to teach me lessons that would help me love myself. I wish they hadn't taken the form of so much criticism and pain. I'm sorry if I hurt you in this life or any other life."

I wanted to make it right. I decided to make a declaration to God. "I decree healing and love between us in all realms and dimensions, throughout all time, space, and consciousness, now and forever throughout our ancestry!" I closed my eyes, letting myself feel the power of that. "So what would you offer me, Dad? As I write these words, are they from you, rolling out of my pen across the page?"

"My beautiful Debra, I know I hurt you and your mother and sister too. My journey through my shadows was never about you. I loved you deeply and completely. Do you remember the time when I said I would die for you? If I could take back all the alcoholic years, I would. I suffered profoundly because of it, and my heart and kidney disease were a direct result of my broken heart. Guided by the grace of Source, I found the strength within to stop drinking when I still had time to love you all and try to make up for the past. From where I am, I can see how deeply you were affected, and my heart grieves for that. I never meant to hurt you. I know you understand karma, and there were other lifetimes filled with more pain than this one together as father and daughter. In this life,

because of who we are, we changed the path of our history and future forever throughout all time and dimensions. There is no need for you to revisit the shame and the pain. Your love, light, and strength were part of why I was able to stop drinking, and I will never forget the day you came to me and gave me the opportunity to ask you what you needed from me. What do you need from me now?"

"I need to know you love me and rejoice in the gifts that I offer through me to the world and that you are proud of me, Dad. I am a writer. I know you always liked my writing. I am writing a memoir. I remember when we sat on your couch, and I shared my love for Ari with you as I grieved, and you opened your heart to me. It was one of the few times you showed me your heart, and I will always treasure it."

"You are a beautiful writer, Debra! I always told you that. I am one hundred percent behind you, beside you. It is an incredible testament to who you are and who you are becoming. You have what it takes to complete it."

I told him about Jonathan, and he listened. He told me not to sell myself short and let a man prove his worth or walk away. "I know I didn't help you to develop confidence in yourself. I couldn't see what you needed. I was too absorbed by life's problems and myself. I grieve that. I never meant to hurt you."

"I forgive you, Dad. I'm having a hard time forgiving myself. I always thought that your drinking was somehow my fault. I couldn't figure out why you needed to take that journey through such pain."

"My drinking was not your fault. This lifetime was the last of it. It was my path to forgiving myself. I love you, Debra. You didn't do anything wrong. Forgive yourself. You are a loving woman. Don't let my behavior speak for my heart. We are here to heal the past. This piece of our journey is done. We will come together again in a healed, conscious relationship. We have only just begun."

"Thank you, Dad. Thank you for coming to me. I love you with all of my heart! Thank you for spending so much time with me. I'm glad I got to be your daughter in this life and glad you were my father. I am blessed."

"We are blessed, my dearest daughter. We are blessed. I will always love you, and I will always be here to support you in your life, your work, and your love. Look for signs of me; I will come to you."

"Please continue to guide me, Dad. You are so important to me. I need you," I spoke aloud as I wrote through tears.

"And you are as well, Debra, more than you will ever know. Let your gifts flow; you know who you are, and there is no need to hide. Let the world love you. Shine your light, your beautiful light. I will see you soon. I will be waiting for you. I am the eagle. You will see me soaring free in the sunny skies."

I put down my pen and let the tears flow freely from my eyes. Something had shifted. Had my father indeed come? Yes. If all that exists is in our hearts, then surely the realness, the wholeness, and purity of who he was, who he is, and what he wanted to offer me in that moment flowed through the unified field as words that joined us as one, expressing itself through the focus of my pen on the page. I felt complete. Authentic and genuine, I could exhale and lay down the burden of the past, could let it be transmuted through love and the eternity of our coming together. I could finally feel my father's love for me, which had always been there, pure and unblemished. He had given me the greatest gift of love; perhaps now, I could start a new relationship with him that was honest, shone like the sun, soared like an eagle, and had nothing to hide.

* * *

I STILL HADN'T RECEIVED what I thought was a significant message from *Wounded Woman* until I read the following words: "Perhaps the greatest wound the man suffers is not to acknowledge his own wound—to be unable to weep."[1] My attention was piqued, and I could feel something shifting. I now knew this book that my father had helped me rediscover would have a critical message.

Leonard said that many men have "lost the power of their tears and they have failed to honor their own young, tender, feminine side…they have sacrificed their 'inner daughter' in the name of their own power."[2]

My body and brain flooded with anticipation. I always knew my father had tears inside! I had always wanted him to be *real*, to cry and release his pain and childhood wounds from his body and heart. His spirit hadn't been "seen" nor honored in some ways as a child, and I knew he was disidentified with his deepest inner needs, feelings, and feminine side.

He had compassion for people, and I saw much greatness in him. As a younger man, he had been an outstanding athlete and had the fortitude to excel and commit himself to what he loved. He took people at face value, without prejudice, and could cut through to the heart of the matter.

I had always seen him as inherently self-contained, narcissistic, walled off, a sort of self-distanced analyst watching life—but not himself—in it. Did he know he was also being observed? That I was paying attention, looking for the littlest signs of genuine vulnerability, where we could connect emotionally rather than intellectually?

Perhaps this was why I sought out the same type of men, within whom their tears were safely tucked away, living life from their mental faculties, denying what was lost to them. In my fantasies, these men I loved always trusted me enough to let those tears be cried, releasing the tender heart within.

Is this what I was chasing? Is this what I saw buried inside them that I thought I had the power and *purpose* of resurrecting? Was I pursuing *their* heart instead of my own? Had Jonathan triggered shame in me because it had equally met its match in him, repressed under a fervent mission and keen intellect? Was it just imaginative folly that I intuited he had received abuse and criticism that was wound tightly around the sinews of his physicality as inflexibility, like in his ankles and feet, as I performed my healing work on him? Was the guinea pig dream offering me something fundamental about his past? What story was his body telling me? What had I wanted him to show me?

In her book, Linda Leonard laid out the differences between the "eternal girl" archetype, or *puella,* and the "armored Amazon," typical patterns or identifications resulting from the wounded father-daughter relationship. As someone who tended to push boundaries in a romantic relationship, I had assumed I would be in the "Amazon" category. I was in for an awakening as I saw the wounded little girl in action.

Leonard referred to a book by Anais Nin, *A Spy in the House of Love,* and one of its characters, Sabina. Although Sabina had decidedly different traits than I, the underpinnings were stunningly similar. My heart was glued to the pages as I read and underlined the passages, as if Linda had pried open the lid of my inner workings and was peering down at the muck that had accumulated in the deep well of my soul, spooning it out onto the page.

Reflecting on Sabina's plight, she writes:

> Guilt, shame, and anxiety begin to overtake her and she realizes that her love anxieties are not so different from those of an addict or a gambler; i.e.

> the same compulsion and irresistible impulse and then the same depression and guilt which follow and then once more the compulsion. Sabina's addiction is love, but the end effect is the same. She feels the dispersion, the desperation, the weakness at the center.[3]

My heart raced as she described Sabina's projections onto her lovers. "Rather than relating to them as individuals and seeing them as they were in reality, she dressed them in costumes of the various myths she wanted to live out."[4] Was this what I had done to Jonathan? Brock? Hunter? Eddie? This crazy crusade that had started when I was fourteen years old?

> For Sabina the change can come only with the tears of acknowledgment for her deception of self and others. Up to now she has been trying to elude her guilt and find self-justification for her lack of commitment and recognition of limitations.[5]

Is this what my ego had been up to all these years? Why hadn't I seen it? Had I *read* this book and not been ready or able to hear its message?

> The difficulty for this type of puella is that she tries to live totally in possibility and ignores the limitations and realities of others and herself. But she needs to accept the boundaries and commit herself to something.[6]

Is this what happened after watching Matias on Gaia's Initiation episode all those months ago that prompted me to "just write"? When I'd realized that dark and light forces were indissoluble parts of the human experience and that I could continue to distract myself by living "totally in possibility," endlessly entangling with my shadows?

A light pulsated inside my brain. For Sabina, as an example of Leonard's "eternal girl" puella, "accepting the paradox of finitude and possibility is her way of resolution…Creating via the various art forms is one way to this end."[7]

I'd had to come down to earth, thrust my fingers into the dirt, and ground my creativity into form! Leonard continues, "Anais Nin transformed the puella existence in herself through her writing, giving form to her intuitions and thus bringing possibility and actuality together."[8] Bingo! My book!

Could it be that I was finally healing, that I had made the shift I had been searching for by loving myself enough to commit to *me*? That this stunningly simple, life-confounding, and elusive solution had existed inside me all along? Had my father seen it? The very man who had cast the net—the *spell*—obscuring it from my child's eyes?

According to Leonard, "The puella lives out her life in the possible, avoiding the actuality of commitment."[9] I swallowed excitedly, absorbing the words like a dry, hungry sponge, each word a droplet of quenching rain, whetting a dormant appetite slumbering deep within me, feeling the realization rise through my bones, an ascending sun of understanding about to burst over the dawn's horizon. Quoting Kierkegaard from *Sickness Unto Death* and describing his viewpoint of this mode of existence as an aspect of (the puella's) despair, Leonard continued:

> The self becomes an abstract possibility which tires itself out with floundering in the possible, but does not budge from the spot, nor get to any spot, for precisely the necessary is the spot; to become oneself is precisely a movement at the spot. To become is a movement from the spot, but to become oneself is a movement at the spot.[10]

Rather than looking inward to express or cultivate what was intrinsically there, I had always looked outward, so any "project" or "program" I pursued was from that perspective (floundering in the possible). It was not birthed *from what was inside* as a specific talent that needed to be *expressed*, but rather as something that I was *missing* that needed to be "found" or "introduced" *from* the outside—something that would "complete" me; I was looking back *at* myself instead of from inside myself projecting that self *out* and held the perspective that I didn't possess what I needed to be fulfilled. I couldn't fathom that what would give meaning was to express who and what I already was!

This is why I'd had no energy for myself! The center of *myself*, my *heart*, was the spot! I had to find *myself at the spot* to reclaim my power, my life force. I had to initiate it, activate it, and move *at* the spot! It was crystal clear to me. This is the path upon which I had been blindly blundering along, thinking the specificity of my plight was staggeringly unique and overwhelming, random, *unnamable*. I'd had to take *action* as opposed to *reacting*! I pressed on, the words drawing my eyes into the page, building to an exquisite crescendo, as a great thunderbolt of enlightened understanding cracked in the heavens, splitting me in two, forever rending the wheat of sweet serendipity from the chaff of despair:

> Possibility then appears to the self ever greater and greater, more and more things become possible, because nothing becomes actual. At last it is as if everything were possible—but this is precisely when the abyss has swallowed up the self.[11]

Exactly! My pattern, my *persona*, had been named and unearthed. I nearly sprung off the sofa as I read the words that were changing my life forever, *here* and *now*!

"For genuine action, the synthesis and integration of both possibility and necessity are required, and it is this synthesis, according to Kierkegaard, which is one of the grounding aspects of selfhood,"[12] Leonard writes. Gaining her sense of identity from outside herself, the puella "needs to accept her potentiality for strength and to develop it,"[13] to actualize the synthesis of her potentialities and limitations.[14]

I'd simply needed to tap into myself and *write*. I knew I had talent, but how much? Accomplishment had always been something out there, as were all the possibilities I envisioned that would save my life. I had to tend to the here and now, merely start from where I was, with whatever talent I had, fanning the tiny flame that existed in me, *that had always been with me,* in my heart, and let it live. There would always be something better, someone better, a shiny new object or a man to distract me, that I would want to grab onto. I had to stop looking outside myself and allow what was *already inside* to be birthed.

Was this, in reality, what Beatrix had offered many years ago when she had said, "if you don't do your healing work, you don't get the man?" That my "healing work" was not the performance of my chiropractic work but the healing of *myself*, the heart that was me that I'd had to discover before I could truly love another? Had she even known?

Leonard references Kierkegaard's view of "The Despair of Weakness," the puella's unwillingness to be herself:

> In this form of despair one realizes that one is not in relationship with the self, but feels too weak to choose the self. Hence the despair is over one's weakness, one's inability to choose a more meaningful way of life.[15]

This is why I could only choose to follow someone *else's* dream. I hadn't known what I wanted, couldn't find my center—Kierkegaard's movement at the spot—or my strength, so I had attached myself to someone else's energy, exalting them in the process! This was why someone else's project was so compelling; it came from outside, matching my idea of my purpose, my power, and where it resided: outside of me. But I'd had to choose the "necessary," I'd had to choose *myself!* Says Leonard:

> Even the inflated puella, the 'high flyer,' remains weak since she doesn't actualize her possibilities but only plays with them. Thus she never becomes a powerful figure in the world. Living perpetually in possibility as the puella tends to do fosters weakness because she never accomplishes anything...she is swallowed up in the abyss of possibility. The puella, once she becomes conscious of her pattern, realizes she is trapped, stopped short in her development.[16]

This is what had happened with Jonathan! He refused to accept a codependent version of me, consciously or unconsciously. The result had hurled me into the abyss, into the darkest of nights, where I was trapped with no one but *me,* where I was forced to look at myself, to see that *I* was my problem, not the men I longed for. The pattern wasn't out there—it was *in my mind,* like a poison, dutifully reflecting an illusion that could not be sustained.

I was incredulous, feeling a tremendous weight lifted off my mind, heart, and shoulders. I sighed and continued to read Linda's words. I was awakening from the dream. At long last!

> For she, too, has something to contribute to the world, although she has not yet found the way to do this. And how frustrating this is—knowing one has something to contribute but not being able to do it. That is the "despair of weakness." And that tension can lead to suicide, withdrawal, adaptation, or rebellion. But it can also lead to transformation.[17]

In her book, Leonard describes this transformation process. First, we had to become conscious that we were out of relation to the self, the higher power of self beyond the ego, and this realization would bring suffering. We then needed to accept that suffering was *meaningful,* and finally, we must surrender to a higher power and that this was the strength within us. We had to accept the strength of the Self, consciously and through choice, that was not "ego-willpower" but the knowingness that dwelled at the core of our being.[18]

"For Kierkegaard, this is ultimately an act of faith requiring all the strength of receptivity."[19] I had been afraid to accept—*to receive*—my Self, because I believed that once I put myself in the hands of God, Source, the Universe, I wouldn't be able to rise to the occasion of what longed to be accomplished through me, or wouldn't like what it offered, wouldn't be able to find the energy to sustain it. As long as I followed someone else's star, I would not have to take responsibility for the content, path, or energy it would take to see their project through. I could understand that now.

> Real understanding of the weakness and acceptance of the suffering involves facing the shadow, that part of oneself that is denied...The shadow of the puella is tied up with power—a power which she has not truly and responsibly accepted. Oftentimes this power has been taken over by another figure in the psyche...and this figure, too, must be confronted.[20]

At a profoundly spiritual level, both Leonard and Kierkegaard saw this acceptance, this confrontation, as a battle with, in their terminology, the "devil."

> When there is a deep wound in the psyche, the negative forces assume a demonic character and must be confronted as such. In Kierkegaard's analysis, when one becomes conscious that one's indulgence in weakness is really a defiant refusal to accept one's strength, a refusal to accept the grace of God, one realizes that the refusal to accept strength is demonic, a prideful clinging to one's ego power. Part of accepting the suffering is to realize one has been in the grips of the devil.[21]

My mind raced over the information Matias had offered in Initiation and the recurring alien nightmare that had terrified me as a child. I didn't resonate with the idea of an actual "devil" and interpreted the term to represent the darkest egoic places in the psyche, but had I actually been in the grips of dark forces? Did these forces have a form, a construct? If not for the string of guidance—*destiny*—that had appeared in my life through myriad forms and individuals, my steadfast commitment to healing my patterns, and learning to trust that I would get what I needed, could I have been vanquished?

Leonard said the final step was to accept the strength within and hold onto it. I knew I would. It was hard-earned. I loved myself too much now to trade it for a pattern so disruptive it had wanted to claim my life.

I was free! Jonathan and all the others had played their parts so well through precise scenarios devised and designed by the Divine, my ego, and the power of my inner being for my ultimate release.

The package was delivered, and I had received the gift! I didn't need to repeat this cycle with men any longer. Jonathan was the last, and that was why my experience with him had been so compelling and intensely painful; the collapse of illusion could only succumb to an unbearable weight, one in which the ego construct could no longer bend, so it broke. The bonds had been disrupted, unraveled. It could no longer exist in the form it once was. I was indeed free. Free to be who I am, who I was *destined to become*, living my life from the center of life itself: my beautiful, beating heart.

CHAPTER 29

Free

I'd been one of the lucky ones, but I'd had to free myself first. My father had helped me, and I had freed us both in the process. What he couldn't give me on earth was surely being offered now. I could feel his presence, like a great pair of eagle wings, wrapped lovingly around me, and in that moment of pure surrender, where heaven meets earth, I knew I had always, and *would always*, be loved. I was complete. Whole. Ready for something new, pure, and sacred.

France had been an impossible gift of grace, a place out of time so many years ago. I was deeply awed by what life and my drive to know myself had shown me. A grand fairy tale, dreamed to life by the sleeping beauty inside me, France had painted a glorious tapestry, an enchanted kingdom, cast over oceans, mountains, and cities, as I navigated the path like a fool, a lover, a warrior, a Queen.

I thought about how I had chased Brock, unaware of a pattern that had defiantly occupied the driver's seat of my person. Unquestionably, Brock had been an emotional dead end for me. How much proof had I needed? I could breathe a romance into the tiniest gesture and create an entire fantasy from it. Everyone was chasing someone or something, I thought. I hadn't seen that then, but it was clear now. I had constructed my life in hot pursuit of the image I had in my mind. But sometimes, life allows us to look at something differently. One thing changes. The mind stops. Everything *we thought we saw* becomes a new set of dominoes, cascading backward in one instant of revelation, birthing a new perception. It was like that after Ari died. One would have thought it would stop me from judging anything, but it didn't; it hasn't. But the one thing that *has* changed was that I didn't have this idea back then; I have it now.

If like attracts like, I reflected, then my unavailability had attracted theirs. This I already knew. And if I had been genuinely available, would I have found an unavailable man attractive? What if the only way they knew they were lovable was by the chase itself? What if they could not receive an open heart coming toward them because they also didn't know how to receive love? What if they were afraid to say yes, for fear they would ultimately be rejected if they did? *Like me.* What if they were just the opposite side of the same coin? If I were *available*, would an unavailable man chase me?

Looking back at my journal while writing this book, I reached an entry that halted me. It wasn't anything special; I had written one like it *many times* before. As I read the description of Brock, I was describing Hunter and Jonathan, and probably Eddie Schechter too. The dashing man of many talents, the cavalier, self-oriented pursuit, oblivious to my longing; the heartbreaker asleep in self-centeredness, unaware of the vulnerable, impressionable, adoring heart before him. The repetition was startling and plucked a deep string in my heart. Why had I thought that any of them were capable of seeing *me*?

Yes, all this had been worth contemplating, but what I saw suddenly, *clearly*, was the exact description of a much younger version of my father and how closely I had patterned my perfect man profile to "look" like him. The him I expected he should become. It shook me. *He hadn't been looking for me; he had been looking for himself!* I spent all those years—tears, inspecting the same facet of the same diamond.

Suddenly, I saw how very stuck my perspective had been. How focused I was on *them* changing. Here it was, written plainly in my journal. The same *exact* story again. The same questions, from inside the same little box. I couldn't ignore it or deny it. It was there, plain as day. Suddenly, all their faces and descriptions merged into one. I put down my journal and cried.

I don't know why I cried. I cried for them. I cried for myself. I felt pain, but it was different. There was understanding, a compassion that included me in it. The shame had turned into grief that simply needed to be released. I realized I hadn't grieved Brock or had ever seen who he was. I had time to grieve Hunter. It took me three years to be able to release him. I was crying for the past, for all those years spent. And here it was again, most recently with Jonathan. I'd had time to grieve him too. I could release them all, but more importantly, I could free myself. I didn't have to wonder why they couldn't love me. Maybe they couldn't love themselves. It didn't matter. I had myself to love now.

I hadn't needed to excavate their hearts; I'd needed to resurrect *my own.* Not from self-query nor from analyzing my personality. I had to stop the story about myself, my past, and them to love myself and connect with my soul. There is no getting to the bottom of personality, I told myself. There *is* no bottom. Personality is an ego construct; it isn't the soul. My analysis would always lead to more analysis. It was another distraction. The only thing that would make me feel lovable was my own belief about it. I was not utterly broken. I had made the choice I needed to make.

For years, I had romanced my patterns, nurturing a false persona. I spent a lifetime trying to reach a solution that wasn't possible through the illusion of trying to control and change these men into someone they could never be. This dead-end thinking should have been starkly evident to my critical mind but was not. Codependency doesn't consider the logical because the child's mind creates it. It's magical thinking. It is transfixed on one facet, trying to perfect an illusion that can't be perfected because *illusions aren't real.* They aren't real because they don't lead to self-love.

The only choice I'd had was to stop that story. Who was I without it? I shook my head again. My objections rose and settled back down into the rawness of the moment. I'd had to choose myself, but could I put it to the test? Would my poor heart be off and running if a Hunter, a Brock, or a Jonathan came along again? I wanted life to prove that real love was better than the illusion I had been chasing.

Until I stopped idolizing and objectifying them, these men couldn't and wouldn't love me. God—*Truth*—cannot sustain an illusion. And why had I needed an idol anyway? If the tables had been turned and a man had treated me the way I treated these men, I would have run too. No one wants someone's fantasies about them to be the reason they are wanted. We want to be seen for who we are.

I had lived through so many emotions. The top and the bottom, it seemed. During the worst of it, I reminded myself of the gift of my heart, the heart that was able to love and hurt so deeply. Wasn't it just two ends of the same stick? To feel the exaltation of one end, would I necessarily have to experience the excruciating end of the other? And where had my soul been in all this? Was my heart my soul? Did I choose this at a level that wanted to expand me in unknowable ways? Did I have a choice? Could I surrender to "not knowing" and trust myself? What "self" was I trusting?

I thought about the caterpillar, decomposing into a putrid mush in its cocoon, dying completely to be reborn into winged, brilliant splendor. I thought about the baby swan, the "ugly duckling" who was the clumsy, necessary ragamuffin of the white majesty of the mature swan. I thought about all the times I had loved and lost, swearing never to love again, only to forget that promise at the dawning of another longing. I thought about the consecration of love, how it is dormant, waiting to be forged clean into a shining diamond. This force had relentlessly driven me, thrusting me forward as I bumped and bumbled through dark nights and brilliant suns, surging and retreating.

And in all this excavating, I had scraped away enough muck to see a tiny glimmer of hope. I could see that I was seeking a heart that wanted to love itself. I was familiar with all the good and bad traits of my ego and personality, the flaws that threatened to swallow me up at every turn. I knew what I liked and what I didn't. And then, I realized that I wouldn't trade any of it. I realized I couldn't have discovered what I was seeking without the actual seeking. And I found that I didn't need to change who I was; I could seek with the parts of me that loved myself. All those parts were there, discovered in the mining.

In Matt Kahn's book, *Everything is Here to Help You,* he asks us to consider, "what if the worst things that ever happened were the greatest opportunities you have ever been given?"[1] That had become my new mantra, a knot at the end of a rope that I could hold onto, a respite from the thoughts that wanted to beat me over the head and tell me I was a misguided fool. And from that place, I could let myself off the hook a tiny bit.

Surging forward with a blindfold on, I could envision it was all for love. I couldn't force Jonathan to love me or *see me,* but I could allow gratitude for the capacity to love at the deepest level of my being. "I'm a lover, Jonathan. My gift is my heart," I had told him in Saddle River as he stared at me wordlessly. I could allow myself to be a journeyer who mattered, a woman whose heart mattered. The deepest part of me wanted to let everything be as it was. I could loosen my grip ever so slightly and trust the Source holding the other end of the rope—even for a few moments. I could put my attention around the area of my heart and breathe. I could give myself all the consideration I had given Jonathan. I could forgive myself as I had forgiven him. I didn't have to control anything. He wasn't really gone, I knew. Once a person enters your life, you can't "unknow" them, but one day, I knew I would be able to release him. It didn't have to be today. It would come, the way it always did, over time.

Something was subtly shifting inside since my dialog with my father and the new story I had written about Jonathan. The breakthrough was real. Small shifts continued to appear, and new images spontaneously appeared in my mind. I bought myself some balloons to celebrate what was undoubtedly a rebirth.

Sitting on my couch, I imagined myself as an infant bouncing out of my crib and landing on my head as my father gaped helplessly, my mother sweeping in to scoop me up off the hardwood floor. I saw myself as a nine-month-old with pneumonia in the hospital, tubes connected to my little body, and my parents, tearfully strained, leaving me for the night as I cried. I saw the eighteen-month-old toddler, shocked by the arrival of a new baby sister who wouldn't stop crying until eighteen months later when that sister was put away in a hospital, leaving a shroud of grief behind.

I held myself as these infants and rocked them as I rocked myself, wrapping my arms around me, comforting them, holding our tears. And, as I sat rocking, embracing us all, an image of myself as a newborn popped into my mind.

There I was, naked, new, delivered, held by the hands of a stranger, cupping my bottom, my head, and I saw my own eyes! Oh, those eyes! The courage and the strength this newly born babe would need for the precious journey ahead, through many challenges, nearly blinding her to her own heart, but she would make it! She would rise to the glory of what was inherently hers, her own precious life, her heart of hearts. I fell in love with her, deeply and exquisitely, longing to touch and kiss her tiny face, to smell her skin as I clutched her to my breast, breathing her into myself. I knew she was there—*here*—an inseparable part of me. This beautiful, brilliant heart would endure and thrive, safe in the light deep inside that would be the very place she would return to time and time again. We were home.

I gazed down at Teensy lying on my lap, the little stuffed, terrycloth puppy-doll my father had given me when I was a little girl. After my closure with him, I had taken her out of the closet where she had rested undisturbed on a blanket, setting her beside me as I wrote. She had been the envy of my childhood friends, and one of my five-year-old playmates had nearly torn her arm off in a jealous tug of war, but she was mine.

My father had gotten her on his way home from work. This was out of the ordinary for him, as my mother did all the gift shopping, and it was neither a holiday nor my birthday. Teensy symbolized the bond between him and me, immortalizing my heart as a little child, and I treasured her.

I picked her up, swathed in a woolen scarf, and put her on my chest. I held and rocked her, and my father's presence hovered lovingly, filling the air with a sweetness that soothed my heart. Yes, this was a big deal indeed. I could feel my entire nervous system restored, rewired, and renewed. It had all been worth it. Nothing needed to be changed; everything had brought me to this moment.

I held on loosely, etching the feelings and sensations into my brain, my memory, my heart, and the very essence of myself. I was free. My father was free. Our oneness, our twoness, united as a trinity through the heart of Love. What I'd been searching for my whole life was here for me now. I celebrated it.

I'd recently had two dreams about Jonathan. In the first one, we were in a room the size of a hotel conference hall with many strangers. I locked eyes with him across the room and walked toward him. He had on a short white blazer with white buttons on either side. "Do I look okay?" he asked modestly. I felt there was something important he was about to embark upon. I could feel our collective power radiating warmly around us.

Stepping closer, I reached for his lapels and gazed into his eyes. A smile spread slowly across my face. "You look beautiful," I offered. Pulling him close, I tucked my face into the crook of his neck. "I love you so much," I half-whispered and kissed him on the side of his head by his ear.

"I know you do," he said, understanding it for the first time. We lingered for a moment, and he headed outside to speak to the strangers seated around a long table. He had something important to tell them. I sensed this was the next part of his journey, and he accepted it with all the grace that made me love him so much. They were eager to hear what he had to say. I watched for a moment, and then I awoke. Who would I be without the love I had felt for him? It was nearly two years ago that he entered my heart. Maybe we were both ready to move on.

* * *

IT HAD BEEN A FEW DAYS since I'd gone to the bay, so I took a drive. I thought about life. Where did it want to take me? I couldn't stay small anymore. I wanted to let life and love fill my sails, to feel the expansion of places inside me waiting to soar, to fly, to live magnificently, wildly open to receiving beyond what I had ever known. I listened to The Council caressing my ears with words otherworldly and dreamed myself there.

> There is [an] intelligence out there that *is* you and is a part of you, that is not separate from you…[a] greater part that knows who you are and knows what's possible for you, and knows, *knows* your divine purpose in this existence that you call Life…and has never forgotten who you are, has been guiding you every step of the way. That is the light within you. It is the energy, the intelligence, the god force, the light within the caterpillar that led it to becoming a butterfly, whether it was conscious of what was happening or not. There is an intelligence in you, [a] source within you. There is energy within you. There is a divine purpose *coded* within *you*, for you to realize your greatness, for the great transformation of you into being all that you are. And all that is asked of you is to allow it. Stop doing…start allowing…start *feeling*…start *being*. There's no more *need* to do, do, do, in order to be enough, to change this and change that. You *realize* your transformation. You *realize* your greatness. You *realize* your divine purpose. Allow it. Feel it. Be it!...All transformation can be

peaceful, harmonious, and loving when you come into a state of realizing that it is done.[2]

***

MORE THAN A DECADE PRIOR, I had taken to working with a man named Elliott, who was looking to advance his agenda and willing to let anyone assist him in this endeavor. He had been developing a program I believed in and wholeheartedly dove into. It wasn't a romance, but it held many dynamics that epitomized my pattern as I focused on *his* dream, using the power and energy that I had displaced outside of me to fuel the endless hours I dedicated to his project. Ultimately, I walked away and never looked back, but my pattern had remained intact.

Surprisingly, I'd had a dream about Elliott and Jonathan. I curiously watched the dream unfold, feeling it had something important to tell me.

Elliott was sitting at the far end of a long table with a younger woman by his side. Their backs were to the wall, and they were sitting on a long bench seat that extended to the other end of the table where Jonathan and I sat. I was seated on the bench; Jonathan sat beside me in a chair at the table. Jonathan scrolled through his phone as I observed the scene with Elliott and the younger woman. They were chatting, laughing, and drinking red wine. I noticed they were crossed at the ankle, just like Jonathan and I had been in the dream with the white cat! Elliott's fly was down, and he was wearing black and white underwear. I was surprised and repulsed. I had a fleeting thought about taking a sip of the red wine, and suddenly Elliott was beside me and tipped the bottle to my lips, forcing me to gulp it down. I spluttered and pushed him away.

"What are you doing?!" I exclaimed as I wiped my mouth with the back of my hand. I heard the unspoken words clearly in my mind: *I don't want that anymore.* Elliott went back to the other end of the table. *That girl used to be me,* I thought. Jonathan sat quietly next to me.

Was Jonathan a witness to the new version of me? Was he just a different version of Elliott? Did Elliott's black and white underwear symbolize the old versus the new—the contrast between who I was then to who I am now? The red wine, temptation—the old pattern that I had overcome?

Contemplating both dreams, I knew the best was yet to come. There were dreams with the white cat, the white rooms with the colors, and now Jonathan's white jacket. There was a purity to our relationship that transcended the unconsciousness of our waking state. I was grateful for the gift of love he had offered me and the gift of release I'd offered myself through him. I had received the closure I needed. Maybe, having finally released my pattern, I was free to create a new possibility in love, a reflection of the love I had found for myself. I was ready.

CHAPTER 30

Rewriting the Fairy Tale

There is a vision, a dream simmering in the back of my mind. It is a gently swirling eddy of a man kissing me on a famous bridge in Paris, cupping my face in his hands, our hair blowing gently in the breeze. It is a kiss we have been waiting for all of our lives.

I laid the story down and reread it to myself, letting it forge a new river in my heart and mind. What was this inspired scrivening? Was it literary folly, or did I have the capacity to create something better in love? Could I rewrite the fairy tale and invoke a new story that spoke of only love?

* * *

WHEN I MET MY BELOVED, *I felt a deep, abiding connection at once. I didn't know his past or what he was born to do. Wise, ripened, humble, he was a man who wanted to feel his own heart. A man whose true path was intimacy, the crown jewel of many accomplishments, a man whose path had led him to me. He had finally allowed himself the grace of forgiving his past, baptized by tears that had been dammed up and released, reborn into one who wanted to love and be loved.*

"There is a palace that opens only to tears," says the Zohar. For me, this had been true. I'd had a sense he, too, had not been seen nor heard, but through this, he had woven a channel of gold that provided the energy to burst forth into the world of mighty causes. Long ago, his heart had stirred, but he was afraid, so he ran away.

Later in time, one foggy, misty day, we stood on that bridge. "I wasn't ready for you then," my Beloved said softly, his heart in his eyes. "I couldn't open my heart to the pain of my past. I felt you in my future. That frightened me, and I closed myself off. I didn't accept the part of me that wanted to love. I should have been honest with myself, but I didn't know how. I didn't want to be weak; I didn't want to get lost." His voice was wistful as he spoke the words coming from deep within. His tone was full and round, rising softly from his chest, and I felt my heart vibrating like another note in the same chord, harmonious, natural, real. "I'm ready for you now," he said, looking into my eyes. "Will you love me?"

"I have always loved you, my dearest Beloved, and waited for you to arrive. Long ago, my idea of love was stained by worship, unequal love teetering on a pedestal, an untrue love. I didn't respect love's boundaries, nor my own. I was rejected and hit the deep, dark bottom with nowhere to go but inward toward a self I never knew was there. And when I stopped fighting, I started to see that everything had happened for me, and there was only love. My infatuation with another turned into a true romance with myself, the self I had abandoned, and I started to forgive myself for what I had done to me. I realized how badly I'd treated my own heart, how deeply I'd rejected, admonished, and punished the love that wanted to flow through me as the pure innocence of Life itself. I dumped it in unworthy places and didn't protect my vulnerability. I let the scabs be ripped open, time and time again. Others' words and deeds sometimes hurt, and yet I stayed. I always saw us together, you holding my face, looking into me with eyes I could only remember on this bridge. And now, here you are, a humble man, a man who wants me, sees me now." I smiled at my Beloved. "I've waited for you my whole life, it seems."

My Beloved looked at me for a long time. I felt his gaze taking in the edges of where my skin met the air, where my hair framed my face, our two sets of eyes fluid and filled with love. Rivers of lifetimes shimmered and sparkled as we beheld each other in the misty, foggy day, the whiteness of the plain white sky. I felt the warmth and the coolness of his fingers as they found my cheeks and wrapped themselves slender and firm around the back of my neck, cupping the base of my skull. I felt his palms as they covered my ears; my head and heart held, buoyed with tender longing, our breath rising in the moment.

He stepped closer to me. His hands gently lifted me toward him, wanting me with the full force of his being. I felt the weight of my body shifting forward onto the balls of my feet, the muscles around my spine responding, my ribs elevating as I leaned toward him, our bodies becoming flush, our separateness merging into one.

I felt his warmth as I let myself be pulled into his embrace. I wanted this moment. The moment before the kiss. The tension, the longing, my heart expanding, beating faster, melting against my chest. I felt his wanting. Oh, how I wanted his wanting! The aliveness of his warm hands, the cool air on my forehead, my chin, the skin of my scalp tingling, my heart and face flushing.

His breath was warm, moister than the air. I knew what it was to be kissed, but oh, this kiss! The kiss I'd been waiting for all of my life. Me in love with my Beloved's heart, materializing into form in this great and ordinary man before me, his two hands cradling me, fingers in my wild hair.

"I've waited so long for you," he whispered, hanging onto the moment, onto me. Slowly our lips met. Softly, sweetly, cymbals crashing as angels raised their golden trumpets thrust high into the mighty white clouds, I let my heart arrive, feeling his body alive at last! He drew me closer, kissing me deeply, pleasure rolling through our tongues, coursing through our veins, our beings.

We stayed there on that bridge for a long time, letting our eternities fully find each other, free each other. Slowly, gently, he pulled away. He looked at me wholly, his heart in his eyes, and I could see only the sun there now. "I love you," he sighed. "I never dreamed I could feel this way. We have so much to share, to offer each other."

"Believe in love, my Beloved. I will always be here for you. Are you ready to hold the heart of another?"

He nodded slowly, his resistance melting away like springtime snow under the rays of a warm sun. We beheld each other, content, self-and-other-contained, the power of love surrounding us. He took my hands in his. "My heart is home in you, Debra. I had to free myself before I could be free to love you. I am joyful, knowing you waited for my heart to arrive."

Softly, I squeezed my Beloved's hands and looked into his ancient eyes. I trusted him. "I always knew you would come for me, to meet me on this bridge."

The palace gates had swung open wide. I didn't have to fall at Love's feet anymore. Through our tears, our triumphs, we had found freedom, liberation, the Heart of another who had loved themself free. And perhaps, like the dewy mist of that day on the bridge, all of our tears had already been cried.

CONCLUSION

After decades of pursuing the path of self-discovery, many of us have humbly learned that the path of the *heart* is the only path that promises true liberation. We have dedicated mountains of time to the pursuit of self-improvement, reflecting family, societal, and cultural values that have taught us to look outside ourselves for salvation. Envisioning something greater for ourselves and fueled by the desire to live more consciously, our journeys are often alchemized through uncountable moments down on our knees as we search for the elusive perfect relationship, career, or external persona in hopes of pleasing ourselves, our families, and the world.

Indeed, much of my past exploration was an attempt to stuff myself into someone else's box, and I regularly failed to follow my heart, convinced that something or someone *other than me* would make me happy. I longed for a deep sense of purpose, to discover, develop and share my gifts, and to be valued as a unique, integral part of society, yet I couldn't do it for myself. I often gave my power away at great expense to my heart and soul because of the core belief of not being good enough.

Unbreakable vividly demonstrates the emotions and behaviors arising from patterns based on this core belief. My intent is not to relive them but to illustrate that most of us do not experience overnight transformation; the awakening process is typically incremental, and there is an integration period between each phase to allow us to assimilate what we have learned. Often it appears we are going backward, but this, in my opinion, is rarely the case. Time and again, we must go down to go up. Imagine two successive revolutions in a vertical coil; the lower side of the top revolution is lower than the top side of the revolution below, but it is, nonetheless, *above* the lower revolution and is still *proceeding* upward.

That your journey has brought you to this moment is a testament to your inviolable, eternal, unbreakable nature. Resilience is part of what invites and creates transformation. It doesn't matter if you've found the love of your life, the perfect career, or anything else you think you need to be happy; you can find your ever-available Self. And as you do this, one moment at a time, you will no longer be able to subordinate yourself to anything *outside* of you that promises a better version of you.

Our decisions about how we live no longer need to be prioritized by what other people think of us, their reactions, or their behaviors based on their perceptions of our actions. They are responsible for their responses, as we are responsible for ours. Knowing this will help us to be vulnerable and to be ourselves.

We are at a place in human evolution to realize our true power. Our extraordinary creative spirit and stories of past events can create the impetus to revolutionize how we live. We must be gentle with ourselves in the process. Too much time has been given to shaming ourselves and others for mistakes whose only purpose is to help us grow as individuals and to realize our true nature. What has happened to us is not who we are but can inform who we become, moving us into a state of abundant living. Through the practice of opening to our creative impulses—the grace within us—we experience what is possible when we access the dreamer inside to *live* our life.

Drawing on the intrinsic wellspring of impeccable creation, we return to wholeness as we experience a revolution back to the innocence of our supreme inner authority. By listening to our hearts, we align with peace because we are in alignment with our own directives, no longer living outside ourselves. Creating a new vision, we step into our greatness—our sovereignty—and begin to experience a more authentic way of living on Earth, where we can indeed have everything our hearts desire.

NOTES

NOTES FOR CHAPTER 16

[1] *A Course In Miracles, Combined Volume: Text, Workbook for Students, and Manual for Teachers, 2nd ed.* (Foundation for Inner Peace, 1992), Manual For Teachers, M-3.1:4-8.

[2] Ibid., Manual for Teachers, M-3.4:1, 3-7.

NOTES FOR CHAPTER 26

[1] "Who is The Council," saralandon.com, accessed October 18, 2022, https://saralandon.com/about-sara-landon-the-council/#WHO.

[2] Matt Kahn, *Everything is Here to Help You: Finding the Gift in Life's Greatest Challenges* (Hay House, Inc., 2018), 41.

NOTES FOR CHAPTER 27

[1] EFT, or Emotional Freedom Techniques, is an evidence-based, self-help therapy technique that may help relieve stress and depression, as well as phobias, PTSD, and other conditions. Acupressure or meridian points typically on the head, face, torso, and hands are stimulated by tapping them in a particular sequence while mentally focusing on or talking through a particular trauma. This helps to release negative emotions stored in the body to improve the body's natural energy balance and reduce or eliminate distress.
https://www.webmd.com/balance/what-is-eft-tapping,
https://www.medicalnewstoday.com/articles/326434,
https://www.tappingsolutionfoundation.org/howdoesitwork/.

NOTES FOR CHAPTER 28

[1] Linda Schierse Leonard, *The Wounded Woman: Healing the Father-Daughter Relationship* (Boston: Shambhala Publications, Inc., 1982), 32.
[2] Ibid., 33.
[3] Ibid., 46-47.
[4] Ibid., 47.
[5] Ibid.
[6] Ibid., 47-48.
[7] Ibid., 48.
[8] Ibid.
[9] Ibid., 53
[10] Søren Kierkegaard, *The Sickness Unto Death*, trans. Walter Lowrie (New York: Doubleday & Co., Inc., 1954): 169, quoted in Linda Schierse Leonard, *The Wounded Woman: Healing the Father-Daughter Relationship* (Boston: Shambhala Publications, Inc., 1982), 53.
[11] Ibid.
[12] Leonard, 54.
[13] Ibid.
[14] Ibid.
[15] Ibid.
[16] Ibid., 54-55.
[17] Ibid., 55.
[18] Ibid.
[19] Ibid.
[20] Ibid., 57.
[21] Ibid.

NOTES FOR CHAPTER 29

[1] Kahn, 89.
[2] The Council, channeled by Sara Landon, "Peaceful Transformation: Choosing the Path of Love & Consciousness," *Revolution 2021: The Importance of Love and Consciousness in Action,* Session 3 (February 6, 2021), MPEG format, 1 hr., 51 min., 14 sec, https://saralandon.com.

ACKNOWLEDGMENTS

It is my greatest honor and privilege to be enveloped and graced by the loving support of my amazing friends, family, and colleagues. I love you all dearly.

So much more than I ever imagined goes into writing a book, and I could not have accomplished it alone. Some individuals helped me directly and some indirectly. All were indispensable in various stages on the road to publication, propelling me emotionally, spiritually, technically, or creatively to get the job done.

A great big thanks to Lynn Komlenic for your extraordinary ability to help me "find" and trust my heart, my gifts, and the process, and for reminding me that my book was "already done." Thank you for your valuable feedback and coaching on my first manuscript and book proposal and for rolling up your sleeves to assist me on so many levels to achieve my long-held dream of writing this book. Your friendship, editing and writing expertise, and keen ability to laser straight to the truth are priceless. You are the Annie Sullivan to my Helen Keller!

To my dear friend Ann D'Angelo, who cheerfully and tirelessly devoted many hours of time and effort to help make this book a success. Thank you for the detailed content feedback to ensure a better experience for my readers and for your written contribution to my book proposal. And just as importantly, thank you for all the insightful Tarot readings, dream shares, and delightful lunchtimes spent at the labyrinth park. I appreciate you beyond words.

Lindsey Cacy, what can I say?? Thank you for showing up to write your first novel at the beach so destiny could bring us together. Your friendship, encouragement, and commitment to helping me and everyone you touch to "shine" are invaluable. Thank you for sparking me to create my website, find the courage to write my first blog, and push me forward with love and inspiration to complete the final steps to publication when I felt I couldn't go on. I miss our bagel breakfasts and masterminding in my living room!

Thank you, Sue Diaz, for your unshakeable faith in my ability and for helping me believe I have something to offer the world through my writing. Thank you, too, for expeditiously binge-reading the final draft of my book, so I could have the confidence to complete it. Your level of integrity is rare and inspiring, and I trust you with all of my heart, dear friend.

To Malinda Zarate, for your indelible friendship, love, and unwavering support in keeping me on track when I felt intense self-judgment and fear of being seen. I am forever grateful for all of our profoundly healing conversations and your deep well of healing modalities. Our friendship and your fine-tuned capacity as a lightworker have expanded me exponentially.

Thanks to Dr. JoAnn Rosen for listening with deep empathy and understanding and teaching me about self-compassion to clear away the clutter of my clamoring mind. I am blessed by your friendship, therapeutic brilliance, infinite kindness, and charitable spirit.

To Carole Bergeron, I am profoundly touched by your cosmic healing work that deeply penetrated the infinite layers and lifetimes of my being; I am forever changed at a magnitude beyond my comprehension. I give thanks for your dedication to liberating humanity and freeing my heart from its cage.

To my trusted friend and colleague, Dr. Guillermo (Willie) Escamilla. Thank you for your incredibly healing hands, our dynamic spiritual conversations over the years, and for seeing my setbacks and foibles as a grand adventure!

To Jane Besso, thank you for listening with a loving heart and being there to hug me when I needed it.

To Grigori Chulaki, thank you for your trusted friendship, genius intellect, extraordinary healing gifts, and for massively expanding my consciousness. My world is a better place because you're in it.

Warmest thanks to my former co-worker Cindy Garcia for your beautiful pure heart and for believing in me long before I started writing this book. I appreciate you more than you will ever know.

Sincere thanks to my friend and colleague Dr. Lawrence Bell for your heartfelt healing sessions and deep intuition in ushering me through the final stages of birthing my book into the world.

To Tamara Rasheed, who coached me through my fears to initiate the publishing process. Thank you for your wisdom, guidance, and enthusiastic support.

Many thanks to the authors, teachers, and spiritual leaders whose knowledge, experience, and contributions to the world changed my life. Notably, Matt Kahn for his incredible gift of showing me how to accept, understand and navigate difficult emotions; and Linda Leonard for her brilliant book *The Wounded Woman: Healing the Father-Daughter Relationship,* which precipitated one of the most significant pattern breakthroughs I have ever experienced, shattering the illusions of a wounded heart. Without your critical synthesis of archetypical relevancy, Linda, my book in this form would not have been possible.

Over the decades, the influences of many other individuals and teachings spawned my yearning to heal my life and write my story. In no particular order, they are *A Course In Miracles* (which catalyzed my spiritual awakening while living in France), The Council (as channeled by Sara Landon), Dr. Joe Dispenza, Eckhart Tolle, Marianne Williamson, Dr. Michael Newton, John Bradshaw and Brené Brown for their outstanding work on healing shame, Melody Beattie for her groundbreaking insights on codependency, Matias DeStefano, Tara Brach, Neale Donald Walsch, Michael Alan Singer, Shakti Gawain, Louise Hay (*You Can Heal Your Life* was my first-ever personal growth book!), Caroline Myss, Martha Beck, Anita Moorjani, Marissa Peer, Seth (as channeled by Jane Roberts), Sonya Sophia and the World Tapping Circle (my EFT life raft), Aleya Dao, Steven Carter and Julia Sokol, Byron Katie, Gail Sheehy, all the way-showers, teachers and guides I discovered on Gaia TV, and numerous others throughout the decades of soul-discovery who collectively fostered my inner and outer journey to help me find my way.

Special thanks to Kelly Notaras, author of *The Book You Were Born to Write.* You inspired me to pick up the pen—or laptop, in my case—and write! Thanks to Rachael Herron for providing a detailed chart for the four-act story structure into which my book snuggled seamlessly, and to Roxana Coumans for your impeccable proofreading skills.

A gigantic thank you to Saqib Arshad, formatter extraordinaire, for countless hours spent perfecting the interior of my book to make it everything I dreamed it would be. Your meticulous precision, tireless patience, and rigorous attention to detail have produced an exceptional book that makes my heart sing.

Of course, this particular story, this journey, would not have been possible without the many people who touched my life as characters within the story itself. Some of you are very dear friends. All of you were part of the gift of helping me find my heart. It has taken a lifetime and is not a permanent state of being, but a state of flux like life itself, changing by the moment. I am deeply grateful to all of you for igniting my desire to become a better version of myself and helping me to take my power back through cultivating self-love.

With deep gratitude, I give thanks to the man who made it all happen, changing the trajectory of my life forever the day we met at the Hotel du Pont. You offered me a rare opportunity, forever planting a seed in my heart and mind that anything is possible. I have carried that idea with me since those magical days in France as I carry you too, “Ari,” knowing your indelible presence will always be with me.

I thank my family for their lifelong support. I am truly blessed to have you in my life. To my mother, Dorothy Hoolahan, thank you for your unconditional love, beautiful artist’s soul, and for demonstrating that creativity can be birthed at any age. Thank you to my sister, Linda, for your ability to soothe my heart during life’s most tender losses. I love you both very much. And thanks to my dad, Robert Hoolahan, who appreciated everything I wrote. You always told me I had a way with words and writing. I hope you are right! I love and miss you and feel your presence beyond space and time.

I thank God, the Divine Source, the Universe, for giving me life and the precious vehicle of my body, mind, and soul to navigate the journey to wholeness. And for anyone I may have forgotten, for any reason or encounter, big or small, I thank you too. In my heart, I know with certainty that everything and everyone matters.

ABOUT THE AUTHOR

Debra Hoolahan was trained as a chiropractor, receiving her doctorate from Northeast College of Health Sciences (formerly New York Chiropractic College). She has a Master of Science degree in human nutrition from Bridgeport University and has practiced energy healing, earning a certification as a Reconnective Healing Foundational Practitioner. Drawing on skills that integrate scientific and holistic approaches, Dr. Hoolahan has helped others achieve greater physical, spiritual, and emotional well-being.

An adventurer at heart, she desires to travel the world writing books that inspire people to deeper levels of fulfillment, connection, joy, and self-love. She believes everyone has a story to tell, and her passion is to use her unique experiences and gifts as a writer to empower others to live from the heart. A first-time memoirist, *Unbreakable* is her literary debut.

Debra is a long-time student of *A Course in Miracles* and many other spiritual teachings and practices. In her spare time, she can be found at the beach, gardening, or hiking a quiet nature trail in the woods. Visit her at www.debrahoolahan.com.

Made in the USA
Middletown, DE
13 July 2023